Praise for *Girt N*

CH00692579

'An entertaining and instructive hist
formative period of Australian nation-making, with a colourful cast
of rhymesters, revolutionaries, rebels, racists, reprobates and rabbits.'
FRANK BONGIORNO, PROFESSOR OF HISTORY,
THE AUSTRALIAN NATIONAL UNIVERSITY

'Insightful, witty and beautifully written, Hunt's latest offering
is as Ozzie as a mozzie in a cozzie.'
MIKEY ROBINS

'I was hooked by the second sentence, and kept asking myself,
"How can this be so horrific, so hilarious, so ridiculous and, most
shocking of all, so true?" But this is not a mere history lesson:
as Hunt deftly brings to life Australia's past in a way that both
illuminates and makes the reader cringe, he also makes us face
our nation's present, and future.'
SUSAN CARLAND

'An instant classic – Hunt's finest work to date. His clever use
of language and insightful analogies connect Australia's past
with its present, showing how our history echoes today.'
CHARLES FIRTH

'Once again, David Hunt uses his sharpened wit to chisel away
at misconceptions from Australian history, leaving us with the
cold, hard truth of how our nation came to be.'
OSHER GÜNSBERG

Praise for *True Girt*

'An engaging, witty and utterly irreverent take on Australian history.'
GRAEME SIMSION

'Astounding, gruesome and frequently hilarious,
True Girt is riveting from beginning to end.'
NICK EARLS

'[A] witty and irreverent romp along the highways
and dirt tracks of Australian history.'
THE WEEKEND AUSTRALIAN

'Bitingly satiricial ... Erudition leavened with wit,
this should be a definite addition to your bookshelf.'
THE BIG ISSUE

'[A] twisted take on Australian history ... Hilarious.'
THE DAILY TELEGRAPH

Praise for *Girt*

'A sneaky, sometimes shocking peek under the
dirty rug of Australian history.'
JOHN BIRMINGHAM

'There is barely a page in *Girt* that won't inspire
a chortle. It's our early history told by a writer with
a wit sharp enough to slice tomatoes.'
THE HERALD SUN

'*Girt* ... cuts an irreverent swathe through the
facts, fools, fantasies and frauds that made this country
what it is today. I was transported.'
SHANE MALONEY, THE AGE

GIRT
NATION

The Unauthorised History of Australia • Volume 3

DAVID HUNT

ILLUSTRATIONS BY AD LONG

Published by Black Inc.,
an imprint of Schwartz Books Pty Ltd
Level 1, 221 Drummond Street
Carlton VIC 3053, Australia
enquiries@blackincbooks.com
www.blackincbooks.com

9781760640156 (paperback)
9781743822043 (ebook)

 A catalogue record for this
book is available from the
National Library of Australia

Book design by Peter Long
Typesetting by Tristan Main
Illustrations by Ad Long
Cover images: Alfred Deakin – unknown photographer, National Library of Australia;
magpie – Shuang Li/Shutterstock; manhole – Yashkin Ilya/Shutterstock;
Parliament House Melbourne – John Henry Harvey, State Library of Victoria
Photograph on p. 296: unknown photographer, studio portrait photograph
of Thomas Hinton, 1900, National Museum of Australia

In memory of Frazer Allan
1966–2021

By David Hunt

The Unauthorised History of Australia

GIRT

TRUE GIRT

GIRT NATION

For children and the young at heart

THE NOSE PIXIES

MY REAL FRIEND

... temper, democratic; bias, offensively Australian.

Joseph Furphy, Summary of His Novel

Such Is Life, 1897

In the land where sport is sacred, where the lab'rer is a god,
You must pander to the people, make a hero of a clod!

Henry Lawson, 'A Song of Southern Writers', 1892

... in another hundred years the average [Australian] will be:
a tall, coarse, strong-jawed, greedy, pushing talented man,
excelling in swimming and horsemanship ... his national policy
a Democracy tempered by the rate of exchange. His wife will
be a thin, narrow woman, very fond of dress and idleness,
caring little for her children, but without sufficient brainpower
to sin with zest.

Marcus Clarke, The Future Australian Race, 1877

Contents

Introduction

... a nation for a continent and a continent for a nation.
Edmund 'Toby Tosspot' Barton, 1897

AUSTRALIA.

How could one word mean so much, yet so little? It might one day be a nation, but who would be its people? Would its bounds encompass the lands of the penniless sand-dwellers to the west, or the atlas-makers' afterthought on the wrong side of Bass Strait? Could the sturdy yeomen of the south, who'd never felt the leg iron's chafe, reconcile themselves with the northern slavers? And how might the citizens of its two great cities join as one when they couldn't even agree on a football code? These disparate peoples shared a continent, but could they share a future?

There were green and gold shoots of possibility. Yes, there were Tasmanians, South Australians, Victorians, Queenslanders, Western Australians and New South Welshmen – and they all considered themselves British – but they also called themselves and each other Australian.[1] There were differences, but also shared values. They believed in democracy (for men), a fair go (for white men) and house-work (for women of all colours). They were committed to a free press, trial by jury and, for the most part, freedom of religion. They trusted in commerce, progress and the queen. And most of all, they shared

---

1   Consideration was also given to calling New Zealanders Australian, but thankfully common sense prevailed.

the bond of losing money betting on ridiculously dressed shortarses engaging in S&M with defenceless animals.

The Melbourne Cup was not so much the race that stopped the nation, as the race that started it. Visiting American writer Mark Twain called Melbourne Cup Day 'the Australasian National Day', with no single event in the world, even the Fourth of July in the United States, able to match its fervour:

> [The] race ground is the Mecca of Australasia. On the great annual day of sacrifice ... business is suspended over a stretch of land and sea as wide as from New York to San Francisco, and deeper than from the northern lakes to the Gulf of Mexico; and every man and woman, of high degree or low, who can afford the expense, put away their other duties and come. They begin to swarm in by ship and rail a fortnight before the day, and they swarm thicker and thicker day after day ... They come a hundred thousand strong ...[2]

Horse racing gave Australians a common sport. More surprisingly, it gave them art, birthing 'a national school of Australian poetry'. Why write about an old Greek pot or some dead Asian guy's pleasure palace when you could dash off a few lines about a jockey being trampled to death in the sixth at Caulfield? It didn't matter whether the poem rhymed or scanned – readers would love it as long as it had a horse in it. The cannier Australian poets didn't just write about horses, they built their identities around them. 'The Breaker' wrote as a horse handler, while 'The Banjo' went one better and wrote as a horse.

Horses weren't just found at the track, but on farms and pastoral runs, and in the untamed expanses of the Australian bush. There were so many wild and remote horsey settings for a poet to choose from – and so poems about racehorses evolved into poems about bush horses and the men who tamed and rode them.

---

2   Victoria remains the only place on earth to hold a public holiday for a horse race.

Australian artists, realising the poets were onto a sure thing, turned their easels bushwards. They abandoned portraits of consumptive girls fondling spaniels for paintings of muscular men fondling sheep, bristling with vitality and facial hair.[3] Landscapes featuring haystacks and flowering meadows were out – slab-huts and gum trees were in. The *Bulletin,* a cynical Sydney paper, remade itself as 'The Bushman's Bible', somehow managing to be both racy and country, like the *Picture* and *People,* but with more bush.

Australia was the most urbanised place on earth in the 1880s.[4] More than half the continent's colonisers lived in cities and large towns, yet when an Australian man looked in the mirror – whether he was short or tall, old or young, from country or from town – a tough, honest, hard-working son of the land stared back at him.

This was the power of the bush legend – the power to make a mild-mannered Sydney accountant who owned an Akubra think he was the Man from Snowy River. Nationalists and Labor, the new workers' party, latched onto the bush legend like blowflies to a jumbuck's jacksy, hoping that a little of its blokey matiness would rub off.[5] Labor, through some weird political alchemy, transformed the mateship of bushmen into the solidarity of workers. The nationalists helped make the bush identity an Australian one.

Australia now had Australians, but something was missing. The answer was un-Australians. To build a nation, you need to know not only who you are, but who you are not. Who would these un-Australians be?

---

3   Both the men and the sheep.

4   If you didn't count First Nations people – which was surprisingly easy in a land whose Constitution would soon provide, 'In reckoning the numbers of the people of the Commonwealth, or of a State or other part of the Commonwealth, aboriginal natives should not be counted.'

5   *Jumbuck* is an Australian word for a male sheep. It is believed to derive from *junbuc,* which Australian poet Charles Harpur claims was an Aboriginal word for a 'shag-haired species of Kangaroo particular to mountain copses', or from the Aboriginal pidgin for 'jump up', which is what a sheep does when you try to spear it.

Larrikins were un-Australian, with their song and dance routines, vegetable-themed double entendres and casual approach to violence. Actually, scratch that – although nobody liked a larrikin (including other larrikins), those things all seemed pretty Australian.[6]

Women looked promising. Most of them rode side-saddle and you couldn't chase a mob of brumbies down a mountain doing that.[7] They were also deficient in the sheep-fondling department. Women had, for the most part, been successfully corralled in the kitchen, laundry and bedroom, and were used to being looked down on. They would do.

It then dawned on Australian men that without Australian women there would be no Australian boys who would become Australian men. And women were increasingly breaking out of the domestic sphere that imprisoned them. They were popping up in all sorts of unexpected places and demanding all sorts of unexpected rights. Australians would have to find an easier target.

What about the natives? It would be tricky to argue that a native of Australia was not Australian – though, given time, some compelling arguments would surely be found. But how could Australians unite against a people who were hiding in reserves and missions? Un-Australians needed to be visible to reinforce feelings of Australianness. And the natives weren't going to be around for much longer anyway – it would be harder to feel Australian if all the un-Australians were dead. A few people even argued that it didn't seem fair to exclude the natives from Project Australia, as we'd 'taken their country from them'.

Hang on a minute ... what if some people took our country from us? Surely, that would be un-Australian. And so, Australians turned their eyes north. To China.

---

6   These sacred larrikin traditions have been handed down through the generations by their custodians – hosts of *The Footy Show*.

7   *Brumby* is an Australian word for a wild horse. It is believed to derive from a lost Aboriginal word, or from Sergeant James Brumby, who left his horses to run wild when he was posted to Tasmania.

The Chinese wanted to invade Australia to take jobs from Australian men and give opium to Australian women. They wanted to infect Australians with leprosy and sell them un-Australian vegetables. And it wasn't just the Chinese (although they were the worst). It was all the other yellow races – and the black and brown ones too! If Australians wanted to keep being Australians, then they needed to be *white* Australians.

The red blood that ran through the blue veins of white Australians would bind the disparate colonies into a nation: itself bound to the red, blue and white of the Union Jack. To keep that nation pure, it would be necessary to keep coloured folk out. It was time to raise the drawbridge of Fortress Australia. Thankfully, its moat was already well stocked with sharks and crocodiles.

There were, of course, things other than racehorses, racism and rugged bearded bushmen that bound the people of Britain's six southern colonies together. There were concerns about all the French and Germans bobbing around the Pacific. There were trains, wars, international expos, droughts, floods, depressions, plagues of rabbits and plagues of Nellie Melba farewell tours. But most of all, there was the simple calculus of geography and a desire to show Mother Britain that her children had grown up, although they still wanted to return home every second weekend with a load of dirty washing.

The people of the Australian colonies achieved great things during their quest to become Australian. They transformed democracy, at home and abroad; they revolutionised women's and workers' rights; they introduced child and adult education reforms that were the envy of the world; they oversaw a second agricultural revolution; they achieved the seemingly impossible in simultaneously increasing jollity levels in both swagmen and jumbucks; they ushered in new freezing and food-preservation technologies and gave man wings; they invented the crouch start and beat the Poms at every sport; they attained the highest standard of living and GDP per capita on the globe; they ate more meat and drank more tea than anyone; and they reduced the incidence of harmful alcohol consumption and even more harmful masturbation.

But we are getting ahead of ourselves.

Let us return to a simpler age, to an unassuming house in Melbourne's Fitzroy. A six-year-old girl sings nursery rhymes in its tidy garden, her father anxiously pacing a narrow hall, his eyes on the door that is closed to him. If he could but open it and step across the threshold, he would see his wife on their bed, sheets spotted with blood, the midwife in attendance. He knew this child would be their last. His wife's cries quieten. A new voice is heard. A voice that will unite a people. A voice that will harness the power of a club of sexist, racist insurance salesmen to transform Australia from an aspiration into a nation. The voice of Alfred Deakin.

I

The PM, the Poet and the Push

I had several faces because I was young and didn't know who I was or wanted to be.

Milan Kundera, *The Joke*, 1967

OF PROPHECY AND COSTERMONGERY

ALFRED DEAKIN WAS A CHILD OF PROPHECY, HIS coming foretold by an ancient gypsy woman encountered by Alfred's father, William, in the west of England. The wizened crone predicted that William would meet and fall in love with his future wife within weeks, that they would travel to the other side of the globe, and that the new Mrs Deakin would bear him two children – standard ancient gypsy woman schtick.

And lo, it came to pass that William, bearing gifts of apple, cabbage and turnip, did travel to the place that is called Abergavenny in the Kingdom of Wales. There he came upon the maid Sarah. And William said unto Sarah, 'Will you marry me?' And Sarah said unto William, 'Sure.' Then did William and Sarah journey even unto the ends of the earth, to a place of sin and darkness called Adelaide, where William begat Catherine. And the Spirit came upon William and called unto him, 'Go ye forth to the lands of the tribe of Melbourne.' William did as the Spirit bade and there, in the place of the Melbournites that is called Fitzroy, he begat Alfred. And it was good.

William Deakin was a humble costermonger when he met Sarah.[1] Costermongers sold fruit and vegetables on the streets, usually from a wheelbarrow. Some, like ancient gypsy women, were travellers – monging their costers by horse, pony, donkey or goat cart.[2]

Prophecy and costermongery had led William Deakin to Australia. Prophecy would guide William's only son, Alfred, and raise him to the prime ministership of Australia. Costermongery would guide Australians in fashion, language and the arts – and in developing a national identity – for it is Australia, not Britain, that is truly a nation of grocers.

ALFRED DEAKIN'S SCHOOL DAYS

Alfred Deakin was named after Alfred, Lord Tennyson, the poet laureate of Great Britain and Ireland. Both his parents dabbled with verse, and poetry would become one of Alfred's great loves.

By the time of Alfred's birth in 1856, William had abandoned his barrow for a stagecoach and vegetables for Victorians, transporting the latter from Melbourne to the Bendigo goldfields. He would rise through the coaching ranks to become the Victorian manager of Cobb & Co, nineteenth-century Australia's largest land transport company. Alfred Deakin's upbringing would be comfortably middle class.

And odd.

Alfred was packed off to boarding school at the unusually young age of four. Even more unusually, he attended Kyneton Ladies' School, an institution that taught young girls how to be young ladies (i.e. chaste, domesticated and cultured). As the only boy among dozens

---

1   Ironmongers mong iron, fishmongers mong fish, and warmongers mong war – but it's not immediately apparent what a costermonger mongs. A costermonger was originally a 'costardmonger', a costard being a variety of apple.

2   Goats were used to pull children and disabled people, as well as fruit and vegetables, with goat cart races popular among working-class gamblers. In Britain, goat carts were called go-carts, while in Australia they became known as billycarts (a billy being a male goat).

of girls, he was cossetted and encouraged to be heard, not just seen – a ladies' school first.

At the age of seven, the aspiring young lady found himself at the all-male Melbourne Church of England Grammar School. Australian grammar schools were modelled on British public schools and, during Deakin's school days, were the sole providers of secondary education.[3]

Alfred didn't make a good first impression at Melbourne Grammar. The other boys teased him for his girlish ways and one of the masters described him as 'the most incorrigible vexatious restless and babbling creature I ever met'. Alfred performed poorly, later admitting that he'd been 'an incessantly restless, random and at times studiously mischievous pupil'.

Alfred escaped the humdrum of class through daydreaming. He loved books and haunting public libraries, and seeing Sir William Don performing in drag sparked a lifelong passion for the theatre.[4] Alfred, who lacked the practical skills of his father, was definitely more arts than crafts.

The young drag fan progressed to Grammar's upper school and applied himself to his studies to please his favourite master, John Henning Thompson, brother of the two sisters who'd run Kyneton Ladies'. Alfred later recalled Thompson as 'over 6 feet, handsome as Apollo, voice like a bugle, eyes beautiful as a woman's ... His influence over me was the most potent yet formed.'

---

3   British private schools were called public schools because members of the public were allowed to attend if they had parents wealthy enough to pay for their education, bowler hats and ritual beatings.

4   Sir William Don, seventh baronet of Newtondon, became a comedian to pay off the debts he'd incurred as an aristocrat (there was much more money in the arts in those days). He toured Australia in 1861–62, playing female characters in a string of burlesques. Burlesques were plays or skits that used overstatement or absurdity to make fun of their targets, rather than the striptease cabaret acts that carry the name today. British burlesque commonly featured large men dressed as unconvincing women, while American burlesque commonly featured blackfaced men dressed as unconvincing African Americans. Both burlesque traditions have thankfully been preserved in Australia by *The Footy Show*.

The pliable young man was also shaped by his headmaster, Dr John Bromby, a clergyman who rose early, chopped wood for exercise, sat down to a spartan breakfast, lectured boys on moral living, encouraged their participation in organised games, sat down to a spartan dinner (definitely no alcohol) and retired early for the night, so that he might wake refreshed to do exactly the same again the following day.

Bromby was a Muscular Christian. Muscular Christians believed that manliness was next to godliness and that Christian men should work out more because Jesus was buff.[5] They were ascetics who insisted Christian men should preserve their God-given bodies by not abusing them with anything enjoyable, for the degradation of a body made in God's image was an assault on God Himself.[6] The Young Men's Christian Association (YMCA) helped spread the doctrine of looking hot for Christ around the globe by encouraging young Christian men to exercise and developing new manly sports, including basketball and volleyball.

The Muscular Christian movement, which began in the mid-nineteenth century, was popularised by two English Christian socialist writers, Thomas Hughes and the Reverend Charles Kingsley.

Hughes was a lawyer, judge and politician who championed workers' cooperatives and the legalisation of trade unions. His works included *Notes for Boys*, *True Manliness* and *The Manliness of Christ*, but today he's best remembered for *Tom Brown's School Days*, in which Tom, an unacademic but athletic pupil at the elite Rugby school, bests the school bully, Flashman, and develops into a manly young man who does not cheat on his homework, says his nightly prayers and is jolly good at ball games.

---

5   Muscular Christians cite Mark 11:15 – '... and Jesus went into the temple, and began to cast out them that sold and bought in the temple, and overthrew the tables of the moneychangers, and the seats of them that sold doves.' You can't trash the joint and kick moneychanger and dove-seller ass if you're a 97-pound weakling.

6   Muscular Christians cite 1 Corinthians 6:19–20 – 'What? know ye not that your body is the temple of the Holy Ghost which is in you, which ye have of God, and ye are not your own? For ye are bought with a price: therefore glorify God in your body, and in your spirit, which are God's.'

FIG. 1: THE YOUNG MEN OF MELBOURNE GRAMMAR KNEW IT WAS FUN
TO STAY AT THE YMCA.

Kingsley was a Church of England clergyman, Cambridge history professor, novelist and poet who championed workers' cooperatives and the liberal education of working-class men. He was also chaplain to Queen Victoria and private tutor to the Prince of Wales – nice work for a socialist, if you can get it.

Kingsley believed the British royal family were descendants of the Norse god Odin, which might explain the muscularity of the superior 'Norse-Saxon race', if not the Christianity. Kingsley didn't like Italians, Turks, Jews, blacks or Americans. Poor Irish Catholics were 'white chimpanzees' and Catholics more generally were slaves to effeminate priests who couldn't relate to women in the manly way God intended. Effeminacy, Kingsley asserted, had also weakened the Church of England. There should be no place in the clergy for sissies – just cissies, born men who were born leaders and proclaimed their masculinity to the world.

Kingsley is today best remembered for his children's novel *The Water-Babies*, in which Tom, a young chimney sweep, drowns after being chased from a rich girl's house and awakens as a 3.87902-inches-long aquatic cherub whose moral education is completed while living in a commune of other tiny aquatic cherubs, and who saves the soul of his also-drowned former master, for which he is returned to life and becomes a great industrialist and scientist.[7]

Kingsley and most early Muscular Christians were 'broad church' liberals who reinterpreted Christianity according to personal experience and reason. A friend of Charles Darwin, Kingsley championed the theory of evolution, arguing that God had 'created a few original forms capable of self-development'.

Dr Bromby included evolutionary theory in Melbourne Grammar's curriculum, and Alfred Deakin, with his inquiring mind and desire to reconcile his spirituality with his observations, integrated this 'new science' into his Christian faith. He believed that God had set the wheels of the universe in motion and then taken a back seat, allowing scientifically observable processes to keep those wheels spinning.

Alfred also embraced Dr Bromby's regimen of self-discipline. The impressionable schoolboy swore off alcohol, coffee and tea, and became a strict vegetarian. Alfred's vegetarianism was motivated by both his commitment to temperance and his belief that animals had rights, not the least of which was the right not to be eaten.[8] Alfred also

---

7   Tom is the Muscular Christian go-to name. Tom is also a sexually mature male
     cat. There is a PhD out there for the first person who can write 80,000 words on
     the links between hyper-masculinism, Anglicanism, socialism, liberalism, racism,
     British public schools, the monarchy, Norse mythology and cats.

8   Alfred was interested in the work of the Society for the Prevention of Cruelty to
     Animals (now the RSPCA), co-founded in England in 1824 by Lewis Gompertz, a
     vegan who refused to wear animal products. The Society may not have been cruel
     to animals, but it was to Jews, with Gompertz expelled after the Society limited
     its membership to Christians. Gompertz is otherwise best known for his 1821
     hand-powered forerunner of the bicycle, which he invented to prevent horses from
     being sat on. The world's first bicycle, the 1817 German *Laufmaschine* (running
     machine) – a balance bicycle propelled by the rider pushing the ground with his
     feet – was also developed as an alternative to the horse, as the massive ash cloud

took up vigorous morning exercise, which became a lifelong habit, although he disdained the organised games that were of growing importance to Muscular Christians and Australians.

Marching was more Alfred's thing. He lied about his age to join the Southern Rifles, a volunteer regiment that embarked on a recruitment drive when Britain withdrew the last of its troops from the Australian colonies in 1870. The Rifles were warrior poets and Alfred joined their debating society, learning to wound with weapons and words alike.

Alfred had become a well-rounded if tediously earnest young man. In 1871, at the age of fifteen, he finished school and passed the exam to study law at the University of Melbourne.

BARTY AND THE BANJO

Rose Paterson gave birth to a healthy baby boy at Narrambla Station, near the New South Wales town of Orange, on 17 February 1864. The baby's birth certificate recorded his name as Baby, suggesting that Rose and her husband, Andrew, were very literal people. He was later christened Andrew Barton Paterson, but everybody called him Barty.

The Patersons were descendants of John Petersen, a Scandinavian who'd changed his surname after moving to Scotland. They were into sport, horses and losing vast sums of money, a common Australian trifecta. Barty's grandfather Captain John Paterson was a champion curler.[9] John Paterson, another relative, bred the first Clydesdale horses. And Barty's ancestor Sir William Paterson convinced Scotland to invest 20 per cent of its money to establish a colony in Panama – the colony failed and Scotland went bust, forcing it to accept union with England.

---

from the 1815 eruption of Mount Tambora in modern Indonesia caused global crop failures during 'the Year Without a Summer' (1816). European horses didn't have enough fodder and those that didn't starve, or hadn't been killed by hungry soldiers during the Napoleonic Wars, were eaten by the crop-starved peasantry.

9   Using brooms to sweep ice in front of a slowly moving rock is 'sport' to the extent that *Fifty Shades of Grey* is 'literature'.

Barty also had poetry in his veins. Captain Paterson wrote verses about his adventures in India, while Barty's grandfather Robert Barton married Emily Darvall after reading her poems aboard the ship they shared to Australia. Barty's early childhood was spent at Buckinbah Station, where he hung out with Jerry the Rhymer, an old convict shepherd and balladeer.

Barty's idyllic years at Buckinbah were interrupted by a broken right arm, which his mother diagnosed as teething. Rose treated the break by slicing Barty's gums and burning him behind the ears in an attempt to drain toxins from his body. This was far less dangerous than standard teething treatments – alcohol syrup, laudanum (a tincture of opium) or chlorodyne (a tincture of opium with some cannabis and chloroform thrown in for good measure).[10]

Barty's break was not detected until he rebroke his arm after falling from a horse. He snapped it again at the age of twelve and was left with a permanently shortened and weakened limb. Rose, on the basis of no evidence whatsoever, blamed Barty's Aboriginal nurse for the original break:

> That horrid Black Fanny must've been climbing trees with him or something of that sort and never let on to us for a moment that anything happened to the child.

Aboriginal women evened the ledger when the accident-prone Barty asked Nora Budgeree, a young Aboriginal girl, for a spear-throwing demonstration. With uncanny accuracy, she threw the spear through his leg.

The Patersons' curse of losing vast sums of money struck when Barty was five. Andrew senior lost the farm (and two others he owned) when a failed Queensland property venture bankrupted him. Andrew

---

10   Children with respiratory complaints were commonly treated with *Cigares de Joy* (cannabis cigarettes). Sick children in nineteenth-century Australia spent a lot of time completely off their faces.

remained station manager at one of his properties, Illawong, a glorified servant on what had once been his own land. He hit the bottle and took laudanum for back pain, slipping into an addict's depression. Rose took to calling her husband 'the old cripple' and lapsed into paranoia, believing Illawong's new owners were listening in on her conversations and engaging her servants as spies.

Barty found solace in riding The Banjo, a family horse, wryly observing that his stunted arm gave him 'a light hand on the rein'. He fell in love with racing at the age of eight when he attended his first meet, at which Pardon won the Bogolong Town Plate. He was not alone in his obsession. Australians loved nothing more than a day at the races with a pint and a punt.[11]

Australians loved horse racing so much they wrote poems about it. Adam Lindsay Gordon wrote 'Visions in the Smoke', in which he hallucinated a Melbourne Cup race in his pipe smoke. The Cup in this drug-induced dream was won by Tim Whiffler, inspiring superstitious racehorse owners to name their horses Tim Whiffler. There were two Tim Whifflers in the 1867 Melbourne Cup. One of the Tim Whifflers won and was put out to stud, siring a colt named Tim Whiffler.[12]

Gordon had left England after his 'strength and health were broken by dissipation and humbug'. After serving as a South Australian mounted policeman, he found work as a horse-breaker and befriended Father Julian Tenison-Woods, a Catholic priest who lent him books and encouraged his love of poetry. After a short stint as a

---

11 Australians are still addicted to racing and sports betting. They lose more than twice as much money through gambling as their UK and US counterparts, punting nearly five times as much as Australia spends on foreign aid.

12 'Melbourne Cup' is a misnomer, as only a few of the early winning owners received anything resembling a cup. The prize for the first race, in 1861, was a gold watch, and the first gold cup wasn't awarded until 1916. An assortment of plates, bowls, trays, tankards, jugs, table ornaments, tea and coffee services, and dessert stands were awarded in the intervening years. The Cup was more the race that stocked a tearoom than stopped a nation.

parliamentarian, Gordon embarked on a career as a poet who wrote about horses. 'The poet of the horse', as Gordon was known, was also a champion steeplechase racer, but his short-sightedness resulted in falls that caused brain damage, manifesting as a profound melancholia. When his 1870 *Bush Ballads and Galloping Rhymes* sold poorly, he trudged into the tea-tree scrub and shot himself. This proved a great career move, with his resulting popularity leaving him the only Australian to be commemorated in Poets' Corner at Westminster Abbey. More importantly, as observed by his contemporary Marcus Clarke, author of the serialised *His Natural Life* (renamed *For the Term of His Natural Life* after his death), Gordon's work formed 'the beginnings of a national school of Australian poetry'.

Barty loved Gordon's work. At age ten, the young poetry fancier went to live with his grandmother, Emily Barton, a society widow whose Gladesville home *Rockend* overlooked Sydney's Parramatta River. Barty was packed off to Sydney Grammar, where he was dux of the junior school.

Barty blamed his subsequent academic slide on 'fish and rabbits', just two of the many animals he delighted in killing.[13] He'd been introduced to cockfighting by his infants teacher and wrote for the Sydney Grammar magazine about the simple childhood pleasures of wasting a platypus and pumping a pelican full of lead. Barty was also into 'wallarooing', a popular Sydney Grammar pastime in which a small boy would be hunted, pushed to the ground and have his mouth stuffed with grass, his boots stolen and his boater trampled, but it was all in good fun.[14]

Sport was another great passion, with Barty's dodgy arm forcing him to learn to play tennis left-handed. He also loved rowing, although

---

13   Barty good-naturedly observed, 'If I had paid as much attention to my lessons as
      to fish and rabbits, I too might have been a Judge of the High Court. There is a lot
      of luck in these things!'

14   *Wallaroo* may refer to a small relative of the kangaroo or a small, terrified Sydney
      Grammar boy with no shoes or hat.

here his arm proved a liability. Still, he'd watch Ned 'The Slab' Trickett, the 1876 world sculling champion (and first Australian world champion in any sport), race Bill 'Gypsy' Beach (Australia's second world sporting champion) on the river below *Rockend*. Barty wrote that their successes gave rise to an 'orgy of sculling' in Australia.[15]

In winter, Sydney Grammar boys played rugby, the sporting vehicle for Muscular Christianity and Empire. In summer, they played cricket, the sporting vehicle for racism and rioting. Cricket, more than any sport, fostered inter-colonial rivalry and, paradoxically, drew the colonies closer together. The colonies loved beating each other, but they loved beating England even more.

Australians thrilled at the success of the cricketers who toured England in 1868, the first Australian sports team to travel overseas. Alright, they were all Victorians, but nobody's perfect. And they were all Aboriginal, but they'd been given proper white names like Dick-a-Dick, Jimmy Mosquito, King Cole, Red Cap, Twopenny, Tiger and Jim Crow.[16]

London's *Daily Telegraph* sniffily reported that Australia produced nothing of interest 'except gold nuggets and black cricketers', although it acknowledged the tourists 'were fully clothed and in their right minds'. The *Times* huffed that the games were a 'travestie upon cricketing at Lords', but Australians were proud that the team won as many games as it lost – although it *was* embarrassing for normal folk to be towelled up by 'conquered natives'.[17]

---

15 Perhaps that's why Australia's most famous rowers were known as the Oarsome Foursome.

16 Jim Crow was named after the famous minstrel character created by international blackface star Thomas Dartmouth 'Daddy' Rice. Rice was also famous for his 'Shadow Dance', in which he'd sing 'Me and My Shadow' while carrying a sack, from which a small child in blackface would emerge and attempt to copy his dance moves in a hilariously incompetent way. Rice's politically incorrect minstrel was so popular that racial segregation laws in southern US states adopted the Jim Crow name.

17 They're called 'cricket whites' for a reason.

Victoria prevented any further embarrassment by passing the
Aboriginal Protection Act in 1869. The Act protected foreign cricketers from being beaten by Aboriginal people by making it illegal to
take Aboriginal people out of Victoria without the approval of a new
Central Board for the Protection of Aborigines.

Which would not be forthcoming.[18]

Still, other Australians could beat the Poms – and they did, when a
combined Victorian and New South Wales XI defeated England in the
world's first test match, held at the Melbourne Cricket Ground in 1877.

Barty was a spectator when England played New South Wales at
the Sydney Cricket Ground during England's 1879 Revenge Tour. Each
team selected an umpire. New South Wales chose one of Barty's distant relatives, Edmund Barton (Toby to his friends), an accomplished
cricketer.[19] Barton was also an excellent rower and fisherman, and an
aspiring politician. England chose George Coulthard, a star footballer
with the Carlton Australian Rules football club.

Coulthard, a treacherous Victorian, judged New South Wales
opening batsman Billy Murdoch run out early in the second innings.
The home captain, Dave Gregory, demanded a new umpire and halted
the game when Lord Harris, the English captain, refused. Barty and
about 2,000 mostly drunk spectators invaded the pitch. Coulthard
was jostled and Lord Harris whipped, before England's two leading
fast bowlers, holding the mob at bay with cricket stumps, escorted
their captain from the field.[20]

---

18   Racism was endemic in Australian cricket. In 1902, the English cricket team
     refused to play against Aboriginal player Jack Marsh, arguably the greatest bowler
     of his era. To save everybody from embarrassment, Marsh was forced out of the
     game by bogus 'no ball' calls. Eddie Gilbert, rated by Don Bradman as the fastest
     bowler he'd faced, couldn't leave his Queensland Aboriginal reserve for games
     without ministerial approval – he was labelled a chucker and barred from the
     game. Australia's first First Nations international cricketer, Jason Gillespie,
     didn't wear the green and gold until 1996.

19   Though, according to the *Australian Dictionary of Biography*, 'an atrocious fieldsman'.

20   Coulthard had a full life before dying of tuberculosis at the age of twenty-seven.
     He was recognised as Australian Rules' 'first bona fide superstar', was the

The Sydney Riot of 1879 relegated Ned Kelly's raid on Jerilderie to the inner pages of Australian newspapers. The *Sydney Morning Herald* called it 'a national humiliation' that 'would remain a blot upon the colony for some years to come'. Barty called it a fun day out.

Barty also attended cricket matches at Gladesville's Hospital for the Insane, where the sports-loving assistant superintendent, Teddy Betts, staged matches between the inmates and some of Australia's leading cricketers. The cricketers participated in Betts' 'therapy for the patients' because they were given 'cold roast suckling pig and all the beer they wanted'. The hospital's wicketkeeper, incarcerated for homicidal mania, once had to be restrained from violently inserting a stump into future Australian captain George Giffen.

With all the sport, hunting, fishing, riding, rioting and stuffing small boys' mouths with grass, Barty had little time for his studies and was awarded a Low in French. Still, his natural ability would have assured him a place at university had he not been quarantined with severe typhoid during his final exams. And he was still able to practise law, because his grandmother's wealth and connections secured him a position at a reputable firm.

Alfred Deakin and Barty Paterson both loved poetry and were interested in the law, but Deakin was inflexible fragile chalk to Paterson's agreeable sweaty cheese. Deakin was drawn to the spiritual – Paterson to the physical. Deakin worked for his success – Paterson trusted it would come naturally. Deakin wanted to protect animals – Paterson wanted to

---

top scorer for New South Wales' Waratah rugby club (which he later briefly convinced to switch to Australian Rules), entered the ring with bare-knuckle boxing champion Jem 'The Gypsy' Mace, fought off a thirteen-foot shark that had dragged him from a boat, and played one cricket test match for Australia (ironically under Billy Murdoch). On his deathbed he announced that he'd dreamed Martini Henry would win the Victory Derby, Dirk Hatteraick would win the Melbourne Cup, and that he would soon die. After Coulthard expired and Martini Henry raced to victory, superstitious folk bet on Dirk Hatteraick in the Cup. The horse, described by one journalist as 'fat as a bacon hog', ran close to last. Coulthard was not only responsible for Australia's first international sporting riot, but its then largest betting plunge.

kill them. Deakin considered exercise necessary – Paterson considered it fun. Deakin sought mastery over himself – Paterson cheerfully surrendered to himself and others.

But both these young men would shape Australia and the very notion of what it was to be Australian.

CHILDREN OF THE COSTERMONGERS

On 7 February 1870, as Alfred and Barty attended school, Melbourne's *Age* ran a story about a group of boys who'd never seen the inside of a classroom.

> A stout six-foot constable next makes his appearance, having in each hand a youngster of the rowdy class, commonly termed 'larrikins,' who have been amusing themselves in company with some twenty others of similar tastes, by insulting every person who passed them.

This was the first time the word *larrikin* appeared in print. The Melbourne press knew it was on to a good thing, with papers soon outdoing each other in the rush to publish stories on the 'larrikin menace'.

There were a lot of young people for old people to whinge about in 1870, as the infants of the gold rush baby boom were now surly teenagers. Old people couldn't flee to the suburbs to escape the disrespectful young folk who spat on the footpath or spoke loudly in the Botanical Gardens, because there were no suburbs to flee to. Australian cities were all city, with the upper and lower classes packed densely together.

Melbourne did disaffected youth far better than Sydney. Sydney had the Cabbage-Tree Mob, young men who wore hats woven from palm fronds and enjoyed giving their betters a 'bonneting' – smacking the tops of their hats to force them over their eyes. Bonneting and wallarooing made Sydney the youth hat vandalism capital of

Australia, but that was about as hardcore as it got.

Australia's first larrikins were members of loose gangs, known as forties and then pushes, the latter term borrowed from the 'flash' language of the convicts.[21] The gangs formed in Alfred Deakin's neighbourhood of Fitzroy and Collingwood in the late 1860s. Their members adopted the name *larrikin*, which meant 'a mischievous youth' in a Warwickshire and Worcestershire dialect. Originally pronounced *learykin*, the name probably also appealed because *leary* was flash for streetwise and *kin* spoke to a common identity.

Most larrikins were unskilled labourers – bootblacks, bottle collectors, newspaper boys, rag sellers, carters and street vendors. They were tuppenny-capitalists who disdained those who'd learned a trade. They first appeared when employment was plentiful and would constantly switch jobs – like millennials, but not as irritating.

Though mostly born of poor, Irish Catholic immigrants, larrikins saw themselves as Australian and their parents' generation as foreign in nationality and attitude. They were the future, and they would remake Australia in their own image. Unfortunately, the image they'd adopted was that of the Cockney costermonger.

Costermongers would attract customers with a rapid-fire sales patter of rhymes, songs and chants. Police regarded them as a traffic hazard and a source of petty crime. Costermongers adopted a

---

21   *Forty* was a slang term for a patch of territory and the gang that claimed it. The term may derive from a unit of area measurement or from the gang of forty thieves who had it in for Ali Baba. The flash language, also known as thieves' cant, was introduced into Australia by convicts and had a profound development on Australian English. James Hardy Vaux, a transported pickpocket and swindler, compiled a *Vocabulary of the Flash Language* that listed slang words used by career criminals. It defined *push* as 'a crowd or concourse of people, either in the streets, or at any public place of amusement'. In Ireland the term came to mean a prison gang, with this meaning brought to Australia by Irish convicts. Other words listed in Vaux's *Vocabulary* included *bash* (hit), *bolt* (run), *cadge* (beg), *chum* (friend), *cove* (master of the house, later meaning boss and then any man), *croak* (die), *dollop* (a large quantity), *galloot* (a soldier), *grub* (food), *out-and-out* (completely), *rum* (good), *snooze* (sleep), *swag* (a bundle of goods), *try it on* (to make an attempt where success is doubtful) and *yarn* (to tell a story).

distinctive dress code, incorporating a kingsman (a large colour-ful neckerchief), long waistcoat and bell-bottomed trousers with mother-of-pearl buttons adorning the seams. The gaudy grocers were known for their rhyming slang, but communicated among themselves in back slang, a coded language in which words are spo-ken backwards – *yob*, for example, which originally meant 'boy', but came to mean 'lout' or 'hooligan'. Without costermongery, Australia would have no yobbos.[22]

Cockney costermonger acts were a music hall staple from the 1860s. Stage costermongers would sing about women, drinking, skiv-ing off work and the foolishness and arrogance of the upper classes. Their skits and songs frequently used catchphrases and fruit and vegetable–themed double entendres.[23]

The stage costermongers, with their faux-aristocratic clothing worn in a streetwise way, modelled their look on the petty street criminals in Charles Dickens' *Oliver Twist*. English authorities had banned stage performances of *Oliver Twist* in 1845 because they were concerned the lower classes would copy the thieving ways and styling of the gang that took in the innocent Oliver. The stage costermongers' adoption of Dickens' flash look was a deliberate 'up yours' to the authorities.

---

22   We Aussies are famous for shortening our words by ending them with one of twenty-four diminutives (e.g. I had brekkie and a ciggie in my cardie with Wazza the garbo), a practice meant to convey that we're so laid-back we can't be arsed finishing a simple word. We later started making short words longer (e.g. yobbo, Barnsey, Deano) because of our love for the diminutive, which entirely defeated the original purpose.

23   Costermonger acts have remained popular in Australia well into the twenty-first century. In 2010, Con Dikaletis, a Greek greengrocer whose name humorously combines *dick* and *lettuce*, toured Australian shopping centres to promote the Australian stoned fruit industry. Con was a 1980s and 1990s television character who loved 'firm juicy melons' and compared the body of his wife, Marika, to less fresh and appealing fruit and veg. He popularised the catchphrases *bewdiful*, *doesn't madda* and *coupla days*. Con the Fruiterer, as he is better known, is Australia's most famous Costamonger.

Early larrikins shared a love of musical theatre. They'd perform scenes from popular melodramas and burlesques, and sing music hall songs on improvised stages. They'd attend singing rooms, dance saloons and theatres, and hold dance-offs in public places.[24] Victims of the first larrikin attacks would have felt like they were being mugged by the cast of *West Side Story*.

Larrikins liked to look *rorty*, costermonger and larrikin slang for rowdily risqué. They aped stage costermonger fashion, wearing flamboyant scarves and handkerchiefs like Austral Oscar Wildes. The 1874 *Victorian Police Gazette* described Collingwood larrikin Garney Cooper as wearing a 'black-cloth sac-coat, soft black felt hat with white horseshoe in band, light tweed trousers, and a showy striped scarf'. Thin moustaches were popular among those old enough to grow them. Hair might be greased, shaved or both. Tattoos were in. At least that was the male larrikin look.

Some larrikin groups included young women known as *donahs*, a demeaning term for 'girlfriend' derived from the Spanish *doña* (Mrs). These low-paid domestics and seamstresses showed an unseemly amount of ankle and hat, with their heavily feathered headpieces an object of popular scorn. Brazenness and bare-knuckle street fights were a donah's stock-in-trade.

The press took the larrikin name and gave it a different meaning. Larrikins were no longer mischievous youths, but yobs. Conservatives were alarmed by young people fighting and dancing in public spaces and offending their elders and betters with their 'saucy words'. The solution, they believed, was intervening before larval street urchins matured into fully formed larrikins. Surely children would be better off out of the streets and into the schools, where some good sense, Christian morality and respect for authority might be thrashed into them.

---

24   Melbourne's Theatre Royal, which charged half the admission price of other city theatres in the 1870s, was noted for attracting 'unsavoury costermongers and foul-mouthed roughlings'.

WE DON'T NEED NO EDUCATION

Liberals were also concerned that many children received no education. Children had historically been treated as a vaguely irritating but
necessary form of parental property, but liberals had come to believe
that children were small people who had rights of their own, including
the right not to be killed while cleaning heavy industrial machinery.
Surely children would be better off out of the factories and into the
schools, where they might learn to improve themselves and society.[25]

With liberals and conservatives in accord, the time was ripe
for reform. In 1872, Victoria became the first Australian colony
(and one of the first places in the world) to provide compulsory, free
and secular public elementary schooling.[26] It also stopped funding
church-run schools.

Churches had traditionally run Australian schools with government financial aid, a few private schools being their only competition.
This heightened sectarian tensions, and most communities lacked the
population to maintain schools for children of different faiths. The solution was state-provided education, but most churches resisted reform.

Enter New South Wales' Robert Lowe, the albino politician
known in less woke times as 'Pink-eyed Bob'. Lowe championed state
schooling, a cause dear to the heart of his young campaign secretary,
Henry Parkes, a bone turner and mediocre poet whose own education
had been cut short when his father was thrown into debtor's prison.
State education was the star that would guide Parkes throughout his
long political career.

---

25   'Child savers', as they were dismissively known, sought to rescue children from
     poverty and vice. They campaigned for the regulation of child labour, compulsory
     education, kindergartens, public parks for children to gambol in, and raising the
     age of sexual consent.

26   Elementary schools were similar to modern primary schools, teaching reading,
     writing, arithmetic (described by world-famous child educator Michael Jackson
     as 'the branches of the learning tree') and religious or secular ethics (not really
     Michael's thing).

Lowe helped introduce the Irish National System of education into New South Wales in 1848, with most other Australian colonies following suit. National Schools, like their Irish counterparts, taught children of different faiths together in an attempt to stop Protestants and Catholics hating on each other. They promoted a generic Christianity, with New Testament passages on the brotherhood of man and turning the other cheek displayed in every classroom.[27]

Henry Parkes' 1866 *Public Schools Act* provided for more government schools and banned new church schools being opened within five miles of them. New South Wales church schools would only receive government funding if they had government-trained teachers, used state school curricula and restricted religious instruction to an hour a day.[28]

Most churches were upset by Parkes' reforms. The Catholic Church, which educated the most students, was furious and refused aid that was tied to limits on the teaching of Catholic dogma.

South Australia, the most religious of all the Australian colonies, had already stopped funding church schools in 1851. Any government involvement in religious affairs, most South Australians believed, compromised freedom of religion.

Tasmania, in 1868, became the first colony to make elementary schooling compulsory, although it didn't get around to enforcing the law until 1916, by which time its earliest truants were approaching retirement.

In 1870, Queensland provided Australia's first free elementary education, but this didn't ensure attendance. Some families weren't prepared to lose the income their children earned from polishing

---

27   The brothers of the religious orders who ran Catholic schools, in contrast, were known for encouraging students to turn both cheeks.

28   The public education system designed by the poorly educated bone turner from England's industrial midlands was the model for the English state education system, introduced in 1870. In 1880, Parkes would make elementary education compulsory and secular and establish government secondary schools, restricted to those expected to pass university entrance exams. Australian secondary education opportunities remained limited until the second decade of the twentieth century.

boots or crawling into small spaces to unclog the gears of dangerous factory machines.

Victoria, with a little help from the larrikins, was the first colony to put all of the pieces of the public education puzzle together. The reforms were vehemently opposed by Archbishop James Goold of Melbourne, Victoria's most powerful Catholic primate.[29] Goold ordered the following read out in every Catholic church during the 1872 election campaign:

> They boldly and defiantly tell you it is their determination to do away with your Schools and substitute them for Godless schools to which they will compel you under penalty (or imprisonment) to send your children.

Goold's scare campaign backfired, mobilising Protestant support for public secular education.

The other Australian colonies, which all established state elementary schools and abolished church school aid by 1895, allowed scripture teachers entry to schools outside class hours. Victoria, however, insisted that religion ended at the school gate. Unlike the other colonies, it stripped all references to Christianity from the curriculum. God was now a generic Creator, a nativity poem became an 'Address to the Deity', and a prose piece, 'Paul at Athens', was replaced by 'The Wonder of Cotton Manufacture'.

The Catholic Church responded to the end of state aid by developing an entirely independent education system, importing predominantly Irish priests, nuns and brothers to teach and beat the bejesus out of nearly a quarter of Australia's children. Parish schools educated the children of some of Australia's poorest families, while the Protestant schools that weren't incorporated into the state system catered for those able to afford their fees. The abolition of state aid was meant to

---

29   A church that was fighting Darwin's claim that man was related to apes should
     have chosen a better word for its archbishops.

defuse religious tensions. Instead it reinforced them by entrenching the Catholic and Protestant socio-economic divide.[30]

Still, the public education reforms pioneered by Victoria were undeniably a success. By the end of the nineteenth century, Australia had much higher child education rates than Europe, and its schools and burgeoning universities communicated new ideas to the masses.

A PORTRAIT OF THE PM AS A YOUNG MAN

Alfred Deakin, newly liberated from Melbourne Grammar, was a sponge for new ideas who sponged off his parents – it's hard to think great thoughts when your mind is needlessly filled with trivialities like paying rent or finding another woman to do your washing.

Like teenagers throughout history, Alfred spent most of his time in his bedroom reading poetry and pretentious novels, which he supplemented with works on philosophy, theology and comparative religion.

Alfred was living in an increasingly secular world and Victoria, the most aggressively secular place in Australia, incubated scepticism. Alfred questioned his faith and, at the age of sixteen, refused to be confirmed into the Church of England, writing, 'Christianity as I understood it was wider than any or even all of the Churches and therefore acceptance of any formal limitations was impossible.'

Many Christians had been struggling with their faith, or had given up on the struggle, in the face of science's assault on Christian orthodoxy. The Bible, orthodox Christians asserted, was the word of an all-knowing god and must therefore be completely true and, according to the more hardcore literalists, truly complete.[31]

---

30 Robert Menzies' Coalition government announced the reintroduction of state aid to non-government schools during the 1963 federal election campaign, in an attempt to gain the votes of Catholics who'd traditionally supported Labor.

31 The most extreme Bibliophiles denied Australia's existence because it wasn't mentioned in the Bible.

Church of England Bibles had since 1701 included Archbishop
James Ussher's calculation, derived from a painstaking study of biblical
text, that the world was created at 6 p.m. on 22 October 4004 B.C.
Charles Lyell sent shockwaves through society when his *Principles of
Geology* (1830–33) insisted the world was millions of years old, with
geologic change the product of slow and continual processes, not
cataclysmic events like Noah's Flood.

Charles Darwin's 1859 *On the Origin of Species* challenged the biblical view that God knocked out animals and humans over two days,
a couple of days after he did plants, while his 1871 *The Descent of Man*
was at odds with the Judeo-Christian orthodoxy that Adam and Eve
were created in God's image to subdue the earth and have dominion
over all living things. At best, the biblical power couple were upwardly
mobile monkeys who'd swapped their bananas for apples.

These revelations of science understandably tested the faith of
Christians who'd nailed themselves to the cross of biblical literalism,
but a real hammer blow was delivered when a Church of England
bishop published *The Pentateuch and Book of Joshua Critically Examined
(Vol. 1)* in 1862. While translating the Bible into Zulu, Bishop John
William Colenso of Natal had been told by his Zulu assistants that
hares did not regurgitate their food for further chewing, in stark
conflict with Deuteronomy 14:7.[32]

Just as a butterfly flapping its wings in the Amazon may change
the world, so might a hare not vomiting grass in Natal. Colenso,
stunned by this revelation, set about testing the accuracy of other early
Old Testament passages. Colenso's book was a publishing sensation
and excited much debate, including in Australia. Rabbits had been
introduced to Victoria in 1859 and inquisitive Victorians could now

---

32   'Nevertheless, of those that chew the cud or have cloven hooves, you shall not
     eat, *such as* these: the camel, the hare, and the rock hyrax; for they chew the
     cud but do not have cloven hooves; they *are* unclean for you.' Leviticus 11:6 also
     provides, 'And the hare, because he cheweth the cud, but divideth not the hoof; he
     is unclean unto you.' Jews really had it in for the hare.

catch one, feed it some grass and observe it steadfastly refusing to eat its own vomit.[33] Scientists confused things with all their hypotheses and theories, but this was the sort of practical testing of the Bible that Australians could understand.

If the parts of the Bible about hares and rabbits were not the words of an infallible God, might not the parts about miracles have been exaggerated a bit? The line that Jesus was just a friendly carpenter from Galilee who liked wine and fish was pushed by Melbourne's Edward William Cole. The English-born Cole had run a night pie stall on Melbourne's Russell Street and spent his days in Melbourne Public Library. There he wrote *The Real Place in History of Jesus and Paul*, in which he argued Jesus' miracles were absurd and the Bible was 'a fallacy originated by spiritual egotism'. After slagging off Allah, Buddha and every Hindu god he could think of, Cole argued that 'All faith should be the product of human reason alone'.[34] He then called for the establishment of a world religion based on the good teachings commonly held by all great faiths.

Publishers ran a mile when Cole pitched his book. Undeterred, he decided to self-publish and traded in his pie-cart for a bookstall from which he could sell his teachings. It soon became the haunt of earnest young men like Alfred Deakin who were determined to test the boundaries of their faith.

Alfred read anything and everything. Reading was a peculiarly Australian pastime. Richard Twopeny, an English-educated journalist and captain of the Adelaide Australian Rules football club, dubbed

---

33   In this, the rabbit may be distinguished from Bon Scott, who was introduced into Victoria in 1952.

34   Several of Cole's ideas mirror the later musings of German philosopher Friedrich Nietzsche. In *The Gay Science*, Nietzsche announced, 'God is dead', arguing that modern science and increasing secularisation had killed God and the Judeo-Christian beliefs that underpinned Western society. In *Ecco Homo*, Nietzsche argued that the idea of 'a Christ' is an impossible and dangerous creation of human imagination. Sigmund Freud believed Nietzsche was homosexual (the book titles may have been a giveaway), although Freud thought that about everyone.

1870s Australia 'the land of newspapers' and estimated that the proportion of people who could afford a newspaper subscription was ten times that of Britain. By 1884, the Australian colonies were the largest overseas market for British publishers – and Victoria's libraries and Mechanics' Institutes held twice as many books as those in New South Wales, despite the colonies having similar populations.[35]

Alfred was determined to add to Victoria's glut of books by writing his own. He penned poems and literary essays. The unpublished novels *Guy Evelyn or In the Far Pacific* and *Raglan Island or the Wreck of the Nelson*, later destroyed by an embarrassed Alfred, suggest the young writer had a taste for boy's own adventures and a pathological indecision when it came to choosing titles. A publisher found Alfred's *Quentin Massys*, a five-act, blank-verse play about a Renaissance Flemish painter, 'too loose and turgid ... words linked together only for a supposed effectiveness, but with entire absence of propriety and often of meaning'. This would not have been a problem for an Australian audience if Alfred had put some horses in it.

Alfred had now moved away from the conservative politics of his parents and embraced the liberalism and scientific materialism of the University of Melbourne circles in which he moved. He was particularly influenced by the radical free-trader Charles Pearson, who'd left his Kings College London professorship in modern history to become an Australian farmer. Pearson, his dreams of a simple life with sheep crushed by drought, had returned to lecturing at the

---

35   Mechanics' Institutes (sometimes known as Schools of Arts) first appeared in Scotland in the 1820s. They were established by local communities to give their citizens, particularly working-class men, access to 'useful knowledge both literary and scientific'. Along with churches, pubs and town halls, Mechanics' Institutes were Australia's main public meeting places. They operated libraries, ran adult education classes, made scientific equipment available to would-be inventors, and hosted public lectures and debates that attracted mass audiences. Australia had more Mechanics' Institutes than any place in the world. Victoria alone had over 1,100 Institutes in the nineteenth century, compared with less than 700 in all of Britain. These forerunners to modern TAFEs made Australia a world leader in adult education.

University of Melbourne and established a Debating Society that attracted youths who wanted to change the world, including Deakin, Henry Bournes Higgins and Richard Hodgson.[36]

Alfred also worked as a librarian for both the Royal Society of Victoria, the colony's principal scientific society, and the Eclectic Association, a sort of standing Festival of Dangerous Ideas for members of Melbourne's progressive elite.

At the age of eighteen, Alfred Deakin delivered his first public speech at an Eclectic Association gathering. The topic was close to the heart of a man who'd enjoyed an all-girls education.

WOMEN'S RIGHTS

---

36   Don't worry, you'll learn more about those other guys later.

2
The Handmaids' Tales

You may try, but you can never imagine, what it is to have a man's force of genius in you, and yet to suffer the slavery of being a girl.

Daniel Deronda, Mary Ann Evans (a.k.a. George Eliot), 1876

THE QUEEN'S TALE

P RINCESS ALEXANDRINA OF KENT WAS AN UNLIKELY British monarch. First, she was fifth in line to the throne when she was born in 1819. Second, she was a she.

England's 1701 *Act of Settlement* looked promising for women's rights, as it declared Electress Sophia of Hanover would be England's next monarch – but it proved a false dawn. It turned out the English parliament hated Catholics and bastards even more than it hated women, and Sophia was the nearest legitimate Protestant descendant of King James I who could be found. Sophia died before she could be crowned, with Britons issuing a collective sigh of relief when her son George ascended the throne.

Britain's Hanoverian monarchs were even better at producing bastards than their predecessors. George I had three, William IV had eleven, and George IV stopped counting.[1] But the later Hanoverians proved spectacularly unsuccessful at producing legitimate sons, and

---

1   Victoria's uncle Ernest Augustus was rumoured to have produced a rare royal double bastard with his sister, Princess Sophia.

Hanoverian women had a disturbing tendency to die in childbirth, in the womb or in infancy.[2]

The collapse of the Hanoverian frontrunners allowed Alexandrina to 'do a Bradbury' in 1837. Queen Alexandrina sounded too foreign, so Alexandrina decreed that she would be known by her middle name: Victoria.

The queen's first job was to produce a male heir and in this she was ably assisted by her favourite cousin, Prince Albert of Saxe-Coburg and Gotha. Victoria was a loving and devoted wife, unusual in her family of German sex-pests, and produced four sons (and five daughters).

Victoria's blissful monogamy made it fashionable not to root around. Sexual morality was catching, particularly among Britain's growing middle class. By the end of Victoria's reign, a glimpse of ankle was deliciously scandalous and the advice of evangelical preacher Henry Varley that husbands and wives should not unnecessarily expose their bodies to each other 'by undress' was just plain common sense.[3] Undergarments, through sheer proximity to naked skin, raised such unnatural passion that they were referred to as 'unmentionables'. Sex was not mentioned at all, at least in polite company.

Victoria herself enjoyed sex, writing of her wedding night:

I NEVER, NEVER spent such an evening!!! MY DEAREST DEAR-EST DEAR Albert ... his excessive love & affection gave me feelings of heavenly love and happiness I never could have *hoped* to have felt before! He clasped me in his arms, & we kissed each other again &

---

2   The Hanoverians and their descendants were notoriously sickly, which is what you get from generations of marrying your cousins (and sleeping with your siblings). Queen Victoria's children introduced haemophilia into most of the royal houses of Europe, with the genetic blood disorder popularly known as 'the royal disease'. The British royal family are commonly described as having 'blue blood', but it's probably just hereditary anaemia.

3   The Dean of Melbourne, the unfortunately named Hussey Macartney, barred his daughters from entering Fitzroy Gardens because some of the statues were inadequately clothed.

again! His beauty, his sweetness & gentleness – really how can I ever be thankful enough to have such a *Husband*! … to be called by names of tenderness, I have never yet heard used to me before – was bliss beyond belief! Oh! This was the happiest day of my life![4]

The queen was the country, so when Victoria lay back and thought of England she was thinking of herself, but other Victorian women were expected to think of the stout British children that two minutes of being squashed in the dark would hopefully produce.

Husbands and children – that's what being a British woman was all about. A woman submitted to her husband and dedicated herself to her children. A woman's place was in the home – she was the 'angel in the house'; the 'Household General'.[5] Victorian men, in contrast, were doers and diers. Theirs was the public sphere: the place of business, the club, the battlefield, the pulpit, the parliament. They laboured for their wages or idled for their inheritances, while their women kept house, or learned how to embroider idyllic pastoral scenes and play the piano. Poor women who had to work outside their homes were not 'proper women'.

The housewife, the husband-provider and their children formed the ideal British family. As Britain moved towards modern constitutional monarchy, eroding Victoria's political power, the queen emphasised the importance of the nuclear family. A stable family built a stable nation. Victoria never permitted a divorced lady to attend court, and she frowned upon widows who remarried (including her own mother) because one man was all a good wife needed. Victoria wore widow's

---

4   The only thing Victoria enjoyed more than sex was the exclamation mark.

5   'An Angel in the House', Coventry Patmore's popular 1854 poem, described the perfect woman as selfless, submissive, sweet, gentle, charming, forgiving and utterly devoted to meeting her wonderful husband's every need. 'The Household General' was the brainchild of Isabella Beeton, author of the 1861 blockbuster *Mrs Beeton's Book of Household Management*. Mrs Beeton believed that what men did for war, women did for washing, and that Britain's Household Generals preserved the Empire with preserves and saved it with savouries.

black for decades after Albert's death, and every bed she slept in had
a photo of the dead prince consort taped to the headboard above his
side of the mattress. This did not stop, in Victoria's words, 'ill-natured
gossip in the higher classes' about her relationship with her Scottish
personal attendant, John Brown, known by some of the bitchier
courtiers as 'the Queen's Stallion'.[6]

The queen ruled the largest and most powerful empire the world
had ever seen, stared down prime ministers, and pushed the limits
parliament had placed on her authority. One might think she'd be
sympathetic to women who sought influence outside the domestic
sphere – but Victoria considered her female subjects objects. The
queen was beside herself when, in 1870, Lady Amberley proposed
that women be granted the vote.[7] Victoria wrote:

> The Queen is most anxious to enlist everyone who can speak or write
> to join in checking this mad, wicked folly of 'Woman's Rights', with
> all its attendant horrors, on which her poor feeble sex is bent, forget-
> ting every womanly sense of feeling and propriety. Lady _____ ought
> to get a GOOD WHIPPING. It is a subject that makes the Queen
> so furious that she cannot contain herself. God created men and
> women different – then let them remain each in their own position ...
> Woman would become the most hateful, heartless, and disgusting
> of human beings were she allowed to unsex herself; and where would
> be the protection which man was intended to give the weaker sex?[8]

---

6   There were unproven rumours that Victoria had secretly married Brown.
     While almost certainly untrue, she did wear Brown's mother's wedding ring
     after Brown's death.

7   Viscountess Amberley, the mother of all-round brainbox Bertrand
     Russell, was concerned by the unhealthy celibacy of her children's live-in
     tutor and, with her husband's support, took him as a lover. She continued
     her destruction of the 'British family' by promoting birth control and
     campaigning for women to work in medicine and other 'men's professions',
     and to receive equal pay.

8   By this stage, Victoria's interest in sex and the exclamation mark had been
     replaced by an overwhelming desire to refer to herself in the third person,

If the most powerful woman in the world held such views, what sorts of lives might women in her far-flung Australian colonies hope to lead?

THE WORDSMITH'S TALE

Catherine Helen Spence was five foot nothing in her shoes (which were sensible). Her fiery hair and fair skin spoke to her Scottish birth, while the cold bath she took each morning and the whisky shot she took each evening spoke to her hearty constitution.

'Australia's first feminist' was indifferent to comments about her thick waist, rounded shoulders and prominent wart. She would be judged on the power of her ideas and the clarity of her expression, not on whether her looks were pleasing to potential suitors. She told herself, 'endeavour to train your mind so as to be a useful and amiable member of society, no one's wife, and no one's mother', later adding, 'although I often envy my friends the happiness they find in their children, I have never envied them their husbands'.

It was unusual for an Australian woman to openly express such a view. Mid-nineteenth-century Australians took marriage even more seriously than the straitlaced Victorian Britons. The British dismissed Australians as criminals and prostitutes. Middle-class Australians responded by marrying each other. That would show the snobs 'back home' how moral the colonies had become! A chip on the shoulder became a ring on the finger.

Marriage was also an economic necessity for most Australian women – women saw inheritances pass to their brothers, and paid work was largely limited to domestic service and clothes making. Marriage

---

a disorder now most commonly displayed by sports stars. Our current long-serving monarch commonly uses gender-neutral pronouns like 'we' (e.g. 'We are not amused') and 'one' (e.g. 'One wishes one's mother had not drunk all one's gin'). Nobody has advanced the self-identification rights of the genderqueer community more than this old queen.

was a market and a woman's looks, accomplishments and virtue were commonly referred to as her 'capital'.

Spence came from a family of real capital and that bought her a first-rate Scottish education. However, her father's loss of the family fortune in a dodgy wheat deal saw the Spences flee to South Australia in disgrace. Fourteen-year-old Catherine arrived in 1839, living in relative poverty until finding work as a governess and opening her own school. Teaching was one of the few professions open to women, as it was really just childminding with books.

Journalism was definitely not women's work, so when Catherine became Australia's first female journalist in the late 1840s, she did so under her brother's name, or as 'A Colonist of 1839'. Spence was not paid much for her newspaper writing and decided to branch out and not be paid much to write novels, complaining that her books earned her 'a coolie's wage'.[9]

Spence, in 1854, was the first woman to write a novel about Australian life. *Clara Morison: A Tale of South Australia During the Gold Fever* was published in England after a Sydney publisher advised Spence, 'the only novels worth publishing in Australia are sporting or political novels'. Spence explained the cultural cringe this way:

> If stories are excessively Australian, they lose the sympathies of the bulk of the public. If they are mildly Australian, the work is thought to lack distinctiveness.[10]

---

9   Men grudgingly admitted women might write fiction, but only as a hobby while waiting to get married, and they should not expect financial or other recognition for their efforts. As poet laureate Robert Southey loftily told Charlotte Brontë, 'Literature cannot be the business of a woman's life: & it ought not to be. The more she is engaged in her proper duties, the less leisure she will have for it.'

10 The British have historically been even more contemptuous of Australian writing. Professor J.I.M. Stewart, an Oxford man appointed professor of English at the University of Adelaide, said in his 1940 Commonwealth Literary Fund lectures, 'I am most grateful to the CLF for providing the funds to give these lectures in Australian literature, but unfortunately they have neglected to provide any literature.'

Spence's books were at best 'mildly Australian'. She increasingly set them in foreign places, and she was determined not to use 'weak fashionable expressions'. *Nightie, comfy, hanky* and other diminutives favoured by Australians were out. Her characters, like her, would honour the English language by speaking it correctly.

Clara Morison was about a young Scottish gentlewoman who arrived in South Australia without resources, and who chose to work as a maid, rather than sell her independence by tying herself to a man – but by book's end, Clara was blissfully married to a pastoralist.

While Spence rejected marriage, the heroines of her early works ended up happily hitched. Most of her novels were 'popular romantic fiction', although her insistence that plots 'should not be merely possible, but probable' meant her works were neither romantic nor popular.[11] Her romantic novels also suffered from her self-acknowledged inability to write male characters:

> Queer that I who have such a distinct idea of what I approve in flesh and blood men, should only achieve in pen and ink a set of impossible people, with an absurd muddy expression of gloom, instead of sublime depth, as I had intended.[12]

Spence's first two novels were published anonymously, although she 'did a Brontë' when she was revealed as the author of her third

---

11 Spence's literary idol was George Eliot, whose essay 'Silly Novels by Lady Novelists' criticised the ridiculous and trivial plots of most contemporary fiction written by and for women. Eliot despised the 'mind and millinery' romantic novel, in which the beautiful, virtuous and extremely intelligent heroine displays an independent streak in her dealings with a man whose difficult nature conceals a noble sensitivity (which she finally recognises). The novel ends when the extremely intelligent heroine marries the misunderstood man, who luckily has enough money to keep her in books and sheet music. Eliot would have hated Spence's earlier works.

12 My next writers' festival presentation will be on why nineteenth-century Australian women should only be allowed to write about nineteenth-century Australian women, rather than culturally appropriate the identities of men and non-binary persons from different places and/or times.

novel, 1865's *Mr Hogarth's Will*.[13]

During the 1860s, Spence increasingly wrote about political reform, in which South Australia led the world. In 1856, it was the first British colony to extend the vote to all men. It also banned polling booths in pubs, breaking with the traditional practice of candidates buying votes with drinks. The colony also established the world's first politically independent electoral body. In 1858, South Australian cricketer turned electoral commissioner William Boothby introduced a ballot paper where an 'X' was to be placed against the names of preferred candidates, with the Boothby Ballot now used around the world.[14]

These reforms did not go far enough for Spence. She was concerned that the votes of minorities were ignored. The answer lay in a minority electoral representation system the Danish had used to elect their *Rigsdag* in 1856, later championed by English barrister Thomas Hare – proportional representation by way of a single transferable vote.

In 1861, 'C.H.S.' published *A Plea for Pure Democracy: Mr Hare's Reform Bill Applied to South Australia*. South Australians were confused. They'd just introduced majority voting (for men) and now someone wanted to honour the votes of minorities? Spence acknowledged her

---

13   The Brontë sisters wrote under the pen names Currer, Ellis and Acton Bell, before coming out as women. Women writers have impersonated men throughout history. In Australia, Ethel Florence Richardson became Henry Handel Richardson, Mary Helena Fortune wrote over 500 detective stories as Waif Wander, and Stella Franklin moonlighted as Miles. Franklin also wrote under other male *noms de plume*, and as the just plain weird 'Brent of Bin Bin' and 'Mr and Mrs Ogniblat L'Artsau'. Why is Australia's most prestigious literary prize named after a gender-appropriating fraud who has reduced the publishing opportunities of real male writers like the author of this book?

14   Boothby was also the first person in the world to propose postal voting, so that people in remote areas might vote. Western Australia, in 1877, is believed to have introduced the world's first postal voting system. Boothby's other great contribution was writing *The Olive: Its Culture and Products in the South of France and Italy*. He also introduced olive growing and pressing in South Australian prisons, establishing a new olive oil industry and enabling prisoners to slip on something other than the soap.

pamphlet 'did not set the Torrens on fire', which was unsurprising as it was small and the Torrens was Adelaide's largest and least flammable river. However, Henry Parkes gave Spence's work to England's leading liberal philosopher, John Stuart Mill, and it was approvingly read by Hare and other leading British reformers. Parkes' promotion of a woman's political views was at odds with an editorial he'd written for his newspaper, the *Empire*, three years earlier:

> ... lovely woman seems to have been placed by nature on a lower platform in regard to the active social duties which are external to the home. The domestic circle seems to be her peculiar sphere. Her physical weakness, amiable timidity, the attributes and accidents of her sex; and her mental conformation, seem to have intended her for something less mundane, more heavenly, than the conduct of public affairs.

When Spence visited England in 1865, her pamphlet provided an entrée into British intellectual society. She stayed at the home of Sir Rowland Hill, whose pre-paid postage system had transformed world communication.[15] There she met Barbara Bodichon, whose *A Brief Summary in Plain Language of the Most Important Laws Concerning Women* briefly and plainly summarised how crap it was to be a woman.

Bodichon fostered Spence's interest in women's rights, and her planting of Australian eucalypts in Algeria to eliminate malaria convinced Spence of the value of philanthropy, if not its effectiveness.

---

15   Mail had historically been paid for by a letter's recipient. This resulted in postmen sitting on doorsteps for hours, waiting for someone to return home and pay them. Sometimes a recipient wouldn't have money, or refused to pay for a letter that might contain unpleasant news. Pre-paid postage made communication vastly more efficient, and soaring postal revenue funded grand post offices that became the centres of the communities they served. Britain's 1840 pre-paid system, using Hill's Penny Black stamp, is commonly claimed as the world's first. However, the world's first pre-paid letters were posted in Sydney in 1838, after postmaster James Raymond read Hill's 1837 pamphlet on postal reform.

Upon returning home, Spence assisted Hill's niece, Emily Clark, to introduce Australia's first foster care program.[16]

Spence was no longer an anonymous figure. In 1866, she was the first woman invited to address South Australia's largest Mechanics' Institute. Spence's voice was 'pronouncedly Scotch and virile' – if she sounded like a bloke, then surely people would respect what she had to say.[17] Spence took to the stage, but remained silent, her 'Reminiscences of a Visit to England' read by a stuttering male friend.

A woman might be seen, but not yet heard.

THE SISTER'S TALE

Mary MacKillop was another unmarried governess and schoolteacher of Scottish descent who'd settled in South Australia. In 1866, she met Father Julian Tenison-Woods, the parish priest of Penola and an eminent geologist.[18] Father Tenison-Woods, who'd earlier inspired Adam Lindsay Gordon to write poems about horses, had an empty stable. Not wanting the space to go to waste, he asked Mary to open a Catholic school in it.[19]

---

16 Spence and Clark believed that 'every dependent child ought to be separated and removed as far as by any means may be possible from pauper moral influences and pauper physical and social degradation'. Their 'boarding out' program was designed to encourage the moral reformation of poor people, as much as to care for children. The common nineteenth-century reformers' views that being poor is a moral failure and that people can be punished out of poverty are now embraced by the Murdoch press and the champions of Newstart.

17 *Bloke* is one of the few Australian words borrowed from Romani (earlier often known as 'Gypsy'). *Loke* means 'man' in a Romani dialect and *bloke* originally meant 'the boss', before coming to mean any man.

18 Catholics were derisively known as *rock choppers*, an Australian slang term that shared initials with 'Roman Catholic' and linked them to Irish convict labourers. As the author of *Geological Observations in South Australia*, Tenison-Woods was a bona fide rock chopper.

19 Being called Mary and tending children in a stable boosted MacKillop's Catholic cred.

Mary asked to be known as Sister Mary of the Cross and became the first Australian to establish a religious institute. She and the women she recruited called themselves the Sisters of St Joseph of the Sacred Heart, which, as a gang name, needed work. The 'Brown Joeys' was more street and acknowledged the gang's colours.

Some may question labelling a congregation of religious sisters a gang, but the Brown Joeys were a close-knit group with strict membership criteria (Catholic women only) and a hierarchical structure (from postulant to Mother General). They had to swear oaths to join (vows of poverty, chastity and obedience) and chose to live outside the law (of the Catholic bishops).

Each Catholic bishop controlled territory known as a diocese and demanded the unconditional loyalty of all Catholics on his turf. The Brown Joeys, who were committed to educating poor children across diocesan boundaries, signed up to a gang charter known as the 'Rules of Life', which placed members under the authority of their own Adelaide clubhouse (a.k.a. the Mother House), rather than the local bishop. Sisters would be doing it for themselves – a revolutionary break from the rules of established religious communities.

By 1869, the Brown Joeys had seventy members and gang operations (i.e. elementary schools) in twenty-one communities. They soon expanded into Queensland and New South Wales and muscled in on the orphanage, neglected children, girls in danger, aged poor, nursing home and palliative care rackets.

However, some priests objected to a woman (and a 24-year-old slip of a thing at that) exercising any independence in church affairs, for was it not said in 1 Timothy 2:12, 'Do not permit women to teach, nor to have dominion over man, but to be in quietness'? A whispering campaign began, and the whispers got louder after the Joeys reported Father Keating of Kapunda for sexually abusing children.[20]

---

20   Father Keating was allowed to return to Ireland to manage his 'drinking'. He
     continued to serve as a priest.

Mary was an alcoholic! Her defenders countered that Mary drank on doctor's orders to manage 'women's issues' (debilitating period pain), and what about all the Catholic priests who enjoyed a tipple or five? Mary had run down the Sisters' finances! Her defenders replied, 'What do you expect from someone who's taken a vow of poverty?'

Adelaide's bishop, Laurence Sheil, listening to his clerics, demanded that the Sisters submit to his authority. Mary refused. Sheil excommunicated her in 1871 (a big deal if you're a Catholic) and closed most of her schools. Six months later, on his deathbed, Sheil lifted the excommunication.

Mary knew the only way she could protect the Sisters' independence was to have their Rules approved by *Il Papa*, the Boss Catholic who directed worldwide operations from the mother chapter in Rome. *Il Papa* obliged, and relaxed the rule of extreme poverty so that the Sisters could own their own convents and accept dowries.[21]

But the Church's hard men weren't backing down. Bishop Matthew Quinn of Bathurst demanded the Sisters follow his orders or leave his diocese. The Sisters who agreed to diocesan control patched out of the Brown Joeys and adopted new colours, forming the rebel Black Joeys. Matthew's brother, Bishop James Quinn of Brisbane, kicked the Sisters out of Queensland in 1880, and in 1883, Bishop Reynolds of Adelaide, who knew women's minds better than they did, told Mary:

> You no longer have the confidence of the Sisterhood, nor is it in the interests of good order and discipline, of peace or religion that you should remain in the Province.

Reynolds ordered Mary's exile from South Australia, so she opened a new Mother House in Sydney. In 1885, Sydney's Cardinal Moran

---

21   The bride's family traditionally paid the groom's family a dowry, as the groom was relieving them of the burden of a useless daughter. Nuns and other sisters were brides of Christ, so it was only fair that their families pay the Church to stick them in a convent.

found Mary's earlier election as Mother General invalid and appointed Mother Bernard leader of the Brown Joeys. At least Bernard was a proper man's name.

The men were back in charge.

THE SCHOLAR'S TALE

Catherine Deakin – Kate to her friends – lived a life of music and the mind. She was a star at school, her little brother Alfred her devoted satellite.

Like Alfred, Kate was schooled by the formidable Thompson sisters, who provided 'a sound English Education, viz., Reading, Writing, Arithmetic (practical and mental), Grammar, Geography, ancient and Modern History, Composition, Chronology, Use of the Globes, with Plain and Ornamental Needlework'. This was an education denied most young women. By the age of thirteen, girls were expected to be able to read and perform basic addition, which was all a homemaker needed. Use of the Globes was very much an optional extra.

Kate's education didn't come cheap, but then again, the Deakins only had to pay for it for seven years. There were no grammar schools for girls, because what man wanted to wake up next to a wife who knew more than he did? Kate would help Mama around the house until a suitable husband could be found. Unfortunately, her family rejected potential suitors – no man was good enough for 'our Kate'. Kate had fallen for John Henning Thompson, but Alfred, who'd had a serious boy crush on his former schoolmaster, spoke out against the match.

Kate was twenty-five and on the shelf, a spinster whose options were rapidly narrowing.[22] Then, in 1875, a door opened – more precisely,

---

22   A spinster was originally a woman who spun wool, but came to mean a woman of marrying age who was likely to remain unmarried, as poor single women commonly worked wool from home. In nineteenth-century romances, spinsters were commonly referred to as 'on the shelf' – i.e. goods that men had passed over for purchase.

the door to Melbourne's Presbyterian Ladies' College (PLC), 'the first major secondary school for young ladies' in Australia that afforded girls the same level of education as boys. Charles Pearson, Alfred Deakin's debating mentor and an advocate for women's higher education, was PLC's inaugural headmaster. Kate did Pearson and PLC proud as the school's first student to pass the University of Melbourne entrance exam with honours.

Of course, there was a world of difference between passing the university entrance and passing through the entrance of the university. A woman might do the former, but actually attending university might distract her from the more important business of getting married and knocked up. And it might upset the chaps.[23]

Kate returned to PLC as a teacher. As she was not as good as a male teacher, it was only fair she received about a third less pay. Kate soon abandoned teaching to study at the Melbourne School of Music, graduating as a concert-level pianist and working occasionally as a music tutor.

Miss Deakin would remain Miss Deakin. Like many unmarried women, she'd live with her parents and care for them until they died. She'd also have plenty of time to support Alfred to fulfil his dreams.

It was a life.

THE DANCER'S TALE

Fanny Osborne had made it. She'd been accepted as a dancer for the Royal Victoria Theatre's 1872 Sydney production of *The Yellow Dwarf and the King of the Hawkins' Hill Gold Mines; Or, The Desert Fairy of*

---

23   The University of Adelaide, in 1874, was the first Australian university that sought to admit women, with its founding mission to be 'open to all classes and denominations of Her Majesty's subjects'. The British government was stunned that the university considered women a class of Her Majesty's subjects and ordered South Australia's governor to bar female students. The university allowed women to 'visit' lectures, but refused them degrees.

Despair, the Gigantic Bon-Bon and the Princess of Pure Delights, which, contrary to the longwinded title and the amusements it advertised, was a one-act pantomime featuring a burlesque adaption of Shakespeare's *Richard III*.

Theatres were dens of vice and iniquity, frequented not just by 'unsavoury costermongers', but by 'the lowest votaries of Venus'. A theatre's vestibule, where these gaudily painted ladies of the night and their bludgers plied their trade, was dubbed 'the saddling paddock'.[24] The moral dangers of the entertainment industry, known well before *Hey Dad..!* and *#MeToo*, meant it was illegal to employ younger children in theatres.

But Fanny was now sixteen and ready for the gaslight. Stage lights were designed 'to illuminate the legs' of dancers, as the gentlemen and businessmen who enjoyed slumming it at the theatre appreciated a well-turned and well-lit leg. Most women on the stage relied on wealthy admirers to further their careers, or discreetly marry them.

Some admirers would dangle offers of marriage, only to vanish after a young woman had surrendered her virtue and good name. The New South Wales government rejected a law to criminalise 'seduction under promise of marriage' on the grounds that men might be wrongly punished for promising to marry a woman who'd seduced *them*! The fact that Premier Henry Parkes was a notorious root rat also made the government gun-shy about laws concerning male sexual morality.

One fateful night, the performance of *The Yellow Dwarf* etc. ended with Fanny, wearing a flimsy ballet costume, reclining by a waterfall that had been installed on the stage. She was playing a mermaid, one of the lesser-known characters in *Richard III*. As the curtain dropped, Fanny leapt up, only to be told to resume her position for the encore. As she hurried back to her spot, her costume brushed against a gaslight

---

24   *Bludger* was flash slang for a pimp and an abbreviation of *bludgeoner*, a reference to the bludgeons some pimps carried to beat and rob their prostitutes' clients. Pimps lived off their prostitutes' earnings and Australians adapted *bludger* to mean any person who sponged off others.

and she went up like a Bundy-soaked barramundi on a barbie. Rather than jumping into the water feature, like any sensible Shakespearean mermaid would, Fanny leapt into the audience, another gaslight igniting the other side of her dress. She died of her burns a few days later.

Burning ballerinas were no rarity, with Jean-Adolphe Carteron responding to the problem by soaking tutus in flame-retardant boric acid. This made tutus heavy, stiff and yellow, with Sydney theatre operator John Bennet advising the inquest into Fanny's death that 'carteronnaged' dresses were unpopular – 'girls will not wear dresses unless they look nice. They would rather run the risk of fire than do so.'

FIG. 2: THE 1877 WORKSAFE-SPONSORED ROYAL VICTORIA THEATRE PRODUCTION OF *SWAN LAKE*.

Ballet dancers were not the only women to wear dresses to die for. In the year of Fanny's fiery demise, four New South Wales women died after their clothes caught fire performing household duties.

The crinoline that pushed a skirt out to a diameter of up to eight feet not only increased the risk of women coming into contact with fireplaces, stoves, candles and kerosene lamps, but created a wind tunnel effect in which trapped air rushed to fuel any errant spark. Crinolined women were also known to be blown into the sea in a strong wind, or have their voluminous skirts tangled in the wheels of moving train carriages. Corsets produced breathing and circulation difficulties, prolapsed uteruses and other compressed organs, and permanently deformed rib cages.

Australian women were fashion victims.

THE PASSING WOMAN'S TALE

Ellen Tremayne had a child out of wedlock – not the done thing in Catholic Ireland. She disappeared from her village, and it was rumoured that she'd fled to Canada or the United States to avoid scandal. Upon her return, she was cast out of her community as an 'immoral woman'. And so we find 26-year-old Ellen aboard the *Ocean Monarch*, bound for a new life in Australia.

Ellen attracted attention on the 1856 voyage. She had a mysterious trunk labelled 'Edward De Lacy Evans', wore a shirt and trousers under her dress, and was unusually attentive to some of her female cabinmates, including 34-year-old governess Mary Delahunty. It was speculated that Ellen was a man masquerading as a woman.

Ellen disappeared after briefly working as a maid at a pub. Soon after, Edmund De Lacy married Mary Delahunty in a Melbourne Catholic church. The union didn't last, with Mary tying the knot with American mining surveyor Lyman Hart in 1862. When queried about this 'blatant act of bigamy', Mary explained that her first marriage had not been legal, as Edmund De Lacy was a woman.

Edmund adopted the name Edward De Lacy Evans and claimed to be the nephew of Crimean War hero General Sir Charles De Lacy Evans. He married two more women, Sarah Moore, who died of tuberculosis in 1867, and Frenchwoman Julia Marquand. Edward became a champion ploughman and also worked as a carter, blacksmith and mining captain.

Edward's world came crashing down in 1877, when Julia gave birth to a daughter. Julia insisted the child was Edward's, but Edward knew better and was 'deeply disturbed by the circumstances in which his wife became pregnant'.[25] In 1879, after a period of depression, Edward was admitted to the Lunacy Ward of Bendigo Hospital. He refused to bathe and was committed to the Kew Asylum, where he was forcibly stripped and found to be biologically female. Not knowing what to do with him, the asylum returned Edward to the hospital.

The *Bendigo Advertiser* attributed Edward's male persona to 'nymphomania', reporting, 'It is evident ... that the woman must have been mad on the subject of sex from the time she left Ireland dressed as a woman.'[26] The edition of the paper sold out, with the *Advertiser* publishing a special supplement on the 'EXTRAORDINARY CASE OF CONCEALMENT OF SEX'.[27] The story of Edward was picked up by national and international papers, and Samuel Lazar, a Sydney theatre impresario, offered to pay the hospital to release Evans to be 'publicly exhibited'.

---

25 In Victorian times, when sex was a mystery and even those who understood the basics thought it should only take place in the dead of night with the curtains fully drawn, it was conceivable that a woman might believe herself married to a cis, rather than a trans, man. Julia's claims of ignorance about Edward's bedtime bits were given credibility by the 1920 trial of Eugenia Falleni. When Harry Crawford was arrested in Sydney for the murder of his first wife, he was discovered to be Ms Falleni. This came as a terrible shock to Harry's second wife. The prosecutor asked the judge to clear the court of women (which was refused) before tendering a strap-on dildo as evidence of Falleni being 'practical in deceit' about his gender.

26 On this confused logic, every woman leaving Ireland dressed as a woman is a nymphomaniac.

27 The *Advertiser* explained, 'As it is almost impossible to give an account of the case without making use of the masculine pronoun when referring to Evans, we propose to use that appellation'. For those of you who think the *Advertiser* was ahead of its time, it was concerned with narrative flow, not Edward's identification as male.

Julia, confronted with the irrefutable evidence that Edward was
not the father of her child, told an enthralled press she believed 'some
strange man entered the house one night about the time her husband
should have returned home'. She later admitted to an affair with her
sister's husband, prominent Bendigo hotelier and businessman Jean
Baptiste Loridan. Edward, released from hospital, gave evidence on
her behalf in a paternity suit. By this stage, journalists were beside
themselves – the story had intra-familial affairs, 'deviance' and French
people, with the third item providing a natural explanation for the
first two.

Julia's suit against Loridan was dismissed, as a woman who couldn't
determine her husband's sex after more than ten years of marriage
could well be mistaken as to the identity of the person with whom
she'd had an affair, even though he was her brother-in-law and the
action allegedly took place in his hotel.

Edward, at a loose end after his release, joined a freak show and
was billed as 'The Wonderful Male Impersonator', with *The Man-
Woman Mystery*, a salacious pamphlet, sold during his appearances.
He later toured Sydney with a trapeze artist and 'The Electric Boy'.
Unable to cope with life as a carnival freak, Edward begged to be
taken back into state care and spent the remaining twenty years of
his life in the Melbourne Immigrants' Home.[28]

Edward's living life as a man has been variously reported as the
product of nymphomania, lesbianism or gender dysphoria. There
may be some truth in the second and third options, but there is also
another possible factor. Life as a Victorian woman, where you could

---

28   Two years after his death, Edward was immortalised in Joseph Furphy's 1903
     classic Australian novel *Such is Life*, where narrator Tom Collins refers to
     Nosey Alf as 'one of those De Lacy Evanses we often read of in novels'. Nosey
     Alf, a disfigured stockman, was born Molly Cooper. Furphy also modelled
     Alf on another 'passing woman', as women who attempted to pass as men were
     known – Johanna Jorgensen, a German-born Australian who lived as a man after
     being kicked in the face by a horse (not a commonly recognised cause of gender
     dysphoria) and became a selector and a soldier with the Victorian Mounted Rifles.

be exiled from your community for falling pregnant, restricted in your career and the public sphere more generally, and otherwise expected to conform to society's expectations of 'the angel in the house', was less than ideal.

If you couldn't beat them, why not join them?

THE WIFE'S TALE

A woman could not only join the ranks of men – she could actually become one ... or at least part of one. She could ascend to this exalted state by marriage, as Sir William Blackstone explained in *The Commentaries on the Laws of England*:

> ... the very being or legal existence of the woman is suspended during the marriage, or at least is incorporated and consolidated into that of the husband.

Louisa Albury saw the suspension of her legal existence as a ticket to a new life. Like most teenage girls, Louisa had a strained relationship with her mother. Mother scolded her more than her eight siblings, gave her more household chores and made her wear her older sister's cast-off dresses.[29] And when 'any strange blackfellows' came to the house when Daddy was away, 'Mother would – by dumbshow, demonstrate the act of hanging by an imaginary knot', which was so 1840.

---

29   Having nine children was downright dangerous. Official records suggest about six in every 1000 Australian pregnancies in the second half of the nineteenth century resulted in maternal death, although the real mortality rate was likely twice that. Caesareans were not an option for most women, as they cost as much as two years' pay for a labourer (of the working, not birthing, kind). A woman who wanted to terminate a pregnancy could visit one of the 'herbalists' or 'fortune tellers', as backyard abortionists euphemistically advertised themselves, although that was even more dangerous and could result in ten years in prison. A woman who wanted to prevent a pregnancy had limited access to family planning information. As providing information on contraception could result in obscenity charges, birth control pamphlets had nonsensical titles like *Fruits of Philosophy*, avoided rude words and pictures, and were generally opaque to the point of uselessness.

Daddy had been a shearer, but he'd wanted better for his family. He'd made a name for himself as a builder and timber-carter in Mudgee, New South Wales, but investing all his money in a brickworks had been a gamble that didn't pay off. The works had been destroyed by flood before a brick was fired, he'd been swindled out of his timber wagon, his bullocks had wandered off, his house had been repossessed and the family had been forced to relocate to Wilbertree, which would have been a one-horse town if his last horse hadn't broken its neck in a fall.

Daddy started drinking and, after gold was found in the area, opened a grog-shanty where he could drink with his miner customers. Louisa didn't like drinkers – they were dirty and handsy – but she had to sing for them because it brought in business. Most of the time, though, she could ride into the bush and pretend she was someone else, somewhere else. She could write poems among the blue gums or decorate her secret shrine. Once she found a giant black snake on her shrine. She called him Judas and killed him, carrying him down the hill on a long stick. Then she burnt him. That was fun.

Mother wouldn't let her have fun. Mother said she couldn't be a teacher. Mother shouted at her when she hadn't eaten for days, even though she wasn't hungry. Mother had stopped the miners from passing a plate around for her to sing in Europe, rather than some backwoods bar. Mother said with so many mouths to feed, Louisa should hurry up and get married. All right, she would! She'd do anything to get away from Wilbertree.

One of the new diggers didn't drink. The other miners called him 'Peter the Swede', even though his name was Niels Hertzberg Larsen and he came from Norway. Peter was thirty-four to her eighteen and knew all about the world. He told her of the exotic lands he'd visited as a sailor, how he'd jumped ship to search for gold and how he wanted to marry her.

Of course, she'd have to obey Peter after marrying him, with Britain's marriage laws drawing on Ephesians 5:22–23: 'Wives, submit yourselves unto your own husbands, as unto the Lord. For the husband is the head of the wife, even as Christ is head of the church.' And all of her property would become Peter's, which wasn't a problem because she didn't really own anything. Anyway, a person who no longer existed didn't need property.

The wedding was nice, but the wedding night was spoiled by Peter's drunk friends singing outside their new hut and demanding she show herself, which she was forced to do after they started tearing off the roof.

But she was leaving her dull life behind! Peter had promised they'd make their fortune on the Weddin Mountain goldfields. They'd start the next chapter of their life with a new, less foreign, name. Lawson would do.

Life as a miner's wife was not as exciting as it had sounded. Louisa stayed in their tent, sewed and wrote poetry, while Peter spent long hours grubbing in the dirt for little reward. Her first child was born during the floods of '67. The midwife wouldn't brave the rising waters and Doc Whiley was on a bender – he only attended after a gun was held to his head. Her midwinter baby, Henry, was small and sickly.

Life just got harder. She returned to the Mudgee area, where Charlie was born in a hut. She wanted a house, but all Peter wanted was to dig. She worked as a dressmaker, bringing in more money than the gold-digger she'd married. And she was pregnant again. The nervous breakdown that followed left her mute for months.

Peter agreed to stop digging and start farming, but the selection he bought was on an old goldfield. He spent every spare second sinking new shafts. Then other miners swarmed the farm and trashed it.

Louisa ran a small store and was the local postmistress, earning barely enough to keep her family's heads above water, and her new twins, Annie and Gertie, were two more mouths to feed. Every night she'd read her children *Robinson Crusoe*, and as soon as she got to the end, she'd start again from page one. That was the pattern of her life – repetition without reward.

Henry had a terrible earache when he was nine, and by fourteen was profoundly deaf. Eight-year-old Charlie ran away from home after Peter flogged him, tied a noose around his neck and threw the other end of the rope over a beam because Charlie had refused to apologise for wagging Sunday School and ruining his best suit. Then Annie's death from a fever in 1878 stripped Louisa of her faith in the Church, with its platitudes about being reunited in Heaven. She replaced sermons and salvation with spiritualism and séances, so she could make contact with Annie in *this* life.

Peter would be absent for months, labouring or mining. OK, mostly mining, but he knew he'd strike it rich on the next dig. Or the one after that.

Louisa Lawson had had enough. In 1883, after seventeen years of marriage, she wrote to Peter to tell him she was leaving. She might move to Sydney. The only thing that was certain was she'd never be back.

THE CAST-OFF'S TALE

'When a woman is separated from her husband,' Miles Franklin wrote in *My Brilliant Career*, 'it is the religion of the world at large to cast the whole blame on the wife.'

While Louisa Lawson kept quiet about the state of her marriage until Peter's death a few years after their split, the circumstances of Martha Terry's separation were gleefully reported by the Australian and international press. A whole world of blame and pain was about to hit.

Martha had married William Terry, a Melbourne grocer and draper turned mesmerist. Mesmerists believed in 'animal magnetism' – the power of the mind to manipulate the invisible force possessed by all living things. A mesmerist might use his powers to heal the sick, control another's thoughts and movements, cause a flower to wilt, and perhaps even make a rabbit eat its own vomit. William was also

Australia's leading necromancer – although, like most modern liberal necromancers, William preferred the term 'spiritualist'.[30]

In 1869, William opened a spiritualist bookstore and herbarium, from which he provided spirit medium, magnetic and trance healing, clairvoyant herbalist, 'how-to' sex advice, and bookselling services.[31] In 1870, he was appointed inaugural secretary of the Victorian Association of Progressive Spiritualists, an organisation that mixed campaigning on health and social reform with telling Victorians how to host supper parties for ghosts. That year he was ordered by a particularly pushy progressive spirit to publish *The Harbinger of Light*, 'a new monthly journal devoted to zoistic [life force] science, free thought, spiritualism and the harmonial philosophy'. The journal soon extended to occultism and the more suspect field of psychology, before moving on to passionately advocate for strict vegetarianism, temperance and women's admission to universities. *Harbinger* established itself as Australia's (and one of the world's) leading publications for fruitcakes.

Martha's first disagreement with William occurred three months after their 1858 wedding. Martha objected to William 'gardening on Sunday', and William, who regarded the Bible as 'all bosh', later took issue with Martha's observance of the Sabbath and teaching their eldest son the Lord's Prayer. Martha also didn't like William holding spiritualist meetings at their house; according to Leviticus 20:27, 'A man or a woman who is a medium, or who has familiar spirits, shall surely be put to death; they shall stone them with stones.'

Britain had passed divorce laws a year before Martha and William's first fight, but an unhappy Australian couple in 1858 could only untie the knot if the governor or parliament passed an Act for their divorce.

---

30   Necromancers summon the dead to seek information or favours. So do spiritualists. The only practical difference between spiritualists and other necromancers (aside from the odd blood sacrifice to animate corpses to lay waste to your enemies) is that necromancy is magic, while spiritualism was considered a science.

31   One of the books Terry sold, *Sinful Saints and Sensual Shepherds*, detailed the sexual acts of clergymen. Customs confiscated it for being both obscene and blasphemous.

It was believed divorce was a slippery slope that led to prostitution and polygamy.[32] As New South Wales politician Charles Campbell argued, divorce would degrade a woman 'from the high position of a Christian matron to the level of a Turkish female – "A soulless toy for a tyrant's lust"'.[33]

Martha and William's case for judicial separation was heard in 1874. Martha objected to William's obsession with Miss Elizabeth Collins, a 22-year-old patient whom he'd 'magnetically healed'. After Miss Collins emerged from her mesmeric trance, William prescribed six herbal remedies for her lung disease, all of which were powerful aphrodisiacs. William took her to the opera twice and a lolly shop once, and wrote her a sleazy letter saying life was too 'limited and transitory' for her to worry about the appropriateness of their developing relationship. He signed it *'Au revoir, carissima'*, to prove his love and inability to distinguish French from Italian.

William refused Martha's demand that he give up Miss Collins, suggesting an open marriage. He even offered to rent Martha a house in the country and give her an eighth of his income – conditional on his being able to see her 'any time he thought fit'. They would still be married and Martha couldn't deny him his conjugal rights.[34]

---

32 Former Liberal senator Cory Bernardi would have also highlighted the inevitability of divorced people hooking up with dogs. Conservative Murdoch press commentator Chris Kenny has made it clear that he personally would not do this.

33 It took until 1873 for all Australian colonies to allow court-ordered divorce. A husband could divorce his wife for adultery, but a wife had to prove her husband's adultery was aggravated by cruelty, desertion, rape, bigamy, incest, sodomy or bestiality. This double standard reflected the prevailing view that most women weren't 'troubled' by sexual feelings and therefore wouldn't succumb to sudden temptation. A wife's adultery couldn't be a momentary lapse, but showed her total loss of affection for her husband. A husband's adultery spoke to his natural passion and momentary weakness, and some argued it was reasonable because wives were frequently 'unavailable' due to pregnancy or childbirth. Divorce was expensive and a man, who owned all the family's assets, could deny his wife funds to pursue it.

34 A husband could sue a wife who refused to sleep with him with desertion, which was sufficient grounds for a court-ordered separation. A woman who deserted her husband would lose any maintenance and custody rights.

During the court hearing, Martha alleged William had caused her to have two miscarriages, one arising from his tying her to a beam after she tried to stop him going out, and one from him beating her 'like a child'. Martha also recounted being drenched with water, kicked, knocked over a sofa, struck in the eye, thrown on the floor and thrown on a rose bush, with her eldest son, a doctor and a neighbour backing up some of those claims.

English and Australian law provided that a husband might 'chastise' his wife. A wife might be beaten to 'correct' her behaviour, 'but not in a violent or cruel way', with the English common law providing that a man might strike his wife with a stick no thicker than his thumb, and the Welsh equivalent frowning on the use of a stick longer than his forearm. Courts were particularly willing to accommodate a husband's violence when his wife denied him his conjugal rights.[35]

William denied striking Martha, but acknowledged he'd threatened to take away their children. He testified that Martha had hit him on the head with a water dipper (Martha claimed this was in self-defence), and that she'd torn his coat, broken his watch-chain and 'seized me by the hair', 'seized me by the tie', 'locked my hat in the pantry to stop me going out', 'snatched a novel by Bulwer-Lytton from my hands', and 'overturned the coffee-pot and the kettle into the fire' (much of which Martha denied).

So, how did Justice Stephen consider Martha's claim for judicial separation on the grounds of William's cruelty? Hang on a minute – sorry – William's claim for judicial separation on the grounds of Martha's cruelty. His Honour found Martha's cruelty proven, rejected

---

35 A jury acquitted a man on five counts of raping his wife, after Justice Derek Bollen of the Supreme Court of South Australia gave them the following instructions: 'There is, of course, nothing wrong with a husband, faced with his wife's initial refusal to engage in intercourse, in attempting, in an acceptable way, to persuade her to change her mind, and that may involve a measure of rougher than usual handling. It may be, in the end, that handling and persuasion will persuade the wife to agree. Sometimes it is a fine line between not agreeing, then changing of the mind, and consenting.' This occurred in 1993.

her submission that separation should not be ordered, ordered William to provide her with minimal maintenance and, ignoring her pleas, gave William custody of nine of their ten children.[36]

Divorce wasn't an option, as Martha hadn't committed adultery. The order of judicial separation meant she couldn't remarry, the principal means by which a woman could achieve financial security and social respectability. She was in a limbo of her husband's devising.

Months after the separation, William Terry wrote and published 'The Missions of Spiritualism'. Three of those Missions were:

1.   To sow the seeds of a general reformation of morals
2.   To cause the rights of woman to be recognised to the full
3.   To cause the wrongs of woman to be redressed to the full

Irony was not dead – it had just passed on to the higher plane of the spirits who gave William Terry his incredible psychic powers.

---

36   Justice Stephen was far more balanced in his judgements than New South Wales' first Divorce judge, Justice John Hargrave, who'd been committed to an asylum by his wife after unremitting study 'unhinged his mind'. After his release, Hargrave could no longer bear his wife's presence, resulting in her return to England. According to Stephen, Hargrave's post-release enmity towards all females made him 'disastrous for women suitors' in divorce and separation proceedings and totally unreliable in cases involving lunacy. Hargrave rorted his judicial expenses, refused to attend court before 11 a.m. and rarely sat after 1 p.m. He relapsed into full-blown insanity in 1882.

3

I See Dead People

I see dead people.

Haley Joel Osment, *The Sixth Sense*, 1999

IF IT QUACKS LIKE A DOC

WILLIAM TERRY USED HIS INCREDIBLE PSYCHIC powers to make the sick well, the lame walk and the gullible poor. Healers were able to peddle all kinds of dubious treatments because there was no consensus on what caused disease.

Most doctors said it was bad air released by rotting matter, although by 1880 blaming tiny organisms was in vogue. Some attributed disease to imbalances in the body's liquid humours, evil spirits or masturbation. And for every argument regarding a disease's cause, there were a hundred as to its cure.

Faith healers like the Nunawading Messiah insisted that the healing power of the Holy Spirit moved through them, into the bodies of true believers.[1]

---

1   James Cowley Morgan Fisher was an escaped convict turned charcoal burner who took over his mother-in-law's religious sect. Followers of the Church of the Firstborn believed the Messiah had chosen the east Melbourne suburb of Nunawading for his second coming, that a hole in Fisher's hand was proof of his crucifixion (rather than an accident with a lump of hot charcoal), that those who believed in Fisher's divinity would never die, and that wandering through the Victorian countryside banging tins on moonlit nights would exorcise the Devil. Fisher was sued by a disciple in 1871 for obtaining money by falsely representing

Herbalists sold pills and potions, while purveyors of patent medicines and aphrodisiacs commonly laced their concoctions with arsenic
for its stimulatory effect.[2] Hucksters hawked snakebite cures containing strychnine (another stimulant that's really bad for you), ammonia,
alcohol, gunpowder, toad urine, or just about anything else you can
think of, but wish you hadn't.

Healing was also popular entertainment and that's where the real
money lay. Everybody loved seeing a snake man like Charles Underwood or Joseph Shires let himself get bitten by snakes, start vomiting,
and then 'cure' himself with his own patent remedy. Underwood's
antidote (boiled bracken fronds) left a lot to be desired, as he died
from snakebite after an 1861 show at the Melbourne Cricket Ground.[3]

In 1869, Shires teamed up for a performance with Melbourne
obstetrician, venereal physician and reputed abortionist Louis Smith.
Shires caused his snakes to bite two dogs, one of which was treated
with Shires' Antidote. The treated dog remained perky, while its
companion apparently died. During Dr Smith's subsequent lecture

---

himself as the Messiah, with a further claim that he enjoyed a polygamous
relationship with his wife's sisters. It is now generally accepted that Fisher was not
the Messiah – just a very naughty boy.

2   People were regularly poisoned by the arsenic in medicines, cosmetics, soaps,
      toothpaste, food-dyes, hair-dyes, fabric-dyes, books, toys, glassware, wallpaper,
      artificial flowers and tobacco wrappings. Louisa Collins, 'the Borgia of Botany',
      terminally over-stimulated both of her husbands with the abundant household
      poison. She was executed in 1889, the last woman to hang in New South Wales.

3   Shires' Antidote (iodine, ammonia and spirits of wine) was tested by police
      magistrate William Drummond in 1867. Drummond wanted to prove Shires' cure
      a 'humbug' and, in order to do so, demanded 'to be bitten by the deadliest and most
      venomous snake he [Shires] had got'. Shires suggested that Drummond think this
      experiment through, but eventually gave in, taking him and a tiger snake to a quiet
      hotel room. Drummond was bitten, the antidote applied, and the snake beheaded.
      Drummond, who'd insisted Shires take off all his clothes during these proceedings
      to prevent any trickery, took the dead snake to Dr George Halford, the only
      professor of medicine in the southern hemisphere, and said he 'would like to know
      whether the snake was of a deadly kind or not'. It was, as Drummond died the
      next day, presumably with the satisfaction of having been proven right. Shires was
      acquitted of manslaughter on the grounds that Drummond was a fucking idiot.

on the medical benefits of electricity, Shires suggested he jumpstart the dead dog.[4] The dog, which had endured the double indignity of being poisoned and shocked, sprang to life and savaged Smith's hand. The doctor, expressing concern that the dog's saliva carried venom, applied Shires' Antidote, but, experiencing 'all the symptoms of snake-poisoning, took stimulants in the form of brandy and champagne plentifully at intervals, and for some time they were partially vomited as fast as they were swallowed'. All the while, Smith kept the crowd entertained by alternately shocking himself and the dog. This 'Snake Bites Dog Bites Man' show, with its deadly reptiles, casual animal cruelty, electrotherapy and boozy chundering, was theatre at its best.[5]

Smith was a medical entrepreneur who established the Royal Polytechnic Institute next to his private hospital. The Institute operated as a theatre, planetarium and museum, with the latter displaying the latest electrical devices, animal and mineral specimens and, most popularly, wax models of reproductive organs. The museum allowed respectable Melburnians to titillate themselves in the name of science, until shut down in 1869 for offending 'taste'.[6]

---

4   Electrotherapy was all the rage in the second half of the nineteenth century. Electric belts, corsets or genital attachments were guaranteed to cure spinal issues, tumours, asthma, epilepsy, palpitations, loss of energy, and masturbatory tendencies and other mental disorders.

5   *Chunder* is an Australian slang term for 'vomit', which Men at Work bought to the world's attention when 'Down Under' became a global #1 hit between 1981 and 1983 ('I come from a land down under / Where beer does flow and men chunder'). There are two different views on the origin of *chunder*. The first speculates it is a contraction of 'watch under', the warning cry of a drunken sailor atop the mast or in the rigging before he vomits on those below. The second is that it is rhyming slang for 'spew', deriving from 'Chunder Loo of Akim Foo', the amusingly subservient cartoon Sikh bootblack who appeared in advertisements for Cobra boot polish in the *Bulletin*, the paper more Australian racists preferred.

6   Anatomical museums were a popular Victorian-era entertainment. They were marketed as 'educational', but paying visitors were really just interested in rude bits. The Melbourne Anthropological Museum of Dr Jordan and Dr Beck displayed a wax model of 'Virgin breasts', with the description, 'This model exhibits those rare beauties so peculiar to the female form, without which she would be despoiled of half of her elegance and loveliness.' The *Age* reported that the proprietors 'accumulate models and casts of the filthiest kinds until the chief

Smith's willingness to do anything for a quid led the *Bulletin* to dub him '££ Smith'. He invested his significant earnings in farms, racehorses, vineyards, art, sponsoring sporting events, and a blood-hound breeding program that enabled him to electrocute as many dogs as he wanted. Victoria's original Geoffrey Edelsten, with his sharp clothes and flashy diamond ring, was so popular that he was regularly elected as an MP between the 1850s and 1890s.[7]

Then there was Thomas Guthrie Carr, who combined religion with pseudoscience and showmanship. Arriving from England in 1865, the self-styled Reverend Carr lectured on the Bible and the evils of spiritualism. Borrowing skulls and busts of criminals and royal family members from Madame Sohier's Waxworks, he took to the stage with a live phrenology act, in which he compared the skulls and personality traits of audience members with those of rapists and royals.[8] Carr soon combined phrenology with mesmerism,

---

feature of the show was the horrible pathological distortions which the instincts of mankind have ever kept as secret as possible'. Anatomical museums were regularly shut down for offending taste.

7   In 1884, Smith met protégé Carl von Ledebur, one of three competitors in the Smith-sponsored Championship of Australia, a six-day walking race. The German-Swiss immigrant had been race-walking under the name of England's world-champion pedestrian, Charles Rowell. Von Ledebur was gaoled for burglary shortly afterwards, when a witness informed police he'd bought stolen jewellery from 'a walking man', one of Melbourne's more unusual criminal identifications. After his release, von Ledebur was hired as a trainer for the Essendon Football Club, which won three titles under his guidance. In 1896, after instruction from Smith, 'Doctor' von Ledebur became a 'medical electro-therapeutist' and advertised 'the new therapeutic method of treating disease by hypodermic injection of organic liquids extracted from the glands etc.' – i.e. injecting the crushed testicles of dogs, sheep, goats and guinea pigs into masturbators to combat the loss of semen believed to cause 'debility and nervous disease'. Who would have thought Essendon Football Club would ever be associated with a bloke giving dodgy performance-enhancing injections to wankers?

8   Waxworks, with their 'life-sized figures, celebrated and atrocious', were another popular Victorian-era entertainment. Parents were particularly keen on showing their children the models of recently hanged local criminals, believing this would keep them on the straight and narrow. Many waxworks also housed live 'freaks', like Sydney's Madame Sohier's nine-year-old 'Esau the Bearded Boy'.

employing audience plants who could be guaranteed to do ridiculous things on stage after Carr mesmerised them by fondling the bumps on their heads.[9]

During his shows, the self-restyled Dr Carr spruiked his new medical practice, promising that his animal magnetism would cure tumours, derangement, deafness, stammering, diseases of the eye, sciatica, rheumatism and neuralgia. Carr successfully employed mesmerism for anaesthetic effect, removing tumours, teeth, fingernails and even fingers from uncomplaining patients, in his private rooms and on stage.

Carr realised that a good showman needed to keep his act fresh. While mesmerism remained his mainstay, he branched out by demonstrating the effect of laughing gas on enthusiastic audience members and delivered lectures on subjects as diverse as temperance, 'The Qualifications requisite for the Pulpit, the Bar and the Press', and 'Man and the Gorilla'.

William Terry took a leaf out of Carr's book, embracing as many mystic practices as he could. His clairvoyance allowed him to diagnose diseases and administer cures. His skills as a mesmerist facilitated the 'trance state' that enabled him to communicate with the spirits of the dead, whose eldritch energies boosted his healing powers.

---

9   Australia's first professional mesmerist, Caroline Dexter (a.k.a. Madame Carole), opened her Mesmeric Institution, complete with electro-magnetic baths, in Melbourne in 1858. Caroline was the wife of William Dexter, the campaigner for miners' voting rights who'd jumped the shark in calling for 'women having the vote as well as men'. Caroline, who'd earlier championed English women trading in their corsets for big comfy bloomers, continued to promote rational dress in Australia through her Institute of Hygiene. She also published Australia's first 'Ladies Almanack'. Professional female mesmerists like Dexter needed other sources of income because they were restricted to a female clientele, as no self-respecting Victorian male would allow a woman to rummage around his psyche. Female stage mesmerists were also a rarity, as public lectures and performances and science and medicine were considered to be within the male public sphere. Madame Sibly (a.k.a. The Wonderful Woman a.k.a. Mary Element) and her daughter Blanche (a.k.a. Zel the Magnetic Lady) were notable exceptions, with their shows combining mesmerism, phrenology, gaudy costumes and tantalising glimpses of exposed flesh.

His herbalism, and his later registration as a pharmacist, allowed him to sell mystic potions and powerful opiates. His advocacy of human levitation served no discernible purpose.

Terry's psychic healing was conducted in a room above his spiritualist bookshop, but country folk could access his services by mailing him a lock of their hair and ten shillings, with Terry sending a patent herbal remedy and a hefty bill for same by return post. Terry pronounced that Mr George Cook's hair showed 'weak lungs, a hard liver, poor digestion, and bad circulation', but, unluckily for Mr Cook, missed his massive heart aneurism.

Sometimes the spirits got it wrong.

THE DEAD DOWN UNDER

Spiritualism, as a new science, was fashionable among Melbourne's medical and free-thinking elite.

Prominent obstetrician Dr Walter Richardson, the inaugural president of the Victorian Association of Progressive Spiritualists, helped Terry make Melbourne the epicentre of Australian spiritualism. Richardson, who apparently had a recreational, as well as professional, interest in lady parts, soon fell ill with syphilis and was committed to an asylum by his wife.[10]

Terry's fellow oddball bookseller, Edward Cole, was also a convert, writing in 1871, 'Modern Spiritualism as a religion ... will, I believe, inevitably become the dominant system of the civilised world.' He enthusiastically attended séances and his wife became a medium.[11]

---

10   Richardson was the inspiration for Australian fiction's best-known syphilitic insane spiritualist, Richard Mahony, the central character of *The Fortunes of Richard Mahony*. The three-novel epic was written by Richardson's male-impersonator daughter, Henry Handel Richardson.

11   Cole married the only serious applicant to an advertisement ('A GOOD WIFE WANTED') he placed in Melbourne's *Herald*, offering a 'TWENTY POUNDS REWARD' to any 'respectable, well intentioned person' who could source him 'a spinster of thirty five or six years of age;

In 1874, the year of his separation from Martha, Terry met a youth who'd been drawn to mesmerism by Charles Dickens' use of 'magnetic powers' in attempting to cure a friend of her 'spectres'.[12] The young man had successfully mesmerised a young lady at a party and compelled a man in a neighbouring room to come to him, before paralysing him with the force of his mind. Frightened by his terrible new powers, he'd sworn off further attempts at psychic control.

The young man had come to Terry to seek psychic healing for his sensitive digestive system. After a dose of ghostly Gaviscon, the youth – his spirit and stomach quietened – became Terry's devoted disciple.

Terry, convinced that children needed to spend more time with dead people, had earlier founded Melbourne's Progressive Lyceum, a spiritualist Sunday School with 'Science and Philosophy as its prophets'. Terry's new acolyte was soon ready to step up and assume the mantle of leadership at the Lyceum, offering spiritual guidance to the flower of Melbourne's youth, while subjecting them to a gruelling regimen of marching, singing and calisthenics.

The young Padawan's name was Alfred Deakin. Strong in the Force he was.

---

good tempered, intelligent, honest, truthful, sober, chaste, cleanly, neat, but not extravagantly or absurdly dressy; industrious, frugal, moderately educated, and a lover of home', before expanding on each of those points for several hundred words because he'd paid for a whole newspaper column. The advertisement acknowledged, 'This may be thought by many an absurd, because an unusual, way of looking for a wife', before concluding, 'if by advertising, I get a good, a sensible, and a suitable wife instead of an unsuitable one, which I would very likely get in the usual way, my temporary exposure is well indemnified and my twenty pounds is well spent.'

12   Dickens experimented with mesmerism, but despite using ghosts in some of his stories, was sceptical of spiritualism. In *Well-Authenticated Rappings*, one of Dickens' characters had 'spiritual experiences' caused by a boozy Christmas lunch and a particularly rich pork pie. Dickens was a founding member of the Ghost Club, a gentlemen's organisation dedicated to investigating fraudulent mediums.

WTF???

TIME OUT!

OK, we've just learned that Australia's greatest Liberal prime minister was a weak-stomached lackey of a notorious snake oil–selling, mystic mumbo-jumbo wife-beater; that he possessed mind-control powers straight out of *The Twilight Zone*; and that he ran happy-clappy necromancy and calisthenics sessions for innocent Aussie kids.

And Louisa Lawson, Edward Cole and a cabal of Melbourne doctors were also into this shit?

Next we'll find out that Alfred Deakin was an extra-terrestrial shapeshifting lizard who forced smallpox vaccinations and those new-fangled telephones on Australians to erase their memories of being abused in the basement of the Lyceum, which doubled as a pizza parlour for Melbourne's Jewish bankers and other liberal/socialist/big-government elites.

To understand what the hell is going on, we need to know a little more about spiritualism.

PRACTICAL NECROMANCY FOR BEGINNERS

Spiritualists believe that the dead pursue self-improvement for eternity, with the afterlife a never-ending Tony Robbins seminar. This quest for personal growth and development makes the dead ideal life coaches. They're happy to pop back to the material plane (you just have to turn off the lights and ask them nicely) to offer guidance on complex moral and ethical issues, reveal hidden truths, divine the future or, most likely, all of the above – because the dead are insufferable know-it-alls.

Sometimes the dead give private counselling sessions, but most of them prefer an audience. Group sessions are known as séances (literally 'sessions' in French), at which one or more dead people may be summoned to impart their spectral wisdom to the ethereally challenged.

Dead people may be summoned by anyone, but specially trained and empathic people known as mediums do a better job. Women, it turns out, are more empathic than men. Female mediums have well and truly broken through the ectoplasmic ceiling and overcome the gender pay gap prevalent in most industries, with more silver crossing their palms than those of their male counterparts.

Spiritualism and feminism were intertwined in their early days, with spiritualists early advocates of women's rights. Both movements originated in 1848 in upstate New York, a hotbed of social and spiritual reform. The feminist movement kicked off at Seneca Falls when Elizabeth Cady Stanton penned the 'Declaration of Rights and Sentiments' at the world's first women's rights convention. The spiritualist movement kicked off some 37 kilometres up the road in Hydesville, when sisters Kate and Margaret Fox summoned the spirit of a peddler who'd been murdered in their house.[13]

---

13   Spiritualism was part of a broader religious revival that took place in rural New York in the first half of the nineteenth century. Mormonism was founded there in the 1820s by a farmer, Joseph Smith Jr, who talked to God, Jesus and some of the more chatty angels, one of whom directed him to some buried golden plates inscribed in a 'reformed Egyptian' script that Joseph was able to translate using 'seer stones'. The translated plates became the Book of Mormon, which explained how all the real Christians had travelled to America in 589 B.C. – as did Jesus after his resurrection, so he could appoint twelve all-American disciples, who were much better than his Middle Eastern ones. Millerism also took off in New York in 1831, after another farmer, William Miller, insisted that Jesus would return to earth sometime in 1843 or 1844. Millerites later checked Jesus' schedule and confirmed 22 October 1844 as his return date. On 23 October 1844, the Millerites endured the 'Great Disappointment', but some of the less disappointed ones formed the Seventh-day Adventist Church, which maintains Jesus will be 'back soon'.

The peddler communicated with the Fox sisters through rapping noises, and Kate and Margaret became the first celebrity mediums. Early conversations with the dead were all a variation of,

Knock, knock.

'Who's there?'

Knock, knock.

... which was unsatisfying for all concerned.

The dead therefore incorporated communication skills into their personal development programs. Some took to tilting tables, with the table legs rapping the floor when relevant letters of the alphabet were called out, spelling messages for the living. This was incredibly laborious and hard on carpets, so the more enterprising dead communicated through an array of devices that would mysteriously move over letters while being held by séance participants – culminating with the Ouija board, invented by an American toy company in 1890.

Dead people who favoured speedier communication used mediums as a kind of psychic telephone exchange, speaking into their minds or through their mouths. Less verbally confident spirits might possess a living person's hand to pen messages from the other side (automatic writing). Others would scrawl spectral notes in chalk on pieces of slate (slate writing), or write on a piece of paper in a sealed envelope that would later be opened by the medium (unnecessarily complicated writing).

During séances, some spirits would make things appear (e.g. a piece of cloth that might pass for a loved one's handkerchief) or disappear (e.g. a participant's money). Others would produce eerie noises from a trumpet or manifest ectoplasm, the nasty slimy stuff that spirits are made from. And exhibitionist dead people would pose for photos with their loved ones, who would part with a not inconsiderable sum for a snapshot of themselves in the dark standing in front of a luminescent blur.

Home séances increased in popularity from the late 1840s, but spiritualism received a massive boost when it was embraced within

America's First Home. In 1862, Mary Todd Lincoln conducted White House séances to talk to her dead sons, Willie and Eddie. Mary later commissioned a spirit portrait in which a ghostly President Lincoln hovered behind her. Shortly after, her sole surviving son committed her to an asylum.

Spiritualism didn't just appeal to the bereaved and feminists; but to vegetarians, teetotallers, sexual abstainers and other killjoys who believed transcending temptations of the flesh would enlighten their lives and afterlives. It appealed to socialists, who saw the netherworld as an undead commune where the spirits of workers were liberated from the chains of capital (but were free to rattle other chains). Robert Owen, the utopian socialist who championed the eight-hour workday, was an enthusiastic convert. And it appealed to liberal reformers because the living dead strove for continuous improvement, and they promised a more inclusive future. Death, after all, is the great equaliser.

As science upped its assaults on Biblical literalism, many people questioned their faith and sought new spiritual meaning. Some found that meaning in the bumpings and scrapings of the dead. Spiritualism, like geology or evolutionary biology, was a new science. Spirits manifested in the material world – they wrote notes in chalk, played trumpets and appeared in photographs. They were simply more *present* than Biblical figures – after all, the Holy Ghost hadn't shaken any table legs since Joseph was a carpenter or produced any ectoplasmic goo since he'd knocked up Mary.

Spiritualism attracted prominent scientists. Alfred Russel Wallace, gazumped by Darwin as the father of evolutionary biology, advanced a theory of spiritual evolution in which eldritch forces directed the development of human intelligence and morality. Vacuum tube pioneer William Crookes saw ghosts in his machines. Sir Oliver Lodge, who arguably beat Marconi to the radio, insisted his dead son Raymond enjoyed whisky and cigars in the spirit world. Pierre Curie believed spiritual phenomena opened up new fields of physics, and Sir Arthur

Conan Doyle, a pioneer in forensic science as well as the creator of
Sherlock Holmes, chased poltergeists and believed sufferers of mental
illness were possessed by malevolent spirits.

Spiritualists spent a lot of time sitting in the dark waiting for table
legs to do something interesting – they had the time and energy to
worry about things beyond the next meal, or how long they'd spend
up a chimney the next day. Spiritualists, like many adherents of other
reform movements, were predominantly upper and middle class.

Spiritualism was one of the USA's first great cultural exports –
McDonald's for the spiritually starved. It was particularly embraced
in English-speaking Christian societies, most notably Britain and its
Australian colonies. And nowhere did it establish a firmer foothold
than in Melbourne.

A HAPPY MEDIUM

Alfred Deakin took to spiritualism like a dead duck to orange sauce.
In 1874, he and his sister, Kate, established a spirit circle in the Deakin
family home. William Deakin, up for anything associated with old
gypsy women, was a keen participant, and Alfred also encouraged his
old debating buddy Richard Hodgson to get in on the act. Medium
George Stow, William Terry's business partner, attended a Deakin
family séance and announced a spirit had told him 'a great medium'
would be present 'who would develop and occupy a very prominent
place' in society. The dead had anointed Deakin for greatness.

Dr James Motherwell, a respected Collins Street physician, ran
Melbourne's most exclusive spirit circle, guided by the spirit of Dr
Elliotson, an English mesmerist who'd died in 1861. Deakin was
invited to join Motherwell's circle, attended by Terry, Stow, Walter
Richardson, and the other movers and shakers and rappers of the
Australian spiritualist scene. The shade of Dr Elliotson ran a tight
ship and ensured that only the better sorts of spirits were in attend-
ance. During one session, Prince Albert materialised and 'expressed

a desire' to speak on national affairs 'to my good friends on earth'. He held forth on Irish nationalism and was later joined by the disincarnate Irish nationalists Daniel O'Connell and Robert Emmet. Motherwell had the prince's communications published as *The 'Prince Consort' on Irish Affairs*.

Deakin, whose unique schooling had given him the empathy of a woman, proved a powerful medium. During a trance speaking session, he channelled a spirit who offered this pearl of post-mortem wisdom:

> Life passes away like a dream, but in reality it rolls slowly along, till purged from earthly impurities, when it gains new speed and brightens from the eternal fires, and souls soar thru'out the vast infinity.

Deakin really proved his spiritual chops in 1876, when he channelled the unearthly remains of John Bunyan during forty-nine gruelling spirit writing sessions. Bunyan controlled Deakin's hand in penning a sequel to his 1678 *The Pilgrim's Progress*, which he unimaginatively named *A New Pilgrim's Progress* – the story of Restless who leaves the City of Worldly Content to seek his destiny as a great prophet. Restless encounters seven spirit guides who gift him seven visions, and marries Wilful, a gifted medium. The marriage transforms Restless and Wilful into Redeemer and Redemptress. Redeemer becomes a preacher of the new Philosophy of Spiritualism and champions 'truth, liberty and spiritualism' against 'error, tyranny and materialism of gross sensuality'. The tale ends with Redeemer's and Redemptress' murders at the hands of agents of a tyrannical city, but their deaths lead to the tyrants' overthrow and 'next morning the city rose free'. Bunyan's shade let go of Deakin's hand for good on this anticlimactic note.

For the bicentenary of *The Pilgrim's Progress*, William Terry published *A New Pilgrim's Progress, Purported to Be Given by John Bunyan Through an Impressional Writing Medium*. It did not set the Yarra on fire.

By now, Deakin was having auditory hallucinations and out-of-body experiences. With his trademark beard growing in, he became a paranormal investigator – a Victorian Shaggy without the talking dog. He gave the psychic seal of approval to Mrs Paton, Terry's sister, certifying that she'd materialised a wet rock and seaweed during a particularly soggy séance.

FIG. 3: ALFRED DEAKIN PUT ON HIS TINFOIL TOP HAT WHENEVER HE NEEDED
TO BLOCK OUT THE VOICES OF THE RESTLESS DEAD.

Terry had become a paranormal promoter, touring international spiritualist acts. He brought out Henry Slade, the father of slate writing, who was later proven to have replaced blank slates with written-on slates during séances, or written on them himself when everyone was looking at jiggling tables.[14] He also promoted Thomas Walker, a child preacher turned spiritualist who'd fled Canada after a coronial inquiry found he'd caused the death of a client who'd sustained burns

---

14   Several mediums who developed novel forms of spirit communication were found to be frauds. The Fox sisters later admitted the rapping peddler had been a hoax. The cacophony that emanated from the instrument of renowned trumpet medium Etta Wriedt was produced by chemical explosions, Mina Crandon's ectoplasmic hand was the sculpted liver of an unfortunate animal, and spirit photographer Helen Duncan's models were made from cheesecloth, rubber gloves and cut-out heads from magazine covers.

from the phosphorous Walker used to make 'illuminated writing' and 'spiritual lights'.

Deakin chaired Walker's first Australian spiritualist lecture, which Walker delivered in a trance while controlled by Giordano Bruno, a Dominican friar, cosmologist and occultist burned at the stake in 1600 for saying sacramental wine was not the blood of Christ and Mary was not a virgin.[15]

Deakin continued to teach at the Progressive Lyceum and, in 1877, took an interest in one of his students, fourteen-year-old Pattie Browne. Pattie was able to summon Shakespeare, which gave her serious spiritualist and literary cred. A medium told Deakin that he would marry Pattie. Who was Deakin to stand in the way of what the spirits had ordained?

But if Deakin were to marry his young charge, he would need to provide for her – and his earthly career was in the doldrums. He'd received few briefs as a barrister, his work at the Gospel Hall Free Night School for urchins was free, his stationery business had failed, his books had been ridiculed or ignored, and his regular chats with dead people precluded him from becoming a Unitarian preacher. He'd submitted regular art reviews of pictures in the National Gallery 'in the style of Ruskin', but Ruskin's style was not appreciated by the philistines who edited the colony's newspapers – and his work on 'the History, Philosophy and Principles of Poetry' was very much 'in progress'. To top it all off, he still lived with his parents.

Still, his spiritualist star was in the ascendant. In 1878, Alfred Deakin was elected president of the Victorian Association of Progressive Spiritualists.

---

15 Sydney radio station 2GB was named for Giordano Bruno. The station was established by the Theosophical Society, a spiritualist offshoot you can learn more about in Chapter 7. The Society, which continued its occult programs on 2GB until 1975, asserted that Bruno had been reincarnated as leading Theosophist and birth control campaigner Dr Annie Besant. Bruno, one of the world's leading undead contrarians and shit-stirrers, is now believed to inhabit the earthly shell of 2GB host Ray Hadley.

THE PROPHET OF PROTECTIONISM

Deakin's work on bringing the dead and children together at the Lyceum brought him into contact with a ghost-curious mother, Annabella Syme. Annabella was married to David Syme, the dour Scots co-owner, publisher and editor of the *Age*, Australia's most read newspaper.

Syme had the appearance and demeanour of an undertaker who'd run out of corpses, acknowledging, 'I'm a man with few friends.' However, Syme understood fear and how to instil it in the politicians he sponsored. He used his newspaper to build the careers of men who backed his agenda, and to destroy those who deviated from the path he'd set them on. He was a proto-Rupert who'd have happily hacked the telephone of a dead schoolgirl for a story, but Melbourne only had two telephones and they belonged to the Robison brothers, the city's leading engineers.[16]

Unlike Rupert, Syme had a soul and believed in something other than himself. Syme believed the Robisons and men like them were the future. In 1860, he realised Victoria's gold would not last forever, and miners would need new jobs. Opening up land for small-scale farmers by breaking the power of the squatters was one solution – but the big pay-off lay in building new manufacturing industries.

The start-ups championed by Syme would not be able to compete with the established factories of Britain, and the gold rush had left Australia with the highest workers' wages in the world. If Victoria was to make things, Syme reasoned, the makers would need government protection. Tariffs on imported goods, including goods from the other Australian colonies, would allow Victorian industries to take root and then flourish.

Free trade, an article of faith for British liberals and the mountebanks from north of the Murray, would only entrench the monopolies

---

16 He could have just hired a spiritualist to interview her.

of British manufacturers. Victoria needed to pursue its own economic policy.

Only a powerful government could challenge the free marketeers, a revelation Syme acknowledged led him 'in the direction of State Socialism'. Governments should invest in transport, communication and infrastructure. Governments should run or regulate key industries, with the American cancer of privatising everything to be cut out of the Australian body politic before it could metastasise. Governments should intervene in the eternal war between labour and capital, maintaining a balance that would advance the common good. Governments knew best. Or rather, governments that thought what Syme thought they should think, and did what Syme told them to do, knew best.

Most Australians supported Syme's big-government agenda. Modern Australia, founded as the world's largest prison, was itself one giant government project. It took time for the churches, charities and cooperative bodies that provided social services elsewhere to establish themselves Down Under, with government filling the vacuum. Australian colonial governments, wary of American-style revolution, hadn't historically directly taxed their people. Instead, they raised revenue through land sales and import duties. Australians were used to the state providing services they didn't have to pay for. This seemed like a pretty good deal. Big government? Bring it on!

The problem was that Victoria's upper house was designed to protect established interests from the common man. Only men of substantial means could sit in, and vote for, the Legislative Council, which had the power to veto legislation passed by the liberal reformers who dominated the Legislative Assembly.

Despite the Council blocking or slowing reform, David Syme had successfully encouraged Victoria's adoption of his beloved tariffs. But more needed to be done and a different administration could undo all his good work.

Syme was always on the lookout for promising young men who could further the protectionist agenda, and Alfred Deakin habitually sought older male role models. Annabella Syme brought the grizzled protectionist and the young, liberal, free-trader necromancer together. It would prove a powerful match.

A HEAD FOR POLITICS

As a spiritualist and free thinker, Alfred Deakin was used to seeing the other side. This, and a job offer from David Syme, allowed him to execute a perfect backflip and pike on his free-trade views.

Deakin worked as a journalist for the *Age* and its weekly stable-mate, the *Leader*, between 1878 and 1883, taking over the 'Under the Verandah' column from the dissipated Marcus Clarke. Deakin was among the twenty pressmen permitted to witness the 1880 hanging of Ned Kelly, his bland report avoiding any reference to the infamous bushranger's last words.

Journalists knew that last words defined a life. More importantly, they sold papers. The journalist from the *Telegraph* claimed Kelly had said, 'Ah, well, I suppose...' This was too equivocal for his counter-part from the *Argus*, who opted for the far more revealing 'Ah, well, I suppose it has come to this.' The *Herald*'s scribe maintained Kelly had said, 'Such is life,' proving that he had a viable second career as a desk calendar copywriter.[17] A reporter of more absurdist bent insisted Kelly's departing words were 'What a nice little garden.'

Deakin could have resolved the dispute by returning home, making himself a pot of tea, drawing the kitchen curtains, and summoning the vengeful shade of Edward Kelly to repeat his last words and explain which bits of the prison garden he'd liked the best. That he did not do so spoke to his growing awareness that most people considered

---

17 EXPLANATION FOR YOUNGER READERS: Boomers used to keep paper calendars on their desks because there were no calendar apps on their mobile phones. In fact, there were no mobile phones. Really, it's true! Ask Siri! Each date on a desk calendar was accompanied by a pithy quote. A quote is like a meme from a boomer influencer, but without any pictures. A copywriter is ... oh, forget it.

talking to the dead a bit suss.

Deakin was concerned about his image because he was now moon-lighting as a member of parliament when his journalistic schedule allowed. In 1879, Syme had suggested he run as a Liberal candidate in the West Bourke by-election. Much to everyone's surprise, including his own, he won.

Deakin ran on Syme's platform of protection, Legislative Council reform, a land tax, and keeping 'priestcraft, dogma and intolerance' out of schools.[18] He wrote glowing editorials about his own campaign, as the idea of impartial reporting had not yet been conceived. He would continue to work for both the people and the press throughout his life.

Deakin's experience as a debater, medium and journalist had made him a powerful communicator. He'd stride the stage like an evangelist preacher, changing pace and tone, one moment gesturing wildly, the next perfectly still. People commented on his command of facts, his arsenal of classical quotes for any occasion, his vigour, his height, his thick dark hair, his statesmanlike beard, his good looks and his mesmeric brown eyes. He was a natural.

It therefore surprised everyone that Deakin, in his maiden par-liamentary speech, announced he'd resign and recontest his seat. His conservative rival had complained a booth had closed early after run-ning out of ballot papers, and Deakin would not have the integrity of his victory questioned. His supporters applauded his principle and his opponents his subsequent loss.

Deakin appeared unperturbed, announcing that he didn't really want to be a politician because of the lack of decency in parliamentary debate. He thought that anyone who entertained political ambition needed their head checked – so he consulted a phrenologist.

Masquerading as a 'Mr Wilson Esquire', Deakin asked Archibald Hamilton to measure his head and provide a full assessment of his character and suitability for political life. Hamilton advised 'Wilson'

---

18   Except for intolerance of priestcraft and dogma.

that his head revealed him to be a man of 'quick observation, penetrating intelligence, lively wit, good language and logical acumen' who may be ready for parliament in a few years, but:

> You are not an original nor profound thinker and have not <u>great</u> force of character. Yours is an intellect of ability not genious.[19]

Hamilton also found Deakin's skull to be well developed in horniness:

> Morally speaking you cannot afford to trifle with your own soaring and ardently affectionate nature, therefore the sooner the better you see your way to a happy matrimonial alliance ... as you are very strong in conjugal desire.

Deakin continued to consult phrenologists, mediums and astrologers on his political options. He ran a failed campaign in February 1880, but was unconcerned, as a medium assured him he'd be in parliament by year's end.

And lo, it came to pass that the parliament was dissolved and Deakin was again flying the Liberal flag in West Bourke. This time he was savaged by the conservative press for his unconventional beliefs. The *Daily Telegraph* noted he was the president of the Victorian Association of Progressive Spiritualists and the author of *A New Pilgrim's Progress*, 'A vile catchpenny publication' and 'the record of the delirious dreams of an illiterate, ignorant and impure mind'. The *Telegraph* was just getting started, condemning Deakin as a 'Spiritist and Comtist and moreover an advocate of free love and an enemy of Christian marriage'.[20]

---

19   Hamilton's own skull had strong underlining bumps, but weak spelling and punctuation bumps.

20   Comtists were followers of Auguste Comte, a Frenchman who urged that theology be replaced by 'a hierarchy of sciences'. Comte developed a 'Humanistic calendar' that started from the French Revolution and comprised thirteen 28-day months and an additional festival day that commemorated the dead (which appealed to

The men of West Bourke must have been up for some free love because Deakin romped it in. The new member refused to be appointed attorney-general, as he felt he lacked sufficient political experience. To remedy this, he committed to a fast-tracked political education from the most experienced operators he could find.

Victorian Liberal premier Richard Heales advised Deakin on negotiations with conservative MPs and assured him he'd be in the next ministry. Heales also convinced Deakin he shouldn't leave political meetings at night alone, as Roman Catholics were plotting to assassinate him for his stance on keeping the Bible out of public schools. Heales' mentorship of Deakin was all the more impressive for his having been dead for sixteen years.

Deakin also received advice on statecraft from the ectoplasmic John Bunyan, John Knox, John Stuart Mill and Thomas Macaulay, the latter urging him to read his history of Charles II to better understand Victoria's Legislative Assembly. These spirits were concerned Deakin was overdoing it, counselling him to rest, eat fruit and avoid stimulants.

Deakin knew he'd change the world – or at least Australia – as the first séance he recorded in his 1880–1882 Spiritual Diary revealed: 'A grand spirit – will lend my words weight – so that I shall convince and conquer in spite of opposition – shall be great Reformer.'

The ever-living dead were not just interested in the great Reformer's political career and fruit intake. Deakin claimed the spirits wanted to help with his finances 'to free and strengthen me for their higher work'. A Ballarat accountant, five years in the coffin, recommended Deakin buy shares in various mining concerns and Dixon Gas, a company that claimed to have discovered 'an easy and practicable method of decomposing water'. Madame Siècle, a medium whose financial

---

spiritualists). Comte named his months after famous men of Western history, and replaced saint's days with days dedicated to slightly less famous men of Western history. The extra day in a leap year was dedicated to holy women, which was all the recognition women got from Comtists. Most Australians distrusted Comtism because it was batshit crazy and, more disturbingly, French.

interest in Dixon Gas is unknown, assured Deakin its shares were certain to rise in value.[21]

Madame Siècle, Mrs Stirling and Mrs Cohen all ran séances for Deakin during his early political career. Deakin's Spiritual Diary recorded the spirits who materialised, the questions he asked them and the answers they gave. When the spirits failed to provide meaningful advice, Deakin acknowledged 'such personal issues were not worthy of the attention of visitors from higher spheres'. In the mid-1890s, Deakin looked back on the spirits' prophecies about his personal and political life and found them 'inexplicably accurate forecasts of the future'.

The new MP was not interested in the petty day-to-day concerns of his constituents, considering them a distraction from 'matters of a purely public nature'. He would not seek to resolve neighbourhood disputes about the height of hedges, lobby for the repair of broken water-pumps or acknowledge the superior qualities of the scones baked by the temperance ladies of West Bourke. He would concern himself solely with great matters of state.

After fourteen months in parliament, Deakin introduced his first bill, which, in keeping with his interest in metaphysics, prohibited putting the cart before the horse. Outlawing the tying of a horse pulling a cart to another cart in front of the horse would minimise horse injuries in horse and cart pile-ups. Deakin told the House it was 'the duty of the Legislature to seek to afford every protection to poor creatures who could not protect themselves or tell of the injuries they received'.[22]

---

21 Taking share advice from mediums and astrologers is not as silly as it sounds (which is very). Astrologer Doreen Daze frequently trounced seasoned financial analysts in the *Sydney Morning Herald*'s stock market game.

22 People think the box jellyfish, tiger snake, funnel-web spider, blue-ringed octopus, great white shark or saltwater crocodile is Australia's deadliest animal. They're wrong. Horses threw people, kicked people, trampled people, ran over people and sent carriages full of people careening into crowds of people. Deakin would have been better served protecting people from horses.

Deakin had given voice to the dead, championed women's rights and protected horses. His political future appeared assured, even though dead people, women and horses couldn't vote. It was time to attend to his personal life and find a wife.

Madame Siècle prophesied that he would soon marry 'a dark lady – brownish', which put Deakin in a quandary because an earlier medium had foretold his marriage to little Pattie from the Lyceum. Pattie had a fair complexion – but wait ... her name was Browne! Madame Siècle's spirit obviously enjoyed wordplay. Prophecy was an art, not a science, and the dead had a perfect right to be Delphic in their pronouncements.

Deakin wrote romantic letters to Pattie, addressing her as 'My dearest child'. Pattie's father, Hugh Browne, was not enthused by the match and failed to stump up the traditional dowry, giving weight to the allegations of 'free love' levelled against Deakin.[23] Alfred and Pattie were married on 3 April 1882 in a private ceremony conducted in a registry office, lending credence to the charge that Deakin was 'an enemy of Christian marriage'. Deakin would later write a poem about his wedding night:

> *Sprinkled with blood and wet with tears,*
> *Timid and tender, since love sears,*
> *How infantile my bride appears.*

Australia's future prime minister could be a bit of a creep.

---

23   Hugh Browne objected to Deakin's poor financial prospects, not his talking to dead people. Browne was a dedicated spiritualist, whose faith was strengthened when two of his sons died in a yacht accident on Port Phillip Bay. A medium told Browne the yacht had capsized at 9 a.m. and that a shark had ripped off his son's limbs, before instructing him to hurry to Frankston pier. Browne claimed he arrived just as a shark was hauled ashore, with its stomach revealing twelve shillings, one of his son's keys and pipe, and a right arm wearing a gold watch stopped at 9 a.m.

4

Exhibitions, Engines and Enemies

Australia for the Australians

The Bulletin's masthead, 14 April 1888 to 30 April 1908

THE EXHIBITIONIST

S IR HENRY PARKES, LIKE ALFRED DEAKIN, HAD transitioned from poet, to pressman, to politician. Deakin wrote of the five-time New South Wales premier:

> He was jealous of equals, bitter with rivals, and remorseless with enemies – vain beyond all measure, without strong attachment to colleagues and with strong animal passions.

The last point was a none-too-subtle reference to Sir Henry's legendary libido. With the highest sperm count in Australian political history, Parkes fathered at least seventeen children and was still on the job at seventy-six.[1]

Parkes' pulling power had nothing to do with his looks. He rarely smiled and his permanently raised left eyebrow conveyed a world-weary

---

[1] Parkes' status as Australia's gold-medal political rooter is all the more impressive given the intermarital escapades of Bob Hawke and John Gorton, the Michael Hutchence-esque final moments of Billy Snedden, and the jaw- and trouser-dropping antics of Prime Minister Scott Morrison's front bench.

contempt for all things not Henry Parkes. With his snowy shock of hair and beard borrowed from one of the rough sleepers in the Domain parklands behind Parliament House, he looked like Santa caught in the act of slipping a naughty child a lump of coal. An American visitor described Parkes as 'a picture to look at' and continued:

> He is fully six feet in his socks; supple as an eel, and wiry as a cork-screw. His face is a compound of wrinkles, 'yallar jaunders', theology and politics ... He has small, keen, grey eyes, and a head shaped like a mammoth goose egg, big end up; his hair, silvery white, much resembling a bag of wool in 'admirable disorder', or a brush-heap in a gale of wind ... Strangers mostly think he is a crazy person escaped from his keepers, and the rest scarcely understand what he's about.

The difficulty in understanding Parkes lay in his contradictions.[2] He was vain, yet wore an ill-fitting frockcoat that *might* have been fashionable decades earlier. He championed the working man, but saw printers at his newspaper gaoled over a pay strike. He condemned Australians who received imperial honours, then pocketed a knighthood. He recommended import duties to protect small manufacturers, only to become one of Australia's most forceful free trade advocates. He cut pub opening hours for the temperance vote, but chugged beer throughout his legendary forty-hour work sprees. He published editorials that belittled women, yet supported their suffrage. He managed the colony's finances, but his bingeing on books, paintings, photographs, autographs and animals for his private zoo made him a multiple bankrupt.[3]

---

2   And in his thick working-class English Midlands accent, which meant he dropped his (h)aitches. Parkes was embarrassed by this until he realised it helped him connect with his working-class political base.

3   Andrew Barton Paterson, who worked for the law firm that represented Parkes, wrote of the premier, 'The old man never had any money, though goodness knows he had opportunities enough of getting it "on the side". But personal finances bored him. He despised money; he was Sir Henry Parkes!' Parkes, in contrast, wrote after one of his bankruptcies, 'My only object is to *make money*. I would

Parkes would have allowed himself a satisfied smile on the afternoon of 16 September 1880. He'd caught a train the previous night,
breakfasted at the end of the New South Wales line in Gerogery,
coached the 22 miles to the Victorian railway terminus in Wodonga,
and here he was, just twenty hours after departing Sydney, stepping
off one of Victoria's slower Irish-gauge trains in Melbourne. His first
overland journey to the southern city had taken twenty-five days!

Parkes was in enemy territory to preview the Melbourne International Exhibition. He'd just overseen the Sydney equivalent, which,
he was keen to point out, was the first international exhibition staged
in the southern hemisphere.[4]

The Sydney International Exhibition was the brainchild of Eliezer
Montefiore, who'd founded the Victorian Academy of Art in 1870
and crossed the Murray to bring a little Melbourne culture to the
northern heathens. Montefiore knew that the practical men of Sydney
wouldn't fork out for an art exhibition, so he co-opted the New South
Wales Agriculture Society to lobby for an international agricultural
show. Hopefully, he'd be able to get some paintings of haystacks or
cows onto the program.

Sydney's exhibition was approved after Melbourne's, but the
Parkes ministry pulled out all stops to get in first and was determined
to build an exhibition hall to rival London's Crystal Palace, the venue
for the world's first international exhibition, the Great Exhibition of
1851. Five hundred men laboured twenty-four hours a day under new-
fangled electric lights to build the Garden Palace, a 224-metre-long
grand edifice in the Domain. The Palace was completed in just eight

---

as soon sell Dung as Divinity if I could only make money by selling it.' The first
money Parkes made in Australia was a sixpenny coin earned from holding a
gentleman's horse. Parkes' numerous creditors never got their hands on his 'lucky
sixpence', which he treasured until his death.

4   Melburnians who note that the Bureau of International Expositions does not
acknowledge Sydney's 1879 exhibition as a World Expo, but does recognise
Melbourne's, are just sore losers.

months and boasted the largest dome in the southern hemisphere (and the sixth-largest in the world). A small wooden 'shanty' was built nearby to house any drawings or paintings the foreigners might bring with them.

A total of 9,345 exhibitors from twenty-three nations and colonies displayed some 14,000 exhibits, spanning agriculture, mining, industry, domestic appliances, homewares, science, art and education. Japan displayed porcelain, India silks, Belgium pianofortes, Austria furniture, Italy statuary and mosaics, and local favourite Mrs Murray showed 'knitted mittens in imitation of lace'.[5] The most popular exhibit was an American hydraulic lift, the first elevator in New South Wales, which visitors could ride to the top of the Palace's northern tower. It was closely followed by, of all things, a painting. *Chloé*, Jules Lefebvre's larger-than-life full-frontal nude of a nineteen-year-old Parisian model, shorn of all bodily hair, drew huge crowds.[6] The men of Sydney might not have known much about art, but they knew what they liked.[7]

The Exhibition received more than 1.1 million visitors. On Anniversary Day, 26 January 1880, 27,500 visitors celebrated the birth of the colony with a temperance holiday. The only thing worse than not being able to have a drink was being forced to listen to 1,000 schoolchildren sing 'Advance Australia Fair'.[8]

---

5   Female exhibitors dominated the 'Lace, Net, Embroidery & Trimmings' and 'Leatherwork, Fancy Articles & Basketwork' classifications. Mrs E.M. Perryman displayed 'a marine clock and striking ships bells' she'd invented, which was considered progressive, though unladylike.

6   In the nineteenth century, the female nude was a symbol of art's highest spiritual ideals. In 1867, a Melbourne customs official described how he distinguished art from pornography, telling a court, 'In art there is no hair.' A lot has changed in the last 150 years.

7   *Chloé*, like all good art, has a tragic backstory. The model, distressed that Lefebvre had married her sister, drank poison at a dinner party. While her suicide upset her guests, it was great for Lefebvre's artistic cred and sales.

8   'Advance Australia Fair', which Peter Dodds McCormick composed one evening in 1878 (straight after knocking off the first verse on his bus trip home), didn't replace

Parkes was confident his exhibition would be better than Melbourne's. Sure, Melbourne might have sixteen more nations and colonies attending, 3,447 more exhibitors, and more than twice as many exhibits – but Victoria's Royal Exhibition Building had a smaller dome and was completely lacking in elevators.[9] And the New South Wales exhibits in Melbourne, featuring a giant sculpture of Parkes carved from coal, were sure to steal the show.[10] However, you had to give it to the Melburnians – they'd managed to secure *Chloé* for an encore tour.[11]

Chloé was not the only woman to attract Parkes' eye in Melbourne. Nellie Dixon, a raven-haired beauty and single mother, forty-three years Parkes' junior, lived around the corner from the exhibition. She would soon leave her child and Carlton home for a discreet Redfern cottage that Parkes would overnight in when parliament was sitting. Parkes' wife, Clarinda, had been conveniently installed at Faulconbridge, his distant Blue Mountains estate.

Parkes had a spring in his step as he left Melbourne for Sydney, and it wasn't just down to Nellie. The exhibitions had cemented the rival cities' places on the world stage. Sydney had showcased its agricultural and mineral resources, and Melbourne its rapidly expanding

---

'God Save the Queen' as the Australian national anthem until 1984. People who believe changing our national anthem is an affront to tradition have short memories.

9   Melbourne, though, secured 200,000 more visitors, including a group of forty Aboriginal people who were mistaken for one of the exhibits. Melburnians followed them back to where they were staying and politely waited for them to do something interesting.

10 Australian politicians love coal, with Prime Minister Scott Morrison once smuggling a lump of it into the House of Representatives and announcing, 'This is coal!', before fondling it like Gollum with the Ring. However, only Parkes had the ego to immortalise himself in coal.

11 *Chloé* was purchased by a local surgeon and hung in the National Gallery of Victoria, before puritanical Melburnians successfully campaigned for her removal. She has hung in the public bar of Young & Jackson Hotel since 1909, starting a proud Australian pub tradition of displaying paintings of naked ladies. The phrase 'As drunk as Chloe' entered the Australian vernacular to describe an extremely pissed person (i.e. a person who is drunk enough to take off all their clothes in public).

manufacturing capacity. Both cities had improved transport and infrastructure, and poured money into grand new buildings, to impress their international guests. They'd secured new trade opportunities and marketed themselves to would-be immigrants, including some visiting artists who'd decided to stay to help develop an Australian arts scene. And they'd exposed their own citizens to new products, culture and ideas. Melbourne and Sydney were each world-class cities in their own right, but together they could be more than the sum of their parts.

On 21 September 1880, Parkes addressed a dinner at Albury's Globe Hotel, on the New South Wales side of the border, predicting, 'The next ten years will disclose to the world an advance in human progress in Australia which has never been witnessed before.'

The planned extension of the New South Wales railway to Albury, connecting to the Victorian line at Wodonga, would do more 'to make the colonies one than all the schemes of politicians under the sun'. Despite Victoria and New South Wales' political differences, Parkes announced to cheers, 'I would never allow, so far as I could command myself, any attachment to New South Wales to interfere with the fairest consideration of any great question affecting Australia as a whole,' with defence and immigration singled out as areas where he was 'prepared to sacrifice much to bring about united action between these great countries'.

Parkes had not dropped the F-bomb, but he was definitely talking Federation. The idea that the colonies might unite had been floating around since Earl Grey, Britain's secretary of state for war and the colonies, flagged it in 1847. However, New South Wales rejected the idea because it had a greater population and was more prosperous than the other colonies, and its superiority would need to be recognised in any union.

The first real champion of Australian Federation was the proud Irish republican and Victorian MP Charles Gavan Duffy, who gained Victorian approval for union in 1857. New South Wales rejected the idea because Victoria now had a greater population and was more prosperous than New South Wales, and its superiority would need *not* to be recognised in any union.

Parkes had tested the federal waters at an intercolonial conference in 1867, musing, 'I think the time has arrived when these colonies should be united by some federal bond of connexion.' However, the idea had sunk, as New South Wales and Victoria were unable to settle their differences on protectionism.

Parkes' raising of Federation from the depths, and giving it the kiss of life on the banks of the Murray, would, he hoped, transform the internationalist sentiment roused by the exhibitions into a nationalist one.

THE LITTLE PAPER

The nationalist cause found a champion in the *Bulletin*, a weekly rag first published by John Haynes and John Feltham Archibald in 1880.

Archibald, who would later give his name to Australia's most prestigious portrait prize, had left sleepy Warrnambool for Melbourne in 1875, but the city editors only offered menial jobs to the young printer who dreamt of becoming a journalist. Archibald found himself working as a lowly Education Department clerk beside Ricciotti Garibaldi, an Italian revolutionary who'd decided to take a break from redrawing the map of Europe in blood by joining the Victorian public service. Ricciotti was the son of revolutionary hero Giuseppe Garibaldi, a republican who'd helped forge the Italian states into a united Italy.

Garibaldi, and other Europeans Archibald met in Melbourne, had a mix of danger, romance, sophistication and culture that Archibald, with his plain Scots and Irish roots, wanted for himself. And so John Feltham reinvented himself as Jules François, and his mother as an exotic French Jew. A more artsy name and compelling backstory would surely pique the interest of the Australian press and literary establishment.[12]

---

12   Australian women writers may have pretended to be men, but Archibald went the full Demidenko in pretending an interesting foreign pedigree. He continued this

In 1879, Archibald got a job with the *News* in Sydney. Haynes, the senior journalist there, ensured the *News* was first with local sports scoops by giving reporters homing pigeons to fly results back to the newsroom.[13] The first piece Haynes assigned Archibald showcased the young cultural appropriator's republican ideals. He praised the recently erected statue of Captain Cook in Sydney's Hyde Park, while noting no colonial government had wanted to purchase the frumpy statue of Queen Victoria unveiled at the Sydney Exhibition.

In the week of Archibald's arrival at the *News*, three young men were sentenced to hang for rape, including Alfred, a 25-year-old Aboriginal man. Following a *News* campaign against the 'proposed judicial murders', the acting-governor postponed, and later commuted, the execution of the two white men, but reasoned nobody would mind if Alfred was hanged. Haynes called out this double standard with a withering piece, 'Hang Him – He Is Only a Black':

> When we reflect upon the treatment which is accorded to this man's aboriginal fellow-countrymen by white settlers, we blush to think it possible that the Executive can sanction his death. Let those who know the country districts best declare how many whites should be hanged for equally gross offences upon the miserable dark women!

Archibald filed a report on Alfred's hanging, 'The Blackfellow Executed', in which he laid into Justice Sir Alfred Stephen:

> But 'Alfred' was black and helpless, and Sir Alfred, who this morning delivered over the body of the unfortunate aboriginal to the octopus-like grip of the brutal hangman, is white and powerful.

---

charade throughout his life, with his 1885 marriage certificate to Jewish woman Rosa Frankenstein recording him as Jules François, a native of France.

13   The pigeons, sacked after the telephone became established across Sydney in the 1880s, were early media industry victims of technological change.

Archibald's vitriolic piece, in which he also attacked the bounties offered for captured Aboriginal people in lands claimed by pastoralists, the murderous Native Police, and white rapes of Aboriginal women on the frontier, made other papers' editors sit up. The French kid wrote with fire.

In late 1879, Sydney's Archbishop Vaughan was concerned the local Catholic newspaper was displaying an unhealthy independence. He commissioned Haynes to produce a rival Catholic publication that would do what it was told, and agreed that Haynes and Archibald, his editorial assistant, could produce their own 'little paper' with the Church's surplus funds. This was like letting Judas open a kissing booth at the Gethsemane Garden Fair.

The *Bulletin*, as the 'little paper' was known, hired a bunch of shit-stirrers who bitched, gossiped, slandered, satirised, lampooned and generally lashed out at authority, including the churches. Vaughan kicked Haynes and Archibald off the Catholic paper after two issues, and they moved the *Bulletin* to a recently vacated boxing hall, billiard saloon, skittle alley and underworld meeting place, digs much more in keeping with their bohemian sensibilities.

The *Bulletin* was fuelled by rage. Its style was distinctly American, with sharp sentences, punchy headlines and biting pen-and-ink cartoons – a break from the turgid blow-by-blow accounts of vice-regal dinners and shipping news favoured by British-inspired publications. The paper's initial run of 3,000 copies grew to over 16,000 within a year, and kept on climbing.

Many of the paper's writers wrote under assumed names – The Bunyip, The Dipsomaniac, Prince Warung and Scotty the Wrinkler, to name a few. The brutal social satirist Theodore Emile Argles did a reverse Archibald – the son of an exotic Frenchwoman who claimed Jewish descent wrote as the respectably Anglo Harold Grey, as well as The Pilgrim, The Devil in Sydney, The Moocher, and Flaneur.

And the pseudonymous Rose de Bohème and Sappho Smith were women! The *Bulletin* boasted it had 'more lady contributors than all the other newspapers in Sydney put together'.[14] While this was in keeping with the subversive image Haynes and Archibald cultivated, some Australian women had openly practised as journalists for several years, although most were confined to pieces on do-it-yourself fashion or stain removal. The *Bulletin*'s employment of women didn't stop it making fun of vicar's wives, posh ladies, drunken prostitutes, battered larrikinesses and women generally. It heaped particular scorn on feminists, with lines like: 'We are to have plenty of female doctors, etc, shortly. We'll then need some female women.'

Engaging women scribes was part of Haynes and Archibald's commitment to the democratisation of writing. They sourced stories not just from journalists, but from anyone they believed could write and had something interesting to say. Archibald, explaining this philosophy, said he would take good copy 'from the man who pastured a pig on my sainted mother's grave'.

Archibald continued his campaign against the death penalty, which he saw as a relic of the oppressive convict system. His lead story in the *Bulletin*'s first edition was a denunciation of the hanging of Australia's most notorious LGBTI bushranger, Captain Moonlite. He also railed against Britain's 'unspeakable callousness of the rich towards the poor; at the denying of meals towards the wan and hungry by the fat and fashionably dressed'. The early *Bulletin* was distinctly socialist in tone, decrying the injustices banks, landlords and governments heaped upon the working man.

The *Bulletin*, Archibald explained, was 'ever cheering for the little dog with its foot in the big dog's mouth', but the paper's support for the underdog did not extend to larrikins, who'd radiated out from Melbourne to infest inner Sydney. On 8 January 1881, the *Bulletin* published William Traill's 'The Larrikin Residuum', a piece on 'the idle, the uncared-for, the willful, and the depraved' larrikins, with their 'evil propensities and outrageous proclivities', at a Boxing Day

---

14   The early *Bulletin* was much like the early *Chaser*, except it gave women a go.

gathering in the Clontarf picnic grounds. The larrikin women were 'cunning, debased, dully sensual ... beauty ... blurred by traces of intemperance and the ravages of excess', but:

> ... amidst the flushed, panting, bevy of young girls, clinging in romping abandon to promiscuous partners, were some unworn childish faces with the devil's mark not yet stamped on their foreheads.

The publicans who owned the Clontarf picnic grounds duly sued the *Bulletin* for defamation. Haynes and Archibald spent two months in debtors' prison after being unable to pay the victorious publicans' legal costs, editing the paper from their cell and starting a new column, 'In the Jug'.

Traill bought Haynes and Archibald out, having already set the *Bulletin* on a nationalist path with his 1 January 1881 story 'Young Australia', which argued, 'It is about time that Young Australia commenced to assume the management of his own affairs.' Traill believed the development of local industry was essential to Australian self-reliance and pivoted the free trade paper towards protectionism. Haynes left, as his creation no longer reflected his views. Archibald, whose sympathies were both nationalist and protectionist, stayed on, and bought back the paper in 1886.

The *Bulletin* was intent on forging a distinct Australian identity. Norman Lindsay, one of the *Bulletin*'s best loved artists and perverts, explained:

> Up to [the *Bulletin*'s] appearance, the Australian-born were wandering in a limbo begotten by a nostalgia in the early settlers, who called England 'home'. The *Bulletin* initiated an amazed discovery that Australia was 'home', and that was the anvil on which Archibald hammered out the rough substance of the national ego, even to the crude device of making the Englishman in Australia a comic figure.

Creating an Australian nation demanded an answer to the question, 'Who is an Australian?' And if there were to be Australians, it followed that there must be un-Australians. The *Bulletin*'s early articles gave a hint as to who some of them might be.

On 15 May 1880, the *Bulletin*'s lead story was on another Aboriginal man sentenced to death. 'Only a Nigger', while condemning the death penalty, felt different to the pieces Hayne and Archibald had written a year earlier in the campaign to save Alfred:

> The wretched aboriginal who is now cast for death is, like all Australian blacks who have been so fortunate as to come into contact with civilization, a worthless, drunken creature ... It is high time that all the dark men living under the British flag in New South Wales left the colony.

Two weeks earlier, the *Bulletin* had opened with 'The Chinese Question':

> There must be no compromise on the part of the people of this country. All the sophistry in the world will not remove these facts – that ... the Chinese bring no women with them, and foster immorality wherever they settle; that the races should not be allowed to mix; that they are mixing to an appreciable extent in the lowest quarters of the large cities; and the presence of the Chinaman must ever be a disturbing element in the at all times sufficiently strained relations between Capital and Labour.

EAST MEETS WEST

The Australian colonies had, between 1825 and 1849, attempted to develop a port on the continent's northern coast, where Chinese migrants and Malay merchants would create a second Singapore, opening Australia to Asian trade.

Australians couldn't start the day without a cup of Chinese tea, laced with sugar from the Philippines. The tea ships that docked in Australian ports also carried exotic spices, silks, furniture and ceramics. Calcutta traders provided the colonists with cloth, manufactured goods and a seemingly inexhaustible supply of Indian cooks.

China, the Asian superpower, was flooding British markets with tea and other household products, causing Britain to rack up significant trade deficits. Britain eschewed tariffs or trade embargos for a simpler solution – flooding the Chinese market with opium it grew in India. When China banned the opium trade in 1839, the world's largest drug dealer sent in its gunboats to keep China high. Britain and France kicked off the Second Opium War in 1856, with Lord Elgin, whose father had looted Greece's Parthenon, continuing the family tradition by looting the emperor's Summer Palaces, razing one to the ground. The Opium Wars forced China to cede territory to Britain, France and Russia; open its ports for European and American trade; legalise opium; and permit its people to practise Christianity.[15]

In 1854, the United States sent Matthew Perry (not the one from *Friends*) and nine warships (not very friendly) to force the shogun to open isolationist Japan to American trade. Britain and France demanded similar concessions, contributing to the fall of the shogunate.

In 1857, India was rocked by rebellions against British East India Company rule, with about 6,000 Britons and 800,000 Indians killed during the 1857–58 uprisings.[16] Britain, acknowledging things had got

---

15 This was a big deal, as Chinese scholar Hong Xiuquan had read a Christian pamphlet when ill in 1837 and converted to Christianity after his recovery. Hong founded the God Worshipping Society, later known as the Taiping, which trained Protestant revolutionaries. The Taiping Rebellion, which kicked off in 1850, resulted in 20 million casualties and almost brought down the Chinese empire.

16 British troops tortured suspects (the application of chilli to the genitals a testament to British ingenuity), executed prisoners, massacred civilians, raped women, tied rebels over the mouths of cannons about to go bang, and forced Muslim or Hindu combatants to eat pork or beef, and lick buildings spattered with the blood of the dead, before publicly hanging them – but the natives came to appreciate Britain's civilising influence.

a bit out of hand, nationalised the British East India Company – and so, the British Raj was born. Indian troops and goods made Queen Victoria the head of the largest, most powerful and richest empire the world had ever seen.

The three great Asian races had been humbled, the West had triumphed over the East, the white man had proved himself superior to the coloured, and Charles Darwin's new theory made all this seem both natural and inevitable.

The introduction of faster clipper vessels in the 1850s allowed the Australian colonies to maintain closer contact with Britain and other Western nations. Resentment of Chinese diggers during the mid-century gold rushes hardened anti-Asian sentiment. The colonists switched to the black tea Britain now grew in India and Ceylon, and Queensland sugar replaced imports. Building links with Asia no longer seemed necessary.

Yet Asians kept coming to Australia. Most of the diggers on Queensland's Palmer River goldfields, which opened in 1873, were Chinese. Many returned to China, but some settled down in nearby Cooktown. In 1877, Queensland adopted lapsed Victorian and New South Wales goldrush laws to tax Chinese residents and prevent incoming ships from carrying more than one Chinese person per 50 tonnes of ship's weight.[17]

But it was the Northern Territory, which New South Wales had transferred to South Australia in 1863, that caused the most concern. In 1869, Palmerston (renamed Darwin in 1911) had been established to serve as the northern terminus of the Australian Overland Telegraph Line. Two years later, an undersea cable was laid between

---

17   The most famous Chinese visitor to Australia during the 1870s was Chang the
      Chinese Giant, a 2.4-metre man who spoke ten languages. Chang's visit as part of
      a freak show tour helped advance the argument that the Chinese were not normal
      folk. After Chang's departure, Australian freak show operators recruited imitators
      like Chonkwicsee the Chinese Giant. It is unclear how immigration quotas linked
      to ship tonnage dealt with giant Chinese people.

Palmerston and Java, connecting Australia to the world's rapid communication network.

Sensible white people didn't want to work in the north, where
they went an ugly pink, caught malaria and were subjected to regular
cyclones. Northern Territory pioneer John Lewis suggested that the
South Australian government import less fussy and more windproof
'Chinese coolies' to develop the Top End, but cautioned, 'They must
not be allowed to enter into any trade or calling to oppose Europeans,
but treated as a subject race.'

South Australia brought out 187 Chinese men from Singapore in
1874 to work on the telegraph line and mine recently discovered gold.
It had been assumed the Chinese would provide low-cost labour for
their European masters, but Ping Que upset the 'subject race' plan
by opening his own mining operations, before branching out into
the retail, hotel, meat and opium trades. Ping brought out hundreds
of Chinese workers, and 3,000 Chinese were later employed to build
the railway line between Port Darwin and the Pine Creek goldmines.
By 1887, 6,000 Chinese called the Northern Territory home, more
than three times the European population.[18]

The European Territorians were rough and ready. Vaiben Louis
Solomon arrived in 1873 with a group of Jewish miners from Adelaide
and entered local politics the following year. He earned the nicknames
'Mr Everything' and 'Black Solomon' – the first for his wide-ranging
business interests, and the second for painting himself black and
walking about town naked after accepting a dare to impersonate an
Aboriginal person because, let's face it, you have to make your own

---

18   Australia had placed the security of its strategic northern port and its international
      communications system in Chinese hands well before the Chinese-owned
      Landbridge Group took out a 99-year lease on Port Darwin in 2015 and Huawei
      arrived on the scene. The Chinese built the Territory's railways prior to New
      South Wales and Victoria recently contracting a China Railway Construction
      Corporation subsidiary (and its happy Uighur workforce) to build Sydney's and
      Melbourne's trains. Australians have historically been able to put aside both their
      xenophobia and their principles in pursuit of an infrastructure deal.

fun in the Northern Territory.[19]

New South Welshmen and Victorians were less tolerant of their Chinese residents than Territorians and Queenslanders were. Cheap Chinese labour drove down wages, and furniture makers had to cut corners to compete with Chinese-run furniture factories. Accusations of Chinese immorality, which had lain dormant after the gold rushes, were revived. And, of course, the Chinese had introduced opium into the British Empire (with the British Empire's introduction of opium into China conveniently forgotten).

While the Chinese were condemned as a race, Victorian and New South Wales political and business leaders enjoyed cordial relations with some Chinese residents, allowing them to start sentences with words like, 'Some of my best friends are ...'

Mei Quong Tart was everybody's best friend. He'd come to Australia in search of gold in 1859, aged just nine. On the day of his arrival, he was enthralled by a performance of the blackface Kentucky Minstrels strumming banjos and jigging down the main street. He soon found work with a Scottish storekeeper and developed the unusual Scots-Chinese accent that would stay with him for life. He also acted as an interpreter for grazier and mining entrepreneur Robert Simpson, and was effectively adopted by Mrs Simpson, who converted him to Anglicanism and taught him to read and write English.

Simpson rewarded his teenage assistant with a small claim that paid out. Quong Tart invested the profits in other mining operations; became a British citizen, Oddfellow and Mason; bought tailored English suits; organised racing meets; and became the established number ten batsman for the Braidwood Cricket Club. At public dinners, he would recite Scottish poetry, murder the bagpipes and sing highland songs in a voice best described as enthusiastic.

---

19   Daryl Somers, Greg Ritchie, Sam Newman and other Australian popular entertainers who have made us laugh with blackface would have been even funnier if they'd followed Vaiben Solomon in developing a full blackbody routine.

Quong Tart became Australia's most prominent anti-opium campaigner, a government advisor on Chinese issues and one of Sydney's
wealthiest men. Returning from an 1881 trip to China, he established
a tea import business and opened his own hugely popular tearooms
across Sydney. Even the *Bulletin* praised the 'Anglo-Mongolian' whose
Asianness was 'only skin deep' – 'a man of the world, a true Briton,
an expert at manly sports who at a recent cricket match ... shone
with refulgence'.

Parkes' good relationship with Quong Tart didn't stop him taking
a hardline anti-Chinese approach at the 1881 Intercolonial Conference, a talkfest held by the Australian colonies on matters of common
concern. Parkes and Victorian premier Graham Berry argued any
Chinese immigration was 'highly undesirable', while South Australia,
Queensland and Tasmania countered that only 'Chinese in large
numbers' posed a risk. Western Australia, which had only 30,000
colonists, surprised everybody by admitting it was actually paying
Chinese people to settle there.

Still, New South Wales and Victoria were ultimately successful
in pushing the colonies to tax Chinese residents and limit Chinese
passengers on incoming ships, although South Australia insisted on
an exemption for the Northern Territory.

The Territory posed a different problem for South Australia.
With Chinese Territorians outnumbering Europeans, they might
elect a Chinaman to parliament! South Australian attorney-general
John Downer introduced laws in 1882 to restrict Territory voting to
'natural-born or naturalised British subjects of European or United
States nationality', stating, 'the Government did not intend to allow
the Asiatics in the Territory to vote'. The colony built on the principle
that all men are equal now asserted that some men were more equal
than others.[20]

---

20   Sir John Downer would become a two-time premier of South Australia and a
     champion of the White Australia policy. His son, Sir Alick Downer, continued to
     make life difficult for non-white folk as the Australian immigration minister from

The same year, the United States passed a law that sent shock-waves through Australia. The *Chinese Exclusion Act* barred 'skilled and unskilled' Chinese labourers from entering the US. As anyone who worked was either skilled or unskilled, the Act effectively ended Chinese migration to the United States.

If the Mongol hordes could no longer descend on America, they would surely turn their funny little eyes south to Australia's bound-less plains, which we didn't want to share. Australians prepared for an Asian invasion.

DIRTY DEEDS, DONE DIRT CHEAP

Alfred Deakin opposed slavery and campaigned for improved pay and conditions in low-paid industries. He also championed a white Australia. However, Deakin didn't let his principles and prejudices stop him investing in Pyramid, a Queensland sugar plantation that employed more than eight basement-wage Chinese or Pacific Island-ers for every white worker.[21]

Between 1880 and 1884, cashed-up Victorians invested heavily in the Queensland sugar industry, which had similar labour problems to the Northern Territory. White people just weren't keen on backbreaking cane-clearing work in the tropics. The Queensland government had gone off yellow people and limited the planters' ability to bring in more of them – and, using its feared Native Police, was killing or driving away its own black people. Queensland needed some new black people to do all the crap jobs – and it really didn't want to pay them much.

The solution was to pay 'labour hire firms' to ship in Melanesian Pacific Islander 'workers' on 'three-year contracts'. The labour hire

---

1958 to 1963. His grandson, Alexander Downer, was an Australian foreign affairs minister and stocking model.

21 Pyramid was established by Jean Baptiste Loridan, who'd fled Victoria after being sued for paternity by his sister-in-law, Julia Evans, who'd married 'The Wonderful Male Impersonator' Ellen Tremayne (a.k.a. Edward De Lacy Evans).

firms were commonly known as 'blackbirders' for catching 'black-birds', a name given to Pacific Island labourers. Some of the Islanders (also known at the time as 'Kanakas', Hawaiian for 'men') were lured aboard blackbirder ships on false pretences, and some were simply kidnapped. Each Islander cost about as much as a horse, with their wage for three years generally less than the blackbirders' 'recruitment fee'. The Islanders were paid once a year, and sometimes not at all. Most were poorly fed and housed in crowded, unsanitary conditions. Those who 'broke their contract' by trying to head back to their island or find alternative work were forcibly returned to plantations by police. Some never received the promised fare home at the end of their contract.[22]

Between 1863 and 1901, some 60,000 labourers from eighty Pacific islands, most notably the New Hebrides (Vanuatu) and Solomon Islands, were shipped to Queensland to work on sugar and cotton plantations, with men like Robert Towns, the founder of Townsville, and Sir Robert Mackenzie, Queensland's premier, making fortunes from using and selling their labour. The blackbird trade, and the labour it provided, were so valuable that the exploited Islanders were dubbed 'black pearls'.

Deakin had his first contact with the Pacific flesh trade in 1879, after a spirit foretold he would travel to foreign lands with a white-haired man. The white-haired man turned out to be Sydney Watson, a spiritualist squatter who invited the promising young Deakin to Fiji as a companion. Watson was travelling there because one of his ships' captains had been charged with kidnapping and murdering some Solomon Islanders who were unenthusiastic about relocating to one of his Fijian plantations, and his son, Archibald, had been charged

---

22   Britain abolished slavery in 1833, with the United States following in 1865. While blackbirded Islanders were not the property of their employers, they were victims of human trafficking; coercion, threats or deception were used to secure their labour; their labour was unfree; and their rights of movement were taken away – all of which would fall foul of modern anti-slavery laws.

with piracy. Watson bailed out Archibald, while Deakin luncheoned with the governor, who characterised Australian settlers in Fiji as 'those who simply desire the extermination of the natives and those who desire to utilise them as serfs or slaves'.[23] Deakin knew what he was investing in when he bought into Pyramid.[24]

Deakin's sponsor, David Syme, was more principled, calling on God 'to send down the fire of heaven to consume the slavers and their ilk'. However, just in case God wasn't up for the job, Syme accepted the proposal of a promising young freelance writer, George Ernest Morrison, to join a blackbirding crew and report on the industry.

In 1880, the seventeen-year-old Morrison had run away from home to walk the 960 kilometres from Geelong to Adelaide, writing to his frantic parents ten days into his trip, 'I do hope you are not anxious about me at all.' He gave Syme his account of the journey, *The Diary of a Tramp*, which the newspaperman published. Later that year, Morrison ran away from medical school to canoe 2,500 kilometres down the Murray, with Syme publishing his unoriginally titled *Down the Murray in a Canoe*.

Morrison's paddling at the expense of studying saw him expelled from Melbourne University, his medical examiner informing his increasingly anxious parents that allowing Morrison to become a doctor would be 'akin to letting a mad dog loose in Collins Street'. Freed from medicine and looking for a new adventure, Morrison became an undercover blackbirder in 1882.

Morrison's eight-part exposé, 'A Cruise in a Queensland Slaver', read like a boy's own adventure, although the jolly japes and ripping

---

23   Archibald Watson skipped bail and fled to Germany, where he studied anatomy. He returned to Australia in 1885, as the first professor of anatomy at Adelaide's new medical school. Adelaide is the best Australian city for finding dead bodies to dissect, although some have already been dissected before they are found.

24   Pyramid's bankers foreclosed on it after the 1884 sugar crash, losing Deakin and its other mainly Victorian investors a tidy sum. In 1990, Victoria's Pyramid Building Society collapsed in one of Australia's largest corporate disasters. Victorians are advised never to invest in anything called Pyramid.

yarns were interrupted by stories of Islander children dying at sea, the use of 'decoy' Islanders to lure others on board with false promises of riches, how the watch would 'vie with each other in the sport of shooting' escapees attempting to swim for shore, and of the Islander women, 'whose presence aboard turns a ship into a "brothel" and whose experience on the mainland almost invariably transformed a pretty, chaste girl into a diseased hag within the three years ashore'.

Morrison's writings on 'the Queensland slave trade' sparked outrage across the colonies, bar Queensland and Western Australia – as Western Australian pearlers were kidnapping or buying Aboriginal people, incarcerating them on isolated islands, forcing them to dive for pearls and not paying them a brass razoo – slavery, pure and simple.[25]

Britain forced the Queensland government to conduct an inquiry into blackbirding, which in 1884 concluded everything was sweet – unsurprising, given the number of Queensland politicians with plantation or blackbirding interests.[26]

Queensland's premier, Sir Thomas McIlwraith, wanted to reduce blackbirders' shipping costs by finding some closer-at-hand black people to exploit. On 4 April 1883, he claimed eastern New Guinea and its islands for his colony, the Dutch having already annexed western New Guinea.

New Guinea excited popular interest as a 'last frontier'. In 1875, 'Captain Lawson' published *Wanderings in the Interior of New Guinea*,

---

25 *Brass razoo* is Australian slang for a non-existent and therefore valueless coin. It may derive from 'brass sou', brass being a cheap metal and the sou being a small-denomination French coin (Brits and Australians enjoy disparaging the French when inventing slang for unpleasant, unsavoury or inferior things). An alternative theory is that it derives from 'arse razoo', a contraction of 'arse raspberry' (i.e. a fart), with 'arse razoo' coined by World War I Aussie diggers in the unpleasantly scented trenches of the Western Front (providing the requisite French connection). In this interpretation, a person who doesn't have a brass razoo owns less than the value of a fart.

26 Exploiting Pacific Islander agricultural labourers continued until 1904, with a brief suspension in the early 1890s. The Gillard government resurrected the practice in 2012, calling it the 'Seasonal Workers Program'.

in which he described his ascent of Mount Hercules (a mountain that dwarfed Everest), falls greater than Niagara, the tallest tree in the world, giant scorpions, daisies the size of sunflowers, a 'striped cat more handsome than the tiger', yak-like cattle and human-like apes. Lawson claimed game was so plentiful that he was able to bring down nineteen ducks with two shots.

Lawson's fictions were likely the work of William Armit, a Queensland Native Police officer 'twice discharged from the government service for drunkenness and misbehaviour', or his brother, Robert, a white shoe brigader who wanted to flog bits of New Guinea to anybody stupid enough to believe Lawson's guff. Lawson and real explorers of the island, like future aviation pioneer Lawrence Hargrave, excited Australian and international interest in New Guinea.

Premier McIlwraith expected little trouble from the annexation, as Britain had approved Queensland's claims over the Torres Strait in 1872 and 1879, in response to Queensland's questionable assertion that it wanted to protect Torres Strait Islanders from violent mariners, and Pacific Islanders employed by pearl-shellers from exploitation.

McIlwraith insisted he'd only moved into New Guinea because Kaiser Wilhelm I was about to do the whole German invasion thing. However, Queensland governor Sir Arthur Kennedy informed the Colonial Office:

> It is useless to disguise from ourselves the fact that in Australia the black races are regarded much in the same light as the African Negroes were regarded by the Jamaica planters a hundred years ago; and not much doubt is entertained by those who know most about the matter that the annexation of New Guinea was intended to supply black labour for the sugar planters.

The other Australian colonies supported Queensland's land grab, as did Syme's *Age*, which could see no reason why 'the great colonising race of Englishmen should be debarred from replenishing this magnificent wilderness'. The anti-imperialist *Bulletin*, however, opposed it, with Archibald writing, 'Australians have more than half of Australia to annex as it is.' To McIlwraith's surprise, Britain disallowed the annexation, fearing it would increase tension with other European Pacific powers, and calling it the act of 'a cheeky young colony'.

With all the interest in New Guinea, Morrison decided to mount a south-to-north crossing of the island. Having finished up as a black-birder, he'd just completed a solo four-month walk from the Gulf of Carpentaria to Melbourne, following the 3,254 kilometre route Burke and Wills would have taken twenty years earlier if they'd packed enough lunch. Morrison cheerily filed reports from the small towns that had sprung up in the continent's interior, writing a lot about snakes and crocodiles, and how the 'wretched Blacks' were 'shot without mercy' by Queensland graziers.

Australians were amazed by Morrison's pedestrian prowess. Syme's *Age* bankrolled his New Guinea expedition, while the rival *Argus* funded William Armit to race him across the island. Neither party made it far out of Port Moresby. Armit got malaria and Morrison got a spear in the stomach and another below his right eye. With his wounds festering, Morrison barely made it back to Melbourne, where a surgeon managed to remove one of the spear tips via a nostril. No one in Australia could treat the abdominal wound, so Morrison set sail to visit the world's best surgeons in Scotland, who extracted a finger-sized spear fragment from his gut.

After finally qualifying as a doctor in Edinburgh, Morrison toured the United States and West Indies, became the medical officer at the Rio Tinto mine in Spain, served as personal physician to the Shereef of Wazan in Morocco and continued his studies in Paris. Returning to Australia in 1890, he spent two years as the resident surgeon at Ballarat Hospital. Restless with this conventional life, the greatest Australian adventurer of his era then set his sights on the land that now exercised such a powerful hold on the Australian mind.

China.

THE IRON WEDDING AND THE ENEMY WITHOUT

The threat of invasion by China, or any one of a number of imagined enemies, put Australian nationalism into overdrive in 1883. So too did trains.

Trains are normally only attractive to large men in anoraks or toddlers who are yet to realise that *Thomas & Friends* is capitalist, colonialist, classist, ageist, racist, sexist, fattist, homophobic, transphobic and climate change denying.[27] Victorian-era Australians were also

---

27   Thomas and his friends live on the island of Sodor, a society that runs entirely on diesel and coal. There they are conditioned by an authoritarian Englishman, The Fat Controller, to believe they are living in a working train's paradise. Sodor is a much better place than the rest of the world, as Gordon, an over-confident Scottish engine, discovers in 'Gordon Goes Foreign'. Thomas the Tank Engine is a collaborator train who keeps the other trains in line, and regularly dobs them in to the Controller. The Controller rewards Thomas by giving him women, Annie and Clarabel, who are forced to roll behind him and do whatever he tells them to do. Thomas is also allowed significant autonomy in running the Ffarquhar Branch Line. The trains compete with each other in being 'Really Useful' because the Controller sends old trains, and other trains unable to work, to the Smelting Yard. Any trains who do unauthorised jobs are punished, as are trains who refuse to work when the Controller tells them to (in 'The Sad Story of Henry', Henry is bricked into a dark tunnel for refusing to work in the rain). The trains are not paid, but compete for new paint jobs, and make fun of trains with old or damaged paint. The steam engines are superior to the 'dirty diesels'. The main diesel is not given a name – he is just called Diesel, or sometimes Devious Diesel. He comes from 'the Other Railway', is black and steals jobi wood, a valuable Sodorian export. Bad engines can be identified from the black smoke they emit and, in the original version of 'Henry's Sneeze', Henry sneezes on two naughty schoolboys who 'ran away as black as niggers'. In 'Tickled Pink', the trains mock James for a pink paint job, but James picks up the Controller's granddaughter and her friends who, being girls, all love pink, so James feels better about himself. Female engines are under-represented and there are no trans trains. The Thomas franchise has recently introduced new lady trains and trains of colour to improve Sodor's diversity. Latin Gina is a stylish head turner, if you are into lady trains. Ashima is a 'fun and feisty' hot-pink lady engine with henna-like decorations, who says, 'Just because we're well painted doesn't mean we can't do anything else' – she wins the Shunting Challenge at the Great Railway Show (an international exhibition for trains), but submissively defers to Thomas in letting him share first place. Frieda is reminiscent of an East German shot putter – a big grumpy German lady train who likes to compete in feats of strength and is mistaken for a male train. Do not let your children watch *Thomas & Friends*.

all of those things, so it's not surprising that track was their crack, and they racked as many lines of it as they could.

'Railway mania' hit in the 1870s, with track addicts from regional communities forming railway leagues to lobby politicians for lines. They were able to do so because, after early experimentation with private ownership, governments assumed responsibility for nearly all Australian railways – in stark contrast to other countries, where railways were privately operated. Throughout the world, railways were built for profit – in Australia they were built for votes.

That's not to say the rail explosion that gave Australia the greatest track mileage per capita in the world was not warranted, but modern Treasury hardheads would gibber and hide under their neat, soulless desks at the thought of more than half the colonies' capital expenditure over several decades being poured into trains.

Australia needed more railways than other countries for two reasons:

1. It was bloody big.
2. It was bloody dry.

Most developed countries had river systems that allowed inland freight to be transported, but Australia had a few piddling trickles near the coast, many of which were unnavigable in times of drought. Railways would be Australia's rivers of iron.

In April 1883, Alfred Deakin, recently installed as Victoria's commissioner for public works, visited Ballarat with other members of Premier James Service's ministry to launch the hundredth locomotive built in the town. Service declared a public holiday to celebrate all things trainy, with his ministers hanging from the doors of an engine festooned with flags and flowers. The crowd of 15,000 got its money's worth when boiling water exploded from the train's funnel, scalding several politicians.

On 14 June 1883, Deakin accompanied Service to celebrate the joining of the Victorian and New South Wales railway lines at Albury.

The Victorians arrived in morning attire, while the New South Wales delegation was resplendent in full evening dress. The colonies' inability to agree on the dress code for the 'Iron Wedding', as the celebration was dubbed, was overshadowed by their failure to agree on the width of their railway tracks. It dawned on the thousand-plus assembled dignitaries that passengers and cargo on the Sydney–Melbourne run would need to be unloaded from one train at the border, and then loaded on to another, an arrangement that would lead the visiting Mark Twain to remark, 'Think of the paralysis of intellect that gave that idea birth.'

Later that evening, at the most lavish dinner in Australia's history, Service expressed the hope that the two colonies 'now looped together with bands of iron' would join in Federation. Sir John Robertson of New South Wales rose to speak:

> I have heard of a something called Federation, but Victoria separated from New South Wales of her own free will. I invite her to return to New South Wales, as a repentant child to her mother.

The marriage had not even lasted as long as Britney Spears'.

Service considered Federation necessary to protect Australia from foreigners. The Chinese would be arriving any day now – and Australian ports had been fortifying themselves against Russian attack since the early 1840s, with Victoria commissioning two warships in response to Russia's 1878 victory in the Russo–Turkish War. The Germans had been bobbing about to Australia's north, and the French were kidnapping Pacific Islanders to slave in the nickel mines of Nouméa, before Queenslanders could kidnap them to slave in a much nicer outdoor setting.

Service's solution was to invade all our neighbours before they could be used as launchpads to invade us. In July 1883, he called on Britain to annex New Guinea and the islands to Australia's east, including the New Hebrides, where French settlers outnumbered the British. 'The islands of Australasia,' he intoned, 'ought to belong to the people of Australia.'

Britain didn't want another war with France and suggested that the colonies might federate before conquering the Pacific. While a stalling tactic, it linked Federation and annexation in the Australian mind.

In September 1883, Australians were shocked by French plans to annually release 5,000 French criminals into the Pacific, granting them liberty (and egality and fraternity) if they promised never to return to France. Alfred Deakin argued that the French criminals would instead come to Australia, that they could never become good citizens and that their children would also be criminals. He said of Paris' plan:

> ... it had sent a thrill of sentiment from one end of the continent to the other ... a desire for a United Australia. Instead of provincial it had made us feel national.

Two months later, leaders of the Australian colonies, New Zealand and Fiji met to plot against the French and Germans. The meeting birthed the Federal Council of Australasia, which would show France and Germany that Britain's Pacific colonies were united in their opposition to all things French and German.

It didn't work out like that. The Council could only pass laws on a narrow range of issues for those colonies that joined it. Most of the colonies signed up, although South Australia joined late and left early. New Zealand opted out altogether, which was no big deal, but Parkes' decision to boycott any federal body dreamt up by someone else effectively neutered the Council. Its members spent most of their time arguing about fish and drinking claret, with Deakin labelling the body as 'little more than a debating society'.

It took three years to get the Federal Council up and running, by which time the Germans had already brought their irritating compound words to Australia's doorstep, annexing north-eastern New Guinea in 1884 and naming it Kaiser-Wilhelmsland. Although

Britain promptly occupied the island's south-east, Australians felt betrayed by the Motherland's earlier inaction.

The Australian Natives' Association (ANA) was a friendly society that provided health and funeral insurance to its members, who had to be:

a) born in Australia;

b) male; and

c) white.[28]

As a result of the Annexation Crisis, it became an unfriendly society towards foreigners, including the British, who'd failed to keep other foreigners away. The ANA became a powerful political pressure group and looked for a white, male, Australian-born politician to champion Federation, an Australian fighting force, compulsory military training, the development of a national culture and the teaching of Australian history (of the right and white kind) in schools. All eighty-six members of Victoria's parliament ticked the first two boxes, but only twelve were native born. Deakin topped that list and largely pursued the ANA's agenda, while it became his political powerbase. The sensitive poet had transformed into an arch-nationalist.

However, a people cannot claim common blood until they have bathed together in the blood of an enemy. Australians got that opportunity after British general Charles 'Chinese' Gordon disobeyed his order to evacuate Egyptians from Khartoum in response to a rebellion against Egyptian rule led by Muhammad Ahmad bin Abd Allah (a.k.a. the Mahdi), an Islamic cleric who wanted to purify the

---

28   Friendly societies were groups of people who shared trade, religious, political or other affiliations and pooled resources for the benefit of individual members or their families when a member was ill, injured, unable to work or dead. Australian friendly societies took on some of the welfare roles performed by churches in Britain, and provided pensions and other assistance before the emergence of government and employer-provided welfare services. Until the advent of the ANA, they were not commonly built around white male nationalism. The ANA merged with the Manchester Unity Independent Order of Oddfellows in 1993, becoming Australian Unity, now Australia's largest friendly society.

faith, enslave his opponents and establish a worldwide caliphate, under which all would 'bow before him' – the usual schtick. Gordon instead occupied the city.

The Mahdi cut Khartoum's telegraph lines and starved the British out. The city fell on 26 January 1885, with 10,000 defenders and civilians killed by the Mahdi and his 'Fuzzy Wuzzies'.[29] Gordon met the foe, wearing his ceremonial uniform and a red fez, a revolver in one hand and a sword in the other. The foe responded by chopping him into pieces and beheading him on the steps of the palace. The Mahdi put Gordon's head on display so 'all who passed it could look in disdain, children could throw stones at it and the hawks of the desert could sweep and circle above' – the usual schtick.

A horrified Britain sent troops to clear the Mahdist forces from an area where it wanted to build a railway. The railway-loving Australians wanted to help, with New South Wales sending 750 soldiers, the first time Australians were deployed overseas.

Two-thirds of Sydney's population lined the streets to farewell 'our boys', and Service saluted his New South Wales counterpart, William Dalley, as a statesman who'd 'precipitated Australia in one short week from a geographical expression to a nation'.

Unfortunately, war was not as glorious as it had been made out to be. The troops sat next to a railway track for seven weeks and returned home without firing a shot, although six died from typhoid or dysentery. 'Our boys' may not have given their blood, but they'd proved to the world that they gave a shit.[30]

---

29   The term for wiry-haired black people, popularised in the Sudan campaign, was abandoned by most Brits (with the notable exception of Prince Philip) in the twentieth century. Australians continued to use the term, dubbing their World War II New Guinean carriers 'Fuzzy Wuzzy Angels'. In 2009, the Australian government began awarding the 'Fuzzy Wuzzy Commemorative Medallion' to those carriers who'd not yet been carried off. It's alright to call a black person a Fuzzy Wuzzy if you give them a trinket.

30   Australian troops arrived in Sudan wearing red and white uniforms, but they've worn khaki ever since.

FIG. 4: AUSTRALIA'S FIRST SOLDIERS DISTINGUISHED THEMSELVES IN THE
SUDAN DURING THE FAMED CHARGE OF THE KHAZI.

Not all Australian nationalists supported the Sudan deployment. Henry Parkes successfully campaigned to re-enter parliament on an anti-war platform, insisting that the colonies should focus on defence, rather than fighting on others' 'home soil'. He also published a poetry collection, *The Beauteous Terrorist* – it had nothing to do with the Mahdi, but still, the timing was off.

The *Bulletin*, which saw the war as a malignant manifestation of British imperialism, editorialised:

> The idea of vengeance for Gordon belongs to the barbaric age, to the days of the Crusades, when swarms of Christian men, smitten with a shameful enthusiasm, which they imagined to be virtuous and noble, flocked to the Syrian deserts to slaughter Saracens for the love of Christ.

And if you think the Digger-Crusader comparison was a big call, the *Bulletin* went one better. It published a poem that ended:

> *And fair Australia, freest of the free,*
> *Is up in arms against the freeman's fight;*
> *And with her mother joined to crush the right – –*

Has left her threatened treasures o'er the sea,
Has left her land of liberty and law
To flesh her maiden sword in this unholy war.
Enough! God never blessed such enterprise – –
England's degenerate Generals yet shall rue
Brave Gordon sacrificed, when soon they view
The children of a thousand deserts rise
To drive them forth like sand before the gale – –
God and the Prophet! Freedom will prevail.

'El Mahdi to the Australian Troops' did not just call out 'our boys' for fighting an illegitimate foreign war – it was close to a call for jihad. The previously unpublished poet signed the poem 'El Mahdi' – with a *nom de plume* probably prudent in the circumstances. But when the *Bulletin* paid for a poem, it had to pay a real person, and that person was Andrew Barton Paterson.

5
Country Matters

I had written him a letter which I had, for want of better
Knowledge, sent to where I met him down the Lachlan, years ago,
He was shearing when I knew him, so I sent the letter to him,
Just 'on spec', addressed as follows, 'Clancy, of The Overflow'.

And an answer came directed in writing unexpected,
(And I think the same was written with a thumb-nail dipped in tar)
'Twas his shearing mate who wrote it, and verbatim I will quote it:
'Clancy's gone to Queensland droving, and we don't know where
he are.'

In my wild erratic fancy visions come to me of Clancy
Gone a-droving 'down the Cooper' where the Western drovers go;
As the stock are slowly stringing, Clancy rides behind them singing,
For the drover's life has pleasures that the townsfolk never know.

And the bush hath friends to meet him, and their kindly voices
greet him
In the murmur of the breezes and the river on its bars,
And he sees the vision splendid of the sunlit plains extended,
And at night the wond'rous glory of the everlasting stars.

'Clancy of the Overflow', 'The Banjo', *The Bulletin*, 1889

THE CITY SOLICITOR AND THE BUSHMAN'S BIBLE

Andrew Barton Paterson lacked the tedious pedantry and inflated sense of self-worth necessary for a distinguished career in the law, placing fourteenth in the field of sixteen who sat the 1883 solicitor's intermediate examination. He was more interested in politics – his idealism not yet dampened, he declared, 'it was up to me to set the world right.'

Paterson's second submission to the *Bulletin*, 'Australia for the Australians – a Political Pamphlet Showing the Necessity of Land Reform Combined with Protection', was 11,000 words of socialism-lite, attacking banks and big business for exploiting rural workers, landlords for profiting from city slums, and governments for supporting rent-seekers at the expense of producers of wealth. It did not set anything on fire, unless Archibald used it to light the *Bulletin*'s wood stove.

Disheartened by Archibald's rejection, Paterson sent him 'The Bushfire', a poem seemingly about the burning of a sheep station, but actually an allegory for Britain's self-harm in refusing Ireland home rule. Paterson had decided he needed a pen-name, so as not to be associated with his failed pamphlet. Continuing to write as the British Empire's most-hated hardcore Islamist might be career limiting, so he'd have to come up with something else. Then inspiration struck. Adam Lindsay Gordon had written about horses, but Paterson would write *as* a horse – choosing the name 'The Banjo', that of his childhood mount.

Archibald liked what he read. He'd encouraged country writers to submit pieces, as he considered the press too city-centric. Country readers responded by subscribing to the *Bulletin*, which was dubbed 'The Bushman's Bible'. City readers also liked articles about fast-living horsemen, sheep and amusing accidents involving alcohol and threshing machines.

There was a growing thirst for Australian stories, whetted by Rolf Boldrewood's 1882–83 bushranger serial, 'Robbery Under Arms'.

And there was a thirst for Australian *voices*. Adam Lindsay Gordon and his spiritual successor, Henry Kendall, may have written about horses and the bush, but they sounded like they were ordering their butler to fetch them crumpets.[1]

Paterson may have submitted a poem about Irish home rule, but he'd inserted references to 'jackeroos', 'coves', 'blue gum', a 'black boy' and 'lots of grog' – and he'd put plenty of sheep in it. This was undeniably an Australian poem, in an unashamedly Australian voice. Paterson explained why he refused to write as an imitation Englishman:

> We were patronised by imported Governors, insulted by imported globetrotting snobs, exploited by imported actors and singers, mostly worn-out and incompetent. These people rode roughshod over us, and we meekly submitted.[2]

Archibald, after reading 'The Bushfire', called Paterson in and asked for more of the same, instructing:

> Alright, have a go at the bush. Have a go at anything that strikes you. Don't write anything like other people if you can help it. Let's see what you can do.

---

1   Kendall, like Gordon, went mad after no one bought his poems. After the commercial failure of *Leaves from Australian Forests*, Kendall hit the bottle, was abandoned by his wife, became a derelict and was locked up in the Gladesville Hospital for the Insane. However, he experienced brief popularity when he wrote the cantata and hymn of praise sung at the Sydney International Exhibition. Given Kendall's knowledge of Australian forests, or at least their leaves, Henry Parkes appointed the rehabilitated poet New South Wales' inspector of forests. After inspecting a particularly cold, damp forest, Kendall caught a chill and died of consumption, the discerning poet's terminal disease of choice. While Kendall had an interesting life, he wrote boring poetry in the style of his English contemporaries, with this extract from 'Aboriginal Death Song' typical of his work:
    Hunter and climber of trees,
    Now doth his tomahawk rust,
    (Dread of the cunning wild bees),
    Hidden in hillocks of dust.

2   Australia later retaliated by sending Britain Jason Donovan.

Paterson's early poems, written while daylighting as a lawyer, included 'The Deficit Demon', a satire of politicians' addiction to public debt, in which Parkes was caricatured as Sir 'Enry the Fishfag, a man whose response to any challenge was personal abuse; 'The Sausage Candidate', featuring a politician rorting expenses during an election campaign; 'The Corner Man', which described a dream about starring in a 'nigger minstrel show'; and 'Our Mat', about the imagined life of a doormat made by the inmates of Darlinghurst Gaol. In 'Who Is Kater Anyhow?', Paterson attacked the political inadequacies of his own uncle, Henry Kater (sensibly using a different pen-name). In 'Only a Jockey', he mourned that a young jockey's death had received less media attention than the injury sustained by the rider's horse. Paterson, like Archibald, stood up for the little man.

Paterson wrote often about racing. He'd followed up 'The Bushfire' with a tribute to Adam Lindsay Gordon's 'Visions in the Smoke', but instead of hallucinating a Melbourne Cup race in pipe fumes, the protagonist in 'The Dream of a Melbourne Cup' dreamt a race in a gluttonous, drunken slumber, only to awaken from indigestion before 'the hook-nosed hog' of a 'Hebrew moneylender' paid out his winnings.

Paterson, like Gordon, was an accomplished steeplechase racer and a keen student of the turf. His racing poems were often tributes to real champions of the track, like Pardon from his first race meet, repackaged as 'Old Pardon, the Son of Reprieve'.[3] Written with a healthy dash of Aussie vernacular, Paterson's racing verse attracted trackside pundits, inveterate gamblers and horse lovers who'd never picked up a poem before.[4]

---

3   Pardon and Reprieve were sisters in real life, but The Banjo never let truth get in the way of a good story.

4   Horses were the Australian sporting heroes of the 1880s and 1890s, and they knew it. Australia's greatest racehorse, Carbine, winner of the 1890 Melbourne Cup and the most painted horse in world history, was a prima donna who refused to leave the saddling paddock unless he received applause. He had 'a great distaste to the rain' and ran in the wet wearing a small umbrella to stop his ears from getting damp. He refused to move when standing in front of an adoring crowd, with his trainer

Paterson's fourth offering was the first of his archetypal works, a poem about horses and the bush. In 'The Mylora Elopement', 'Jim the Ringer, "cocky" on Mylora Run', elopes with the station manager's daughter, while the manager rides out on his black steed Sambo to recover a horse that has joined a mob of brumbies.[5] Jim, feeling guilty, stops mid-elopement to 'ride like a white man' and help the manager round up the wild horses. The horses in the poem foam at the mouth as they are flogged into exhaustion. Whipping, spurring and gouts of blood would become staples of Paterson's outback and racing poems – yet Paterson's horses always relished the chase or race, a masochistic embodiment of pluck and country grit.[6]

Jim, too, was typical of Paterson's heroes: a strapping country man, lover of horses and hard work, brave and confident, quick to laugh, beholden to no authority but his own, at one with the natural world around him and determined to live life to the full. Paterson, more than anyone else, made the country bushman the classic Aussie hero, and built a sense of Australian identity for a people seeking self-definition as they moved towards nationhood.[7]

The influence of earlier archetypes had waned. The convict's chains were rust, the independent gold digger had made way for the

---

encouraging him to leave his fans by opening an umbrella and looking nervously at the sky. He was rivalled only by 1920 Caulfield Cup winner Eurythmic, an equine Mariah Carey who threw tantrums if his track riders didn't wear the same jacket, would only ride by train if given specially designed earplugs, and couldn't function at all without his cat, which slept in his stall and toured the country with him.

5   *Cocky*, a contraction of cockatoo, was originally a derisive Australian term for a small-scale farmer or country worker, but it was embraced by countryfolk and lost its negative connotation.

6   Paterson, with his childhood love of cockfighting and shooting anything that moved, continued to regard animals as a source of both blood and sport. In 1885, he bought a dog that he entered in illegal dogfights, writing, 'But it was not cruel to the animals ... The dogs are born fighters, anxious and eager to fight, desiring nothing better. Whatever limited intelligence they have is all directed to the one consuming passion.'

7   Everybody loved the bushman except the New South Wales town of Bushman's, which changed its name to Parkes in honour of the city-dwelling Sir Henry.

company man and his machines, and the bushranger was incompatible with a people seeking international respect for themselves and
the new world they had built.

Australian cities were very much old world, islands of marble in
a sea of urban squalor that washed against the rose-strewn gardens
of suburbia. The bush, though, was distinctly un-British – it allowed
Young Australia to distinguish herself from her mother.

The farmer on his selection was an ideal symbol of the new people Australians wanted to be. He was a David who'd stood up to the
Goliaths of the squattocracy and the banks. He was industrious,
toiling to build a better life for himself, his family and the emerging
nation. He had tamed the land and remade it in his own image. And
he was invariably the right colour.

Pastoralists were not considered bushmen, but rather land-grabbers
backed by city banks. However, the shearers, shepherds, stockmen,
station hands, boundary riders, fencers and land clearers they employed
joined – and then surpassed – the yeoman farmer as bush icons. These
men – and they were all men – had no cosy farmhouse and family
to return to after a hard day's labour on the land. They camped out
together, often moving from place to place in search of work.

British literary titan Anthony Trollope, in recounting his 1870s
visit to Australia, wrote that the most distinctive feature of colonial
life was the emergence of a 'nomad tribe of pastoral labourer'. These
wanderers, who often travelled and worked together in pairs, called
each other 'mate'.

Bush mateship was more than friendship. Mates were equals. They
were brothers. They had your back, no matter what. At least, this was
the ideal that mates aspired or pretended to. And as the bushman
became the archetypal new Australian, mateship was elevated above
all other virtues.[8]

---

8   Mateship has exerted such a profound influence on the Australian psyche that
    former prime minister John Howard wanted to incorporate it into a preamble to

Richard Daintree had also proved the bushman's matey appeal
to the aspirational British workers who wanted to make new lives
in Australia. Daintree's touched-up photos of muscular bearded
bushmen having picnics, smoking, chatting and laughing on logs,
boiling billies, eating damper and generally enjoying a healthy (and
not terribly arduous) outdoors life, were key to a successful 1860s–70s
Queensland immigration campaign.[9]

In 1889, a group of city artists staged the 9 by 5 Impression Exhibition in Melbourne, moving away from the staged scenes favoured
by Daintree and other Australian photographers and painters. Their
183 9x5-inch painted cigar lids were testament to their originality and
nicotine addictions. They'd left their studios to paint naturalistic
impressions of the Australian landscape and its people, an approach
borrowed from the French that outraged the *Argus'* conservative art
critic, James Smith:

> The modern impressionist asks you to see pictures in splashes of
> colour, in slapdash brushwork ... Of the 180 exhibits catalogued
> on this occasion four-fifths are a pain to the eye. Some look like
> faded pictures seen through gauze; others that a paint-pot has
> been accidentally upset over a panel nine inches by five; others
> resemble the first essays of a small boy who has been apprenticed
> to a house painter ...

---

the Australian Constitution. Australians would feel more of a connection with
their founding document if it started, 'How ya fuckin' goin', mate?'

9   *Billy*, a simple container used to boil water over an open fire (usually to make tea),
    probably derives from the Scottish *bally*, an abbreviation of *bally-cog* (a milk pail).
    Alternatively, it may be a contraction of *Royal William*, the name given to a large
    bush kettle during the 1830s reign of King William IV. The term may have been
    further popularised by the 1850s advent of bouilli tins – tins of preserved *boeuf
    bouilli* (which Australians called bully beef to avoid French contamination of their
    language) – used by bushmen to boil water after the horrible-tasting beef had been
    removed. Damper, the simple, unleavened bread baked in the ashes of an outdoor
    fire, was named for its dampening of the appetite.

The group became known as the Heidelberg School, for its artists' camp in rural Heidelberg, now a Melbourne suburb. It was led by Tom Roberts, who enjoyed painting men doing things to sheep – a subject, tutted the *Argus*, 'altogether unworthy of depiction'. Frederick McCubbin specialised in melancholic, yet noble, country characters, while Arthur Streeton was more a landscape guy. Charles Conder, a recently arrived dandy, learned how to be a painter of Australian beaches under Roberts, and how to be a rent boy under his landlady, Mrs Read, who gave him free board, lodging and syphilis in return for sexual favours. Walter Withers was the Pete Best of Australia's impressionist band, and Jane Sutherland was sometimes allowed to paint with the men, but Streeton made it clear what he thought of women in the arts – 'no woman was ever Shakespeare, or Wagner or Michelangelo.'

Depicting country people in art was not new, with Bruegel having cornered the paint-a-peasant market four centuries earlier. Bruegel's rural characters were gaunt, stooped, covered in warts and frequently deformed – and those were their good features – but the Heidelberg

BEFORE   AFTER

FIG. 5: BUSH EYE FOR THE TOWN GUY

School painted countryfolk as ruggedly vital men, rosy-cheeked women and angelic children.

Art historians credit the Heidelberg School with developing a national style of painting, which is a polite way of saying that the Heidelberg artists (with the exception of Conder) never experienced international success.[10] Still, along with Paterson and his fellow 'bush poets', the Heidelberg artists helped define the ideal Australian.

BIG FARMER

Alfred Deakin was living his own version of the ideal Australian life, one of spiritual inquiry, 'family values' and friendly neighbours who were never more than a white picket fence away. Deakin played with his new daughter in the morning, attended parliament during the day, and returned home in the evening to enjoy the chops Pattie had prepared for him, having renounced vegetarianism after realising voters considered not eating meat un-Australian. He'd stepped down as president of the Victorian Association of Progressive Spiritualists, though his fascination with the dead remained, and started a prayer diary, in which to record his one-sided conversations with God, a habit he'd keep for twenty-nine years.

Deakin was a man of the city, but he knew that the politicians, lawyers, accountants and shopkeepers with whom he rubbed shoulders were not the stock from which a master race could spring. If the healthy, happy bushman was to remain the nationalist pin-up boy, Deakin realised, further rural investment and development would be required.

In the early days of the Australian colonies, agricultural industries were limited by the size of the domestic market. Once the colonists

---

10   Conder didn't get to enjoy his success for long, as the syphilis contracted from
     Mrs Read sent him mad. He died in an asylum for the incurably insane in 1909,
     aged just forty.

had sufficient food, additional lands could only be opened if they produced goods for export. Unfortunately, Australia was not just dry and hot, it was also thousands of miles away from potential markets. Shipping costs were going to be a bugger. And, surprisingly, horse and ox costs were going to be a double-bugger with a triple-pike. Wheat could only be transported overland for about 50 kilometres before the cost of cartage became too high. Other crops had an even lower transport range.

Sheep came to Australia's rescue. Fine wool from the descendants of the Merino flocks of John Macarthur, Australia's first supervillain sheep whisperer, was prized in European markets. European sheep had to be hand-fed and housed in winter, while Australian sheep could graze outside all year, reducing the cost of wool production.

Sheep originally wandered in search of food and water as they saw fit, with shepherds and dingoes following dutifully behind. The 1850s gold rush, which decimated the labour force and blew out wages, forced efficiencies. Land was fenced, dingoes poisoned and dams dug, allowing sheep to stay put and one boundary rider to do the work previously performed by nine shepherds. Eugenic principles were diligently applied to build a larger, woollier race of master-sheep.

Sheep yards and shearing sheds were built to a standard Australian design, with sheep sorted, dipped, dried, housed, shorn and pushed down a chute in the most labour-efficient manner possible. In the shed, shearers were supported by tarboys, who applied hot tar to sheep's shaving cuts; rouseabouts, who carried fleeces; wool skirters, who trimmed fleeces; wool classers, who sorted fleeces by quality; and wool pressers, who packaged fleeces, aided by mechanical baling machines developed in the late 1870s. These were wool factories, built around a production line of which Henry Ford would have been proud – and they made the eastern Australian colonies the world's wool superpowers.

Shearing seasons were staggered throughout the eastern colonies, with local workers supplemented by a mobile workforce that fleeced sheep and gullible graziers as they travelled from station to station.

These walk-in walk-out (WIWO) workers would commonly go on a 'spree' at shearing season's end, blowing their savings on alcohol and/ or prostitutes. On the trek back home, they might get work fencing or building dams.

Station-owners provided shearers with enough rations to walk to the next station, which they carried in a calico bag – the 'nose bag'. The nose bag was tied to a towel that ran across the shearer's shoulders, with the other end of the towel connected to a blanket rolled around the shearer's meagre possessions. The blanket was known as a 'swag' and travelling shearers and other itinerant workers, with a water bag in one hand and a billy in the other, became known as 'swagmen' or 'swaggies'.[11]

The swaggie, who walked the length of the country with his mates in search of work, foregoing home comforts and female companionship, before blowing his dough on booze and hookers, was one of the bush foundations upon which Australian masculinity was built.

Cattle were Australia's second agricultural success. They were originally farmed for their hides, but Australians soon realised they tasted great. They could graze in lands too harsh for sheep and, like their woolly counterparts, could be walked to where they were slaughtered, eliminating cartage costs. Most Australians enjoyed a steak or chop for breakfast, cold cuts for lunch and a meaty pudding or roast for dinner – and they still couldn't get through the mountains of meat on offer.[12]

---

11 *Swag* was originally a bundle of stolen goods in the flash language. A swag was also known as a *bluey*, as a blue blanket was commonly used, with a swagman's travelling referred to as *humping bluey*. A swag was also known as a *matilda*, and a travelling swagman would *waltz matilda*, believed to derive from the German *auf die Walze gehen* (to go a-wandering). *Matilda* is also of German-Australian origin, with the name Mathilde used from the eleventh century to denote a prostitute who followed soldiers or itinerant apprentices. Itinerant Australian workers, who didn't have a girlfriend to provide warmth and comfort at night, turned instead to their blankets – literally *humping bluey*. That Australian rural workers replaced women with blankets, and that the chorus of Australia's most popular traditional song, Banjo Paterson's 'Waltzing Matilda', is about a country hobo's wank-rag, says a lot about Australia.

12 Australia was unable to successfully export meat until 1880. Fresh meat spoiled during the seventy-day voyage to European markets, the price of barrels made

Wheat was more of a slow burn, largely confined to land near Tasmanian and South Australian ports until the second half of the nineteenth century. In the 1840s, South Australians John Wrathall Bull and John Ridley both claimed credit for inventing the world's first mechanical grain harvester, which reduced harvesting costs by almost 60 per cent. Ridley's Stripper, as the machine became known to Bull's disgust, only worked on wheat grown in hot, dry climates, giving Australian wheat growers an edge.

In the 1870s, South Australia's Charles Mullen revolutionised land clearing by rolling an old boiler across mallee scrub, burning the crushed vegetation, and rolling a spiked log (a.k.a. a mulleniser) across the fired earth to loosen it for sowing wheat. In 1876, South Australia's Richard Bowyer Smith invented the stump-jump plough, a hinged contraption that could leap over tough mallee roots and other obstructions, meaning fields no longer needed to be laboriously dug out before planting. And in 1885, Victoria's Hugh Victor McKay patented the Sunshine Harvester, the world's first mass-produced combine harvester – able to simultaneously strip grain and winnow the chaff.

The reason Victorians had got in on the act was trains. Rail had cut domestic freight costs by about 90 per cent. It had brought city and country closer together, enabling farmers to push further into the interior and grow wheat and other crops for urban markets. Wheat, which could survive long sea voyages without spoiling, could now also be exported in large quantities. By 1890, economies of scale delivered by Australia's sprawling wheat farms, combined with Australian land-clearing and harvesting innovations, meant Australian wheat was cheaper in Britain than the local product, even though Australian yields per acre were half those of Britain, and Australian labour was much more expensive.

---

exporting cured meat cost-prohibitive, and Australian canned meat was known as 'tinned dog' – attempts to export the nauseating grey paste to feed British prisoners foundered after the prisoners simply refused to eat it.

The railways profoundly changed the Australian diet. Before the tracks came to town, Australia was the epicentre of the local food movement – but not the kind promoted by the wannabe celebrity chef who serves you a pigeon ethically sourced from the nearest park bench, stuffed with weeds lovingly harvested from the nature strip outside his over-priced gastro-wankery. The Australian local food movement was born of necessity. If you ate unprocessed food sourced from a distance, it was likely to kill you, so many Australians lived entirely on locally slaughtered cattle or sheep, along with flour, sugar, salt, butter, tea and other preserved foods. The railways allowed fresh fruit, vegetables, seafood and dairy products to be transported further, and animals to be discreetly murdered outside towns.[13] Trains were able to transport food even further after Sydney entrepreneur Thomas Mort built the world's first mass-freezing works in 1875, followed by the world's first refrigerated train carriages.[14]

The final key to unlock Australia's agricultural potential was water. Australia had the lowest rainfall and highest levels of evaporation of all the world's continents, bar Antarctica. Other continents had mighty mountain ranges that stored water as snow and released it in summer, but at 2,228 metres, Australia's highest point was more

13   While rail gave Australians a varied diet, most still prepared plain meals, with
     dishes involving any level of complexity seen as pretentious. In 1883, French
     immigrant Edmond Marie Marin la Meslée sniffed, 'It is true to say that no other
     country on earth offers more of everything needed to make a good meal, or offers
     it more cheaply, than Australia; but there is no other country either where the
     cuisine is more elementary, not to say abominable.'

14   Australia is not just bloody big and bloody dry. It's also bloody hot. It's therefore
     unsurprising that Australia led the world in cooling technology. Geelong's James
     Harrison built the world's first commercial ice-making machine in 1854, meaning
     lake ice no longer needed to be imported from Massachusetts. Two years later,
     Harrison thrilled Australians, and infuriated Englishmen, with the world's first
     beer chiller. Thomas Mort teamed up with Eugène Nicolle in 1867 to produce
     the world's first artificially frozen food, but it was left to Queensland premier
     and entrepreneur Sir Thomas McIlwraith to unload Australia's first cargo of
     frozen meat in England in 1880 (although it lost colour and flavour when thawed,
     with Australian beef and mutton exports largely unsuccessful until new freezing
     technologies emerged in the 1930s).

pimple than peak, and nobody could pronounce its ridiculous Polish name, let alone water the country with its run-off.[15]

If large tracts of Australia were too dry for farming, Alfred Deakin reasoned, why not make them wetter? Deakin was one of the only people who listened to Hugh 'Water on the Brain' McColl, a fellow Victorian MP, who'd hijack parliamentary debate on any subject to rabbit on about how farmers needed more water.

In 1884, Deakin decided that Victoria needed a royal commission on water supply and irrigation, and that he should head it. Deakin travelled to the United States, where he was traumatised by a bullfight and shocked that 'Most people are stout here. Meals are enormous and very rich.' He was, however, impressed by Ontario and Etiwanda, irrigation colonies founded by brothers George and William Chaffey. The Chaffeys had built perfectly laid-out towns in the Californian desert, where alcohol was banned and fruit trees blossomed in once-barren sands.

The Americans, being Americans, had privatised water, selling it to the Chaffeys to develop their model temperance orchard-towns. This was a break from Britain, where anyone whose land adjoined a waterway inherited a confusing jumble of ancient rights over drinking water, irrigation water, swimming, boating, the erection of piers, and what one could or couldn't do to swans and otters. Irrigation rights in European countries, by contrast, were generally collectively owned and run by local communities.

Deakin returned to Victoria and mounted an argument for irrigation that Australians would understand – an argument based on race. Indians, with their low wages and expectations, could produce cheaper wheat and rice than Australians could. 'The white farmer of the future' could only compete with the Indian, Deakin stated, if he brought 'his

---

15   Until the Snowy Mountains Scheme was built between 1949 and 1974 – but no one could conceive of, let alone build, one of the modern engineering wonders of the world in the nineteenth century.

superior qualities' (i.e. his mighty white brain and bulldog determination) 'into full play'.

Deakin was determined to emulate the success of the Chaffeys, but with a twist:

> ... the State should exercise the supreme control and ownership over all rivers, lakes, streams and sources of water supply, except springs arising on private lands.

The laws subsequently introduced by Deakin transferred water rights from private citizens to the state, and gave local bodies public funds to build irrigation works. Deakin had just socialised water, and the other colonies followed suit.[16]

The Chaffeys immigrated to Australia and decided to open the 'hissing desert' of Mildura for irrigation and settlement, with Deakin experimenting with water privatisation there. South Australian premier Sir John Downer also granted the Chaffeys land to make wetter at Renmark.

There can be no doubt that Deakin's irrigation reforms benefitted Victorian farmers, who collectively pocketed £2.2 million in the first decade of widespread irrigation. However, the government spent £2.904 million on irrigation infrastructure during this period, and recovered only £217,000 from landholders. The taxpayer bore the cost and the farmer reaped the benefit, a model that generations of Australians would come to accept as the norm, because when it came down to it, weren't all Australians hardy sons and daughters of the bush?

THE PROTECTION RACKET

Throughout the 1880s, there was a growing nationalist narrative that Australian colonists had treated Aboriginal people with kindness and

---

16   If you think the Murray—Darling Basin Plan is a mess, you can thank Alfred Deakin.

done everything possible to ensure their survival. This was news to Aboriginal people, who were being driven off their land by pastoralists and farmers enjoying the agricultural boom.

In Queensland, this was all too often at the point of a gun, with the Native Police – paramilitary death squads led by Europeans and manned by Aboriginal troops from the south – believed to have killed some 24,000 Aboriginal people between 1859 and 1897. In 1884, 600 Kalkatungu warriors charged a force of settlers and Native Police at Battle Mountain, near Mount Isa, losing 200 men in this engagement alone.[17]

Queensland cattlemen drove their herds into the Northern Territory during the 1880s and 'encouraged' Aboriginal people to work as stockmen. Some pastoralists sought accommodation with the tribes, trading the 'right' to continued occupation of ancestral lands for labour. Most Aboriginal stockmen were paid in rations or credits that could only be redeemed at their station's store.

Paul Foelsche was the South Australian inspector of police for Central Australia.[18] He reported on the innovative labour hire practices of less culturally sensitive pastoralists:

> … in many instances boys who assist in station work were, and perhaps are still obtained by what is termed 'running them down' and forcibly taking them from tribes to stations some distance away

---

17 In fairness to Queensland, it did not shoot all of its Aboriginal people. It helped some of them become successful international performance artists. In 1883, Robert Cunningham took nine Palm Island people to America to join Barnum & Bailey's Greatest Show on Earth, where they were displayed as part of the circus's 'Ethnological Congress of Strange and Savage Tribes'. After the tour, Cunningham showed them in dime museums, with the body of one of his exhibits, Tambo, embalmed and mounted in an Ohio museum for the next thirty-six years. The survivors toured European theatres, parks and zoos as 'specimens of the lowest order of man', 'ferocious, treacherous, uncivilized savages', and 'ranting man-eaters'; had their skulls measured by scientists; and contracted consumption, the discerning Aboriginal performer's terminal disease of choice. Three made it back to Palm Island.

18 It was common for Northern Territory residents to have multiple jobs, given the Territory's small non-Aboriginal population. The German-born Foelsche was also the Territory's leading dentist and photographer.

from the tribe, and young girls were and, I believe, are still obtained in a similar manner ...

Aboriginal men who retaliated when their children were abducted, or who otherwise made a nuisance of themselves, were targeted in what Foelsche called 'nigger hunts'. The *Northern Territory Times*, which described Aboriginal people as 'a race of creatures resembling men in form, but with no more trace of feeling in their natures than Siberian wolves', outlined how such a hunt should be run:

> ... we feel equally sure that the party will save themselves the trouble of bringing their prisoners such a distance to serve no sensible purpose. The only things that have hitherto proved of any value in bringing the niggers to their senses have been dogs and revolvers; and we trust the party now gone out will not be afraid to use them.

Reverend John Gribble moved to Western Australia in 1885. He'd earlier impressed Ned Kelly with his demand that the outlaw return a girl's much-loved pet horse, which Ned had stolen during the Jerilderie hold-up. (Ned had obliged.) He'd also impressed his fellow missionaries with *A Plea for the Aborigines of New South Wales* and *Black but Comely*, in which he encouraged settlers to stop raping Aboriginal girls, no matter how good looking they were:

> ... black girls are ruined by white men ... And what, I ask, is the consequence? The up-rising of a wild race of half-castes in the very midst of a Christian community.[19]

Gribble didn't impress Western Australians, who objected to his 1886 *Dark Deeds in a Sunny Land*, in which he denounced the shooting murders of 'sixty natives, men, women and children' in a single

---

19   OK, he loses some points for the last sentence. Gribble's son Ernest and daughter Ethel would both later contribute to the 'wild race of half-caste' 'problem' by having children with First Nations people.

day in the Pilbara, the rape of Aboriginal women, forced Aboriginal labour and the use of neck chains. Gribble was called 'a lying, canting humbug' by the *West Australian*, he was bashed, his bishop revoked his licence to preach and his mission was shut down.

The same year, the Western Australian government established an Aboriginal Protection Board. The Board had the power to establish and run Aboriginal reserves, government-administered alternatives to the church-run missions, where those on the government payroll could be trusted not to publish embarrassing pamphlets.

Western Australia was following Victoria, which from 1860 had encouraged Aboriginal people to live on reserves, and in 1869 established the Central Board for the Protection of Aborigines. The Victorian Board had powers beyond preventing Aboriginal cricketers from showing up their betters. It controlled almost every aspect of reserve life: it could tell Aboriginal people where to live, the work they must do, and who they could associate with and marry. It could also take action for the 'care, custody and education of the children of Aborigines' – or, more bluntly, their removal from their families.

The Aboriginal people of Coranderrk and a number of other Victorian reserves established self-sufficient agricultural communities, and preserved aspects of their traditional lives - despite Board interventions, being mixed with people from different cultural and language groups, and a 50 per cent infant mortality rate. The Coranderrkians successfully campaigned against the Board's attempt to assign their land to white farmers, with the government making Coranderrk a permanent reserve.

In 1883, New South Wales opened its first government-run reserve and established its own Aboriginal Protection Board, which, at least early on, had less intrusive powers than its Victorian counterpart.[20]

---

20   The athletics world can thank the New South Wales reserve system for producing the crouch start, pioneered in 1887 by Yorta Yorta man Bobby McDonald from the Cummeragunja Reserve. McDonald developed the 'sitting start', as he called

Western Australia decided to be more intrusive than the Victorians. Justices of the Peace could order any Aboriginal person judged not 'decently clothed from neck to knee' to leave any city or town. Magistrates could indenture Aboriginal children from 'a suitable age' until they turned twenty-one, removing them from their families and forcing them to work. The Western Australian Act also introduced contracts between employers and Aboriginal workers over fourteen years of age, with employers to provide 'substantial, good, and sufficient rations, clothing and blankets', with any mention of wages conspicuously absent.[21] The powers of the Board were soon expanded to allow Aboriginal people to be whipped for certain offences, and to allow pastoralist magistrates to adjudicate cases involving Aboriginal people spearing or stealing their stock.

The year 1886 was not a good one for Aboriginal people (but, in fairness, neither was any other year in the nineteenth century). Alfred Deakin, freshly elected as leader of Victoria's Liberal MPs, and the second most senior figure in the colony's Conservative-Liberal coalition government, introduced a law that differentiated between those of full Aboriginal blood and 'half-castes' (as those of mixed race were called).[22]

The *Half-Caste Act*, as Deakin's law became known, upset the precarious balance of reserve life. A key purpose of the Act, according to Deakin, was 'making the half-castes useful members of society, and

---

it, to protect himself from cold winds while waiting for the starter's gun, and was pleasantly surprised to discover that it enabled him to get an early lead on his rivals.

21   The Act made it clear that Aboriginal people did not own any of the 'blankets, bedding, clothing, and other articles' provided to them in accordance with the Act. These goods were government property and Aboriginal people could be prosecuted for their sale or other disposal.

22   In Western Australia, the grandchildren of a mixed-race union were considered to have had their Aboriginality bred out of them. Over time, some of the Australian colonies (and later the states), attempted to apply different policies to different classes of mixed-race people, determined by the amount of Aboriginal 'blood' they had. A person with one Aboriginal grandparent was a 'quadroon', while a person with one Aboriginal great-grandparent was an 'octoroon'. It all got pretty silly.

gradually relieving the State of the cost of their maintenance'. 'Half-castes' aged between eight and thirty-five would be removed from reserves and trained for manual or domestic work, and so absorbed into the general community. They, or at least their children, would be made white.

The *Half-Caste Act* broke up families and deprived the reserves of many working-age men and women who'd helped them achieve self-sufficiency. Coranderrk, with fewer people, obviously required less land – so parliament assigned half of it to white farmers in 1893, notwithstanding its earlier permanent status.

Mixed-race people moved into a world in which, despite Deakin's best intentions, they would never be accepted. Those they had left behind, broken by the breaking of their communities, would become more reliant on the scraps thrown to them from the Protection Board's table, and fall further under Board control.

The plan for these 'full-blood' Aboriginal people, and the older 'half-castes' who would stay on the reserves, was less clear. However, despite the narrative that the colonies had done everything to ensure Aboriginal survival, the *Age* articulated Victorian thinking:

> ... where two races whose stages of progression differ greatly are brought into contact, the inferior race is doomed to wither and disappear ... clearly beneficial to mankind at large by providing for the survival of the fittest.

Social Darwinism had decreed that Aboriginal people were a 'doomed race'. It was not their fault, and it certainly wasn't ours. It was just the way of things.[23]

Protection boards were ultimately rolled out across Australia, with the exception of Tasmania, which believed all its Aboriginal people were safely deceased. Queensland proved that it could be simultaneously

---

23   When something is someone's fault, the someone is expected to say sorry. It follows that if someone doesn't say sorry, then there was no fault for them to be sorry for.

racist and sexist by restricting the definition of 'half-caste' to the child of an Aboriginal mother and non-Aboriginal father, it being unthinkable that a white woman, free of the lusts that bedevilled men, would sleep with an Aboriginal man. It also banned the supply of alcohol or opium to Aboriginal people, with Aboriginal protection used to justify banning the non-medicinal use of opium in the broader community.[24]

Aboriginal protection resulted in the increased removal of children, particularly those of mixed race, from their families and communities. Some were fostered; some were 'apprenticed'; some were sent to reformatory or training schools; some were raised on church missions or in other institutions. All were protected. All were saved.

These were the Stolen Generations.

If all the unstolen Aboriginal people would be dead soon, then they would not need the rights that other people had. In 1891, the *Bulletin* had this to say on Premier Henry Parkes' refusal to strip Aboriginal men of their New South Wales voting rights, as had occurred in Queensland in 1885, and would occur in Western Australia in 1893:

> ... as soon as he learns anything of civilisation, he gives up being independent then and forever. It is his pride and joy to be MR DANGAR's blackfellow, or JACK HAMILTON's nigger ... the idea of being his own aboriginal never enters his head. His constant desire is to have a patron who will keep him in tobacco and occasional drinks, and he will vote for his patron just as every other man will vote for the party that fills his political programme .... The nigger doesn't want a vote, apart from the question of rum and tobacco, any more than the black snake needs a new hat ... And, anyhow, a ballot-box is a hard substance with which to console a dying race, and if the nigger is dying it is more to the point to let him down easy with grub and blankets and tobacco.

---

24 Queensland was the last Australian state to dismantle Aboriginal protection and reserves. It did so in 1981, as it feared African nations would accuse it of racism and boycott the 1982 Brisbane Commonwealth Games.

New South Wales did, however, conclude that Aboriginal children didn't need the same education as white children – and recognised that Aboriginal children playing with white children made some white parents feel uncomfortable.

In 1883, George Reid, the then New South Wales minister for education, expelled fifteen Aboriginal children from Yass Public School after white parents complained about racially mixed classrooms. Reid explained that differences in creed or colour should generally not exclude a child from school, but 'cases may arise, especially amongst the Aboriginal tribes, where the admission of a child or children may be prejudicial to the whole school'.

Reid favoured separate Aboriginal schools in areas with large Aboriginal populations. Aboriginal schools were poorly resourced, teachers were often unqualified, and a separate syllabus focusing on manual activities was imposed. Aboriginal kids in other areas could attend public schools if they were 'habitually clean, decently clad and they conduct themselves with propriety'. Many non-Aboriginal children would have failed the 'clean, clad and courteous' test, if it had been applied to them.

In 1902, the New South Wales government instructed public schools to remove Aboriginal students whenever non-Aboriginal parents complained. Western Australia had similar exclusion policies. Queensland allowed neglected children to be placed in industrial and reformatory schools and defined '[a]ny child born of an Aboriginal or half-caste mother' as neglected. The Northern Territory didn't provide formal schooling for Aboriginal children until 1950.

There would be no quick fix to Australia's educational apartheid. School principals in New South Wales could exclude Aboriginal students on the grounds of community opposition or unsatisfactory home conditions until 1971.

Again, none of this was anyone's fault. It was just the way of things.

6

The Big Smoke

I am sitting in my dingy little office, where a stingy
Ray of sunlight struggles feebly down between the houses tall,
And the foetid air and gritty of the dusty, dirty city
Through the open window floating, spreads its foulness over all.

And in place of lowing cattle, I can hear the fiendish rattle
Of the tramways and the buses making hurry down the street,
And the language uninviting of the gutter children fighting,
Comes fitfully and faintly through the ceaseless tramp of feet.

And the hurrying people daunt me, and their pallid faces haunt me
As they shoulder one another in their rush and nervous haste,
With their eager eyes and greedy, and their stunted forms and weedy,
For townsfolk have no time to grow, they have no time to waste.
'Clancy of the Overflow', 'The Banjo', *The Bulletin*, 1889

LOUISA LAWSON COMES TO TOWN

L OUISA LAWSON HAD HAD A GUTFUL OF THE BUSH, with its provincialism, snakes, handsy miners, feckless husbands and backbreaking toil for little reward. Youthful romance and hope had given way to a steely pragmatism and a desire for self-transformation. The city would be her chrysalis.

When Lawson arrived in Sydney in 1883, almost a third of the colony's non-Aboriginal residents were waiting there for her, filling

the city's narrow, winding streets with an unceasing din.¹ Rank scents
mugged her nostrils – the waft of ammonia from urine-stained alleys
and the whiff of stale beer, rotting food and death from Sydney's
many malodorous pubs.²

The steam tram, originally a novelty to convey gawping tourists to the International Exhibition, was so popular that new lines
soon snaked out from the city's centre. Along with the half-hourly
train services to Homebush and horse-drawn omnibuses, the trams
transformed villages into suburbs, with urban sprawl radiating from
their routes.³

New foundries opened to make trams, trains and the tracks
that writhed across the Australian landscape like the tentacles of an
epileptic octopus. Railways didn't just allow cities to import farm
produce from the country – they allowed goods to be more cheaply
exported there. With Aunty Mabel from West Woop-Woop now
able to afford the latest mangle from the big smoke, manufacturing
boomed and New South Wales transitioned from a pastoral to an
industrial economy.

The factories that started belching fumes into Sydney's once
sea-scented air in the 1870s didn't just make engines and ironwork.
They processed food – making white bread, biscuits, confectionery,
jams, cordials and pickles, all liberally laced with preservatives, each
batch tasting exactly like the last. Cheap alternatives to established

---

1   Town-planning advocate John Fitzgerald condemned Sydney as 'a city without a
    plan, save whatever planning was due to the errant goat. Wherever this animal
    made a track through the bush, there are the streets of today.'

2   New South Wales pubs were required to accommodate corpses for the coronial
    inquests that were routinely held on their premises, although publicans had the
    right to refuse corpses in an 'offensive state of decomposition', or corpses of
    persons who'd succumbed to infectious diseases.

3   Horses remained the principal mode of transport for travel of any distance.
    Sydney's horses bought noise, smells and flies to the city. Clearing the streets of
    manure was a full-time occupation for hundreds of youths, known as *blockboys* or
    sparrow starvers.

products emerged, with Frederick Phillips mixing beef offal fat with skim milk and 'Danish Butter Colouring' to make butterine.[4] Where shopkeepers previously promoted products ('Try our milk arrowroot biscuits'), they now promoted brands ('We sell Arnott's Milk Arrowroot biscuits'). Australia was changing, and the services sector was booming too – soon, guys with fast mouths and floppy hair would start adding extra vowels to their names and telling you why you really, really needed Arnott's Milk Arrowroot biscuits.[5]

This was a brave new world for Louisa Lawson – and it was not an easy one for a single mother caring for three children, two of whom were deaf and spoke haltingly. Lawson was too busy and too strict to show her children much affection.

Lawson complained that, as a separated woman, she suffered an 'undeserved loss of caste', her disreputable character confirmed by her decision to take in boarders, washing and sewing.[6] But her boarders, many of whom were printers, fostered her interest in writing and publishing.

Sydney's Progressive Spiritualist Lyceum also exposed Lawson to new and radical ideas, with the socialists, republicans, feminists, trade unionists and dead-botherers she met there making her boarding house their second home. She was particularly close to Thomas Walker, the guy who'd toured Australia with his spiritualist show after burning one of his Canadian séance attendees to death with stage phosphoros.

---

4   Australians didn't like the word *margarine* because it was French.

5   Arnott's Milk Arrowroot and Full of Fruit biscuits arrived in Sydney a few months before Louisa Lawson. Arnott's SAO biscuits appeared in 1906 – named either after a boat, or to celebrate Arthur Arnott being a Salvation Army Officer. Arnott's Golliwog biscuit could still be enjoyed in Sydney until the 1990s, with its brief rebranding as Scallywag not satisfying the PC police who objected to eating smilingly subservient black children with large afros and no trousers. Following its axing, some fast-mouthed, floppy-haired, bevowelled idiot told Coles that calling their new brown and white biscuits Creole Creams would be a great idea.

6   A 'boarding house' was sometimes a euphemism for a bawdy house, and prostitutes commonly claimed to be laundresses, seamstresses or actresses (and sometimes they were).

Walker had admitted his act was a fraud; founded the Australasian Secular Association; lobbied for art galleries, libraries and museums to open on Sundays; campaigned against war, imperialism and the death penalty; been convicted for exhibiting obscene pictures while advocating birth control (he conducted his own appeal and won); had his bush poetry published; staged his hit adaptation of Marcus Clarke's *His Natural Life*; and donned blackface in his own play, *Marmondelle the Moor*. Shy, stuttering Henry, Lawson's son, apprenticed as a coach painter, attended the Lyceum's Sunday school and hung out with Walker and other members of his mother's eclectic coterie, developing his own radical political ideas.

Louisa Lawson, whose love of poetry remained undimmed, had been moved to tears when visiting the grave of Henry Kendall, the insane poet who'd died of consumption after inspecting a forest for Sir Henry Parkes. A simple wooden cross was an unworthy monument to a man who could write so movingly about Aborigines climbing trees and being afraid of bees – a true master of rhyme.

Lawson, in her campaign to build Kendall a fitting monument, received donations from Parkes, Lady Carrington (the governor's wife) and the *Bulletin*. More importantly, it drew her into a circle of bored, middle-aged society ladies who had nothing better to do with their time than debate what sort of stone and font Kendall would have chosen for his memorial, had he not coughed up his lungs in a forest. Those women would help make Louisa Lawson a household name.

YOU DON'T GET ME, I'M PART OF THE UNION

Although the Australian union movement would attach itself to the bush myth, it was originally a creature of the city.

Before the 1880s, most workers saw employers as workers who'd made good, and who were therefore sympathetic to their wants and needs. Australian workers had high wages and, unlike those in Britain, most could vote (if they were men). They believed in democracy (for men) and they'd backed the liberals in their attempts to bring down the squatters and their conservative political representatives – but they were into aspiration, not class warfare. They wanted to rent a bigger hovel, be able to afford the latest model cart and send their kids to school until the age of twelve – they wanted to live the liberal dream of self-advancement.[7]

Liberals like Alfred Deakin didn't need to be working men to know what was best for working men. A few workers had actually entered politics, but most of them sought to represent 'the people', not just workers, and their ascent proved the liberal dream was no dream at all. Charles Don, a stonemason whose 1859 election to the Victorian seat of Collingwood made him the first worker elected to any legislature in the British Empire, claimed he 'punched bluestone by day and squatters by night' and that the 'horny-handed sons of toil' were 'the source of all wealth', which all sounded dangerously nutty.[8] Most workers didn't see themselves first and foremost as workers – they were individuals, with their own interests and ambitions.

That isn't to say that workers in the same industry and local area didn't share common goals or work together. If you were a Sydney stonemason, you didn't want any Sydney idiot picking up a hammer

---

7   These were the pre-Howard Howard's battlers. Humphrey McQueen, an Australian Marxist historian and spear carrier for the New Left, argues that the workers who gave rise to the Australian Labor movement were a bunch of racist, imperialist social climbers who'd sell out their mates for a house in the suburbs and piano lessons for their kids.

8   Don was described by one journalist as 'a cross between a poet and a pirate'. His reference to punching bluestone and squatters was a complaint about MPs being unpaid, forcing him to work in a quarry by day and only attend evening sessions of parliament. British MPs had traditionally been remunerated by their constituents, although not always with money (the 1463 representative for Dunwich was paid in herrings). In the early modern era, a decision was made not to pay MPs, ostensibly to ensure the people were represented by those motivated by the ideal of public service. In reality, the decision ensured that only men of independent means could attain office. The payment of MPs was one of the six key reforms demanded by the mid-nineteenth century Chartist movement to enable working class men to have the same democratic rights as wealthy men.

and giving Sydney stonemasons a bad name. No, you formed a craft union, and anybody who wanted to hit rocks with a hammer in Sydney had to become your apprentice and pay you to learn how to hit rocks properly. And if you controlled who could hit rocks, you controlled the price that people who needed rocks hit would pay.

Craft unions charged hefty membership fees to keep the riffraff out, but those fees were used to help members who'd been injured at work (a frequent occurrence in the days before safety regulations), or who'd otherwise fallen on hard times. Some provided their members with libraries, journals, lectures and debates, to assist them to 'improve' themselves. Some even welcomed employers as honorary members! This all seemed to work very well, as long as you were an urban skilled male worker who wanted to live in a bigger house and one day employ other urban skilled male workers.

In 1871, some Sydney unions decided they shared interests beyond those of a single trade, forming the Trades and Labour Council of Sydney (TLC), a union of unions. The TLC encouraged unskilled workers, and workers from regional areas around Sydney, to organise.

This was, of course, illegal. Workers who stopped work, or went on strike, could be prosecuted for breaching their employment contracts. Workers who picketed a workplace could be done for intimidation or inducing other workers to breach their contracts. Workers who talked about any such action could be charged with conspiracy. Any collective organisation of workers was illegal, which made unions criminal enterprises, but employers were willing to look the other way as long as things didn't get out of hand. So were the authorities, as politicians didn't want to alienate large numbers of people who could vote.[9]

In Victoria, unions and manufacturers enjoyed a symbiotic relationship in their pursuit of protectionism. The Amalgamated Miners'

---

9   In 1855 and 1856, the rock hitters of Sydney and Melbourne committed all sorts of crimes in their successful campaign to win the world's first industry-wide eight-hour workdays, but the outcome was so popular that the authorities let it slide.

Association of Victoria adopted a motto in 1874 that would never fly today: 'United we stand; divided we fall – Labor and Capital United'. The first Australian Intercolonial Trades Union Congress (ITUC), held in 1879, also agreed that labourers should embrace capitalism and aspire to join 'the fortunate classes'.

The first chinks in the compact between organised labour and capital appeared when the Australasian Steam Navigation Company employed low-wage Chinese sailors. In 1878, trade unions, with government and press support, organised widespread and effective strikes against the company.

Emboldened by its success, the union movement latched onto race as a way to win popular support. The movement was a champion of equality – and that could only be achieved if all the unequal people were sent back to where they came from. When governments refused the ITUC's demands for blanket bans on Asians, the ITUC claimed that unions alone spoke for the people. Labour was getting political.

The labour movement's anti-Chinese rhetoric grew increasingly hysterical. J.V. Wiley, an ITUC delegate, told the 1886 ITUC he'd personally witnessed a teenage hooker sex party in a Chinese opium den:

> Young girls of 14 and 15 were decoyed into dens by offers of lollies, &c. and the most degrading scenes were then enacted. When a girl had once taken to that sort of thing she never rose again, but went downward till she died diseased in the gutter.[10]

Every good unionist knew that white women had to be protected from Chinamen – and white men had to be protected from white women. Victorian ITUC delegate H.A. Harwood, who represented furniture makers threatened by Chinese-owned furniture factories, complained:

---

10   Strangely, none of the other delegates asked J.V. Wiley why he'd attended a teenage hooker sex party in a Chinese opium den.

Women were the greatest supporters of Chinamen, as they bought
from them vegetables and fancy goods, probably not considering
that by so doing they were helping the Chinese to strangle their
white brethren.[11]

Women, like Chinamen, were also taking white men's jobs. The
only people members of the Tailors' Union hated more than Chinamen
were members of the Tailoresses' Union. Although the Trades Halls
that emerged in Australia's large cities during the 1870s and 1880s
tried to broker peace between male and female workers, and help male
and female unions work together, the growth of factories heightened
these gender tensions.

As factories grew, small workshops diminished. Skilled self-
employed craftsmen were replaced by machines and their operators.
Women and children could be paid less than men, they were smaller
and could more easily access hard-to-reach machine parts, and most
of them didn't have beards that could get caught in the wheels of
industry. You could pack them in like sardines and make them work
long hours because they were less likely to complain than men and,
even if they did, who'd listen? Sweatshops had come to Australia.

Even better, you could tell women and kids not to turn up for work
at the factory, but to make clothing at home – in short, you could
make them independent contractors. You could pay for each piece
of clothing delivered, you didn't have to worry about work hours or
conditions, and you really saved on overheads.

The labour movement wanted to free women from sweatshops
and piecework, but not so they could work in factories. Women workers made factories 'hotbeds of vice and immorality'. Women should

---

11   The links between Chinese, vegetables, vice and venereal disease became so
      strongly embedded in the Australian consciousness that the New South Wales
      1891 Royal Commission on Alleged Chinese Gambling and Immorality inquired
      into whether women could contract syphilis from vegetables purchased from
      Chinese market gardeners.

be freed from work to protect their virtue and enable them to fulfil their proper calling as housewives.

After having a go at foreign and female workers, unions turned their attention to people who employed foreigners and females. In 1885, H.A. Harwood said of the 'race traitors' who supported the importation of coloured labour:

> They live in fine houses, pleasantly situated, and are surrounded by refined associations. Their daughters are not tempted, and drugged, and degraded. Their callings and incomes are not interfered with hence they see no harm in thousands of Chinese being allowed to come here.

The politics of envy had entered the Australian Eden, and Australian unions began to embrace the language of class. Class war could not be won in the streets of a single city, so local unions made way for industry bodies that organised across the colony. Some, like the Amalgamated Miners' Association of Australasia, began to operate across colonial borders, in anticipation of the nation that was to come.

Alfred Deakin shared many of the aims of the labour movement. In 1884, he legalised trade unions in Victoria, following similar reforms in Britain, South Australia and New South Wales. In 1885, he introduced the *Factories and Shops Act*, which provided for health and safety inspections and workers compensation, and cracked down on the employment of women and children in factories.

Even so, Deakin was distressed he hadn't been able to do enough for workers in the face of a hostile Legislative Council. In late 1885, he succumbed to one of the bouts of depression that would darken his life, writing in his prayer book:

> Me shallow & poor & frail in spirit, in mind & in flesh. Me selfish & barren, even to bitterness & blackness of soul. Me the mere creature of other wills, though closed to Thine. Me the mere counter of the ideas of others, producing none. Me the figure upon the stage of

life letting all power slip past me, without use or benefit. Me sunk
in dreamy sloth & wayward idleness. Me humiliated – me shamed.

ON THE WATERFRONT

Employers felt humiliated by the unions' success in the 1878 Australasian Steam Navigation Company strikes. Then, in 1884, the Victorian
Operative Bootmakers' Union, led by former Hobart lightweight
boxing champion Billy Trenwith, gave the capitalist shoe-lords a good
steel-capped kicking and brought them to heel. Unionists, employers
believed, were growing too big for their boots.

Shipping magnate Bruce Smith regarded unionists as whingers,
claiming 'the second engineer of a steamship had threatened to report
his firm to the Trades Hall if the sweets served on board were not
more varied'. The Bootmakers' Strike convinced Smith that employers
had a problem and, if they were to counter the unions' growing influence, they needed to form an anti-union union. Smith founded the
Victorian Employers' Union, which backed him and other Melbourne
shipowners in not paying wharfies who didn't work on the holiday
celebrating the eight-hour workday. Giving workers time off work
to celebrate their winning time off work stuck in employers' craws,
with Smith arguing the eight-hour day was an attack on the liberty
of the working man who wanted to work longer hours for more pay.

On 1 January 1886, 900 wharfies walked off the job. Seamen,
stewards and ship's cooks followed. The unions got most of what
they wanted after some employers broke ranks.

The *Age*, although it had backed the strikers, expressed concern
about the fracturing of the alliance between capital and labour. The
Bulletin pooh-poohed this, opining, 'There is no common brotherhood between Capital and Labour, any more than there is a common
interest between the vampire and the sleeping Indian.' In 1886,
Bulletin cartoonist Livingston Hopkins created Mr Fat Man, who

later appeared as Fat Man, or just Fat. Fat was a morbidly obese old man who wore gentlemen's clothes and a top hat, carried a cane and was often pictured with a large cigar. Fat, the representation of capitalism, was adopted by other publications, and was commonly accompanied by talon-clawed Orientals, savage Pacific Islanders and Jewish moneylenders.[12]

Fat, who would appear in Australian newspapers for decades, was commonly opposed by an Australian worker. While British, European and American publications commonly depicted workers as down-and-out scarecrows, the Australian worker was always a tall, superbly muscled Aryan who'd just stepped straight off the cover of an R.M. Williams catalogue. The union movement and its media backers were desperate to make the worker synonymous with the bushman.

BRINGING BACK THE BIFF

Unionists weren't all about work. They were also about play – the eight-hour workday was promoted to allow eight hours' rest and eight hours' recreation. Unionists were just as into picnicking as picketing.

Union picnics were fun affairs, if your idea of fun is hanging out in a park with a bunch of white supremacists. There were earnest speeches about solidarity and Chinamen wanting to pimp out your daughters, and union links with the temperance movement meant you were unlikely to find a drink, but you could dance and play football with your comrades – at least until the larrikins arrived.

---

12   Jews were popularly believed to hoard vast sums of cash. The Australian word *motza*, meaning a large sum of money (e.g. 'He made a motza'), probably derives from the Yiddish *matzah* – unleavened bread (bread being another word for money). Other Australian words or phrases with probable Yiddish roots include *to put the moz on*, meaning to exert a malign influence, from the Yiddish *mazzal*, meaning 'luck' – and the most Australian word of them all, *cobber*, meaning 'mate', which most likely derives from *chaber*, Yiddish for 'comrade'. *To carry on like a pork chop*, meaning 'to behave foolishly, make a fuss, or rant' – probably derives from the older *like a pork chop in a synagogue*, a phrase used to convey that something was inappropriate or unpopular.

Larrikins were small-time entrepreneurs who despised the unions' attempts to regulate work, and crashing union picnics was a favourite larrikin sport. At the 1882 Sydney Journeymen Tailors' annual picnic, larrikins seized a football and hurled it at the seated picnickers. At a wharf and coal labourers' picnic at Chowder Bay, larrikins ran through the dance pavilion with a stretched rope, felling jigging wharfies and coalies.[13] Larrikins disrupted union parades and pickets, hurling abuse and rotten food at the marching or striking workers.

Larrikins also despised God-botherers. The open-air meetings of the Salvation Army, which brought its good deeds and tambourines to Australia in 1882, were disrupted by larrikins who sang obscene versions of Salvo hymns and pelted the congregation with vegetables, rocks, soot, flour and dead cats.[14]

Larrikins naturally despised the police. The 1880s saw the highest arrest rates in Australian history, as police were given new powers to deal with vagrants, neglected children, truants, prostitutes, gamblers, illegal sport and theatre operators, and people who looked like they were enjoying themselves on a Sunday. Many arrests were for minor public order matters, like public drunkenness or offensive language – offences commonly committed by larrikins.

Larrikins delighted in baiting and assaulting coppers. In 1884, more than twenty members of the Surry Hills Bummer Gang climbed

---

13   In the grand Australian tradition of the rabbit-proof fence, the dingo-proof fence and the emu-proof fence, the owners of the Chowder Bay dance pavilion later built a ten-foot larrikin-proof fence.

14   In 1880s Sydney, there wasn't enough room to swing a dead cat without hitting another dead cat. The 1886 annual report of Sydney's Inspector of Nuisances reported that 3,519 dead cats, 2,689 dead dogs and 20,757 dead fowls had been removed from the city's streets that year. Throwing dead cats and other objects at participants in Salvo street-meetings and marches was a popular sport, with several councils victim-blaming the Salvos by declaring their getting beaten up was a public nuisance. Between 1881 and 1907, over a hundred Salvos were fined or gaoled for gathering in public.

through a window into the ladies' dressing room at the Bondi Pavilion.[15] The arrival of the police kicked off the infamous Bondi Riot, with the Bummers throwing stones and attacking the constables with staves. Twenty Bummers were tried for rioting and other offences.[16]

The Sydney larrikins' love of a bit of biff is not surprising, as a number of pushes formed around the boxing gyms that emerged in Sydney during the 1880s. Late-nineteenth-century boxing was different to the genteel sport of today, with fighters allowed to wrestle and throw each other. Each round lasted until a fighter was knocked down. There were no judges or points decisions, with the fight only ending when one of the combatants was knocked out or could not return to the scratch, a line marked in the middle of the ring, within eight seconds of the round being called (hence the term *not up to scratch*).

Former champion bare-knuckle boxer Larry Foley opened a Surry Hills boxing gym/fight club next to his White Horse Hotel. A larrikin fan squad attended his fights and local theatre shows in which he was given vanity roles.

Foley's most famous fighter was Albert Griffiths, a Millers Point street brawler and larrikin icon. Although Young Griffo, as he was known, was an alcoholic who'd drink between rounds, he was famous for his lightning reflexes. He'd bet against members of the public who thought they could hit him, standing in front of them on a handkerchief and inviting them to take a swing, ducking and weaving away from their blows without ever stepping off the handkerchief. Once, when completely spannered in a pub, he famously dodged a spittoon thrown at the back of his head by rival Mysterious Billy Smith, having seen it hurtling towards him in the mirror above the bar.

---

15 The Bummer Gang took its name from the call push members made when police attempted to arrest them. When a member shouted 'Bummer!', that was the signal for nearby Bummers to flood the scene and mount a rescue.

16 Sydney's beaches are world-renowned for their pristine sands, aquamarine waters and riots. The 1884 Bondi Riot was similar to the 2005 Cronulla Riots, only whiter.

In 1889, Young Griffo won the Australian featherweight title from
Nipper Peakes. When he looked like losing to 'the Negro Jerry Marshall' in 1892, his larrikin supporters invaded the ring and threatened
Marshall and the referee. Young Griffo left for the United States in
1893.[17] His departure was triggered by the Australian colonies making the un-Australian decision to ban sports betting, in response to
a church and temperance organisation campaign that highlighted
match-fixing, particularly in the latest Australian sporting craze,
safety-bicycle racing.[18] Horse racing, to Andrew Barton Paterson's
delight, was exempted.[19]

---

17 Young Griffo starred in the first American film ever shown to a paying movie
    audience, 1895's *Young Griffo versus Battling Charles Barnett*. Shot on the roof of
    Madison Square Garden, the film was a recreation of the fight they'd held earlier that
    day. Young Griffo controversially lost one world title fight and drew three others.
    He was regularly arrested for drunkenness and resisting arrest, killed an opponent in
    the ring, and was gaoled for a year for assaulting a twelve-year-old boy while drunk.
    Young Griffo was admitted to an inebriates' home at twenty-six years of age. After
    his release, he became a stuntman and was arrested for vagrancy and begging. He
    spent his last years camped out on the steps of the Rialto Theatre on Broadway.

18 Safety bicycles, as modern bicycles are known, arrived in Australia in the
    late 1880s, replacing dangerous penny-farthings, upon which a rider would
    precariously perch atop a giant front wheel, some five feet above the ground.
    Safety-bicycle racing attracted shady types like Carl von Ledebur, the former race
    walker and Essendon football trainer who'd injected his charges with crushed
    guinea pig testicles (such treatments becoming synonymous with competitive
    cycling in the twentieth and twenty-first centuries). In 1896, his three attempts
    at breaking the cycling record from Dunedin to Christchurch failed, due to a
    flat tyre, a broken pedal and getting lost (with the likely common factor being
    his betting against his own success). Von Ledebur continued to lead a colourful
    life. His wife, Lizzie, left him after his affair with their housemaid, establishing
    an electro-therapeutic, palm reading, prostitution and abortion business in
    Melbourne under the name of Madame Olga Radalyski. Lizzie killed a woman
    while using electricity to induce an abortion and was convicted of murder after the
    woman's body was found in a suitcase in the Yarra. After his return to Australia
    from cycling in New Zealand and gold prospecting in Canada, Von Ledebur was
    prosecuted for representing himself as a doctor, selling cocaine, carnal knowledge
    and 'defrauding a deaf girl for the price of a massacon' (an ear-massaging device).
    As an old man, the triple bigamist was charged with injecting his nurse with
    barbiturates and cocaine in an attempt to stupefy her. Von Ledebur also holds the
    dubious honour of being interned as an enemy alien in both world wars.

19 South Australia banned gambling on horse races in 1883, believing fans would
    still come to the track for the love of the sport. They didn't. The decision was

Paterson paid tribute to the larrikins' love of violence in his 1888 *Bulletin* poem 'Uncle Bill: The Larrikin's Lament':

> *When sounds of fight rang sharply out,*
> *Then Bill was bound to be about,*
> *The foremost figure in 'the scrap',*
> *A terror to the local 'trap'.*
> *To drink, or fight, or maim, or kill,*
> *Came all alike to Uncle Bill.*

The larrikins' only redeeming features, in Paterson's eyes, were that they hurled stones and dead cats at Chinese people and vandalised Chinese shops.

THE MONGOLIAN OCTOPUS

Paterson was worried about the impact of cheap Chinese labour on working men's wages and 'the danger of Oriental invasion', referring to the Chinese as 'the cheap and nasty Chow' and 'Chinky' in his anti-Chinese *Bulletin* articles. The hero of Paterson's 'A Bushman's Song' leaves a shearing shed that employs Chinese labour because of 'the leprosy about', a reference to the popular belief that Chinese spread the disease (and diseases generally).[20]

Paterson's writing was tame in comparison to that of some of his peers at the *Bulletin*, which had moved from periodically attacking the Chinese to sustained xenophobic nutbaggery, starting with 'The Chinese in Australia: Their Vices and Their Victims' in 1886.

---

overturned and horse racing remained exempt from the later sports betting bans. Betting on sports other than horse and greyhound racing remained illegal in Australia until the Northern Territory broke ranks in 1992. Now it's impossible to watch television without being assaulted by ads featuring blokes enjoying the company of other blokes while getting on the punt.

20 *China virus* and *kung flu* would have been rapturously received in late-nineteenth-century Australia.

The 12,000-word feature commenced:

> Disease, defilement, depravity, misery and crime – these are the
> indispensable adjuncts which make Chinese camps and quarters
> loathsome to the senses and faculties of civilised nations. What-
> ever the neighbourhood the Chinese choose for the curse of their
> presence forthwith begins to reek with the abominations which are
> ever associated with their vile habitations. Wherever the pig-tailed
> pagans herd on Australasian soil, they introduce and practise vices
> the most detestable and damnable – vices that attack everything
> sacred in the system of European civilisation – vices which cannot be
> named in print, and others infinitely worse, so horrible and heinous
> that they cannot be spoken of by man to man.

The feature continued with the usual stuff about the 'degradation
of the thoughtless or innocent' white girl by 'moon eyed whoremongers'
and 'that potent ally of Mongolian lust, the omnipresent opium pipe',
but the truly extraordinary thing was the unknown author's ability
to write 12,000 words without resorting to specificity. The author
charged the people of New South Wales with buying cabbages from
the Chinese, 'never asking how those cabbages have been grown'.
Were they grown in sewerage, watered with lepers' pus, or fertilised
with the blood of kidnapped white babies???

The author avoided entertaining any particular fancy, coyly explaining at article's end, 'We give the facts generally, because details are
disgusting and particularisation dangerous.' This was Propaganda
101 – make as many non-specific allegations as possible, raise questions without providing answers, and let the fevered imagination of
each reader fill in its own blanks and connect dots that no sane mind
has ever connected before.

The author then seamlessly switched to enumerating the many
unpleasant features of the octopus ('The whole world of land produces no form of animal life so repulsive'), before introducing the

now thoroughly confused and frightened reader to 'the Mongolian Octopus'. The fearsome Asioaquatic supervillain was brought to life in a double-page cartoon of a grotesque caricature Chinaman with eight black tentacles crushing innocent Australian men, women and children. The tentacles were labelled Cheap Labour, Immorality, Bribery, Customs Robbery, Opium, Smallpox and Typhoid, Fan-Tan and Pak-Ah-Pu.[21] The author concluded:

> Until the leopard changes his spots and the Ethiop his colour, the Mongols will continue to be an ulcer in the fair bosom of Australia. Expulsion, and expulsion only, can meet the necessities of the case.

FIG. 6: 'SEE HERE, WAITER. I ORDERED THE MONGOLIAN LAMB.'

Other publications followed the *Bulletin*'s lead, with the *Boomerang*, a Queensland paper, particularly vociferous. The *Boomerang* was established by William Lane, a British radical who'd arrived in Brisbane in 1885, following a stint as a journalist in the United

---

21   Fan-Tan and Pak-Ah-Pu were gambling games, and therefore prima facie not un-Australian. However, as readers had no idea what they actually were, and they sounded suitably foreign, they were perfect for stoking fear and resentment.

States. Lane attacked the 'selfish rich', who 'cry down as unreliable the stories of Chinese outrages against women and children ... and deface the manhoods of their own race'. 'The Chinese must go,' Lane thundered, 'and their friends, these white traitors had better be flung out with them.'

Lane's obsession with the Chinese led him, in 1888, to write *White or Yellow? A Story of the Race-War of A.D. 1908*, a dystopian futuristic novel about Chinese immigrants overrunning Australia, with only a few heroic Anglo-Australian warriors standing in the way of a new southern Mongolian empire.

Writings of this kind both reflected and reinforced the Sinophobia that had found a voice in local Anti-Chinese Leagues, formed in 1886 to lobby politicians to exclude and expel the Chinese from Australia.

Lane and the *Bulletin*, however, saw no need to stop at the Chinese. Lane wrote he'd rather his daughter was 'dead in her coffin than kissing a black man on the mouth or nursing a little coffee-coloured brat that she was mother to'. The *Bulletin*, in its 2 July 1887 editorial, 'Australia for the Australians!', made it clear: 'No nigger, no Chinaman, no laksar, no kanaka ... is an Australian.' The following year, the *Bulletin*, now an opponent of all coloured immigration, adopted 'Australia for the Australians!' as its slogan.

Despite these tensions, Quong Tart's life was looking up. In 1886, he married Margaret Scarlett, who'd kept newspaper clippings of his escapades since she was a schoolgirl. Margaret's family erased her name from the family Bible, but Jack Want, the New South Wales attorney-general and a friend of Quong Tart, stood in for her absent father in giving her away on her wedding day. The newlyweds honeymooned in Ballarat, where the mayor and MPs staged a public banquet for them. Quong Tart gave a concert the following night, with Victoria's Scottish governor, Sir Henry Loch, listening to the honorary Scot murdering Highland ballads down a specially installed telephone line. Even the *Bulletin* wished the couple well, although it delivered a backhander in expressing 'tᵣ fervent hope that the lovely bride, though Tart in name, will never become Tart in nature'.

Quong Tart's tearooms were doing a roaring trade, and in 1887 he helped arrange a three-month tour of the colonies for two commissioners sent by the Qing emperor to inquire into the 'circumstances, commerce and condition' of Chinese residents in Australia – for which the emperor conferred on him the rank of Mandarin of the Crystal Button (apparently a big deal).

The commissioners received every diplomatic courtesy from New South Wales, South Australia and Victoria.[22] Queensland officials, however, refused to meet them. The press was also hostile, with the relatively staid *Sydney Morning Herald* accusing the commissioners of:

> [coming] to Australia, not only to discover how the Chinese who are already here are getting on, but with the object of paving the way for the arrival of others ... We have made up our minds not to be overrun by the Chinese or any other inferior race.

The commissioners' visit inflamed anti-Chinese sentiment, which ratcheted up further in early 1888 when China lodged a formal protest that the colonies' anti-Chinese laws were inconsistent with the Britain–China treaty that guaranteed Chinese freedom of movement throughout the British Empire. Edmund Barton, the one-time cricket umpire turned politician, dubbed Toby Tosspot by the *Bulletin* for his love of a drink or six, responded that this was a nonsense and that the Australian people had the right to 'preserve the soil of Australia for the Anglo-Saxon race'.

---

22 The Melbourne Club made the commissioners honorary members, even though Chinese, Catholics and Jews were excluded from the club, the latter being particularly problematic when Benjamin Benjamin became Melbourne's first Jewish lord mayor in 1887. Today, the Melbourne Club only excludes women.

ırkes asked Britain to enter into a new treaty with
ıich China would agree to block its citizens from
ıy part of Australasia. However, in April 1888, before
ımatic progress had been made, the Victorian government
prevented the SS *Afghan* from unloading its Hong Kong passengers,
alleging most carried forged British papers. Victorian law provided
that Chinese could enter the colony if they paid a £10 tax, but the
collector of customs, Mr Musgrove, simply refused to collect it, having been instructed by his minister that refusal of payment was now
government policy.[23] Chinese passengers on another ship were placed
in quarantine, pending deportation, after Premier Duncan Gillies
falsely claimed they'd come from infected ports.

The *Afghan* sailed for Sydney. Its arrival, along with three other
Chinese passenger vessels, caused 5,000 protestors to storm the New
South Wales parliament. A shaken Parkes gave a written guarantee
that the passengers would not be unloaded in New South Wales,
ignoring the legal rights of those with proper papers.

Parkes recognised he didn't have time to wait for a diplomatic
solution and, submitting to the will of the mob, rushed the Chinese

---

23 Mr Ah Toy sued Musgrove for not accepting his £10 and letting him enter Victoria,
insisting that the government and its officials needed to comply with their own
laws. The government argued the queen didn't have to comply with Victorian
laws, which meant her Victorian representative, the governor, didn't have to
either – and, as the minister exercised the delegated powers of the governor,
he could do whatever the hell he wanted and Musgrove had to obey his orders.
The government was appalled when the majority of judges found it was obliged
to comply with Victorian law and that government ministers were responsible
to the parliament that made those laws. While South Australia had provided for
responsible government in its Constitution, this was the first time an Australian
court had held a government accountable to its parliament and its people –
a principle later enshrined in the Australian Constitution. A pissed-off Chinese
person had transformed Australian constitutional arrangements – but it did him
no good, as he'd been deported before the decision was handed down. This relieved
Justice Williams, who expressed regret at the precedent he'd helped set: '... it leaves
us in this most unpleasant and invidious position, that we are at present without
the legal means of preventing the scum or desperadoes of alien nationalities from
landing on our territory whenever it may suit them to come here.'

Restriction Bill through the Legislative Assembly, arguing that if New South Wales was 'to maintain the fabric of its liberties ... it cannot admit into its population any element that of necessity must be of an inferior nature and character'.

When the Legislative Council refused to be rushed and the Supreme Court found that the government was illegally detaining immigrants who had a right to enter New South Wales, 40–50,000 protestors gathered in the Domain to demand Chinese exclusion.[24] The Council ultimately passed the bill, which increased the Chinese poll tax from £10 to £100, reduced by two-thirds the number of Chinese immigrants ships could carry, prevented Chinese from being granted citizenship in the colony and banned Chinese mining.

Quong Tart, serving as Parkes' intermediary, convinced passengers who'd meanwhile arrived without the correct papers to accept Parkes' offer of work on an offshore plantation.[25] Alternatively, they could return to Hong Kong, with the cost of their passage refunded.

In June 1888, New South Wales hosted the Intercolonial Conference on the Chinese Question, during which the white residents of the Queensland town of Normanton responded to the alleged murder of three whites by a Malay sailor by burning all the houses, businesses, boats and fishing equipment of the town's non-white residents, who were then arrested 'for their own protection' and dumped on Thursday Island, where many were forced to work as pearl shellers in slave-like

---

24   The Parkes government argued that passengers weren't detained, as they'd voluntarily boarded the *Afghan* and were at liberty to disembark anywhere except New South Wales. It also argued that it could expel any foreigner it liked, or detain a foreigner for the purpose of expelling them, in the absence of any law conferring such powers. The Supreme Court threw out these arguments, but Parkes was vindicated in 2001, when the Federal Court accepted them in ruling that the Australian government could prevent would-be immigrants aboard the MV *Tampa* from disembarking on Australian soil. In both the *Afghan* and *Tampa* cases, the government retrospectively validated any unlawful acts it may have committed.

25   A precursor to Manus Island.

conditions.[26] A number of newspapers reported that the Normanton murder victims were killed as 'a blood sacrifice' at the culmination of a Malay festival, and a packed courtroom erupted in cheers when the Normantonians charged with burning out the foreigners were all acquitted.

Against this backdrop, the Conference resolved that 'the further restriction of Chinese immigration is essential to the welfare of the people of Australasia'. The colonies were to lower the number of Chinese immigrants per ship to a level that would make transporting them economically unviable, and South Australia was to extend its Chinese restrictions to the Chinese-dominated Northern Territory. The Conference also resolved to prevent Chinese residents from moving between the Australian colonies without government approval. Victoria, South Australia and Western Australia followed New South Wales' lead in prohibiting Chinese naturalisation.

The resolutions of the Intercolonial Conference were drafted by Alfred Deakin, who didn't share the prevailing sentiment that the Chinese were a lesser race. Deakin's support for Chinese exclusion was based on his beliefs that most white Australians couldn't live harmoniously with coloured people and that Australian unity was necessary to progress Australian nationhood. Deakin's resolutions were the foundations of the White Australia policy he would later champion.

SONS OF THE SOUTH

For Alfred Deakin, Australian nationhood was a step on the path to Imperial Federation.

The Imperial Federation League, which established branches throughout the British Empire in 1884, called for an 'Imperial Federal

---

26 Thursday Island was a postcursor to the precursor to Manus Island. Australians' enthusiasm for dumping unwanted immigrants on islands has remained undimmed to this day.

Government', comprising representatives of Britain and its colonies, to be responsible for imperial foreign affairs, trade and defence. Australia and other imperial states would otherwise run their own affairs, although those with a majority-coloured population would be subject to greater federal oversight.[27]

A spirit had earlier prophesied that Deakin would be sent to London to appear before a great tribunal that would deal with the interests of Victoria, Australia and the British Empire. And lo, it came to pass that the thirty-year-old Deakin led the Victorian delegation to the Colonial Conference of 1887, which doubled as an official celebration of the fiftieth anniversary of Queen Victoria's rule.

Deakin was the only Australian-born conference attendee and he proceeded to do what Australians do best – get right up the noses of the Brits. He particularly irritated Britain's prime minister, Lord Salisbury (a.k.a. Robert Cecil), who lived by the conservative credo, 'Whatever happens will be for the worse, and therefore it is in our interest that as little should happen as possible.' Salisbury's suffering at the hands of bullies at Eton had given him a low opinion of humanity, which fed his dislike of democracy. He once said of politicians' constituents, 'It's a pity you can't carry around a powder pesticide to get rid of vermin of that kind.'

---

27   Edward Cole supported both Australian and Imperial Federation, but didn't think they went far enough. He wanted 'the Federation of the World', believing 'the spread of education and literature' and improvements to transport and communication would make 'the Brotherhood of Man' inevitable by 2000 A.D. He presciently predicted, 'A network of railways, telegraphs, telephones, and later inventions will cover the entire earth, bringing nearer together, associating, and fraternizing all nations,' and 'Flying machines will be in general use, passing and re-passing over every spot on earth.' There would be an end to war; one world religion; English, supplemented by the best words of other tongues, would be the world language; 'universal suffrage will prevail' and the 'reasonable rights of women will be established throughout the world'. Cole, atypical of Australians, wanted an end to 'the enmities of races', although he predicted, 'All savage and barbarous races will be subjugated by more advanced nations, civilized, and then, like-grown-up children, allowed the rights of equals.'

Salisbury also had a low opinion of Victorians, about whom he'd written bitchy things while slumming it on the colony's goldfields thirty-five years earlier.[28] Deakin had a similarly low opinion of Salisbury. He wrote of his encounter with the prime minister as if he were having one of his out-of-body experiences:

> Deakin ... broke quite new ground not only with unrestrained vigour and enthusiasm ... but because he did so in a more spirited manner, challenging Lord Salisbury's arguments one by one and mercilessly analysing the inconsistencies of his speech ... Lord Salisbury several times stared at the speaker, as well he might, in considerable amazement at his plain speaking and in some discomfort at the stern debating retorts to his inharmonious contentions.

Deakin wanted Britain to provide the Australian colonies with warships, which the colonies would crew and maintain. An Australian navy would help the colonies assert their rights over the New Hebrides and other Pacific islands, and keep the French and Germans at bay. Deakin quipped that although 'we are a remarkably pacific people, we intend to be masters of the Pacific'.[29]

Deakin and the other Australian delegates got their wish on the ships, and Salisbury said Britain wouldn't surrender its Pacific territories, but neither would it countenance military conflict with France. The warmongering Australians, complained Salisbury, were 'the most unreasonable people I have ever heard or dreamt of'.

Still, Deakin's get-up-and-go impressed Britain's colonial secretary, Sir Henry Holland, with Deakin claiming Sir Henry 'has fallen in love with me as other elders have done'. The increasingly egotistical

---

28 Salisbury was a champion whinger, whose complaints about Australian people, · drunkenness, violence, punctuality, literacy, roads, horses and property prices are detailed in *True Girt*.

29 Deakin's zingers remained unrivalled in Australian political history until the advent of Bill Shorten.

Victorian schmoozed and hobnobbed with all the right people, finally realising that being a teetotaller was a political liability. He abandoned abstinence and embraced claret, but remained sober enough to rebuff the advances of garden designer Maria Theresa Earle and the daughter of the Earl of Carnarvon. He also turned down the offer of a knighthood, later explaining, 'Titles don't grow out of a man or a woman – they are stuck on from the outside, and are always artificial and often ridiculous.'

His refusal to accept imperial honours, unlike the turncoat Parkes, further cemented his reputation with the Australian Natives' Association (ANA) and the *Bulletin*, which claimed that Australians who accepted knighthoods were 'in the scale of creation beneath a formless, organless, boneless, stomachless, brainless polyp'.

The *Bulletin*, though, was a staunch opponent of Imperial Federation. Its famous 'Australia for the Australians!' editorial rhetorically asked:

> What similarity of race or aspirations exists between Australians, Burmese, Hindoos, Chinese, Maltese, and the hundred or so distinct peoples which combine to make up the heterogeneous Empire known as the British? If England cannot convince Ireland that the two countries have an identity of interests, how much less can she convince us that the centre of political gravity is London?'

While the ANA defined Australians with reference to birthplace and colour, the *Bulletin* took a more nuanced, and arguably crazy, view:

> By the term Australian we mean not those who have been merely born in Australia. All white men who come to these shores – with a clean record – and who leave behind them the memory of the class distinctions and the religious differences of the old world; all men who place the happiness, the prosperity, the advancement of their adopted country before the interests of Imperialism, are Australian ... all men who leave the tyrant-ridden lands of Europe for freedom

of speech and right of personal liberty are Australians before they
set foot on the ship which brings them hither. Those who fly from
an odious military conscription; those who leave their fatherland
because they cannot swallow the worm-eaten lie of the divine right
of kings to murder peasants, are Australian by instinct – Australian
and Republican are synonymous.

Australia might one day be a state, but Australian was a state of mind.

Sir Henry Parkes proposed an even narrower definition of an Australian: a person from New South Wales. In 1887, he introduced a law
to rename New South Wales Australia. In part, this was to assert New
South Wales' primacy among the Australian colonies in the lead-up
to the 1888 centenary celebrations, but mainly he did it to piss off the
Victorians. Victoria's premier, Duncan Gillies, rose to the bait like
a saltwater croc to a Japanese tourist, snapping that another colony
should go 'one higher still' and call itself 'the Southern Hemisphere',
while a quicker wit suggested that New South Wales might instead
rename itself Convictoria. Parkes' law went nowhere, but he had some
fun with it.

Parkes, who'd flirted with republicanism early in his political career,
now rejected it.[30] He therefore clashed with Thomas Walker, who'd
moved on from setting fire to Canadians and performing blackface
plays to become New South Wales' most prominent republican MP.
Walker and the radical labour propagandist John Norton, the self-
styled 'bastard son of a parson' and a madwoman, had been involved
in republicans infiltrating a 3 June 1887 public meeting to plan events
for Queen Victoria's Golden Jubilee. The meeting's organisers had
put forward a resolution that all of Sydney's Sunday-school children
be invited to a grand fete to celebrate the monarch's reign, but the
republicans successfully amended it to read:

---

30   Think Malcolm Turnbull with a beard and a spine.

That, in the opinion of this meeting, the proposal to impress upon the children of the colony the value of the Jubilee year of a Sovereign is unwise and calculated to injure the democratic spirit of the country.

The mayor of Sydney, Alban Riley, hurriedly closed the meeting and arranged for a second gathering, open only to those carefully screened monarchists able to produce an invitation. Norton simply forged invitations for his fellow republicans, who again disrupted the meeting as Riley and Parkes looked on helplessly.

Twelve thousand people attended the third meeting on 15 June 1887, the largest public meeting Sydney had seen. Mayor Riley kicked off proceedings by presenting a petition signed by 15,000 people who'd declared their loyalty to the queen. The republicans responded by cheering 'Mrs John Brown', a reference to Victoria's rumoured relationship with her Scots servant. Parkes successfully rescinded the earlier resolution passed by the republicans, whom he labelled 'a clique of seditious and cowardly tyrants', while political up-and-comer Edmund Barton accused the republicans of denying the Jubilee planners the 'liberty of speech'. Some of the attending republicans were assaulted. The Empire had struck back.

Louisa Lawson was fired up by the Jubilee meetings. With the financial backing of Thomas Walker, she published the *Republican* under the pseudonym Archie Lawson. Louisa encouraged her now twenty-year-old son Henry, odd-jobbing as a house painter, to write for her paper. While Henry avoided speaking, his pen was his tongue and he used it to lash 'landlordism, the title-worship, the class distinctions and privileges, the oppression of the poor, the monarchy, and all the dust-covered customs that England has humped out of the middle ages where she properly belongs.' The *Republican* also published Henry's 'A Neglected History', in which he damned schools for teaching children about distant kings and queens while ignoring Australia's past. And, just for good measure, Henry decided to have a crack at poetry:

Sons of the South, awake! arise!
Sons of the South, and do.
Banish from under your bonny skies
Those old-world errors and wrongs and lies.
Making a hell in a Paradise
That belongs to your sons and you.

Sons of the South, make choice between
(Sons of the South, choose true),
The Land of Morn and the Land of E'en,
The Old Dead Tree and the Young Tree Green,
The Land that belongs to the lord and the Queen,
And the Land that belongs to you.
.....
Sons of the South, aroused at last!
Sons of the South are few!
But your ranks grow longer and deeper fast,
And ye shall swell to an army vast,
And free from the wrongs of the North and Past
The land that belongs to you.

Henry rushed into the *Bulletin*'s office and gave 'Sons of the South'
to the newspaper's surprised cleaning woman, before rushing off
again. He couldn't bear the thought of his work being rejected by
one of the *Bulletin*'s manly, self-assured editors.

He needn't have worried. An excited Archibald felt he'd discovered a Sydney Springsteen or Down-Under Dylan who'd rouse the
masses to revolution. Archibald renamed Henry's poem 'A Song of
the Republic' and, for once, decided he'd publish something under
an author's real name – although he'd talk up Henry's 'imperfect
education' and working-class background, and shave three years off
his age so Henry could be marketed as a boy genius.

Henry's second *Bulletin* poem, 'The Wreck of the "Derry Castle"', was about the foundering of a wheat ship out of Geelong and the drowning of most of its crew. Its verses included:

> *Pray for souls of ghastly, sodden*
> *Corpses, floating round untrodden*
> *Cliffs, where nought but sea-drift strays;*
> *Souls of dead men, in whose faces*
> *Of humanity no trace is —*
> *Not a mark to show their races —*
> *Floating round for days and days.*

Scratch Dylan or Springsteen – the kid was more Nick Cave – and tragedy, misery and hardship would become his stock in trade.

7
Pride and the Fall

I saw bank booms, land booms, silver booms, Northern Territory booms,
and they all had one thing in common — they always burst.

Banjo Paterson, *The Sydney Morning Herald*, 1939

PARTY LIKE IT'S 1888

THE CENTENARY OF NEW SOUTH WALES' SETTLEMENT by Britain was met by an outpouring of patriotic fervour. On 24 January 1888, a crowd of 50,000 gathered in Sydney to watch the governor, Lord Carrington, unveil yet another bloody statue of the Queen.[1] Most of the revels, however, had a more Australian feel. The emphasis was less on the act of settlement, and more on the manner in which the settlers had survived, and then thrived, over the following hundred years.

On 26 January, Sir Henry Parkes marked the anniversary by opening Centennial Park on swamplands that Sydney's unemployed had been press-ganged to drain and clear for the occasion, a forerunner to the Howard government's Work for the Dole program.[2]

---

1   Charles Robert Carington was titled Lord Carrington, his title coming with an extra 'r' because that's the sort of incomprehensible thing British aristocrats do. He was assisted by aide-de-camp Lord Montague Peregrine Albemarle Bertie, who distinguished himself from his father, Lord Montagu Bertie, by having an extra 'e' added to his first name. Carington and Bertie are prime examples of the sort of gormless *Tatler* garden-party refugees that the Brits used to foist on us.

2   Sydneysiders celebrate every hundred years of British settlement by building a park on the nearest shithole. In 1988, Bicentennial Park was opened on a

Parkes had rejected the suggestion that Aboriginal people might be invited to the opening party, retorting, 'And remind them we have robbed them?' However, Sydney's non-Aboriginal poor were welcomed to 'the people's park' with free hampers of bread, cheese, meat, vegetables and tobacco, while a thousand assorted worthies from across the colonies retired to Government House to enjoy a seven-course banquet, washed down with three French champagnes, two French clarets, and various lesser wines, sherries, ports and liqueurs, some of which were even local.[3] There were bands, fireworks, boat races and an intercolonial cricket exhibition.

The centenary was very much an intercolonial affair, with sporting events held across the continent – the most novel being an ANA-sponsored battle-of-the-sexes cricket match in Brisbane, in which the ladies played with broomsticks instead of bats (the gentlemen chivalrously let the ladies win).

Victoria, for the first time, held a public holiday on 26 January. This brought it into line with New South Wales, which held its Anniversary Day on that date, and met a key demand of the ANA, which reasoned that the colonies' acknowledgement of a common past would help them embrace a common future. However, it insisted on adopting a different name for the precursor to Australia Day – Foundation Day – which more explicitly linked the celebration to the act of colonisation. The other colonies also agreed to hold a public holiday on the centenary, except convict-free South Australia, which was reluctant to celebrate the foundation of a prison state.[4]

---

former rubbish dump filled with toxic chemicals, petroleum waste, asbestos and unexploded ordnance.

3   As much as the British and Australians despised the French, they acknowledged that France produced superior wines and cuisine. The menu for the banquet was in French, as was fashionable among Australia's foodanistas, with *Gelée a l'Australienne* the only dish that suggested Australians might have learned to cook something in the preceding hundred years.

4   The first 'Australia Day' was an Irish celebration of the release of an Italian pope by a French emperor after a German battle, which says a lot about Australian

Victoria also ran with Alfred Deakin's idea to stage a Centennial
International Exhibition, with Premier Gillies writing to his New
South Wales counterpart, Patrick Jennings, in 1886:

> Victoria could aid you, and contribute to your success, may I not
> say our joint success, for we too have an interest in the memorable
> events you will celebrate, as it marked the beginning of our Australian
> history as well as yours. What at present you want we have – a grand
> exhibition building ...

The Victorians just couldn't pass up the opportunity to remind
New South Wales that its Garden Palace had burned down in 1882.[5]
Still, they gave New South Wales the central court in the main exhibition building for a display of the mother colony's history. Victoria's
court, in contrast, looked to the future, with its machines and manufactured goods lit by the largest installation of electric arc lighting
the world had ever seen.[6]

---

multiculturalism. It was sponsored by Sydney's Irish Catholic church leaders
and held on 24 May 1911, the Empire Day public holiday, as the Irish didn't want
to celebrate the British Empire. The Catholics liked 24 May as a national day
because it was the feast day of the Virgin Mary Our Lady Help of Christians, the
Patron Saint of Australia. That feast day celebrates the return of Pope Pius VII
to Rome on 24 May 1814, after his arrest by Napoleon. The pope attributed his
release, and the defeat of Napoleon at the Battle of Leipzig that preceded it, to the
intercession of Our Lady. The second 'Australia Day', was held on 30 July 1915 as
a state-supported Red Cross Society fundraiser for servicemen injured in World
War I. The ANA lobbied for Foundation Day, or ANA Day, as it was sometimes
known, to be rebranded as Australia Day in 1930. Victoria held the first modern
Australia Day in 1931, with the other states following by 1935 (although New South
Wales clung to calling it Anniversary Day for a while). The Australian states and
territories didn't all recognise 26 January as Australia Day until 1946, or all hold
a public holiday on that day until 1994. People who believe changing our national
day is an affront to tradition have short memories.

5   Parkes had realised his dream of bettering the London Exhibition's Crystal Palace,
     which took until 1936 to burn down. Some historians speculate that prominent
     New South Welshmen may have paid arsonists to torch the Garden Palace, as it
     contained convict records that could embarrass them.

6   New South Wales got one up on Victoria later in 1888, when rural Tamworth
     became the first place in Australia to install electric street lighting.

The southern entrance to the Exhibition drew visitors' attention to the wealth of Australia as a whole, with a giant gilt obelisk representing 'in bulk the total quantity of gold raised in the Australasian colonies from the first discovery to the 31st December 1887'. This was a gleaming one-fingered salute to the continent's impoverished past, when Britain outlawed a domestic currency, suppressed trade and discouraged the production of wealth. It was vulgar. It was brash. It was very Australian.

Parkes, who was sulking that Victoria had stolen an event that was rightfully New South Wales', was the only Australian premier to miss its opening, preferring to visit Darlinghurst Gaol instead. The *Bulletin* sniped, 'After all, when you come to think of it, 'twas a much more appropriate way of celebrating the Centenary.'

Archibald's rag had labelled the New South Wales festivities 'a feeble, fifth-rate drunk – a sort of combined scalp-dance and gin conversazione – in honour of the meanest event in her short history', 'the day she was lagged' (i.e. sent to prison). Now it attacked the celebration of Anniversary Day:

> Australia began her political history as a crouching serf kept in subjection by the whip of a ruffian gaoler, and her progress, so far, consists merely in a change of masters. Instead of a foreign slave-driver, she has a foreign admiral; the loud-mouthed tyrant has given place to the suave hireling in uniform ... Rather than 'the day we were lagged', Australia's national day should be December 3, the anniversary of the Eureka rebellion, 'the day that Australia set her teeth in the face of the British Lion'.

The *Bulletin*, with its republican ideals and admiration of the United States, wanted Australians to have their own Boston Tea Party – a defining moment in the struggle against British rule. A bunch of tax-evading miners armed with medieval weapons and theatre props, who hid in a DIY fort and were shot up by troopers before some of their leaders escaped in drag, was as close as Australia got to revolution-ary uprising. These men, including the ones dressed as women, were models of Australian masculinity, joining the bushman to form the master stock in which Australian identity simmered.

While the *Bulletin* saw the partying as 'empty and artificial glee', Australians had a lot to celebrate. They earned and spent more than any people on earth, their workers enjoyed more leisure time, food was plentiful and cheap, and the gap between rich and poor was narrower than in more established societies, where inequities had become entrenched.

Immigration (white) had boomed during the 1880s, with an influx of families and young women ending a century of gender imbalance. Australian women were, on average, squeezing out six kids, with this impressive 'Double Costello' ensuring the colonies' native-born (white) population outnumbered immigrants for the first time.[7] By 1888, more than three million people called Australia home, with the growing population driving an economic boom that had lasted for decades, except in the backwaters of Tasmania and Western Australia.

Melbourne grew by 75 per cent during the 1880s, its 420,000 people in 1888 making it one of the largest cities in the British Empire, and larger than all but three US cities. Victoria's Parliament House was the grandest in the Empire, outside Westminster, its ballroom intentionally designed to be larger than Buckingham Palace's. New hydraulic lifts – far superior to Sydney's clunky exhibition elevator – birthed skyscrapers, with Melbourne joining Chicago and New York as the world's first high-rise metropolises. In 1888, construction began on a 46-metre-tall building, which Melburnians claimed was the highest in the world.[8]

---

7   In 2002, Treasurer Peter Costello launched the Howard government's 'Fucking for Growth' policy, which provided financial incentives for Australian families to have more babies. Each family, Costello urged, should 'have one for Mum, one for Dad and one for the country'. Australian women in the 1880s were more patriotic than their modern counterparts, having four kids for the country.

8   It was probably the third highest. Melburnians talked bigger than their buildings.

Edward Cole, the pie seller turned crank religious author and bookseller, presided over the world's largest bookstore. Cole's Book Arcade featured an entrance flanked by mechanical men, giant mirrors and ornate brass columns, bustling staff in brilliant scarlet jackets, wind-up toys, curios from around the world, and an art gallery, band and sideshows. (Cole later added a fernery, a 'Smiling Gallery' of funny mirrors, a 'Black Man Who Turned White', and cages of monkeys and talking birds.)[9]

'Marvellous Melbourne', as it was dubbed by a British journalist, was a world city, admired by the increasing number of foreign businessmen and entertainers who visited it. And Melbourne was putting Australia on the global map in other ways, too. In 1888, Helen Mitchell, who'd adopted the name Nellie Melba in honour of her hometown, was the leading soprano at London's Covent Garden, while lawyer Fergusson Wright Hume's 1886 *The Mystery of a Hansom Cab*, a murder mystery that explored the seamy underbelly of Melbourne's Little Bourke Street, was the world's bestselling detective novel of the nineteenth and early twentieth centuries.[10]

---

9   Cole is today best remembered for *Cole's Funny Picture Book*, which included 'funny' stories, poems, jokes, puzzles and cartoons (including a frankly worrying one of 'Cole's Patent Whipping Machine for Flogging Naughty Boys in School'). In 1889, Cole also became briefly infamous for Cole's smutty words books, after Alfred Deakin ordered raids on booksellers suspected of stocking the racy French novels of Émile Zola. Cole was found to have imported 162 French novels of the kind that Deakin had ordered be seized at the border, the start of Australia's use of Customs to restrict obscene publications. The *Daily Telegraph*, a supporter of such censorship, sermonised, 'Are we prepared to allow the more subtle and deadly infection of French literary vice to be emptied upon our bookstalls, and into the imaginations of our children?' Cole destroyed the books to avoid prosecution.

10 Hume self-published after Melbourne publishers 'refused even to look at the manuscript on the ground that no Colonial could write anything worth reading'. He then sold the rights to a group of Australian speculators for £50 and received nothing for the more than 750,000 copies that subsequently sold. *The Mystery of a Hansom Cab* and its protagonist, Detective Gorby, 'who looked keenly round the room, and his estimate of the dead man's character was formed at once', reputedly inspired Sir Arthur Conan Doyle to write the Sherlock Holmes novels, with *A Study in Scarlet* published a year after Hume's work.

Sydney, with its stately sandstone buildings and 360,000 people, was also a truly global city. The populations of the other colonial capitals ranged from Perth's 9,000 to Adelaide's 115,000.[11] And nearly all of those people were obsessed with real estate.

Throughout the world, property rights being the preserve of the few seemed as natural as the sun rising in the east – but in egalitarian Australia, even the poorest aspired to home ownership. The *Australasian Building Societies and Mortgage Companies' Gazette* seductively cooed, 'Every owner of property is a better citizen, and the feeling such proprietorship gives him is one to be envied.'

In European cities, several generations might be crammed into a tiny apartment, but Australians were all about upsizing. Between 1861 and 1891, the average number of rooms in an Australian city house rose from three to five, and for those who'd moved to the new suburbs, a substantial garden was no longer an idle pipedream, but a must-have. The land of sweeping plains had become the land of quarter-acre blocks.

Australians invested their savings in residential property, supported by easy credit from new building societies and land banks (private real estate investment schemes) fattened on British capital. Property values soared, with investors driven into a frenzy by the ever-increasing capital gains on offer. Melbourne's flash elevators allowed landowners to build up, contributing to the rapid tripling of Melbourne land values. As demand for property increased, owners cashed in by subdividing their land and property speculators swarmed the market. An 1886 *Table Talk* article noted:

> The previous summer about 100,000 allotments were sold. Melbourne's population stands at about 65,000 households. So if every household moved out of its existing dwelling right now, there would still be 35,000 allotments to spare.

---

11 Adelaide distinguished itself by being the only Australian city to have a sewer system, its citizens being expert at digging underground chambers in which to hide each other's bodies.

By 1890, almost half of building society loans were for speculatively built houses. Alfred Deakin raked it in as chairman of the City of Melbourne Building Society and a director of four property speculation companies.

Deakin also speculated with public money. He oversaw the Centennial International Exhibition, which cost almost ten times the budgeted amount, and approved Victoria taking out its largest-ever loan to build more railways. But money wasn't a problem – Victoria's 1888 budget had produced the colony's biggest surplus to date. The good times, Deakin reassured parliamentary debt hawks, would keep on rolling.

Deakin's family life mirrored the fortunes of his colony. Pattie was devoted to him and his career; he doted on his two young daughters, Ivy and Stella; sister Kate was always around, helping Ivy with her music and letters; and his beloved parents lived nearby.

The spirits had blessed Alfred Deakin.

THE BANJO AND THE BREAKER

Andrew Barton Paterson's father had joined the spirits in 1889, his cause of death an 'overdose of opium (laudanum) ... accentuated by continued heavy drinking' – but Paterson, ever the optimist, wasn't going to let this get in the way of him having a good time.

Paterson led a charmed life. Few were aware he was The Banjo – Sydney society knew him as a successful lawyer, the fiancé of the elegant Sarah Ann Riley, a keen track athlete and amateur rider at Sydney Turf Club meets, and a 'front rank [tennis] player in New South Wales', who played equally well right- and left-handed.[12]

12　In the nineteenth century, all tennis in Australia was played on grass, with lawn tennis an elitist sport. The later introduction of clay courts opened the game to the broader population. In most parts of Australia, clay courts are known as ant bed courts, although in Victoria they are known as en-tout-cas (in any case), conclusively proving that Victorians are wankers.

While poetry would remain his staple, The Banjo turned his hand to prose, as the *Bulletin* was seeking short stories to fill unsold advertising space. It was writing by numbers, with stories commissioned by the column inch. Character development, plot and pace were determined by whether or not the latest shipment of 'DR SCOTT'S ELECTRIC CORSET (A Great Boon to Delicate Ladies)' had hit the shelves.

High on Aussie vernacular, low on plot, The Banjo's scribblings were more sketch than story. He debuted with 'Hughey's Dog', the tale of a station butcher and his fighting dog Stumpy, which was killed, skinned and hung in the meat house by the station's Dutch cook. In 'The Cast-Iron Canvasser', two publishers respond to country folk attacking their door-to-door book salesmen by replacing their salesmen with a robot that fights back and ends up drowning a local policeman. Death, violence, threats and deception were common themes in The Banjo's stories, but his tales were not tragedies – they were light comedies written for men who liked horses, sport, drinking and fighting.

Paterson's poetry had more emotional range, but talking up the bush and deprecating the city remained his trademarks. An 1889 stay with the Mitchell brothers in the Snowy Mountains, during which he encountered Jack Riley, a weather-beaten brumby hunter and horse-breaker, helped cement The Banjo's popularity.[13]

'The Man from Snowy River', which drew heavily on Riley and the stories he told, didn't have the most auspicious beginning, being printed on page thirteen of an 1890 edition of the *Bulletin*, above an advertisement for 'Scott's Emulsion of Cod Liver Oil'. It was startlingly

---

13   During Paterson's visit to his station, Peter Mitchell asked his friend, 'Why should you not improve men?' A keen eugenicist who wanted to apply his horse-breeding skills to humans, Mitchell left £178,478 in his will to establish competitions to improve the white race, as he was 'keenly interested in the development of a vigorous manhood' to reduce 'the aggregate of human misery and suffering around the globe'. More assertive white men was the answer.

unoriginal – The Banjo didn't even take the time to steal someone else's plot, instead rehashing his own 'The Mylora Elopement', with a prize horse joining a mob of brumbies that are chased down by bushmen lashing their mounts, etc, etc. He also couldn't be arsed thinking up new characters: the poem's two named (non-horse) protagonists, Harrison and Clancy, were borrowed from his earlier 'Old Pardon, the Son of Reprieve' and 'Clancy of the Overflow'. However, this story of the little guy on a little horse who outrode Clancy to single-handedly capture the brumbies connected with Australian readers.

The poem's hero is 'a stripling on a small and weedy beast' – literally a little Aussie battler. So is his 'hardy mountain pony', which, typical of Paterson's plucky mounts, gets off on being spurred into blood-soaked exhaustion. The poem concludes, 'The man from Snowy River is a household word to-day/ And the stockmen tell the story of his ride.' Yet he is never named, and never says a word – an everyman who is instinctive action personified. You can't get more 'Strayan than that.

Paterson himself, according to Norman Lindsay, 'preferred to consort with men of action' and 'did not care to mix with writers or artists or other self-elected intellectuals'.[14] And so his interest in horses and men who sweated testosterone inevitably brought him into contact with, in Paterson's words, 'a bronzed, clean-shaven man of about thirty, well set up, with the quick walk of a man used to getting on young horses, clear, confident eyes, radiating health and vitality'. This was Harry Harbord Morant, pen-name 'The Breaker' – the 'horse-breaker, drover, steeplechaser, polo player, drinker and womanizer' who in 1891 started writing bush poems for the *Bulletin*.

Edwin Henry Murrant, the son of an English workhouse master, had arrived in Queensland in 1883. He moved from station to station, generally when asked to repay money he'd borrowed. He convinced the

---

14   This is not strictly true. It's just that Paterson didn't hang out with Lindsay, who was a creepy little perve.

Reverend Barlow to perform his marriage to an Irish station governess, Daisy O'Dwyer, on credit – claiming to be a gentleman awaiting
his remittance. Barlow never saw a penny and Daisy was forced to
return Murrant's gifts, which he had neglected to pay for. A month
after the wedding, Murrant was tried for stealing pigs. Although he
was acquitted, Daisy left him.[15]

Murrant's first known use of the name Harry Harbord Morant was
on a cheque that bounced. As Morant, the young conman claimed to
be the son of Admiral Sir George Digby Morant, a connection he used
to gain entry into the social circles and wallets of respectable men.

Paterson's poem 'Jim Carew', likely modelled on Morant, recounted
the life of a charming, athletic English rogue who found work as a stockman, living hard and fast before falling into alcoholic despair. It ends:

> *Such is the end of the ne'er-do-well –*
> *Jimmy the Boozer, all down at heel;*
> *But he straightens up when he's asked to tell*
> *His name and race, and a flash of steel*
> *Still lightens up in those eyes of blue –*
> *'I am, or -- no, I was -- Jim Carew.'*

Still, Morant was good fun, and Paterson, rode, hunted and played
polo with him.

In 1895, The Banjo released *The Man from Snowy River and Other
Verses*. With his famous 1890 poem as a centrepiece, the book was

---

15   After two further unsuccessful marriages, a return to Britain, and a stint editing the
     psychic quarterly *Borderlands*, Daisy returned to Australia with a commission from
     the *Times* to report on the mistreatment of Aboriginal people in Western Australia.
     Daisy Bates, as she was then known, became a world-renowned ethnographer who
     lived among Aboriginal people for the next several decades, writing *The Passing of
     the Aborigines* and the grammatically correct and politically incorrect *My Natives
     and I*. She was a staunch defender of tribal Aboriginal people, whom she considered
     a dying race, but was vehemently opposed to interracial unions, writing, 'with very
     few exceptions, the only good half-caste is a dead one.' With friends like Daisy
     Bates, Australia's First Nations people didn't need enemies.

declared by the *Oxford Companion to Australian Literature* to be 'the most successful volume of poetry ever published in Australia'. It even earned the praise (faint) of Rudyard Kipling, the British literary titan Paterson would soon befriend.

Fortune had blessed Andrew Barton Paterson.

HOW THE WEST WAS WON

The partying that swept Australia in 1888 was more restrained in the west, which hadn't shared the eastern colonies' growth. Western Australia remained a Crown colony, its small population ruled by Britain and its man on the ground, Governor Sir Napier Broome. Its fire- and termite-prone wooden telegraph poles, strung with cheap wire, meant communications with the rest of the world regularly dropped out; its capital, lacking a dam, was plagued by waterborne diseases; and its second largest export, after wool, was bird shit.

Sir John Quick's 1901 *The Annotated Constitution of the Australian Commonwealth* (a surprisingly good read) perfectly summed up the purgatory that was Western Australia: 'For fifty years the history of the colony was uneventful except for the explorations of Major Warburton, Mr. Ernest Giles, and Mr. (afterwards Sir) John Forrest.'

Peter Egerton Warburton made the first crossing of the Great Sandy Desert in 1874, and Ernest Giles discovered routes across the Great Victoria and Gibson deserts between 1873 and 1876. Two guys walking across sand rated as among the most exciting things to happen in Western Australia – but neither guy made his mark on the west like John Forrest.

Forrest, the son of Scottish servants, was a surveyor. He'd led an 1869 expedition to search for the one-man Bermuda Triangle of Australian exploration, Ludwig Leichhardt. The following year, with brother Alexander, Forrest made the first Perth-to-Adelaide trek, setting the route for Western Australia's dodgy telegraph line. In 1874, he led the first west-to-east expedition through the western centre

of Australia, earning him acclaim during an 1875 visit to London as
'The Young Explorer', the nineteenth-century equivalent of fronting
a boy band (except the groupies were all old white men).

In 1879, Alexander Forrest explored the Kimberley and promoted
the area for grazing, leading Patrick Durack to drive 7,250 cattle
across the continent, a 5,000-kilometre trek that took twenty-eight
months and cost half the cattle (and a handful of drovers) their lives.
Still, Western Australia had a new industry, and John, promoted to
the positions of surveyor-general and commissioner of Crown lands,
was responsible for opening the Kimberley for business.

On Christmas Day in 1885, Charles Hall received the traditional
gift of gold (but lucked out on the frankincense and myrrh) when he
found an 870-gram nugget in the Kimberley creek that now bears his
name. Three years later, Thomas Risely and Mick Toomey followed
five stars, rather than the traditional one, to the Southern Cross goldfields, which they named after the guiding constellation. These finds
sparked short-lived gold rushes, boosting the colony's population.

Henry Lawson decided to try his luck in Western Australia, spending a few months odd-jobbing in Albany, interspersed with bouts of
drinking and writing. Like Paterson, he'd added short stories to his
repertoire. Unconstrained by rhyme or metre, Lawson found it even
easier to be miserable in prose.

The population surge that followed the discovery of gold led
Britain to grant Western Australia self-government, notwithstanding
House of Commons concerns about the wisdom of handing nearly
half a continent to 40,000 people. Britain required the governor to
nominate members of the colony's Legislative Council for the first
six years of self-government, or until the colony's settler population
reached 60,000. Governor Broome's support for home rule had been
conditional on setting aside 1 per cent of colonial revenue, or a minimum
£5,000 pounds a year, to feed, clothe and educate Aboriginal people.
Forrest and co reluctantly accepted this being built into Western Australia's new Constitution, seeing it as the price for greater autonomy.

The first Legislative Assembly elections were held in 1890, although Western Australians were slow to grasp the finer points of democracy. John Forrest was the sole candidate for the seat of Bunbury and was similarly unopposed in claiming the premiership and role of colonial treasurer. He saw no point in building a parliamentary faction, sacked cabinet members who disagreed with him, took on the additional role of colonial secretary, and ruled Western Australia, without any real opposition, for the remainder of its colonial existence.

Forrest didn't have the silver tongue, oily hands or vestigial spine commonly found in modern Australian politicians. He said what he thought and did what he said. While conservative by nature, he was a pragmatist, rolling out Deakinesque reforms to a constituency eager to taste the exotic freedoms of the liberal east.

Forrest had the money to bankroll his reforms after 1892, when Arthur Wellesley Bayley discovered gold at Coolgardie, in the arid interior. While this find had no apparent link to the Nativity, normal programming resumed the following year, when three wise men from the east discovered gold at Kalgoorlie, 40 kilometres north-west of Coolgardie.[16] The Golden Mile, as their find was known, became the richest square mile on earth.[17]

The Coolgardie and Kalgoorlie finds triggered a mega-rush. Most fortune-hunters were migrants from the eastern colonies, supplemented by old hands from the Californian goldfields. Western Australia reached the 60,000-population target for a fully elected government in 1893.

Resources also flooded into the colony, with hundreds of British companies investing in mining ventures. Twenty-three-year-old

---

16   Paddy Hannan, Tom Flanagan and Daniel Shea, Irish prospectors from the
      eastern colonies, encouraged the rest of their party to move on from the area of
      their find, claiming they needed to stay behind 'to look for a lost horse'. If this
      didn't demonstrate wisdom, it certainly showed a high degree of rat cunning.

17   It was lucky for Victorians that these finds were not made several years earlier, as
      they would have had to fork out for a much bigger obelisk.

American mining engineer Herbert Hoover recommended an English firm buy out the Welsh-backed Sons of Gwalia mine, and was
appointed its manager. In his first week, he increased work hours,
scrapped safety rules and abolished bonuses and double pay for Sunday work. He then imported cheap Italian and Slav labourers, free
of the taint of trade unionism. Hoover's American know-how and
bastardry made Sons of Gwalia and other Western Australian mines
he restructured the world's most successful goldmining operations.[18]

Hoover was forced to employ cheap European labour because
Forrest had excluded Chinese people from the goldfields.[19] The Japanese, however, were welcome, as the male-dominated mining towns
demanded prostitutes, and city girls were curiously unenthusiastic
about shagging dirty miners in the desert.[20] Kalgoorlie established a
separate red-light district, which respectable folk could avoid and the
police closely supervise, with the *karayuki-san* only allowed to leave
their brothels to visit the doctor or a hairdresser. This 'Containment
Policy', it was explained, was for their own protection.[21]

---

18   Hoover would go on to become the thirty-first president of the United States
      of America and take a keen interest in the construction of the mega-dam that
      bears his name. He would have approved of the dam's project managers cutting
      wages, abolishing paid lunch breaks and forcing work to continue in extreme
      temperatures, which resulted in sixteen workers dying from heat exhaustion.

19   In South Australia, Vaiben Solomon, recently elected as the Northern Territory's
      first representative in the South Australian parliament, led the charge to bar
      Chinese from mining or owning land in the Territory. The Territory's federal
      electorate of Solomon is named after Vaiben. It's surprising that cancel culture
      hasn't yet caught up with the Territory's leading Sinophobe and full blackbody
      Aboriginal impersonator and streaker.

20   Thankfully, modern Australian ladies are not so narrow-minded. Kalgoorlie
      now proudly advertises its Skimpies – clothing-limited ladies who escort
      mineworkers and pervy tourists into bars. The Skimpies were sadly shut
      down by Covid-19, with some transitioning to clothing-limited food
      delivery marketed as Boober Eats.

21   Queensland similarly imported Japanese prostitutes, largely for the benefit of
      its Pacific Islander workforce. Queensland police commissioner William Parry-
      Okeden explained, 'The supply of Japanese women for the Kanaka demand is
      less revolting and degrading than would be the case were it met by white women.'

Forrest borrowed against the colony's newfound mineral wealth to fund a massive infrastructure program, ordering the construction of a dam to end Perth's dysentery epidemic and hiring New Zealand whizz Charles Yelverton O'Connor as the colony's engineer-in-chief and general manager of government railways. O'Connor built a harbour at Fremantle that could berth any steamer, laid down miles of track and convinced Forrest to nationalise the colony's largest private railway.

Running steam trains to the desert mining towns was tricky, as deserts are, by definition, incompatible with the principal ingredient of steam. As Coolgardie grew into the colony's third-largest town, its situation became more dire, as water was also the principal ingredient of the beverages favoured by miners (beer) and Japanese prostitutes (green tea). O'Connor had a solution – the Coolgardie Water Supply Scheme would pipe over five million gallons of water a day from just outside Perth to Coolgardie, 528 kilometres away. This involved pumping the water 300 vertical metres over the Darling Ranges and building the world's tallest overflow dam and longest freshwater pipeline. O'Connor got to work.

There was one group of people who didn't share in Western Australia's success. Aboriginal people never received the food, clothing and education funding required by the Constitution, and Forrest secured British support to remove the requirement in 1897. They did, however, receive a surfeit of pastoralists, pipelayers, prospectors and prostitutes.

Conflict with the unwanted newcomers was greatest in the Kimberley, where Jandamarra, a Bunuba stockman and police tracker, killed his sleeping friend, fellow policeman Bill Richardson, during an 1894 operation that captured sixteen Bunuba. After releasing his countrymen, Jandamarra led a guerrilla campaign against the colonists. He was shot and beheaded in 1897, his preserved noggin sent

---

Australians should be proud that their government-sanctioned prostitution programs were all about protecting women.

to the English manufacturer of the rifle that killed him and used to promote the firearm's effectiveness.[22]

John Forrest's head remained very much in the game. As Western Australia's finances improved, so too did Forrest's, in no small part due to the kickbacks brother Alexander, now Perth's mayor, provided when Forrest's policies advanced his many commercial interests.[23] Forrest's marriage to Margaret Hamersley, the daughter of an establishment family, brought him additional business and social connections, and provided him with a loving and stable home that he valued more than power or riches.

God had blessed John Forrest.

THE MAN WHO LUNCHED A NATION

Sir Henry Parkes had less luck than Deakin, Paterson or Forrest with his personal life and finances, combining the two in calamitous fashion. It's hard to support a large family while paying for the upkeep of a mistress, her parents and two illegitimate kids.[24]

In 1881, Parkes had taken Bella Murray, his attractive 21-year-old step-granddaughter, as his companion on a nine-month tour of America and Europe, causing him to further fall out with his wife and daughters, who considered his behaviour a bit Woody Allenish. Bella had not helped the situation, telling one of Parkes' daughters, 'Your father loves me so much he has told me he would be glad to die so long as he

---

22 Another Bunuba person's head was put on display in Perth and labelled as Jandamarra's. Readers who want to learn more about displaying Aboriginal people's heads, or pickling or smoking them and posting them to Britain, can read the stories of the Appin Massacre and Aboriginal resistance leaders Pemulwuy and Yagan in *Girt* and *True Girt*.

23 The Western Australian power family's commercial interests have been further expanded by Andrew 'Twiggy' Forrest, the great-grandson of John and Alexander's otherwise uninteresting brother, David.

24 By 1890, he'd have another three kids with Nellie Dixon, further straining his wallet and Parkes family Christmas gatherings.

could do so in my company!' Parkes' son Varney was also distressed, as he'd married Bella's sister, but transferred his attentions to Bella after his wife's death. Parkes left wife Clarinda and moved in with mistress Nellie, while Varney married Bella. Parkes' life was *The Bold and the Beautiful* meets *Wife Swap*, with readings of *Hansard* during the ad breaks.

Parkes commenced his fourth premiership in 1887. For the first time in Australian history, politicians broke from voting on each issue according to conscience or self-interest in ever-shifting coalitions to form a relatively stable political bloc that united behind the cause of free trade. Parkes may not have had a political party, but he'd sent out the invitations and hired the clowns.

Parkes owed creditors an eye-popping £39,000 by 1887 – at a time when an £80 debt was cause to file for bankruptcy. The *Bulletin* accused him of trading government positions for personal loans, dubbing his ministry 'the I.O.U. Cabinet'. Parkes' friends ran a subscription fund to save him from ruin, but it was not enough to salvage his Blue Mountains home. He rented in Balmain, with Clarinda and two of his daughters joining him for the sake of propriety and financial necessity, although they remained estranged. Clarinda died a week after the centenary bash, her obese body unable to fit in her casket. An unhappy life had come to an undignified end.

Parkes married Nellie during the 1889 election campaign, without telling his family. His daughter Menie visited him, only to find her two sisters moving out as the newly installed Lady Parkes took charge of the house. Menie told her father his second marriage was 'the most sorrowfully disastrous mistake of your whole life'.

The *Bulletin*'s none-too-subtle reports on 'the little affair' of Parkes' marriage failed to dent his political appeal, with the septuagenarian swinger securing his fifth and final premiership – but this was not enough to secure respectability for Nellie, who was barred from Government House by Lord Carrington and excluded from polite society.

FIG. 7: LADY PARKES HAD TO BE STABLED WHENEVER SIR HENRY VISITED GOVERNMENT HOUSE.

Parkes had bigger concerns. While the New South Wales economy continued to thrive, his government was weighed down by debt, forcing him to take an axe to the public service. This did not stop Louisa Lawson dropping in to seek a government post for her son, Henry, given Parkes' history of appointing mentally unstable poets to plum positions. Young Henry was already well down the rabbit hole – drunk whenever he wasn't hungover and consumed by self-loathing in both states, which confirmed Henry's moral weakness in the eyes of his teetotaller mother. Parkes politely received Louisa, but hadn't forgiven Henry for penning a mocking verse about him. Henry would have to continue to write and paint houses for a living.

Ruling New South Wales no longer excited Parkes. He'd been there, done that, five times over. Each day in parliament was ground-hog day. The old man needed a new challenge. He got one from Lord Carrington.

On 15 June 1889, Parkes luncheoned with Carrington at Government House, after making sure Nellie hadn't followed him. As the governor popped another bottle of champagne, he confessed that the 1867 confederation of the Canadian provinces into a single dominion meant Canadians were much easier to deal with than Australians.[25]

Parkes acknowledged, 'That must be so, until we federate', before boasting, 'I could confederate these colonies in twelve months!' Carrington retorted, 'Then why don't you do it? It would be a glorious finish to your life.' Australia is the only nation on earth to have been established as the result of a lunchtime dare.

Parkes sensed the time was ripe for nationhood when Major-General Sir James Bevan Edwards' October 1889 review of Australia's defences concluded that land defence was 'quite impossible without a federation of the forces of the different colonies', and that Australian troops would be unable to quickly engage an invading foe if they had to change trains at every colonial border.

After reading Edwards' report, Parkes travelled to Brisbane to meet liberal premier Sir Samuel Griffith and Griffith's onetime nemesis, former conservative premier Sir Thomas McIlwraith, who'd formed a coalition known as 'the Griffilwraith', a fantastic two-headed political beast that surpassed any creation of Lewis Carroll or J.K. Rowling. After sounding out their support for a federal push, Parkes headed home via Tenterfield in northern New South Wales, the New England electorate he'd represented in 1882–83.[26]

New Englanders were no fans of the colonial status quo. They sold most of their produce in Queensland, which imposed tariffs on their goods, and lived closer to Brisbane than to Sydney. Sydney ignored

---

25 This is historical licence, as it's not absolutely certain champagne was served – although it is highly likely. Carrington was known as 'Champagne Charlie' for having his first bubbly at breakfast, which set the tone for the rest of his day. Parkes was also a pedigree champagne hound, who wined and dined those who might prove useful to him – a friend declaring that the wily premier had 'great faith in gastronomy as a political force'.

26 Colonial New South Wales electorates held their elections at slightly different times, allowing Parkes to run for Tenterfield a few hours after losing the vote in East Sydney. He visited the electorate on a couple of occasions, spending thirteen months of his term overseas. For some, Henry Parkes will forever be remembered as the champion of Australian Federation. For others, he was just the warm-up act for George Christensen.

their interests and they rarely saw their elected representatives, who spent most of their time in the capital or, in the case of Henry Parkes, swanning about Europe with young women. They wanted change.[27]

Federation would reduce Sydney's influence, free New Englanders from Brisbane's import duties and better support the farmers' sons who formed the backbone of New South Wales' light horse units.

Parkes, at a banquet held at the Tenterfield School of Arts on 24 October 1889, delivered a speech that had something for everyone. Those afraid of invasion were reassured by Parkes' call for 'one great federal army'. Trainspotters wept into their timetables when presented with Parkes' joyous vision of 'a nation wide uniform gauge railway line'. People who liked Tasmania jokes chuckled at Parkes' dismissal of the Federal Council, which 'sat in Tasmania and held sessions which never appeared to interest anyone'. Poetry lovers admired Parkes' deft segue from a dry dissertation on the machinery of government to a reading from 'The Dominion of Australia', a work by Brunton Stephens, one of Australia's most patriotic and racist poets.[28] But all of them sat up

---

27 New Englanders are New South Wales' most rebellious citizens. During World War I, future prime minister Earle Page founded the Northern Separation Movement (later rebadged the New England New State Movement), which campaigned for New England's secession from New South Wales. A referendum was held on New England statehood in 1967, with 54 per cent of New Englanders voting 'Remain', the votes of townies in Newcastle effectively killing the dream to Make Armidale Great Again.

28 **WARNING – THIS IS THE MOST DISTURBING FOOTNOTE IN THE BOOK**

Stephens was lauded by critics as Australia's second-greatest nineteenth-century poet after Adam Lindsay Gordon. Like all proper Australian poets, Stephens wrote about horses – his book *The Godolphin Arabian: The Story of a Horse* was a heroic verse about Scham, the ancestral thoroughbred, delivered in the style of Byron. However, Stephens was better known for his works promoting Australian independence and denigrating foreigners and Aboriginal people. 'My Chinee Cook' is the tale of a Chinaman whose work as a cook was a front for his jewel thieving, while 'My Other Chinee Cook' tells of his replacement, who fed the narrator's family 'rabbit pie' filled with dead puppies. 'King Billy's Skull' is a humorous verse about William Lanne, Tasmania's so-called 'last [male] Aborigine', in which the narrator holds a conversation with Lanne's skull, which was kept in a rosewood box by the doctor who'd stolen it from Lanne's desecrated corpse. In 'A Piccaninny', Stephens implores a three-year-old Aboriginal girl to die before she is abducted,

and took note of the words at the heart of the Tenterfield Oration, as Parkes' address became known:

> The great question which we have to consider is, whether the time has not now arisen for the creation on this Australian continent of an Australian government and an Australian parliament.

This was the first time a colonial leader had directly proposed Federation to the people, rather than showboating in parliament or the papers, or to sworn federalists. Parkes, in his oration, also called for a 'convention of leading men from all the colonies' (no sheilas) to devise an Australian Constitution.[29]

The colonies agreed to further Federation talks, with Victoria's support conditional on it hosting them. Former Victorian premier James Service, who'd hoped the 'bands of iron' that linked New South Wales and Victoria would herald their union, delivered a toast to 'A United Australasia' at the February 1890 Australasian Federation Conference banquet.[30] He then poured cold water on a United Australasia by saying Federation would remain impossible until free traders and protectionists settled their differences on tariffs.

---

beaten and raped by Aboriginal men and becomes a haggard, pipe-smoking, sexless drunk like her mother. In 'To a Black Gin', Stephens devotes all its eighty-eight lines to telling an Aboriginal woman she is not human and is the ugliest thing he's ever seen, with stanzas like:

> Thy skull development mine eye displeases
> Thou wilt not suffer much from brain diseases
> Thy facial angle forty-five degrees is.

The fact that this guy's poem was chosen for the defining speech on Australian nationhood says something.

29 Constitutions set out the structure, functions and powers of government and, in many cases, certain rights of the governed. It's nice, but not strictly necessary, to have a written constitution. New Zealand, for example, doesn't have one, as someone stole its only pen.

30 'Australasia' reflected New Zealand's participation in the Conference. Even if it didn't join the Federation, one of the other participants would hopefully lend it a pen.

Parkes rose in reply:

This question of a common tariff is a mere trifle compared with
the great overshadowing question of a living and eternal national
existence.

'The crimson thread of kinship runs through us all,' he intoned,
condemning Service's 'bands of iron' to the graveyard of second-rate
metaphors.

The majority of Conference attendees, including Alfred Deakin,
backed Parkes over Service, endorsing a National Australasian Federation Convention to draft a national Constitution. Parkes, increasingly
infirm after a cab accident had left his right foot hanging by a strip
of ancient flesh, was elected president of Sydney's 1891 Convention.

Deakin and Edmund Barton came to admire each other at the
1891 Convention, laying the foundations for their later partnership.
Deakin's initial judgment of Barton was informed by phrenology,
describing him as having 'eyes of remarkable beauty and expression,
glowing like jewels in the ardour of his inspiration', but a fish-like
mouth and large jaw 'pointing not only to strength of will but love of
ease and indulgence'.

While Parkes' proposals to the 1891 Convention that the new nation
be named the 'Commonwealth of Australia', and that its flag bear 'Our
starry cross, our glorious sign', would ultimately bear fruit, his ideas
that the Australian states have no governors, and that the larger states
have more seats in the Senate, were rejected. The smaller colonies
rightly feared they'd be trampled by New South Wales and Victoria if
they had fewer seats in the 'states' house'. The only republican among
1891's 'Founding Fathers', Tasmanian attorney-general Andrew Inglis
Clark, was also disappointed that state governors would be appointed
by the British monarch, rather than by Australian parliaments.

Clark's republicanism and nationalism bordered on the obses-
sive, as evidenced by his keeping a picture of Giuseppe Mazzini, the

republican revolutionary who'd help forge a unified Italy, in every room of his house. A lover of all things American, Clark had forwarded Parkes, Deakin and other Convention heavies a draft Australian Constitution, modelled on that of the United States.

Sir Samuel Griffith took Clark's Constitution and ran with it. He invited Edmund Barton and South Australian radical liberal MP Charles Kingston to cruise the Hawkesbury River with him aboard his government's super-steamer, *Lucinda*, a floating pleasure palace decorated with Japanese tapestry panels that seemed at odds with Queensland's rabid xenophobia.[31] During this three-day Easter break, the trio knocked out a Constitution that the Convention approved, with only minor changes, for presentation to the colonial parliaments.

Parkes was hailed as the Father of Federation, a title that stuck in the craw of Charles Gavan Duffy, who'd retired to France in disgust after his twenty-five-year Federation campaign bore no fruit, due in no small part to Parkes' obstructionism. A bitter Duffy wrote to Parkes: 'In the Federal movement, I not merely took the principal part but practically did everything ... The flowers gathered from so much seed make but a scanty bouquet.'

The other colonies waited for Parkes' lead in putting the proposed Constitution to the New South Wales parliament, but the old man

---

31   Griffith and Kingston rivalled Sir Henry Parkes in the trouser action stakes. Griffith had a youthful liaison with a married woman and, after proposing to Brisbane's 'loveliest daughter', Etta Bulgin, pursued her three cousins. Kingston's application to join the South Australian bar was contested by Lucy McCarthy's elder brother, who accused the young lawyer of gross immorality in seducing his sister. Kingston is believed to have had at least two illegitimate children with other women before marrying Lucy. His political career was almost derailed when, as attorney-general, he was named co-respondent in an 1886 divorce case for seducing Mrs Elizabeth Watson, who'd given birth to Kevin Kingston. Kingston begged the public's forgiveness, swore he wouldn't stray again, and adopted Kevin with Lucy. Socially shunned by stitched-up South Australians, Kingston is believed to have later fathered at least two more illegitimate children, with Lucy burning all his personal papers after his death. In 2008, the South Australian government approved the unusual request to exhume Kingston, so that his DNA could be compared with those claiming descent from his dalliances, a move that will ensure more Australian politicians elect to be cremated.

dithered, concerned that he didn't have the numbers. Parkes' greatest worry was George Reid, the portly free-trader who'd demonstrated his liberal principles by excluding Aboriginal children from schools in 1883. Reid, despite his ponderous manner, was a canny political operator with a sharp wit and even sharper tongue. When a heckler inquired about his vast gut, Reid retorted, 'It's all piss and wind. I'll call it after you.'

Reid was concerned that the draft Constitution lacked democratic safeguards and that the failure to resolve differences on protectionism might jeopardise New South Wales' free-trade principles:

> New South Wales by joining would be acting like a reformed alcoholic who set up house with five drunkards, leaving the question of beverages to be decided later by a majority vote.

Reid's opposition earned him the eternal enmity of Alfred Deakin. Deakin later compared Reid's gait to that of a hippopotamus that 'had climbed into a ferry boat and was determined to upset it unless given his own way'. Then he really let rip:

> Every caricature has been unable to travesty his extraordinary appearance, his immense, unwieldy, jelly-like stomach, always threatening to break his waistband, his little legs apparently bowed under the weight to the verge of their endurance, his thick neck rising behind his ears rounding to his many folded chin. His protuberant blue eyes were expressionless until roused or half hidden in cunning, a blond complexion and infantile breadth of baldness gave him an air of insolent juvenility. He walked with a staggering roll like that of a sailor, helping himself as he went by resting on the backs of chairs as if he were reminiscent of some far-off arboreal ancestor ... He never slept in a public gathering for more than a moment or two, being quickly awakened by his own snore. His extreme fatness appeared to induce this state and for that his self-indulgence was chiefly responsible since he denied himself nothing he fancied,

sucking ice or sweetmeats between meals and eating and drinking according to his fancy.[32]

Parkes ultimately lacked the political will to take on Reid. His prodigious energies diminished, he'd already left most of the heavy lifting on Federation to Edmund Barton. In October 1891, he surrendered the premiership for the final time, resigning 'in joyful satisfaction'.

The Constitution was left gathering dust, the momentum lost. But Australians now had a much bigger issue than Federation to worry about.

THE GREATEST DEPRESSION

Australia's 1890s depression was more severe than anything experienced before or since, with the colonies' GDP falling 17 per cent during 1892–93, the worst years of the downturn.

The omens were there, for those prepared to take time out from the real estate pages to read them. In 1891, the year the bubble burst, Melbourne, Australia's hardest hit city, was beset by a great flood and a plague of locusts. Then, the very symbol of Victorian democracy, the ceremonial mace used to open and close parliament, was ripped from its sacred resting place in the dark dead of night. There were rumours most foul that a cabal of MPs partied hard and long within parliament's hallowed halls, joined most unnaturally by sex workers from the red-light district conveniently located across the road. The revellers, the press reported, continued their bacchanal at a nearby bordello, where the mace was used in 'fearful orgies' and 'low travesties of parliamentary procedure'. Unable to smuggle the slightly worse-for-wear

---

32 The fat-shaming Deakin is the only Australian politician who could hold a candle to Prime Minister Paul Keating in delivering political insults, although Keating delivered his vitriol with far greater economy. Keating's descriptions of Liberal leader John Hewson as a 'feral abacus' and 'a shiver looking for a spine to run up' will never be surpassed.

ornamental weapon back into parliament the next morning, the MPs
(according to parliament's electrician) paid two crooks to dump it in
the Maribyrnong River. These disasters and depravities could only
herald Melbourne's doom.[33]

How did things go so wrong?

During the 1880s property boom, banks and other lenders issued
loans like there was no tomorrow. When property prices started to
fall in 1889, there would be no tomorrow for many of them. Property
investors left holding the parcel when the music stopped were unable
to service their mortgages, triggering a spate of building society
failures and a run on the land banks. The contagion spread to the
traditional banking sector, as worried customers withdrew their
deposits. In Victoria, the government shut the banks for five days,
heightening customer concerns that they'd never see their money
again. Of the sixty-four financial organisations that solicited public
deposits in Australia in 1891, fifty-four had closed by the peak of the
crisis in mid-1893, thirty-four of them permanently.

Colonial governments were largely unable to cushion the financial shock, as they'd spent all their money on trains. The price of
Australia's primary export, wool, was heading south, and the cost
of imports rising. Britain had closed its chequebook to the colonies
in late 1890, as Barings Bank, one of its largest financial institutions,
only survived bad loans it had made in Argentina through a Bank
of England bailout. Investment in the new world no longer seemed
such a safe bet.

Australian banks tried to stay afloat by calling in their loans.
Smaller repossessed rural properties was sold on the cheap to large
landholders, again concentrating land ownership in the hands of the
pastoralists. One in ten houses was repossessed, with the bailiffs
marching Sir Henry Parkes, a newly minted backbencher, from his

---

33   An alternative story is that the mace continued to be displayed at Annie Wilson's
     Boccaccio House, the discerning Victorian politician's brothel of choice.

Annandale home in 1892. Nellie, five of his children and two of his sisters were evicted with him. This was particularly hard on Nellie, who was fighting uterine cancer and losing. Although forced to sell many of his curios, Parkes thankfully had enough put away to continue to employ Nellie's maid and carer, Julia Lynch, a twenty-year-old Irish lass who, he couldn't help noticing, was hotter than a hot potato at a Belfast barbecue.

Thousands of the cities' new homeless took up the swag and trudged the countryside, begging for work. There was little to be found, with unemployment peaking at more than 30 per cent. Other economic refugees set sail for Western Australia, which was rolling in gold and had escaped the carnage. The immigration boom, which had driven economic development in the other colonies, ended in 1891, accompanied by a sharp decline in marriages and births. The Australian population grew by only 7,000 people over the remainder of the decade.

Alfred Deakin had a job and a home but, like Parkes, had taken himself to the backbench. His mood in late 1891 mirrored that of Australia:

O God, once more the waters have gone over me, I am drowned ... as I sink inward to the coreless emptiness of things almost without a struggle or a sensation except that I know my loss and my loneliness ... Strip my lethargy, scorch my wavering faith so that I may accept my part and perform it without the endless questioning and weary round of iterated unrealties. Make me real.

It was not reality, but realty, that was Deakin's problem. Having sunk much of his own and his father's fortune into get-rich-quick property schemes, he lost big. Then he lost his father. After William Deakin's death in 1892, Alfred asked his mother and sister Kate to live with his family, but Pattie, who resented Kate's superior airs in teaching her daughters, swore she'd move out if Kate moved in. On the day of the largest family row he'd ever had, Deakin, usually a prolific diarist, simply recorded that he'd shot twenty-six rabbits. A man had to take out his frustrations somewhere.

Having enjoyed a relatively conventional religious life of late, Deakin returned to spiritualism and the darkened room of Mrs Cohen, who had the recently departed William Deakin on speed dial. William (sounding suspiciously like Mrs Cohen) requested chloroform to ease his spiritual pain, promised to regularly haunt his wife and daughter, and told his family he'd joined an astronomy club so he could travel to other planets. (He admitted to having already travelled a good deal, an unexpected perk of being dead.)

Deakin returned to the law to supplement his income, sensationally representing mass murderer Frederick Deeming, who claimed his long-dead mother had ordered him to murder his two wives and four children. Australia's very own Norman Bates, who'd slain his first family during a brief return to Britain, was identified by the *New York Times* as a suspect in the 1888 Whitechapel murders, with some of today's Ripperologists maintaining Deeming was Jack the Ripper.

Deakin remained chair of the City of Melbourne Building Society, which suspended payments to its customers. He prayed:

> Disaster has overtaken me at last O God! And upon me lies in some
> degree the responsibility for disaster to many others. Grant that it
> may be mitigated for them.

Deakin's genuine remorse didn't stop him spruiking the building society to investors, or telling its customers their money was safe. Those investors and customers lost out when the company went to the wall in 1892.

Deakin represented financial institutions in cases against distressed investors, and also took on the cases of friends and parliamentary colleagues implicated in fraud. He mounted an unusual and unsuccessful defence for Charles Staples, chair of the Anglo-Australian

Bank: 'Who should go free in the city of Melbourne if rash and even reckless speculation were considered criminal?'

Premier James Munro, chair of the Real Estate Mortgage and Deposit Bank, used funds from the financial institutions he controlled to pay for personal investments, and lent to family and friends with little or no security. As the depression deepened, Munro rammed the *Voluntary Liquidation Act* through parliament in a day, blocking minority shareholders who suspected fraud from initiating public inquiries into company operations. The next day, Munro used these laws to voluntarily shut down a bank and a building society he controlled, without his dirty laundry being aired.

An old school pal of Deakin's, Theodore Fink, devised a scheme that took advantage of laws allowing three-quarters of a company's creditors to agree to an insolvent company's continued trading as an alternative to winding it up. The solution was to lend a tiny amount to lots of friends, who would then stack creditors' meetings. Those friends' companies would similarly extend small loans to you, and you'd turn up at meetings to keep their creditors at bay. A company owner who entered into such a cosy arrangement – in which they drained every penny from their dying company and avoided the shame of bankruptcy, while real creditors received nothing – was said to have 'finked it'.

The Chaffey brothers, the beneficiaries of Deakin's experiment of privatising the Murray, went into liquidation, surprisingly easy to do when your business is water. Fresh fruit was a luxury, with sales plummeting in the tough times, and Mildura's growers refused to pay the Chaffeys' water rates. The wet dream of irrigating north-west Victoria was dust.

Irrigation and religion remained two of Deakin's great passions: he published *Irrigation in India* and *Temple and Tomb in India* in 1893, and delivered lectures on Hinduism, Buddhism and Islam. Deakin had written *The Gospel According to Swedenborg*, a 600-page exploration of the Swedish mystic's views on the spirit world, revelation, religion, ethical living and duty, before his attraction to Eastern religions led

him to embrace Theosophy and take on the role of secretary of a new
Theosophical Lodge in Melbourne.

Theosophy was an offshoot of spiritualism developed by the
aristocratic Ukrainian occultist Madame Blavatsky, publisher of
the Theosophical magazine *Lucifer* and author of the faith's sacred
texts *Isis Unveiled: A Master-Key to the Mysteries of Ancient and Modern
Science and Theology*, *The Key to Theosophy*, *The Voice of the Silence* and
The Secret Doctrine, the contents of which had been revealed to her
by a secret brotherhood of spiritual adepts known as 'the Masters'.
Theosophists believe that all the world's religions devolved from a
single 'Ancient Wisdom'; that personal growth through reincarnation
will allow a person to reclaim this wisdom; that humans comprise a
physical body, an astral fluid body and a divine spark; and that the
universe and all the important things in it have a connection with
the number seven (for example, seven intelligent rays, the Dhyan
Chohans, created the universe with a cosmic lifeforce known as
Fohat). Deakin had now well and truly reached the Tom Cruise stage
of his spiritual journey.[34]

The 1890s depression was not all doom and gloom. Andrew Barton
Paterson, for one, was determined to make the best of it. As the jobless
queues grew in 1891, Paterson was appointed honorary treasurer of the
Lawn Tennis Association of New South Wales and joined the Sydney

---

34 Deakin's old debating buddy Richard Hodgson, whom Deakin had introduced
    to spiritualism, had, as a leading member of Britain's Society for Psychical
    Research (SPR), published reports that accused Blavatsky of fraud in establishing
    Theosophy, faking psychic powers and being a Russian spy. Hodgson, who
    supplemented his work for the SPR by lecturing at Cambridge and self-
    experimenting with hallucinatory drugs, was visited by Deakin in 1887, shortly
    after he blew the whistle on Blavatsky. Hodgson moved to Boston later that year,
    became the secretary of the American Society for Psychical Research, and lived
    in a small room to which no one was admitted, lest they disturb his supernatural
    studies. He was restless to explore the other side, remarking, 'I can hardly wait
    to die.' Hodgson's wish was granted in 1905, after suffering heart failure during a
    particularly vigorous game of handball. His friendship with Deakin had continued
    throughout his life, and perhaps beyond it, notwithstanding their different views
    on Theosophy.

Club, a new polo fraternity. In 1892, he joined the Australian Club, sponsored by his uncle, Henry Kater, whom he'd earlier anonymously attacked in verse. While Paterson wrote poems about fee-grasping lawyers and heartless bankers, he also did debt-recovery work for three banks during the depression years. The man who'd once raged against elites was now very much part of the establishment.

The hard times also encouraged innovation. In 1891, Hobart's Henry Jones recognised that people who were worried about the future wanted to buy food that lasted.[35] Jones opened a jam factory that was soon exporting preserves throughout the British Empire, with IXL becoming a household name.[36]

In 1892, Coolgardie miner Arthur McCormick invented a powerless, iceless 'fridge' that relied on wind passing through a water-soaked hessian covering, with the resulting evaporation drawing heat from its interior – a trick Aboriginal people had discovered millennia earlier in wetting their hide waterbags. The Coolgardie safe, as McCormick's invention was known, was widely used throughout Australia until electric refrigerators became common in the 1950s.[37]

In the 1880s, Lawrence Hargrave, the New Guinea explorer and son of the woman-hating divorce judge John Hargrave, invented new adding machines and, less successfully, shoes to enable a man to walk on water. By 1893, he had turned his attention to the skies, developing a radial rotary engine later incorporated into French World War I planes, curved wing surfaces and aerofoils capable of providing lift, and a box kite that proved a heavier-than-air machine was capable of stable flight.[38] In 1894, he ascended 16 feet into the air, tethered to

35 Although he would have been as confused as everyone else about why later generations would want to stockpile toilet paper over all other goods.

36 IXL took its name from Jones' self-regarding motto, 'I excel in everything I do.'

37 That a technology requiring regular watering emerged in the desert is surprisingly typical of Australian innovation.

38 In 1882, Edward Cole predicted that people would soon travel by flying machine. He offered a £1,000 reward to anyone who could invent such a contraption within

four of his box kites and, sensibly, the ground.[39] Hargrave's designs informed the Wright brothers' first powered and sustained aeroplane flight at Kitty Hawk nine years later.

Hargrave, like many other Australian inventors of his era, was an open-source kind of guy who believed men of science were morally obliged to share their discoveries with the world, so they could be improved upon by others. McCormick also never patented his invention. Both of their designs were later commercially exploited by others, consistent with the proud Australian tradition of being great at coming up with ideas and terrible at making money from them.[40]

The industrial unrest of the depression years, which failed to secure workers the wages and conditions they demanded, also encouraged political innovation. It was time for the workers to leave their pickets and their picnics for the parliament.

It was time for the rise of Labor.

---

two years, subject to the provisos that it not be powered by gas and that it fly at least 100 miles before landing outside Cole's Book Arcade.

39   Baronet Sir George Caley had proved that a glider could carry a person in 1848, when he asked a ten-year-old boy on his estate to strap himself into the untested machine. It is a quirk of history that the name of the world's first winged flight 'pilot' is unknown. The first adult pilot is believed to be Caley's coachman, John Appleby, who survived the first manned winged flight crash and promptly resigned from Caley's service. Hargrave, a decent and considerate man, would not have dreamed of testing his flying machines on anyone else.

40   For example, the CSIRO's Doug Waterhouse developed the active ingredient for Aerogard after years of sticking his arm into a perspex box filled with starving mosquitoes. CSIRO sold Doug's invention to Mortein for a song, and Mortein made millions. All Doug received for his work was a box of Aerogard and a very itchy arm.

8

Take the 'U' Out of Labour and It's ...[1]

Socialism is being mates.

William Lane, *The Hummer*, 1892

SHEARERS, SEAMEN AND SCABS

N 1888, HUNTER VALLEY COALMINERS WENT ON STRIKE
over wages and conditions. Mine owners responded by bringing blackleg (scab) labourers, many of whom were Italian, up
from Sydney.[2]

While colonial governments had backed those who took industrial action against Chinese labour, Italians were white. Artillery

---

1   *Labour* and *Labor* are both used in this chapter, which is simultaneously confusing
and irritating. This is in no way the fault of the author – Labour/Labor is solely to
blame, as both spellings were used, with little rhyme or reason, during the first
decades of its existence. How a party that couldn't agree on its own spelling ever
came to power is a question that defies rational answer.

2   *Blackleg* and *scab* were both used in the 1880s to describe strikebreaking workers.
Scab, which would largely displace *blackleg*, was similarly used to describe a worker
who refused to join a trade union. *Blackleg* and *scab* were also sheep diseases, with
shearers' unions amplifying the link between disease and industrial treachery
in the popular Australian consciousness. William Lane's weekly, the *Worker*,
reinforced the negative connotations of *scab* by injecting a little of Lane's usual
Trumpian xenophobia and introducing his readers to an animal even more
dastardly than the octopus: 'The "skunk" is the meanest and least bearable of all
animals, and the "scab" is twenty degrees lower in social grade than the skunk.
It is said both originated in China.'

troops were sent to support police protecting the blacklegs, with machine gun emplacements erected at the New Lambton and West Wallsend collieries. The *Newcastle Morning Herald* pointed out that the proper job of a defence force is to kill foreigners, and asked if the Parkes government was actually prepared to machine gun its own citizens.

The strike ended with the mine owners and the Amalgamated Miners' Association of Australasia (AMAA) reaching agreement, but the AMAA again flexed its muscles at Broken Hill the following year.

Mining commenced at Broken Hill in 1883, after German boundary rider Hieronymous Salvator Lopez von Pereira (who sensibly chose to be known as Charles Rasp) thought there might be some tin lying around. There was no tin, but Rasp found the largest source of silver, lead and zinc in the world. In 1885, he formed the Broken Hill Proprietary Company to mine it.

The Broken Hill strikers demanded BHP run a closed shop (i.e. only employ union members). The company agreed, but not before a group of local women formed the strike-supporting Women's Brigade and doused picket-breaking shift managers with hot tar and whitewash, causing significant injuries.

The 1888–89 mining disputes demonstrated that local communities would rally behind industrial action. The belief that organised labour could improve society had taken root, inspiring women such as Mary Cameron, a schoolteacher from near Broken Hill, to commit themselves to the labour cause. In 1890, Cameron took a teaching post in Sydney, writing poetry and stories about oppressed newspaper boys for the *Bulletin* on the side. Cameron refused Henry Lawson's marriage proposal, but remained his muse and lifelong friend.

In 1890, about 20 per cent of the Australian workforce was unionised, believed to be the highest rate in the world. Fired up by their successes, unions went all in after Melbourne shipowners refused to allow maritime officers to affiliate with Melbourne Trades Hall. Sixty thousand seamen, wharfies, transport workers, shearers, miners and

gas stokers from across the eastern and southern colonies walked off
the job in support, the largest industrial action Australia had seen.
The 1890 Maritime Strike quickly broadened into a dispute about
the right of employers to contract non-union workers.

In Victoria, a rattled Deakin (not yet retired to the backbench)
responded to a planned rally of 50,000 strike supporters by declaring he wouldn't leave the city to 'mob law and the tender mercies
of roughs and rascals'. He ordered the Mounted Rifles, under the
command of Colonel Tom Price, to deploy to Melbourne. Price
told his men:

> You will each be supplied with forty rounds of ammunition, leaden
> bullets, and if the order is given to fire, don't let me see any rifle
> pointed in the air; fire low and lay them out so that the duty will
> not have to be performed again.[3]

The Mounted Rifles stayed in their Melbourne barracks and
Price clarified he'd only meant for his troops to shoot protestors in
the knees, so what was all the fuss about? However, Deakin's calling
in the armed forces, and swearing in hundreds of shopkeepers and
white-collar workers as special constables to protect scabs, fractured
relations between liberals and labour.

In New South Wales, Bruce Smith, the founder of the Victorian
Employers' Union who'd fought wharfies' holiday leave and was now
Parkes' secretary for public works, denied urging his fellow ministers to 'shoot down' the strikers 'like bloody dogs'. Parkes certainly
adopted a more moderate approach, countermanding his deputy's
order to deploy 5,000 troops. He did, however, issue special constables with firearms to clear the way for strikebreakers to load wool
at Circular Quay.

---

3   The Patrick Stevedores wharfies who whinged about a few private security guards
    bringing their dogs and balaclavas to work during the 1998 Australian waterfront
    dispute didn't know how good they had it.

The Maritime Strike collapsed after eleven weeks, partly because governments and the courts cracked down, but mostly because employers heeded the lesson Smith had earlier tried to teach them – they, like workers, needed to organise and maintain solidarity. The unions achieved none of their goals. Some of their leaders were imprisoned and others, like Queenslander Andrew Fisher, who'd worked in coalmines from the age of ten, were told they'd never work again.

The closed-shop campaign had ended in a union rout, but nobody had bothered to tell Queensland's shearers. During the 1880s, shearers had successfully gone on strike against non-union labour and unsuccessfully against the introduction of mechanical shears.[4] On 5 January 1891, shearers at Logan Downs walked off the job over proposed changes to conditions and closed-shop arrangements, with the strike spreading faster than foot-and-mouth at a sheep-'n'-shearer swingers club. The *Shearers' and General Labourers' Record* put the case of the shearers and pastoral workers who joined them in language that would pass the Queensland pub test:

---

4   In 1888, Dunlop Station in western New South Wales was the first place in the world to fit out its shed with mechanical shears, invented by Irish-Australian station-owner Frederick Wolseley. Dunlop's shearers, concerned that mechanisation would open their industry to less-skilled workers, responded by sabotaging the machines' drive system – although, like machine-breakers before them, they discovered that they couldn't jam the wheels of progress. The machines, originally powered by horse, steam or a shearer on a bicycle pedalling like buggery, removed over a kilogram more wool per sheep, increasing the colonies' dominance as wool superpowers. However, a skilled shearer with hand blades was still quicker than a machine shearer. Jackie Howe, an imposing man with 'a hand the size of a small tennis racquet', 'reputed to have run 100 yards in eleven seconds in his socks', set an even more impressive record in shearing 321 sheep in seven hours and forty minutes, which wasn't bettered by a machine shearer until 1950. The world record was all the more impressive as it was achieved despite Jackie's workmates trying to slow him down by tickling him and jumping on his back. The blue singlet Jackie had worn setting the record (which he'd made by removing the sleeves from a flannel shirt) inspired generations of Australian labourers to wear blue singlets, which in Queensland are still known as 'Jackie Howes'.

The squatters forced the men off their runs by giving them the choice of leaving or taking a Chinkee or a Kanaka for a mate.[5]

The 1891 Shearers' Strike, and the widespread social unrest it unleashed, owed much to uber-racist William Lane and just-a-little-bit-less-racist William Spence.

Lane, in 1889, was the prime mover in organising Queensland unions to form the Australian Labour Federation, which adopted the platform of nationalising 'all sources of wealth and all means of producing and exchanging wealth' (which sounded disturbingly socialist). He was also the inaugural editor of the Federation's newspaper, the *Worker*. Although Lane wasn't directly involved in strike action, his organisational skills supported the shearers and his writing inflamed them, leading a Brisbane newspaper to label him 'the man behind the curtain' – the prototype 'faceless man' of Labor.[6]

William Spence had no formal schooling, having enjoyed careers as a shepherd, butcher's boy and miner by age fourteen. After taking mining unions trans-colonial in establishing the AMAA, Spence did the same for shearers. As foundation president of the Amalgamated Shearers' Union of Australasia and editor of the *Shearers' and General Labourers' Record*, Spence ushered in closed shops on most of Australia's southern sheep stations.

Spence saw the bush as a new Eden, in which socialist Adam would slay the serpent of capitalism while Eve baked apple pie. Lane

---

5   Henry Lawson played down the racial element of the 1890s shearers strikes in his
     1901 poem 'The Shearers':
        And though he may be brown or black,
        Or wrong man there or right man,
        The mate that's honest to his mates
        They call that man a "white man"!
     Australians used the term *white man* to denote a man who is fair and decent,
     similar to the American expression, 'That's mighty white of you.'

6   Lane's faceless-man status led him to write under pseudonyms including Bystander,
     The Sketcher and John Miller. He was also sometimes a faceless woman, writing as
     Martha Guy to broaden the labour movement's appeal among women.

broadly supported this vision but, as an advocate for sexual equality, saw Eve as Adam's co-revolutionary. Both drew on the bush legend and mateship in defining what it was to be a labour man/person. The sacred bush–labour relationship, Spence believed, flowed both ways:

> Unionism came to the Australian bushman as a religion. It came bringing salvation from years of tyranny. It had in it the feeling of mateship which he understood already and which characterised the action of one white man to another ... Unionism extended the idea, so a man's character was gauged by whether he stood true to the Union rules or 'scabbed' it on his fellows.

The mateship of bushmen had been hijacked by these two fathers of Australian Labor, who transformed the concept into solidarity among workers. This solidarity was seen on 1 February 1891, when the shearers' strike committee met under a ghost gum in the small town of Barcaldine, declaring, 'the Queensland bush is to be a battleground whereon is to be decided whether capitalism can crush Australian unionism altogether into the dust.' It was seen when shearers cut telegraph lines and set fire to grasslands, woolsheds, fences, effigies of Premier Griffith and, less successfully, sheep. It was seen when shearers tried to derail a train full of police, and attacked squatters and scabs at Clermont, under the leadership of 24-year-old ex-schoolteacher Julian Stuart.[7] It was seen when shearers faced down soldiers kitted out with cannons and machine guns, and rallied to the cry of Frederick Vosper, editor of the *Australian Republican*, whose 'BREAD or BLOOD' editorial called for 'revolution throughout Australasia' and

---

7   Julian's real name was John, but he changed his name because he wanted to be a poet and Julian sounded more artsy. Here's a little of his work:
          I am deformed by labor
          I am the working man
          Cursing the fate that holds me
          A dull-browed Caliban
     Julian didn't give up his day job.

urged the shearers, 'If your oppressors will not listen to reason, let them feel cold lead and steel.'

The Queensland government sent a message to the unions in choosing to try the shearers' ringleaders for sedition and conspiracy on 1 May 1891 – May Day, the day international workers set aside to campaign for the eight-hour day.[8] As the accused were taken into Rockhampton Court in chains, 1,340 shearers and their families gathered around the Barcaldine ghost gum and set off on a May Day march under the Eureka flag, cheering 'the boys in gaol'.[9]

A fired-up Henry Lawson composed a paean to the strikers, 'Freedom on the Wallaby'.[10] The poem ended with the revolutionary cry:

> *So we must fly a rebel flag,*
> *As others did before us,*
> *And we must sing a rebel song*
> *And join in rebel chorus.*
>
> *We'll make the tyrants feel the sting*
> *O' those that they would throttle;*
> *They needn't say the fault is ours*
> *If blood should stain the wattle!*

---

8   During their arrest at Clermont on 24 March 1891, one of the shearers' leaders asked a pastoralists' representative who was present, 'Do you call this a fair go, Mr Ranking?' The *Brisbane Courier* report of the arrests is the first time the term *fair go* is known to have appeared in print. This Australian term for fair treatment, which underpins the notion of Aussie egalitarianism, originally had industrial connotations, as did the similarly jingoistic term *true blue*, which first appeared in the 1890s with the meaning 'loyal to workers and union values'.

9   The Eureka rebels' Southern Cross flag was later adopted by the broader union movement. It has since been embraced by Australian nationalists, communists, fascists, anarchists, outlaw motorcyclists, tattooists and assorted other ists.

10   This title has confused generations of Australian schoolchildren, who quite reasonably ask their teachers, 'What does a small marsupial have to do with freedom?' and 'Isn't this meant to be a poem about shearers?' If they'd bothered to read their crib notes, they'd know 'the Wallaby' is a reference to a track made by wallabies and used by shearers.

Lawson's work was published in Lane's *Worker*, but its promised sting was not felt by the tyrants. The Pastoralists' Federal Council of Australia, an umbrella group for pastoral employers, held firm. With unemployment rising as the depression took off, scabs were easier to find. The striking shearers, having foregone pay and rations for five months, were starved out a couple of weeks after Lawson's poem went to print. Twelve of their leaders, including Julian Stuart, were sentenced to three years' imprisonment with hard labour.

On 20 June 1891, six days after the strikers folded, what was left of the Barcaldine strike committee met under the ghost gum and issued a defiant manifesto that called for unionists to register on electoral rolls. Politicians might think twice about sending troops out against workers if the workers could unite to vote them out. The ballot might succeed where the picket had failed.[11]

Writers who'd backed the shearers also maintained the rage. Frederick Vosper, twice acquitted of seditious libel for 'BREAD or BLOOD', was sentenced to three months' hard labour for inciting a miners' riot. William Lane wrote *The Working Man's Paradise* (a turgid novel about an earnest young man who liked sheep and socialism) to

---

11   In the days before compulsory voting, elections were won and lost on how effectively candidates could enrol their supporters and get them out to vote. Unions, with their organisational skills and in-house presses, were well placed to get out or suppress the worker vote – and use this power to pressure the liberal candidates for whom workers traditionally voted. Alfred Deakin had tried to introduce compulsory voting in Victoria in 1888, five years before the world's first compulsory-voting laws were passed in Belgium. He believed voting was a civic duty, and that compulsory voting would encourage moderates to vote and end the practice of candidates offering their constituents inducements. Deakin also found electioneering distasteful, with compulsory voting promising an end to kissing babies and patting dogs, or vice versa. He withdrew his compulsory-voting laws from parliament after they were universally panned by the press, with the *Leader*, published by Deakin backer David Syme, calling them 'reckless' and 'thoughtless', and expressing outrage that 'the citizens are to be driven to the polls by the police'. Queensland adopted compulsory voting in 1914, with the Commonwealth following in 1924. South Australia, in 1985, was the last state to make voting compulsory for both houses of parliament. Australia remains the only English-speaking democracy in the world that requires its citizens to vote.

raise funds for the families of the imprisoned shearers. Lane modelled his novel's heroine on Mary Cameron, now a writer for the *Worker*, although his admiring words to her, 'You can reason like a man,' undercut his cred on the sexual equality front.

In Queensland's Legislative Council, during a 'Vote of Thanks' to the police who broke up the Barcaldine strike camp, Frederick Brentnall, quoting the last two verses of 'Freedom on the Wallaby', led the charge for Henry Lawson to be arrested for sedition. Lawson responded by addressing a poem to Brentnall, published in the *Worker*. 'The Vote of Thanks Debate' was one of Lawson's more clearly titled works. In it, the young poet nailed his socialist colours to the mast and expressed his contempt for politicians and the vested interests they served:

> *The other night in Parliament you quoted something true,*
> *Where truth is very seldom heard except from one or two.*
> *You know that when the people rise the other side must fall,*
> *And you are on the other side, and that explains it all.*
> *You hate the Cause by instinct, the instinct of your class,*
> *And fear the reformation that shall surely come to pass;*
> *Your nest is feathered by the 'laws' which you of course defend,*
> *Your daily bread is buttered on the upper crust, my friend.*

BATTLE OF THE BARDS

Henry Lawson was a true believer, his 1892 'A Song of Southern Writers' envisioning a trade union for Australian writers, musicians and artists:

> *We have learned the rights of labour. Let the Southern writers start*
> *Agitating, too, for letters and for music and for art*[12]

---

12   Writers had their own scabs. E.J. Brady, a Woolloomooloo wharfie whose verse appeared in *Australian Workman*, stole one of Lawson's poems and had it published under his own name. It must have been hard for Lawson to go in to bat for Australian writers when the bastards were ripping him off.

The poem was first and foremost a plaintive cry for the recognition of Australian art and a rejection of the cultural cringe:

> *Talent goes for little here. To be aided, to be known,*
> *You must fly to Northern critics who are juster than our own.*
> *Oh! the critics of your country will be very proud of you,*
> *When you're recognised in London by an editor or two.*
> *You may write above the standard, but your work is seldom seen*
> *Till it's noticed and reprinted in an English magazine.*

It also bitched about Australians' love of sport over art, and the anti-intellectualism this fostered:

> *In the land where sport is sacred, where the lab'rer is a god,*
> *You must pander to the people, make a hero of a clod!*[13]

On one level, 'A Song of Southern Writers' was classic Lawson whinging, as the Australian public loved his writing. On another, Lawson had a point, as the Australian public was reluctant to pay him for it. Lawson made a better living from odd-jobbing than from writing. The lack of appreciation (and money) was enough to drive a poet over the edge:

> *Banish envy, Southern writer! Strike with no uncertain hand,*
> *For the sound of Gordon's rifle still is ringing through the land!*
> *Ah! the niggard recognition! Ah! the 'fame' that came in vain*
> *To the poor dead poet lying with a bullet though his brain!*
> *'Gone, my friends!' (he thought it better to be gone away from here),*
> *Gone, my friends, with 'last year's dead leaves ... at the falling of*
> *the year'.*

---

13   Lawson was right on the sports front. Banjo Paterson had taken his name
      from a horse and Arthur Hoey Davis called himself Steele Rudder because it
      sounded suitably boaty, rowing being the sport at which Australians excelled
      internationally – in 1895, he'd write the first of his quintessentially Australian
      'On Our Selection' pieces for the *Bulletin* under the shortened name Steele Rudd.

During the depression years, a number of Australian poets joined Adam Lindsay Gordon's Dead Poets Society. In 1892, financial and female problems led the drover-poet Barcroft Boake to hang himself with his own stockwhip. In 1893, the republican poet Francis Adams calmly asked his wife to hand him the revolver he'd kept for years on the off-chance he might one day want to top himself.[14]

Lawson, who was feeling even more maudlin than usual in 1892, wrote in 'The Poets of the Tomb':

> *The world has had enough of bards who wish that they were dead,*
> *'Tis time the people passed a law to knock 'em on the head,*
> *For 'twould be lovely if their friends could grant the rest they crave –*
> *Those bards of 'tears' and 'vanished hopes', those poets of the grave.*

Lawson, described by Norman Lindsay as 'sodden with self-pity', was undoubtedly Australia's leading bard of tears and vanished hopes. While Paterson was action, Lawson was heart – one most often broken.

Lawson's bush bore no resemblance to Paterson's. It was harsh and cruel, 'burning wastes of barren soil and sand with their everlasting fences' that ground men and women into its gritty red dust. Women had it particularly tough, with Lawson drawing on his mother's early life in his works. His most acclaimed story, *The Drover's Wife*, incorporated the childhood tales Louisa had told him of her poverty, isolation and absent husband; the need for a dog to protect her from predatory swagmen; and a burning black snake at the end of a stick.

Men might survive such hardship through mateship. In *For Auld Lang Syne*, Lawson told of the parting of a group of mates during the depression:

---

14   When the coroner asked Mrs Adams if she could have prevented the act by not giving her husband the gun, she replied that she would have considered herself a 'contemptible coward' had she done so.

There were between us the bonds of graft, of old times, of poverty, of vagabondage and sin, and in spite of all the right-thinking person may think, say or write, there was between us that sympathy which in our times and conditions is the strongest and perhaps the truest of all human qualities, the sympathy of drink.

Drink was Lawson's major problem and his benders were legendary in the publishing world. Paterson acted as Lawson's lawyer and, although the two were acquaintances rather than friends, it was Paterson Lawson turned to in the depression's early days. Why should they not both earn a bit of extra coin by staging a Battle of the Bards, with the *Bulletin*'s readers to determine which of their takes on life was correct?

Lawson and Paterson addressed a series of poems to each other, Lawson damning the bush and Paterson praising it. It got a little personal. Paterson told Lawson:

> *You had better stick to Sydney and make merry with the 'push',*
> *For the bush will never suit you, and you'll never suit the bush.*

Lawson returned fire with:

> *It was pleasant up the country, City Bushman, where you went,*
> *For you sought the greener patches and you travelled like a gent.*[15]

Archibald, worried that expressing hatred for the bush might prove career-limiting for a bush poet, expressed concern for Lawson:

He is coming here in the morning with tobacco juice running down his

---

15   Archibald stopped the battle before things got out of hand, although Lawson had the final word over a decade later:
> *No I am no longer snarling,*
> *Long ago we had our row –*
> *Don't be angry Banjo, darling,*
> *Though I'm fashionable now.*

jaw, smelling of stale beer, and he has begun to write about 'The Rocks'. The next thing he will be known as 'the Poet of the Rocks'.

Archibald packed his derelict poet off to Bourke to dry out and reconnect with his inner bushman. Lawson wrote to his aunt upon arrival, 'The bush between here and Bathurst is horrible. I was right, and Banjo wrong.'

Bourke was no place to go straight, with Lawson dubbing the town 'Comeanaveadrink' on account of its nineteen pubs and countless locals who wanted to shout the visiting celebrity. The relationship Lawson developed with seventeen-year-old Jim Gordon, an itinerant worker, suggests that Lawson may not have wanted to go straight. Jim described their meeting:

> I had noticed this long-necked, flat-chested stripling eyeing me off each time we passed and I noticed too that he had the most beautiful and remarkable eyes I have ever seen on a human being ... soft as velvet and of a depth of brownness that is indescribable.

Lawson invited Jim to 'Come and camp with me', and when Jim lost his job as a painter the two men walked hundreds of miles in search of work, sleeping under the stars. Jim recalled they 'talked and talked' and, in his poem 'When Lawson Walked with Me', he wrote, 'Henry gripped my fingers tight' and 'linked arms with me'. Lawson's daughter Barta recalled, 'Dad loved Jim very much. And Jim loved him ... Dad said, "After all, I think he's about the best thing I ever did."'[16]

---

16 Lawson wrote movingly of mateship in his poems and prose. For Lawson, this exclusively male bond was the strongest emotional attachment a man could have. In *Mateship*, one of his short stories, he wrote: 'The grandest stories ever written were the stories of two men ... The man who hasn't a male mate is a lonely man indeed, or a strange man, though he have a wife and family. I believe there are few such men. If the mate isn't here, he is somewhere else in the world, or perhaps he is dead.' In *The Australian Legend* historian Russel Ward theorised that the mateship between convicts, and then the mateship between bushmen, might be forms of 'sublimated homosexuality'. Australian literary heavyweight Frank Moorhouse

If Lawson loved Jim, his hatred for bush life was greater. He tried his hand at shearing, complaining, 'A shearing shed is perhaps the most degrading hell on the face of this earth,' a far cry from his romanticisation of the shearer's life in 'Freedom on the Wallaby'. He wrote to his aunt:

> You have no idea of the horrors of the country out here; men tramp and live like dogs ... The physical hardship was bad enough, but the sense of degradation was worse.

Lawson abruptly parted ways with Jim after several months and travelled back to Sydney, determined 'never to face the bush again' and decrying the lot of 'the poor, hopeless, half-starved wretches who carry swags through it and look in vain for work – and ask in vain for tucker very often'. Lawson had returned the same as he'd left – broke, depressed, drunk – but his sense of injustice about the exploitation of rural workers had hardened, and his support for the labour cause strengthened.

Catherine Helen Spence disliked the 'offensively Australian' writing of Lawson, Paterson and their fellow bush writers. She particularly had it in for those who traded in misery, with their stories of 'the "deadbeat" – the remittance man, the gaunt shepherd with his starving flocks and herds, the free selector on an arid patch, the drink shanty where the rouseabouts and shearers knock down their cheques, the race meeting where high and low, rich and poor, are filled with the gambler's ill luck'. 'The one-sided pictures which our pessimistic poets and writers present,' Spence concluded, 'are false in the impression they make on the outside world and on ourselves.'

Spence recognised that Lawson's depression down-and-outer was just as influential as Paterson's sun-kissed bushman in forging a distinct Australian identity, one she considered distressingly

---

was open to dropping the 'sublimated' in the case of Lawson, speculating that he may very well have considered himself bisexual if he'd lived in a more tolerant age.

provincial and blokey. The labour movement would also latch on to the Ausploitation genre popularised by Lawson in forging a distinct Labor identity built on the bedrock of mateship.

NEW LABOR

Lawson's view that politicians were opposed to reforms that would raise the working class, expressed in 'The Vote of Thanks Debate', was widely shared within the union movement.

The movement had earlier called on workers to vote. Now it called on them to be *voted for*. Union leaders drew on the rhetoric of American populism in asserting that electing workers to parliament was the only way to cleanse colonial politics of its corruption. It was time to drain the swamp.

Australian Labor Party mythology traces the party's birth to the reading of the Manifesto of the Queensland Labour Party to a gathering of workers under the Barcaldine ghost gum on 9 September 1892. The Manifesto decried the worker's lot; dissed employers, pastoralists and the government; and promised social and economic justice for all. The assembled workers nominated Tommy Ryan, secretary of the 1891 shearers' strike committee, as a candidate for the new party. Ryan won an 1892 by-election, becoming the first Labour man in Queensland's parliament.

The Australian Labor Party is big on mythology, with its ability to look back in time and up its own arse unrivalled in political history. Why talk about building a better future when you can crack open a Toohey's Old with your mates, sing all fourteen verses of 'Red Fly the Banners, O', and reminisce about the Light on the Hill, the DLP split of '55, the Dismissal and how Johnno stacked Balmain in '76?

The Barcaldine ghost gum is part of this mythology, forever linking the party to the bush and the heroic shearers. It helps that the story has a tree in it: trees, symbols of life and revelation, are common in origin stories. Viking folklore has it that the many worlds of the cosmos radiate from Yggdrasil, the World Tree, while Enid Blyton folklore ascribes a similar function to the Magic Faraway Tree. Siddhārtha Gautama achieved enlightenment and launched Buddhism while sitting under the Bodhi Tree, while Isaac Newton achieved a sore head and launched gravitational physics while sitting under an apple tree. Another apple tree, the Tree of the Knowledge of Good and Evil, was the catalyst for Adam and Eve's exile from Eden. Labor drew from this well in naming the Barcaldine ghost gum the Tree of Knowledge.[17]

The story of Labor's birth under the Tree of Knowledge is classic propaganda, another thing the Australian Labor Party is big on, as acknowledged by William Spence in *Australia's Awakening, Thirty Years in the Life of an Australian Agitator*:

> Labor ... is a political as well as a propagandist movement. Its leaders realise that before we can have social reform the people must be educated to demand and carry out ... reforms ... It is slow work getting the right ideas knocked into the masses. They are mostly so mentally lazy that they take their views ready-made from a misleading press.

There are, of course, other Labor origin stories. One traces the party's birth to the 1891 May Day march at Barcaldine, which also features the tree. Both tree stories overlook Thomas Glassey, the signatory to the 1892 Manifesto who'd been elected to Queensland's Legislative Assembly in 1888, on a trade union platform with union support.

There's also the treeless, and therefore less romantic, New South Wales origin story, which traces the birth of the party to quarryman Charles Hart convening the first Labour Electoral League meeting

---

17   As in, 'I sat with my fellow workers under a tree in Barcaldine, where Democratic Socialism was suddenly revealed to us, and we knew that it was good.' Labor should have continued to read the tree-leaves in divining the party's fortune: the 1990 discovery that the tree was infested by termites was a sign of Paul Keating's white-anting of Bob Hawke, and the deliberate killing of the tree with Roundup in 2006 a portent of the fate of all future Labor leaders at the hands of their own caucuses.

at Balmain's Unity Hall Hotel on 4 April 1891.[18] South Australians, by contrast, insist they founded the Labor Party, when the United Trades and Labor Council met on 7 January 1891 to form the United Labor Party of South Australia (ULP).[19]

All and none of these stories are true. There was no angelic trumpet, or even the drunken cry of a striking shearer tripping over an unshorn sheep, to herald Labor's birth. There were instead a number of meetings of unionists, socialists and radicals, held across the colonies, where it was agreed that the failed Maritime Strike (and, later, the Shearers' Strike) was a sign of things to come – and that industrial action, in the absence of political representation, was insufficient to advance workers' rights. Those meetings birthed political parties that sought to improve the lot of 'producers of wealth' (socialist code for 'workers') and otherwise pursue a broadly liberal agenda, in all the Australian colonies, bar Western Australia and Tasmania.[20]

It was not so much ideology as organisation that made Labour an overnight success. The colonial parties had a clearly identifiable constituency (workers) and unions campaigned for their members to support Labour candidates. The union movement also provided ongoing administrative support, while parliamentary candidates had historically only received such assistance in the lead-up to an election.

In 1891, the Conference of the Labour Electoral League was formed to determine Labour's policy platform. League candidates

---

18 Labour Electoral Leagues, representing Labour members in local areas, became known as branches, in keeping with Labor's tree fetish. Charles Hart was one of the first Labour splitters, declaring that the party was 'out of touch with its members' within months of its formation.

19 This meeting almost certainly took place at a far creepier location than a pub or a tree.

20 It was harder to establish a workers' party in those two colonies, which still linked voting rights to property ownership or rental value, and wouldn't introduce universal male suffrage until 1901 and 1907 respectively. Although most colonies introduced payments for MPs between 1870 (Victoria) and 1890 (Tasmania), allowing workers to seek office, Western Australia held out until 1900, further hindering the formation of a Labour party in that colony.

had to sign a pledge they'd promote that platform and, while parliamentary tactics were a matter for MPs, they pledged to vote in line with the majority decision of the Labour caucus. Most readers will have drifted off to sleep reading this, but these actions fundamentally reshaped Australian democracy. Labour MPs would be bound to the policies determined by the Conference's unelected 'faceless men' and import union solidarity into parliamentary politics, rather than vote according to their conscience or self-interest.

In 1891, Alfred Deakin characterised Labour's entry into parliamentary politics as 'more significant and more cosmic than the Crusades', believing liberals could ride that cosmic wave in forging and controlling an anti-conservative liberal–labour alliance. This was the case in Victoria, where the earliest iteration of Labor, the Progressive Political League, won only ten of ninety seats in the 1892 election. Most League candidates were liberals and, in 1894, the League changed its name to the United Labor and Liberal Party. Led by boxer turned bootmaker Billy Trenwith, the party gave its support to the Liberal government.[21]

---

21   Victorian Labor was more intellectual and less blokey than its colonial
     counterparts. While other colonies' labour presses adopted names like the
     Worker or *New Order*, Victorians had *Tocsin*, which sounded more like a posh
     restaurant or Italian light opera than a newspaper for the working man (it's
     actually a French alarm bell). *Tocsin* was co-founded by poet Bernard O'Dowd,
     who, unusually for a Labor man, considered racial exclusion to be 'unbrotherly,
     undemocratic and unscientific'. O'Dowd also admitted to 'having something
     of the woman-soul' and 'in my psychic experiences had often the woman-body
     too'. O'Dowd's commitment to the rugged bush worker was, however, beyond
     question – as evidenced by his poem to close boyhood friend, turned swagman,
     Ted Machefer:
       Well, Ted, I sit down to address you
       (Excuse my bad metres and rhymes)
       With longings to see and caress you
       With ardour and joy of old times.
     Racially tolerant, swagmen-loving, gender-diverse poets may play well to a
     modern Labor audience (indeed, there's probably a whole Labor subcommittee
     devoted to them), but they would have gone down like a scab at a picnic with
     1890s Melbourne dockworkers.

In South Australia, the ULP won three Legislative Council seats in 1891. South Australian conservatives were quicker than their colonial counterparts to recognise the threat Labor posed. In 1891, conservative MP Sir Richard Baker established the National Defence League to oppose Labor, the trade union movement, state conciliation and arbitration of industrial disputes, socialism, the eight-hour workday and anything else Labor considered worthwhile. The League won more than a third of the seats in the 1893 South Australian election.

However, the ten seats secured by the ULP in 1893 gave it the balance of power. ULP backing enabled liberal Charles Kingston to seize government and the premiership from conservative John Downer, even though Kingston was still serving an 1892 sentence for challenging Baker to a duel for calling him a coward, a bully and a disgrace to the legal profession; providing Baker with a pistol; and turning up at Adelaide's Victoria Square to blow Baker away.[22]

Labour's rise in New South Wales was meteoric, with the League securing a quarter of the seats in the June 1891 election, giving it the balance of power – a world first for a workers' party. Labour backed Sir Henry Parkes' Free Traders to stay in government, over George Dibbs' Protectionists.

Labour wanted to abolish plural voting, which enabled men to vote in any electorate where they owned property and gave additional voting rights to male university graduates – effectively devaluing workers' votes. New South Wales Labour's threat to block government

---

22   In 1895, Premier Kingston again turned up in Victoria Square to fight the Adelaide manager of the South Australian Company, who thrashed Kingston with a whip for his offensive remarks. The larger and stronger Kingston then seized the whip and laid into his opponent, later quipping, 'Who can now say that I have not shed blood for South Australia? "What a pity," my capitalistic friends will say, "that there was not more of it."' Kingston could be a vindictive bastard. Adelaide's leading barrister, Paris Nesbit QC, a friend of Kingston described as an 'absinthe-drinking, woman-loving, tobacco-enslaved ... Prince of Bohemia', became a political opponent and was committed to an asylum. Despite the medical superintendent determining Nesbit was fit for release, Kingston illegally ordered his continued detention.

legislation saw them get their way on this in 1894.[23] Trading parliamentary support for government concessions on key planks of Labour's platform became the party's modus operandi, ensuring much of Labour's agenda was progressed by Liberal, Conservative, Free Trade and Protectionist governments.

The New South Wales parliamentary Labour party, in keeping with its socialist origins, was originally directed by a five-man politburo, before Joseph Cook was elected its first leader in 1893. Cook had worked down English coalpits as a child, relocating to the New South Wales coal town of Lithgow in the mid-1880s. He 'eschewed alcohol, gambling, sport and other forms of entertainment, and sought self-improvement through study at home', typical of the boring Methodists who dominated early Australian Labour parties.[24] The most exciting thing he'd ever done was change his name from Cooke to Cook. While poncy aristos like Lord Carrington and Lord Bertie might garnish their names with additional letters, Cook regarded his 'e' as an ostentation unbefitting a working man.

THE TRUE BELIEVERS

Labour was at first a broad church. Many of its earliest members, including John Tanck, hailed from the union movement. Tanck arrived in Australia from New Zealand in 1886 and found work in

---

23 South Australia never had plural voting. The rest of Australia followed New South Wales, although Western Australia held until 1907.

24 Early Labour members, who were often Methodists or other Protestant dissenters, argued that colonial parliaments had been corrupted by the brewers and publicans who sat on their benches, with the election of Labour men necessary to ensure fair and sober reform. Early Labour platforms called for reduced pub opening hours, though some members argued the party should not interfere in the leisure pursuits of workers. By the end of the 1890s, the temperance movement had aligned itself with the Liberals, and Labour had become the party of brewers and publicans. Over time, Catholics, many of Irish origin, came to dominate Labor, and getting on the piss became central to Labor culture.

Sydney mucking out the stables of Government House. He then landed a job as a typesetter, rising through the ranks of the New South Wales Typographical Association and being elected to the Trades and Labour Council. Tanck had more ambition than Cook: he didn't just remove the redundant 'c' from his name – he changed it altogether. And so, Chilean John Tanck, the son of a Germano-Chilean sailor and a New Zealand mother, became Chris Watson, a knockabout bloke of honest British descent. Watson successfully carried the secret of his true identity to the grave.

Billy Trenwith, blacklisted miner Andrew Fisher and fellow Queensland miner Andrew Dawson, along with at least three of the imprisoned 1891 shearers, including wannabe poet Julian Stuart, also numbered among the unionists elected as early Labour MPs. William Spence merged the shearers and other rural workers to form the Australian Workers' Union (AWU), a bush super-union that cemented his power in the party and launched his parliamentary career. Mary Cameron was the AWU's first female member and sat on its executive, although this didn't launch her parliamentary career because she was a woman.

Labour also appealed to socialists and single-taxers. Socialists believed in communal ownership of the means of production, distribution and exchange, while single-taxers were disciples of America's great nineteenth-century economist Henry George. George's 1879 *Progress and Poverty* posited that wealth in a free-market economy is concentrated in the hands of landowners and monopolists, who profit from their ownership through non-productive rents. This unfair distribution of wealth is the main cause of poverty, and can be remedied by replacing all taxes on productive activity with a tax on the unimproved value of land. Governments can then invest land-tax revenue in providing a universal basic income, pensions and disability services, infrastructure and other worthy things.

George toured the colonies in 1890, packing out town halls and stadiums because land ownership and taxation were sexy topics in Australia. Property speculation was rife, and landowners were convinced George wanted to ruin them, while the un-landed were convinced by George that the system was stacked against them.

Victoria directly taxed Australian residents for the first time, introducing a modest land tax in 1877. South Australia followed suit in 1884, and supplemented it with Australia's first income tax. Free-trade New South Wales, looking for new sources of revenue to replace its protectionist tariffs, introduced land and income taxes in 1895.

None of these colonial taxes made owning land without improving it unprofitable, to the disgust of Billy Hughes, who was both a socialist and a single-taxer. Hughes had no problems reconciling socialism, single taxation and the many other radical policies to which he subscribed – he was a political weathercock capable of holding five different views before breakfast.

Hughes, recently arrived from England, was five-foot-six in heels and so slight that his shadow filed for divorce. His delicate frame, combined with an overly large head, glittering eyes and long bony hands, gave him the appearance of an escapee from Area 51. He also suffered from profound deafness and indigestion. He was, incongruously, a fitness fanatic who excelled at cricket and rowing.

Hughes was moving up in the world, having transitioned from ship's cook to oven-hinge maker, to self-employed umbrella repairman and purveyor of mixed goods. Those goods included political pamphlets, and Hughes' small Balmain shop became a meeting place for socialists, single-taxers and other radicals. In those rare moments when he was not reading political economy, selling smallgoods or repairing umbrellas, Hughes could be found on a Balmain street corner, delivering soapbox lectures on the single tax in a harsh but mesmeric voice.[25] The little radical couldn't be faulted for want of energy, involving himself in the Balmain Labour Electoral League,

25   Hughes needed to stand on two soapboxes.

working as a shearers' industrial organiser and publishing the pro-Labour *New Order* weekly newspaper.

Even anarchists joined Labour, proving that they really hadn't thought their politics through.[26] Larry Petrie was a socialist-anarchist who claimed to have lost an arm in a freak quarry accident and to have suffered an unspecified disability in a freak coach accident. He normally went by the name George Frederick Howard, which he claimed was in deference to his uncle, a Scottish baronet. The false name also proved useful when organising the 'Social Revolution' that would bring down the corrupt capitalist state.

Petrie helped found the Social Democratic League and Melbourne's Knights of Labour, the latter modelled on a secret organisation of American garment-cutters whose members dedicated themselves to liberating workers while conducting mystic rituals involving scissors and cloth in the dark. Concerned that the eight-hour movement was not sufficiently hardcore, Petrie vigorously (but ineffectively) campaigned for a six-hour workday.

Petrie's lack of limbs, casual relationship with the truth, industrial zealotry, cloth-cutting nutbaggery, revolutionary fervour, and being a Melburnian, didn't halt his rise in the New South Wales labour movement. While AWU secretary-organiser in Sydney, Petrie printed revolutionary pamphlets by day and pasted them onto walls by night.

Mary Cameron, in her later years, fondly recalled Petrie's confession to her that he'd planted a bomb in a Circular Quay sewer, and reminisced about how she'd stood watch while Chris Watson and Labour MP Arthur Rae removed it. In 1893, Petrie was charged with detonating explosives aboard the *Aramac*, a Brisbane ship crewed

---

26 Anarchists are opposed to authority and hierarchy, while political parties (and groups generally) rely on them to maintain cohesion. Anarchists are generally anti-establishment. Melbourne anarchists, by contrast, were so much part of the establishment that there was a Melbourne Anarchist Club, although club attendees insisted they were all individuals who'd simply decided to turn up at the same place at the same time.

by non-union workers, with the *Sydney Morning Herald* reporting,
'In some circles it [the *Aramac* attack] is held to be the death-knell
of unionism in the colonies.'

The case against Petrie was eventually dropped, and the labour
movement quietly dropped him, as bombing non-unionists was bad
PR. Labour might tolerate the rhetoric of revolution, but not its
practice. The party's early success suggested that it might soon win
government, so why would it want to bring the political establishment down?

William Spence was typical of this New Labour in claiming to
be an evolutionary, rather than revolutionary, socialist. While intellectuals might theorise about how best to seize control of the means
of production, Labour men would be pragmatic in cutting deals with
Liberals to get pro-worker laws through parliament. They would
change the system from within, confident that the system would not
change them. Spence and co saw themselves as 'practical idealists'.
Their critics saw this as having a bet each way.[27]

With its power on the rise, and its revolutionary fringe quietened,
it was time for Labour to do what it did best – viciously turn on its own.

RATS IN THE RANKS

Labor had more splits than an Elizabeth Taylor–hosted party for
the US gymnastics team, with the first occurring over spelling. Different colonies, and different branches within a colony, adopted
different spellings, regularly switching between Labour and Labor
and then switching back again. The press generally favoured *Labour*,
the accepted British spelling, irrespective of what local Labor/Labour
was actually calling itself. It was a branding nightmare.

---

27   Labour's non-evolutionary socialists were dismayed by the party's gradualism –
      'What do we want? *State ownership of the means of production!* When do we want it?
      In five or six terms!'

The Great Labor Spelling Split can be traced back to Noah Webster, the American language reformer who attempted to standardise American speech and spelling. Webster believed the British aristocracy had corrupted the English language by adding unnecessary letters and encouraging fruity pronunciation, and that overly complex English spelling rules should be replaced by simpler ones that Americans might understand. His 1828 *An American Dictionary of the English Language* (now the *Merriam-Webster Dictionary*) adopted more phonetic spelling, favouring 'o' over 'ou' in many words.[28] Webster saw his dictionary as providing an intellectual foundation for American nationalism, the break from British spelling reinforcing the United States' break from Britain.

Australian colonial speech, in contrast to that of Britain and America, was remarkably homogenous. In the convict era, people with differing languages, dialects and accents were forced to live together. The early colonists had to flatten their accents and adopt consistent pronunciation in order to understand each other. A distinct Australian accent had appeared by the middle of the nineteenth century, and a highly mobile population ensured new regional accents never had the opportunity to develop (although, if you listen closely, South Australians sound a bit funny).

Back in Britain, the elocution movement was promoting the overly pronounced and slow 'standard southern English' favoured by Eton boys and chinless aristos now known as 'BBC'. In the 1880s, Australian social climbers began to look down on their own accent, deliberately adopting the 'correct English' of the elocution movement. In reaction to this 'cultivated' accent, many working-class Australians, or those with strong nationalist sympathies, adopted a 'broad' accent that

---

28 *Melbournians* changed their name to *Melburnians* in 1876, although this was not a simplification, but an exercise in elitism. They wanted a Latin name and, given there is no 'ou' in Latin, they dropped the 'o' – notwithstanding Lord Melbourne, after whom the city was named, being an out-and-proud 'ou' guy.

dropped letters and ran syllables together.[29] Those who thought that adopters of the 'cultivated' or 'broad' accent were wankers retained the flat 'general' Australian accent.

The Great Labor Spelling Split was a symptom of a broader debate on how Australians should speak and write. Joseph Cook, who'd dropped an 'e', was typical of those who wanted a simpler English, broadly modelled on American lines. *Labor*, spelling reformers believed, reflected the party's modernity and was a rejection of aristocracy that spoke to a classless Australian future, rather than the class-riven British past. It also saved on ink.

It took until 1918 (with numerous name switches and passionate spelling debates at conferences) for 'Australian Labor Party' to be consistently adopted at both federal and state level, with a few die-hards holding out until the 1950s.[30]

The second Labor split occurred in late 1891, after Sir Henry Parkes' final resignation as premier. Parkes' successor, Protectionist George Dibbs, introduced a customs bill that split New South Wales Labor into free trade and protectionist factions, with the latter securing Dibbs the premiership over his Free Trade rival, George Reid (although Labor would later jump ship and back Reid).

In 1892, the New South Wales Labor executive voted eleven to seven against a proposal that all workers be employed by the state, with hardcore socialists effectively purged from the party by 1898. The following year, a motion to make the single tax part of the party's platform lost by one vote.

Tensions also grew between city and country members. The party platform supported an eight-hour workday for all. The AWU didn't

---

29   The broadest Australian accent is known as *Strine*, which is how those who speak it say *Australian*. In Strine, *didn't go* sounds like *dingo* and *couple of minutes* sounds like *garbler mince*.

30   I'm very glad that Labor spent its first quarter of a century so productively, as I can now settle on a single spelling for the remainder of this book, regardless of the spelling in vogue at any particular place and time. So, from now on, *Labor* it is.

want this, as bush shifts were set by the sun, rather than clocks, and the type and amount of work available varied with the seasons.[31]

In 1893, the New South Wales party, still reeling from the free trade/protectionist split, decided it would no longer tolerate splitters. A motion was carried that any person causing dissension in the ranks 'must be regarded as an enemy of Labor and a traitor to its cause'. Groupthink was enforced, and a Labor member who publicly deviated from the party line was a 'rat' – an even lower life form than the scab.[32]

Chris Watson, now president of both the Labor Electoral League Conference and the Trades and Labour Council, worked with Billy Hughes and others to require Labor MPs to sign a new pledge – one that further bound them to the decisions of the union-dominated Conference. Labor fractured into Solidarities (those who signed the solidarity pledge) and Independents (those who didn't), and the groups ran separate tickets in the 1894 election, with the division contributing to the loss of about half Labor's seats.

A disillusioned Joseph Cook, who'd refused the pledge, accepted a ministry in George Reid's Free Trade government. Billy Trenwith also repudiated the pledge later demanded by the Victorian party. Tommy Ryan, uncomfortable with the ease with which his comrades had adapted to political life, explained his decision to quit parliament:

> The friends are too warm, the whiskey too strong, and the seats too soft for Tommy Ryan. His place is out among the shearers and the billabongs.[33]

---

31 Queenslanders know that clocks are a Trojan horse for daylight savings, a degenerate southern reform that must be resisted at any cost.

32 J.K. Rowling, a Labour supporter who acknowledges socialist influences in her literary work, plays with scab and rat tropes in the character of Peter Pettigrew, who transforms into a rat named Scabbers after selling out his friends. All good Marxist-Leninists should keep a copy of *Harry Potter* besides *Das Kapital*.

33 For foreign readers, a billabong is a pool of water left behind after a flood. The Wiradjuri word was first recorded by New South Wales surveyor-general Major

Solidarities like Billy Hughes came to dominate Labor. After winning the Sydney seat of Lang in 1894, Hughes' supporters celebrated by buying him a decent suit and staging a victory parade, in which he was drawn through the streets in a dogcart.[34]

One of the things that all Labor parties and factions could agree on was that the Chinese were up to no good. The original New South Wales Labor platform, with its muted complaints about Chinese furniture, was only mildly Sinophobic – but in 1892, it railed against 'Chinese, coolies, and other undesirable labourers entering the colony'. It even had a go at Asian animals that were taking the jobs of honest, hard-working oxen and horses. Camels, Labor declared, were un-Australian.

The colonial Labor parties adjusted their immigration and employment platforms until they broadly aligned with Queensland Labor's full-throttle xenophobia.[35] So too did the trade union movement, with William Spence explaining that the AWU embraced all workers, 'no matter what their occupation or sex may be', but:

> No Chinese, Japanese, Kanakas, or Afghans or coloured aliens other than Maoris, American negroes, and children of mixed parentage born in Australia shall be admitted to membership.

Jews were another popular Labor target. Didn't they control the banks that were stealing the deposits and land of workers and farmers? Even though the banks were controlled by men like Deakin and Premier Munro, there were more votes in promoting an international Zionist banking conspiracy. An 1892 *Worker* cartoon depicting a suitably foreign-looking Jew abusing an unemployed white man was captioned:

Thomas Mitchell in 1836 and soon incorporated into Australian English, as was another Aboriginal word – *bunyip*, an aquatic monster that lurks in billabongs.

34   Two decades later, the Little Dogger would become the Little Digger.

35   One Queensland Labor delegate boasted 'he had been two years without vegetables because he would not buy them from the Chinese'.

QUEENSLAND
MILLIONS of ACRES
TONS OF GOLD
SHEEP CATTLE HORSES
ALL BELONG TO THE JEWS
NOTHING BELONGS TO THE PEOPLE

John Tanck had made a sensible decision in becoming Chris Watson. While undeniably white, South Americans like Watson were perhaps just a little too foreign for comfort. It therefore surprised everyone in Labor when William Lane, the most virulently racist of its founding fathers, decided to split and become a South American.

LANETOWN

Lane, who'd believed Australia was set to become the world's first socialist state, was disillusioned by the failed maritime and shearers' strikes. Then, in 1892, Broken Hill's miners went on strike over employer demands that they be paid for ore extracted, rather than hours worked. The strike was crushed, although the Women's Brigade put on another good show, assaulting strike-breakers with 'sticks, broom handles and axe handles'.

Workers were losing faith in unions. Sure, the picnics were nice, but what was the point of paying your dues and going hungry on the picket line, only to be shafted? By 1896, union membership would drop from 20 to 5 per cent of the workforce, with many smaller unions going to the wall. Lane wasn't going to hang around to see his dreams turn to ash.

He decided Australia needed to start all over again if it were to become a worker's paradise. Australia would do this in Paraguay. Lane would establish a utopian socialist commune called New Australia, where he would 'practically demonstrate that men and women can live together in perfect peace and contentment if absolute equality and absolute mateship is taken as the basis of the movement'.

Once he and his followers had 'become accustomed to being mates, and our children are born and bred into the same atmosphere', Lane predicted, 'all need for legislation or for state-force of any kind will pass away' – 'we shall all love being mates, and all hate the very notion of competing with each other as we do now'.

Lane was clearly into mates in a big way – so much so that he elevated mateship to a religion, which he, as its primate, would bring to the world (or at least a remote corner of South America):

> ... men are being driven into mateship by the overwhelming Destiny which our forefathers termed God ... And it is to bring this idea of mateship from vague and casual happening into the domain of actual and persistent experience that we New Australians surrender all other things, and devote all our energies to proving the reality of the supreme Truth in which we believe.

Before we go any further, it's important to understand a few things about socialists and communes. In the late nineteenth century, socialists fell broadly into two groups: those who believed socialism was a choice and those who believed it an inevitability.

The first group included Christian socialists like Thomas Hughes (the *Tom Brown's School Days* guy), ethical socialists like William Spence (the racist shearer guy) and utopian socialists like Robert Owen (the eight-hour workday guy). Christian socialists are motivated by God, ethical socialists by morality, and utopian socialists by rationalism. There's a fair amount of crossover between these schools, and they're all generally comfortable with gradual, localised reform. Their members have, at various times, shown an interest in finding a quiet bit of countryside and building a cosy little commune on it.

The second group included anarcho-socialists like Larry Petrie (the one-armed, sit in the dark chanting over cloth, hey let's blow up a ship guy), who wanted to dismantle all state structures – and, in the twentieth century, Leninists, Maoists and other revolutionary descendants of Karl Marx. The members of these schools believe that socialism is the necessary endpoint of capitalism and that it will be achieved through revolution. There's not much crossover between revolutionary socialist schools, because if you leave their members alone with each other for more than five minutes, one lot will have purged all the others. Members of this group are motivated by blowing up people who disagree with them and by charismatic, populist leaders who build palaces for the glory of the workers, which they then symbolically occupy. Their leaders have, at various times, shown an interest in finding a quiet bit of countryside and building a cosy little re-education and/or death camp on it.

This means William Lane was one of the good guys. In founding a socialist commune, he was following in the footsteps of Robert Owen and Thomas Hughes. Owen established a utopian socialist commune in the US state of Indiana in 1825, buying the German religious commune of Harmony after all the religious Germans moved to a new commune, Economy.[36] Owen's New Harmony lasted only two years.

---

36 Members of religious sects are, like socialists, big on communes. Australia's most influential spiritual communist was John Alexander Dowie, a Congregational pastor turned independent evangelist faith healer who moved to America in 1888 to establish the International Divine Healing Association – a lucrative telephone, telegram and mail-order faith-healing empire. In 1896, he founded the Christian Catholic Church in Zion (which he later rebranded as the Christian Catholic Apostolic Church) and announced he was Elijah the Restorer, the third incarnation of the prophet Elijah and the herald of Christ's second coming. In 1900, he established Zion City, a massive commune in which he owned all the property and insisted that his followers keep all their money in the Zion bank (which he also owned). He wore flowing robes and jewelled turbans, travelled by private train, engaged some of his more muscular followers as uniformed bodyguards, and generally lived a life of wealth and luxury. Several of his followers were influential in the twentieth-century Pentecostal movement, and members of the Zionist Churches that sprang from his ministry are the largest group of Christians in South Africa. Dowie also provided the blueprint for modern televangelism. Not bad for a guy who started out as an Adelaide bootmaker.

Hughes established the Christian socialist commune of Rugby
(named after his posh school) in the US state of Tennessee in 1880.
Rugby was an unusual socialist commune in that it was built for the
younger sons of the English gentry, whose only hope of an inheritance
lay in all their older brothers dying. Hughes hoped to give these poor
deprived souls the opportunity to become healthy, manly, Christian
cooperative farmers. The first wave of colonists constructed tennis
and croquet courts and, by 1884, Rugby's 400 residents had established a tennis team, a social club and a literary and dramatic society.
An attempt to establish a tomato-canning operation failed, as the
Rugbyans couldn't grow enough tomatoes – in selecting Rugby's
location, its poor soil had been ignored because of the site's potential
as a mountain resort. The 'pleasure picnic', as London's *Daily News*
dubbed Rugby, was effectively wound up in 1887, but not before giving chardonnay socialists a bad name.

Lane selected South America for his mateship cult to discourage
the weak from joining. Over 220 hardy Australians drank his Kool-Aid,
relocating to the Paraguayan jungle in 1893. Henry Lawson wanted
to join them, but couldn't afford the fare.

The *Bulletin*, usually a Lane supporter, labelled the venture 'one
of the most feather-headed expeditions ever conceived since Ponce
de Leon started out to find the Fountain of Eternal Youth, or Sir
Galahad pursued the Holy Grail'. It prophesied 'schemings, and
heart-burnings and bitterness'.

The *Bulletin* was remarkably prescient. Lane's idea of absolute
equality involved some people (him) being more equal than others
(everyone else). His dictatorial qualities manifested on the voyage
out, with one of his colonists lamenting:

> 'Mateship', the word we conjured with, is forgotten. It died as we
> crossed the Pacific Ocean, and it was as dead when we landed as if
> it had been formally buried in the sea.

Several of the colonists engaged in an alcohol-fuelled brawl when the party arrived at the Uruguayan capital of Montevideo. Lane decreed that this was NOT MATEY and demanded *his* colonists foreswear alcohol altogether.[37] Within a few weeks of starting the commune, he started expelling the unmatey. 'The crooked ones will have to go', Lane proclaimed. 'If any man has not ... absolute faith in the righteousness of mateship and in the certainty of its final success ... don't let him even think of joining New Australia.' Others left of their own accord.

The following year, in keeping with Labor tradition, Lane split. With his family and sixty-three of the righteously matey, Lane moved 72 kilometres down the road to build a New New Australia, which he named Cosme. He continued to look for new recruits and found William Petrie.

Mrs Lane returned to Australia to raise funds for Cosme, supported by Mary Cameron, who acted as honorary treasurer for the venture. In 1895, Cameron relocated to Paraguay to become Cosme's schoolteacher, edit its daily paper, cook, clean and garden. In her spare time (not much), she wrote poetry, mostly about how much she loved the man she'd met there – her husband, ex-shearer William Gilmore.

Lane's continued despotic behavior brought New Australia to breaking point. 'He is a madman,' Petrie wrote of Lane, 'a knave seized with the madness of ambition, overpowered with a sense of the divinity of himself and his mission, and for that he will barter truth, justice and the whole world plus the handful of bigots he terms the faithful'.

Petrie left for the Paraguayan town of Villarrica, where he was run over by a train while attempting to rescue a child on the tracks, a noble way for an anarchist bomber to go. The Gilmores drifted from Cosme in 1899, settling in freezing Patagonia, where Mary taught

---

37   Henry Lawson would now have been thanking his lucky gods he'd had no money
      for the fare to Paraguay.

FIG. 8: UNLIKE HER GREAT-GREAT-NEPHEW, AUSTRALIAN PRIME MINISTER
SCOTT MORRISON, MARY GILMORE HELD A HOSE.

children English and William introduced Argentinians to mechanical shears. A bitter William Lane immigrated to New Zealand the
same year, where he edited a conservative newspaper and made the
transition from republican to imperialist. Writing as 'Tohunga' (the
Maori word for prophet), he denounced trade union lawlessness and
called for universal military training.

Still, Lane's ideas of communal socialism were influential in
Australia, albeit for a short time. In late 1893, months after the New
Australians set sail, colonial parliaments passed laws to establish
cooperative village settlements for the depression unemployed, with
Chris Watson treasurer of one such community. The same year, South
Australia established Murtho, a Christian ethical socialist settlement
on the Murray River for men and women 'with the true mateship

spirit', several of whom were family members of New Australians.[38] Murtho's constitution provided that the sexes were 'to be recognised as equally entitled to full membership' – women had the same rights as men in determining how the settlement was to be run.

While William Lane was failing to provide 'absolute equality' in the Paraguayan jungle, something strange was happening in South Australia.[39] Women were demanding the vote.

And even more amazingly, they were getting it.

---

38 Eleven cooperative villages for the unemployed were established on the Murray in the 1890s, all but one failing by 1905 (although socialists would say they failed in practice, not in theory). These villages were championed by the Forward Movement, a loose grouping of South Australian progressives, including Catherine Helen Spence, who variously pursued socialism, trade unionism, a single tax, temperance, women's rights and assorted other worthy concerns.

39 Too much shouldn't be read into this, as something strange is always happening in South Australia.

9
Let Us Be Up and Doing

Nineteenth century civilisation has accorded to women the same political status as to the idiot and the criminal. Such is the basis of our reverence for the person of women and of our estimate of her work.

Mary Lee, 1889

FANNY AND THE FRANCHISE

ON 22 JANUARY 1856, FANNY FINCH BECAME THE FIRST woman to vote in an Australian election. A woman voting was an embarrassment to all right-minded Victorians, but a black single mother voting was a complete clusterfuck.

The child of African-English servants, Finch was raised in a London orphanage that trained her in dusting, polishing and saying 'Yes, ma'am' whenever she was ordered to dust or polish something. After travelling to South Australia as a domestic servant in 1837, Finch married, had four children, left her husband and set out for the Victorian goldfields, eventually settling in Castlemaine. By 1854, she was a successful restaurateur.

Finch heard miners complaining about paying tax to the government while the government denied them the vote, and saw the government grant them suffrage after the 1854 Eureka Rebellion. Well, didn't she pay rates on the property she owned? Wasn't she also a victim of taxation without representation?

From 1854, ratepaying 'persons' were entitled to vote in Victorian local government elections, so Fanny and another woman rocked up to a Castlemaine polling booth. Their ballots were taken by election officials, but later rejected on the grounds that 'they had no right to vote'. Finch had got the wrong end of the stick in presuming that women were persons.

The men of Victoria's parliament considered the subhuman status of women settled when they legislated in 1863 that all voters in local elections could vote in the colonial polls. They were therefore surprised by the following 1864 *Argus* report:

> At one of the polling booths ... a novel sight was witnessed. A coach filled with ladies drove up, and the fair occupants alighted and recorded their votes ...

Some of the more enterprising candidates were prepared to advance the argument that women were people and had arranged for members of this hitherto untapped electoral resource to be bussed to the polls. The women's votes were counted, a first at the Australian colonial level. Gobsmacked MPs responded by closing the loophole that had made Victoria an international laughing-stock. Their insertion of the word 'male' before 'persons' restored women to their proper place.

In 1867, Britain extended voting rights to all male heads of households. The following year, 4,000 Manchester women attempted to vote, with their lawyer, Richard Pankhurst, arguing that the reference to 'man' in British voting laws should be interpreted to include 'woman'. He lost.[1]

The legal argument that a woman was a man remained untested in Australia, where the colonies were still grappling with whether a woman might be a person. As extensions of their husbands, married women had no rights to property in their own name (unless, like Finch, they'd

---

[1]   In 1878, Pankhurst married Emmeline Goulden, who became Britain's leading suffragist, with their daughters Christabel, Adela and Sylvia also prominent fighters for the female vote.

separated).[2] Even the wages they earned belonged to their husbands, making their husbands little more than pimps.

In 1869, Victorian radical liberal MP George Higinbotham failed to gain support for a bill to grant married women property rights. After the British parliament passed laws in 1870 for married women to keep their own wages and inherit certain property in their own name, Higinbotham had another crack. This time he succeeded. The result went far beyond the British law, with wives given absolute control of their property and earnings, including all their property at the time of marriage.[3]

Still, Henrietta Dugdale thought Higinbotham hadn't gone far enough. She'd lost her property to a wastrel husband whom she couldn't live with and had difficulty living without. In an 1869 letter to the *Argus*, she described Higinbotham's bill as 'a poor and partial remedy for a great and crying evil', calling on him to 'lay the axe to the root of the tree' by liberalising divorce laws so that the separated or deserted might remarry. She wrote:

> In the case of a young woman so deserted it is three to one but she either falls a victim to some vile seducer, and ultimately ends her shortened career in Bourke-street or the River Yarra, or she forms some other connexion which may or may not turn out happy, but which, under the best conditions, the law does not recognise.

While the other Australian colonies followed Victoria's lead on married women's property, divorce would prove a tougher nut to crack.

Meanwhile, Higinbotham again sought to bridge the gender divide. In 1873 he appealed to his fellow MPs:

---

2   Married women didn't even have their own names. When Fanny Combe tied the knot with Joseph Finch she became Mrs Joseph Finch.

3   Brits still like to claim credit for being the first to give wives full control of their property and earnings, but Richard Pankhurst, who developed Britain's 1882 *Married Women's Property Act*, essentially did a cut-and-paste job of Victoria's revolutionary law.

Giving the right of voting to females will be one step towards that general and complete political equality which it appears to be the chief purpose of this age to effect.

Premier James Francis was having none of it:

Although I entertain great respect and regard for the female sex, I consider the qualification of the ladies to be already sufficiently charming without adding to their influence in society by conferring on them the right to vote for members of the legislature.

Higinbotham had gone too far, but Henrietta Dugdale was determined to go further. She didn't just want to push the envelope, but lick it, put a stamp on it and post it, so that it might be opened in a fairer future. In 1883, she published a utopian novel dedicated to Higinbotham, 'in earnest admiration of the brave attacks made by that gentleman upon ... the greatest obstacle to human advancement, the most irrational, fiercest and most powerful of our world's monsters – the only devil – MALE IGNORANCE'.

Dugdale's unnamed female Australian narrator of *A Few Hours in a Far-Off Age* dreamt of Alethia, a model democracy thousands of years in the future. The Alethians ate two vegetarian meals a day, spent their mornings working and learning, and devoted their afternoons to pleasure. They wore loose, comfortable clothes, in contrast to the 'hideously shaped' 1880s women, whose constricting garments were designed by 'cunning men' to make them 'weak-brained tools'. Man, the narrator informed her female readers, ensnared them with fashion so that he might 'make laws affecting you and your children ... as he does over any other animal he possesses.'

The Alethians had no religion, consistent with Dugdale's view that all faiths, being designed by men, were oppressive. Alethian women had equal access to education, co-designed the flying machines owned by every Alethian household and had made great discoveries, including the use of petroleum as a fertiliser.[4] And Alethian women had the vote, with the narrator concluding this was the only way to end 'man's tyrannical laws' and usher in *just legislation* ... for the progress of all humankind'.

Dugdale lived the values of Alethia. She wore a homemade 'bloomer suit' of baggy trousers and tunic, and championed rational dress for women in an attempt to save them from open flames, train wheels and compressed organs. She adhered to 'true ethics' rather than religious morality, believed the monarchy perpetuated social and sexual inequality, condemned alcohol and illiteracy, and supported birth control. And in 1884, with Annie Lowe, she co-founded the Victorian Women's Suffrage Society, Australia's first organisation dedicated to achieving the vote for women.

A HEN AMONG COCKS

Victoria may have started women's suffrage in Britain's southern colonies, but it was South Australia that gave momentum to the cause. In 1861, it *deliberately* gave women ratepayers the vote – but only in local elections, because councils were responsible for collecting rubbish, cleaning footpaths and dealing with complaints about neighbours' hedges – matters that encroached on the domestic sphere. Colonial parliaments dealt with great affairs of state, finance, railways, post and telegraph services, shipping, lighthouses and other serious and important matters only comprehensible to the male brain.

The person who did the most to convince South Australian men that women might be capable of rational thought on matters unconnected to the home was Catherine Helen Spence.

In 1866, Spence had sat silently on stage while a male friend stumbled his way through the speech she'd penned, later writing, 'law and custom have put a bridle on the tongue of women'. In 1871, she became

---

4   Dugdale was a better feminist than horticulturist.

the first woman to address the South Australian Institute, delivering two lectures on the poetry of Robert and Elizabeth Barrett Browning. Spence was determined to overcome her nerves 'to make easier henceforward for any woman who felt she had something to say to stand up and say it'. Developing into a confident speaker, she took to the pulpit as a Unitarian preacher, delivering sermons in Adelaide, and later in Sydney, Melbourne and the United States.

Spence cast off her journalistic invisibility cloak in 1876, writing for the *Melbourne Review* under her own name. From 1878 until 1893, the *South Australian Register* proudly advertised the widely ranging articles she wrote for it. Spence offered her opinions on land policy, taxation, wages and labour, agriculture and Imperial Federation – matters far removed from the domestic sphere. She claimed credit for South Australia's introduction of Australia's first income tax in 1884, and the same year became Australia's first champion of 'compulsory providence', a scheme to reduce poverty by requiring workers to save a portion of their earnings until retirement – now known as superannuation.

Not all of Spence's writing was so weighty. She published domestic tips, word games, literary reviews and children's stories, although some of these had political messages. 'The Hen's Language', a somewhat risqué children's verse, asked why a rooster had a harem of fifteen hens, with the hens complaining, 'Why not one hen to fifteen cocks?'

Having abandoned the staid romances that saw her rise to prominence, Spence, like Henrietta Dugdale, turned her hand to utopian fiction. *Handfasted*, written in 1879, was set in an American commune where unmarried couples were allowed to live together for a year and a day to see whether they were compatible, with any little bastards born during an unsuccessful trial partnership honoured as 'God's bairns', given the best education and employed as public servants.[5]

---

5   *Handfasted* was submitted for a literary competition, with the judge reporting, 'it
    was calculated to loosen the marriage tie – it was too socialistic, and consequently
    dangerous.' It was not published until 1984, a good year for futuristic novels.

The protagonist of 1889's *A Week in the Future*, Emily Bethel, was an unmarried Adelaide woman who exchanged the last two years of her life for a week in 1988 London. Emily finds herself in a wonderful world of communal living, where women are 'set free' from domestic work 'to pursue bread-winning avocations' and provided with contraceptives to prevent them from having more than three children. Newspapers are thinner because 'universal peace' means there is less news, and advertising is unnecessary because everything can be bought at cooperative stores. Britain's railways have been nationalised, workers work six-hour days, factories have been replaced by public gardens, amateurs have their paintings hung in the National Gallery, children attend coeducational state schools, women have premarital sex at universities and lead religious services, the Catholic Church supports 'easy divorce', and the monarchy has been replaced by a republic. Less idyllically, birthday cards are expensive, 'idiot children' are euthanised at birth, and immigration restrictions prevent 'Chinese coming to destroy all we have struggled for!'

Spence was a forerunner of futuristic feminist writers like Margaret Atwood, although women in her imagined worlds had a much better time than those in *The Handmaid's Tale*, unless they were Chinese or idiots, or it was their birthday.

Spence was passionate about female education, considering it essential for women to enter the workforce and compete with men 'on a fair field'. Education, she explained, would allow a woman to choose 'not between destitution and marriage but between the modest competence she can earn and the modest competence her lover offers'.

In 1877, Spence was the first woman appointed to a South Australian school board and, in 1879, she was instrumental in establishing Australia's first government secondary school, Adelaide's Advanced School for Girls, founded on the principle that its students should receive the same education as boys. The same year, the University of Melbourne started enrolling women for most of its degrees, with Bella Guerin's 1883 Bachelor of Arts making her Australia's first female tertiary graduate. Other Australian universities followed Melbourne's lead.

The government asked Spence to write about South Australia's laws and institutions for the colony's senior students. *The Laws We Live Under*, published in 1880, was the first Australian school textbook that addressed economics or politics. As Spence explained in its first chapter:

> The progress of the world ... depends on the character and conduct of its women as much as on that of its men; and there can be no greater mistake for girls to make than to suppose they have nothing to do with good citizenship and good government.

THE WOMAN IN BLACK

Fifty-eight-year-old Mary Lee arrived in Adelaide in 1879. Swaddled in layers of clothing that ranged in colour from black to blacker, she sweated under an alien sun. No matter. She'd lived through the Irish Potato Famine, so she wouldn't let a little heat stop her from doing what was right. Her widow's weeds and the heaped bun that added inches to her stout five-foot frame would become her trademarks in Adelaide society.

Lee had come to South Australia to nurse her sick son, John, who died within a year of her arrival. Lacking the return fare to Ireland, she was stuck in Adelaide.[6]

Adelaide was the city of churches, which suited Lee just fine. She'd been a dutiful attendee of Armagh Cathedral (the Protestant one) and her personal trials had not dimmed her faith. She soon fell into the orbit of Reverend Joseph Coles Kirby of the Port Adelaide Congregational Church.

---

6   Adelaide is the Hotel California of Australia.

Adelaide was also the city of prostitutes, having overtaken Sydney as Australia's sin city.[7] Kirby was concerned that men were debauching respectable Adelaide girls, turning them into prostitutes. With all the prostitutes around, men delayed marrying respectable Adelaide girls, increasing the likelihood of the girls being debauched. It was a vicious circle.

There was too much sex in the world, Kirby believed, and if people insisted on adding to it, they should at least do so within the confines of marriage – preferably no more than once a month, in a darkened bedroom, on a hard and scratchy mattress that would reduce any pleasure either of the parties might inadvertently experience.

When it came to sex, men were the problem. They initiated it and sometimes even enjoyed it, while women consented to it out of familial duty, financial need or feeblemindedness. However, sexual laws protected men and punished women. South Australia needed new laws that would reduce men's sexual opportunities and empower women to say 'NO!', which they'd find easier if there were greater equality between the sexes.

Kirby, emulating the moral purity movements that had flourished in his native England during the 1870s, founded the South Australian Society for the Promotion of Social Purity in 1882 (Social Purity being a way of saying 'Not Having Sex' without mentioning the S-word). Men and women, mainly middle-class Nonconformist Protestants, signed up to make South Australia less sexy. Mary Lee joined the Society's Ladies Division and took the Social Purity Pledge to 'protect ... all women and children from degradation'; abstain from 'jests and conversation, and behaviour derogatory to women'; ensure 'equal obligation of the law of purity to men and women alike'; and, first and foremost, 'fulfil the apostolic injunction,

---

7   In fairness, there's not a lot else to do in Adelaide. The fact that it was often the
     first Australian port of call for international sailors may have also had something
     to do with it.

"Keep thyself pure".[8]

Lee was at the forefront of the Society's campaign to raise the age of consent.[9] If men could be stopped from having sex with children, she reasoned, then those children, a few years older and wiser, might have the wherewithal to tell men they were disgusting old perverts.

South Australia had already raised the age of consent from ten to thirteen in 1876, which parliamentarians considered about right.[10] Lee wrote outraged letters to the papers. She spoke to church groups and anyone else who would listen. She buttonholed MPs.

In 1884, the South Australian parliament concluded that the colony's prostitutes were 'a benefit to society, as they might in some instances be a sort of safety-valve by which the crimes against children ... were rendered more unfrequent'. However, the following year it accepted Lee's arguments to set the age of consent at sixteen, helping to keep younger girls out of brothels and off the street.

Social Purity Societies sprang up across the continent during the 1880s. They highlighted the unfairness of Queensland, Victorian and Tasmanian contagious disease laws that permitted the compulsory genital examination of women suspected of having syphilis (being a prostitute was sufficient cause) and the imprisonment of syphilitic women to protect men from infection. A woman who was found not to have syphilis was issued with a medical certificate authorising her to work as a prostitute, even if she'd never entertained the thought of such work. The Victorian parliament rejected the suggestion that such laws might equally apply to syphilitic men, as it would be

8 Paul the Apostle wrote a letter to Timothy to this effect when he was concerned his pupil was thinking dirty thoughts. Paul's circumcision of the adult Timothy would have also helped keep him pure (see next page).

9 According to a 2021 Australian government sex-education campaign, this is the age at which you can have a milkshake.

10 Reformers often looked to the United States for progressive policies, but most American states at that time set the age of consent at ten, with Delaware considering seven-year-olds fair game. Victoria followed South Australia in 1891, with the other states all having an age of consent of at least sixteen by 1910.

unreasonable to 'go into a family and take the father of a family and punish him'.

In 1887, the New South Wales Social Purity Society spearheaded an attempt to criminalise seduction under the promise of marriage, as 'women, as a rule were chaste, and very few went wrong unless they were deluded by some unprincipled vagabond'. As age had not slowed Premier Parkes' unprincipled vagabondery, and purity was generally in short supply on the parliamentary benches, the Seduction Punishment Bill went nowhere.

Social Purity Societies recommended parents educate their children about sex to prevent them from having it. Children were taught how to stay vigilant against fleshly temptations, with social purity campaigners recommending that young people suspected of masturbation be referred to a doctor.

The social puritans waged a war on wanking, advocating vigorous exercise and early marriage as preventatives. Dr Alexander Paterson, author of *On Nervous Debility*, prescribed cold baths, hard mattresses, not going back to sleep after waking, electrocution and placing the penis in an uncomfortable device that he just happened to sell. Dr Richard Arthur recommended circumcision as both a preventative and cure in *The Innocence of Children*.[11]

Social purity types were opposed to people having sex with themselves because it set them on the slippery slope to sex with others. So too did the 'cure' of early marriage, but at least a teenage wedding avoided the terrible consequences of self-stimulation, which included nervousness, depression, over-eating, insanity, degeneration of the brain, impotence, blindness, shrinking of the penis and scrotum, and walking funny. Prominent Geelong butcher and anti-masturbation campaigner Henry Varley preached that 'self-pollution' led to 'simpering

---

11   Arthur, a prominent social purity campaigner, also wrote movingly of the 'bright and innocent girl' yielding to temptation, only to become a 'painted, gin-sodden harlot ... whose consumptive cough drowns her hoarse and despairing laughter'.

effeminacy' and 'lewd speech', while Dr Bottrell's *At Once or Never! A Pamphlet with a Purpose* warned:

> The hands are either feverishly dry, or else clammy with moisture. There is no animation in the gait of these phantoms, and they start at the nearest sound. They are shy and reserved, especially in the society of women.

Female fiddlers, Doctors Freeman and Wallace cautioned in *Rescued at Last: Being Clinical Experiences on Nervous and Private Diseases, by Sydney's Leading Specialists*, would develop flat chests and round shoulders and sleep on their left sides.[12]

Wankmania held middle-class Australia in its feverish grip, with Ted Machefer, the swagman whom Labor poet Bernard O'Dowd yearned to caress, planning an 1890 campaign against 'the nation-destroying practice of self-abuse'. Wanking was un-Australian, and any widespread outbreak of onanism would lead to racial and national degeneration, lowering the white man to the level of the Chinaman and opening the colonies to Chinese invasion.[13]

The social purity movement had given Mary Lee a platform that she'd used to achieve real change – and the one-time 'slip of an old red-hot Tory stem' was not yet done with radical reform. But she realised that if she and her social purity sisters really wanted to convince politicians to improve the lot of women, then they needed some skin in the political game. They needed the vote.

---

12   The good doctors also marketed a device for reformed male masturbators, promising 'the flabby, soft, and pallid penis, more like that of a delicate child than the organ of a full-grown man, renews its former healthy condition and accomplishes with natural energy the part for which it is intended'.

13   *Onanism* derives from Genesis 38:7–10, which tells how Onan's brother Er was slain by God; how Onan was ordered by his father to sleep with Er's widow; how Onan was not happy with this arrangement and 'spilled his seed on the ground'; and how God slew Onan for his seed-spilling.

WOWSERS!

The 1880s weren't all about stopping people from having sex – they were also about stopping them from having a drink. There was, social-purity types concluded, a clear link between the two vices. If people stopped getting drunk, then they might keep their pants on.

Women had a particular interest in reducing alcohol consumption. Drunk men weren't only more likely to abuse women and children, but also to neglect and desert them – and mire their families in poverty by spending all their money on booze. Henrietta Dugdale was among those who believed liquor reform was necessary to better protect women and children from 'ill-usage'.

Temperance had become fashionable among Australia's Nonconformist Protestant elite in the 1830s, but it was seen as a personal choice, with an emphasis on moderation, rather than abstinence. In 1843, the International Order of Rechabites, founded eight years earlier in northern England, set up shop in Australia. The International Order, a.k.a. the Sons and Daughters of Rechab, was a healthcare-focused friendly society whose members swore an oath of total abstinence.[14]

By the 1880s, many Nonconformists embraced militant temperance (words that, unlike vodka and vermouth, traditionally don't mix). They denounced alcohol as a major social and moral evil. Their children joined Bands of Hope, juvenile temperance chapters, and signed pledges of lifelong abstinence. And they lobbied politicians.

New South Wales justice minister John Foster (not to be confused with the beer) was dubbed 'Water Jug Foster' by the *Bulletin* for his

---

14   The Rechabite founders established their own friendly society because they didn't like hanging out in the pubs where most friendly societies met. The Rechabites took their name from the biblical tribe of Jehonadab, son of Rechab. Jehonadab ordered the Rechabites to drink no wine and to live in tents, and the modern Rechabites call their local groups 'tents' and their governing body 'the Movable Committee' in honour of the ancient nomadic tribe of buzz killers. Both ancient and modern Rechabites would have objected to Amy Winehouse's name, lifestyle and lyrics, as the 192-proof chanteuse rejected both Rechab and Rehab.

crusade against the demon drink, while member for Carlton (not
to be confused with the beer) and future Victorian premier James
Munro founded the Perseverance Tent of the International Order
of Rechabites, chaired international temperance conferences during
the 1880 and 1888 international exhibitions, and was president of the
Melbourne Total Abstinence Society and the Victorian Alliance for
the Suppression of the Liquor Traffic. In 1881, Alfred Deakin moved
a resolution at the Alliance's inaugural meeting:

> That the traffic in intoxicating liquors for consumption as bever-
> ages is detrimental to the best interests of society, and retards its
> progress, physically, morally, and religiously.

In 1883, the Blue Ribbon movement started pinning blue ribbons
on Victorian teetotallers, giving the temperance movement increased
public visibility.[15] The Women's Christian Temperance Union (WCTU),
established in Ohio in 1874, opened its first Victorian chapters in 1885,
with members wearing a 'bow of pure white ribbon'.[16] Chapters had spread
across Australia from 1882, as England's Margaret Hampson and the
United States' Mary Leavitt toured the country, preaching the temperance message at packed-out churches, public halls and sporting venues.

Nearly a quarter of Victoria's adult female population – 44,501
women – successfully lobbied parliament in 1885 to allow people to
vote against liquor licenses in their local communities. Alfred Deakin
almost gave himself a hernia carrying their cart-wheel-sized petition
into the Legislative Assembly.[17]

---

15   The movement, founded in the United States a decade earlier, took its inspiration
     from Numbers 15:38–39: 'Speak unto the children of Israel, and bid them that
     they make them fringes in the borders of their garments, throughout their
     generations, and that they put upon the fringe of the borders a ribband of blue:
     and it shall be unto you for a fringe, that ye may look upon it, and remember all the
     commandments of the Lord, and do them.'

16   Victoria's ribbon-makers really loved the temperance movement.

17   Other colonies established similar 'local options' in the 1890s and, with the
     exception of Western Australia, heeded the temperance movement's call to close

Victoria was the place to go to not have a drink, with temperance hotels proliferating during the 1880s. A temperance hotel, to borrow from Slim Dusty, was a pub with no beer. These 'dry' hotels served tea, coffee, cordials and new specially created 'temperance drinks', like America's Coca-Cola, in which the loss of alcohol was more than offset by the cocaine hit.[18] The Federal Hotel and Coffee Palace was one of Melbourne's grandest buildings, boasting 370 guest bedrooms, with nary a minibar to be found. It opened days before the 1888 International Exhibition, so Victorians could show the world how uptight they were.

South Australians were determined to prove they could be just as prissy as Victorians. In 1886, Methodist Sunday school teacher Elizabeth Nicholls helped Mary Leavitt found Adelaide's WCTU and, like Mary Lee, Nicholls soon realised that her organisation would have more clout if its members could vote.

The same year, Lord Carrington established the Intoxicating Drink Inquiry Commission to 'make a diligent and full inquiry into the excessive use of intoxicating drink by the people of this colony and the deterioration it has produced in public morality', which was a brave call from a guy who popped a magnum of champagne every breakfast.

---

pubs on Sundays. During World War I, the movement helped usher in 6 p.m. pub closings, an Australian norm until the 1960s. Victoria went further than the other states in allowing communities to vote to establish dry areas and close all their hotels, with Camberwell and Nunawading going dry in 1920. Victoria still has designated dry areas, in which the community must vote in support of any new pub or club license.

18   John Pemberton produced *Pemberton's French Wine Coca*, a mix of wine, ethyl alcohol, cocaine and the caffeine-laden kola nut, marketing it as a patent medicine that would aid those 'devoted to extreme mental exertion' and be 'a most wonderful invigorator of sexual organs'. In 1886, after parts of his native Georgia embraced prohibition, Pemberton produced a non-alcoholic version that he marketed as *Coca-Cola: The temperance drink*, the name taken from the cocaine-producing coca leaf and the kola nut. Members of the temperance movement don't appear to have objected to their drinks being spiked with cocaine, which was only removed in 1903 because black people had started to enjoy it.

FIG. 9: COKE IS IT!

The Commission found Sydneysiders drank more spirits and wine, and less beer, than most British citizens. Australian spirits and wine were cheaper and nastier than European ones and 'very injurious to health', causing insanity, 'deterioration of vital organs' and, for the committed inebriate, death. Alcohol ruined 'women of every class, from the most rude to the most refined'. Sir Alfred Stephen, the one-time chief justice now comfortably ensconced on the Legislative Council's padded benches, aired his concern that drink was responsible for a surge in larrikin crime.

Not everyone was worried about alcohol. *Truth*, Australia's grubbiest little rag, enjoyed nothing more than savaging temperance and purity campaigners. The paper's owner-editor was John Norton, the republican who'd disrupted the public meetings in support of Queen Victoria's Golden Jubilee. During the 1890s, he'd been dismissed as editor of the *Newcastle Morning Herald* for repeated drunkenness and elected a Protectionist MP, sitting in parliament when his editorial

muckraking allowed.[19] In 1899, he ran an article about the sancti-
monious folk of Sydney's Lower North Shore under the headline
'Willoughby Wowsers Worried'. Australians had a new word for
the moralising puritans who sought to drain the world of all its joy.[20]

But before *Truth* gave us *wowser*, J.F. Archibald was already well
and truly on the case. The *Bulletin* railed against those who sought to
interfere with a man's right to get on the turps and otherwise enjoy
himself, reserving particular contempt for women and moralising
clergymen.[21] When the WCTU suggested barmaids pursue 'some
more womanly occupation', the *Bulletin* asked what could be more
'womanly' than 'the serving-out of refreshments to males'?

Archibald had a problem with women. In 1885, he married Rosa
Frankenstein, the daughter of a Jewish merchant from London's
East End. In 1886, the couple lost their only child a day after his

---

19   *Truth* was a Sydney paper first published in 1879, promising 'Verbatim reports
     of all divorce cases and any interesting and instructive rape and murder cases'.
     It failed, but was revived in 1890 under editor Adolphus Taylor, a former MP
     known as 'the Mudgee camel' who would soon after die of syphilis in the Callan
     Park Hospital for the Insane. Norton was sacked as *Truth* editor for drunkenness
     in 1891, but later bought the paper. He observed how low other papers went and
     then went lower, while proving he was still a true republican in describing Queen
     Victoria as 'a dull and brainless woman' and 'a flabby, fat and flatulent-looking
     scion of the most ignoble line of Royal Georges', and her son the Prince of Wales
     as 'a turf swindling, card sharping, wife debauching rascal'. Norton also penned
     'comic' stories on the physical assaults he and his wife committed against each
     other. A Melbourne spin-off of *Truth*, also known as *Truth*, lasted until 1993. It
     was noted for its pictures of topless women, form guide and catchy headlines like
     'Snedden "Died on the Job"', a reference to former Liberal leader Billy Snedden
     expiring during a motel sexual encounter after attending John Howard's 1987
     campaign launch.

20   Norton claimed to have coined the term as an acronym for 'We Only Want Social
     Evils Remedied', although some linguists believe it derives from *wow*, an English
     dialect word meaning to 'howl or whine like a dog'. Australian poet C.J. Dennis
     later defined a *wowser* as 'an ineffably pious person who mistakes the world for
     a penitentiary and himself for a warder'. Americans who don't like cussing use
     Wowser! as an exclamation of surprise.

21   The *Bulletin*, in 1904, was the first publication in the world to use the term
     Bible-basher. It also referred to clergymen as *Bible-bangers, amen-snorters, gospel-
     punchers, devil-dodgers* and *sky-pilots*.

birth. Archibald became a workaholic, Rosa an alcoholic. Theirs was an increasingly distant relationship, with Rosa pawning the jewels Archibald gave her for whisky.

Archibald turned his attention to other women, with serial sex-pest Norman Lindsay later recounting how 'Archie' once ogled 'a young girl in short skirts with long curls down her back; one of those full-breasted, big-legged girls who sprout into full maturity about the age of fourteen'. Lindsay continued:

> Archie loved looking at girls ... Of that one he said, 'By George, now, look at that kid's legs. Now there'a pair of legs that could get a man a jail sentence and a lashing into the bargain, with half a dozen words to a policeman!' ... That was to touch on another of Archie's obsessions: the iniquitous administration of the law in cases of alleged rape. In those days any blackmailing slavey could go into the witness-box and swear away a man's liberty and reputation on her unsupported statement. It was Archie's long fight against the law's malevolent wowserism in that respect that brought about its present rationality over rape cases.

Archie's contempt for rape victims and all-round male chauvinist piggery was on full display for all to see after 9 September 1886.

#METOO 1886

On 9 September 1886, sixteen-year-old Mary Jane Hicks accepted a lift from cab driver Charles Sweetman. Instead of driving Mary to her appointment, Sweetman took her to Mount Rennie, a low bushy hill that is now part of Sydney's Moore Park Golf Club. Mary screamed for help when Sweetman commenced his assault, attracting the attention of a knight in shining armour.

Leaving with the young knight proved a mistake. He asked her to rest while he picked her some flowers, only to return with a group of

between twelve and twenty friends who gang-raped her. Alerted by
a witness, the police arrived during Mary's terrible ordeal. Although
unable to capture the fleeing offenders, they later arrested eleven
young larrikins and the cabman.

The larrikins from Waterloo's 'Irish Town', which adjoined Mount
Rennie, were members of the Waterloo Push. Three years earlier,
push members had been acquitted of raping and beating to death
53-year-old prostitute Margaret Owen in a paddock beside Our Lady
of Mount Carmel Church.

Owen was only one of many Australian gang-rape victims during
the 1880s and '90s, some of whom were tortured and beaten to death.
The public blamed larrikins for most such assaults. The community
sentiment against larrikins did little to secure rape convictions. Women
were considered insufficiently rational and overly emotional for jury
duty.[22] The prevailing male view was that a girl who smiled at a man
or looked attractive while unchaperoned in public was asking for it. In
fact, just about any woman who put herself in a position to be raped
was leading men on, as Archibald opined on the Mount Rennie case:

> ... you may search the records of Australia for the last 70 years
> without finding more than three authenticated cases where even
> in the lonely bush, a really virtuous woman has been successfully
> assailed by a satyr.

But Archibald had misread the public mood. While prostitutes like
Margaret Owen couldn't be raped because, well, they were prostitutes,
a sixteen-year-old convent-educated orphan girl from the country
seemed somehow different. The *Sydney Morning Herald* tried to head
off the 'But she was good looking' defence by reporting Mary was

---

22 Queensland, in 1923, was the first state to allow women jurors, but none were
appointed until 1945. Victoria, in 1962, was the last state to permit women jurors,
but they effectively remained disqualified until 1977. Tasmania, in 1991, was the
last state to pass gender-neutral jury laws.

'plain, and altogether unattractive', before defusing the 'But she's not good looking enough' defence with, 'Her general bearing, however, is by no means repulsive.'

The Waterloo and Redfern communities rallied around the eleven youths charged with Mary's rape. The local MP represented some of them in early appearances, saying six had attended mass at Our Lady of Mount Carmel shortly before the crime. Good mass-attending boys could not be guilty of such an offence. Neither, according to Reverend T.J. Curtis, the ranking local Presbyterian, could the two 'exceptionally good' boys from his congregation.

The jury found otherwise for nine of those charged. Justice William Windeyer declared them guilty of 'a most atrocious crime, a crime so horrible that every lover of his country must feel that it is a disgrace to our civilisation'. Not only were the Mount Rennie Nine gang-rapists, they were un-Australian – an even worse crime in the eyes of many. The nine death sentences handed down by Windeyer were, collectively, the most severe punishment imposed in Australian history.

The *Daily Telegraph* and *Sydney Morning Herald* applauded the sentences, the latter arguing, 'Crimes of this particular nature do not happen in other parts of the world' (a bravely incorrect assertion) and that gang-rape had replaced bushranging as Australia's crime *du jour*.

Truth, in contrast, accused Mary of being 'a female fiend' and 'partially a consenting party'.[23] The *Bulletin* called her a 'lying little street tramp' who'd 'voluntarily entered into immoral relations' with a number of 'dirty little larrikins', and had this take:

> The chief lesson of the Mount Rennie affair has been overlooked, and it is this – that no woman should, by voluntarily or carelessly breaking down the first barrier between herself and the brutal man, encourage the latter to deeds of which they would not dream save

---

23   Partial consent is like being a little bit pregnant.

for her own readiness to walk in the crooked path. A woman's best protection is not the lash or the gallows, but her own virtue.

In the week of the executions, the *Bulletin* complained, 'we don't see why men, however degraded, should be hanged to protect female vice instead of female virtue.' It similarly doubled down on cabbie Sweetman's sentence of fourteen years' imprisonment and fifty lashes: 'If the prisoner's deed deserved so frightful a penalty, where is there "a man of the world" who would go unwhipped?'

Archibald didn't try the 'All men are a little bit rapey, so it's OK' line with Lord Carrington, but he wrote to the governor after the death sentences were imposed:

> My Lord, there are worse offences possible than Mount Rennie Outrages: a rape may be committed on the person of the Goddess of Justice, whose guardian you are.

Archibald had come to public attention through his attempt to save convicted Aboriginal rapist Alfred from the hangman, and he'd continued to rail against capital and corporal punishment, but his advocacy for the Mount Rennie rapists and his slut-shaming of Mary had taken his campaigns against the death penalty and women to a whole new level.

The fired-up editor arrived on Carrington's doorstep, leading a delegation of death-penalty opponents including recent acting premier William Dalley, Cardinal Moran, Rabbi Davis and Henry Parkes, with the grand old man of colonial politics warning of 'the great harm which would accrue to the colony if these youths were hanged a year before the Centennial'.

After the longest Executive Council meeting in colonial history, Carrington commuted three of the rapists' sentences to hard labour for life, with a further two commutations to follow. Four were hanged.

Time passed and the *Bulletin* and *Truth* continued to campaign for the release of the surviving 'Mount Rennie Boys', who were freed in 1896, ten years after their crime. One of them, Michael Donnellan, became an organist and sacristan for Our Lady of Mount Carmel Church, a writer for the Catholic *Freeman's Journal* and a Waterloo alderman. He represented Waterloo Council at the coronation of King George V and was president of the Fresh Air League, with his 1941 obituary describing him as 'a prince in his charity, generosity and kindness to the poor, the unfortunate and little children' (other than sixteen-year-old girls).[24] Mary Jane Hicks, in contrast, quietly faded into history.

Yet the Mount Rennie Outrage had a lasting impact. It forced Australians to confront questions about sex, violence, the justice system, young people and inter-generational poverty. And, most importantly, it placed a lens on society's attitudes towards women.

Henrietta Dugdale and temperance advocate Bessie Lee called for the castration of rapists and serial seducers – but the big takeaway from Mount Rennie was how little sway women had in the chambers of justice and corridors of power. In 1884, Dugdale had written to the *Melbourne Herald* about the courts' treatment of female victims of male violence:

> Women's anger was compounded by the fact that those who inflicted violence upon women had a share in making the laws while their victims did not.

More women came around to Dugdale's view after Mount Rennie – and if they wanted a share in making the laws that affected them, then they needed a say in electing the men who made those laws.

DAWN

Louisa Lawson was thrilled when, in 1887, Sir Henry Parkes rose to his feet in the Legislative Assembly and called for women to have the vote. The *Daily Telegraph* was on board, advocating that women

---

24   The City of Sydney website for Sydney's aldermen contains a laudatory biography of Donnellan that makes no reference to his crime.

be placed 'on an equal footing with men in every respect affecting their place in the social and political system'.

The *Bulletin* was having none of it. An article titled 'The Great Woman Question' opened with, 'The dependence of a woman upon her husband is, after all, the chief incentive to marriage', before letting rip:

> Women are far from that stage of progressive rationalism when they can take their stand on the same platform with men. The equality argument is an absurd one.

The *Telegraph*, the *Bulletin* sneered, only supported the vote for women because it was a Tory rag that wanted to emasculate working men:

> Tories champion the alleged cause of woman because the women of today are, as a rule, Tories; almost every woman is a queen-worshipper, a prince-worshipper, a parson-worshipper.

On suffrage, it concluded, 'Women's enfranchisement just now means man's enslavement.'

Lawson was determined to return fire. If the *Bulletin* was to be a megaphone for males, then she'd be a foghorn for females. She wound up the *Republican*, which had struggled as support for the monarchy surged during Queen Victoria's 1887 jubilee. In its place, she published the *Dawn* and took on the roles of editor and principal writer. On the front page of the 15 May 1888 debut edition, she wrote:

> Every eccentricity of belief, and every variety of bias in mankind allies itself with a printing machine, and gets its singularities bruited about in type, but where is the printing-ink champion of mankind's better half? There has hitherto been no trumpet through which the concentrated voice of womankind could publish their grievances and their opinions ... Here then is DAWN, the Australian Woman's

Journal and mouthpiece – phonograph to wind out audibly the whispers, pleadings and demands of the sisterhood ... This most potent constituency we seek to represent, and for their suffrages we sue.

The *Dawn* was a clever mix of the political and practical, combining essays on women's employment, spousal abuse and the vote with tips on 'Sensible Use of Onions for Medicinal Value', how to get insects out of your ears (pour oil in them), and curing nervous disorders by going barefoot to tap into the earth's 'vast reservoir of electricity and magnetism'.[25]

Lawson contended, 'Half of Australia's women's lives are unhappy' and, more than any other Australian writer, pressed for divorce reform. She didn't hold back. In 1890's 'The Divorce Extension Bill or, The Drunkard's Wife', she wrote:

> What sober, strong, cleanly man would submit to share his bed with another in the worst state of drunkenness? But the confirmed sot, if he possesses enough command of his tottering limbs to bring him to his lawful wife's chamber, may then collapse in abandoned beastliness upon the floor or conjugal couch if he reaches it, and proceed to make the night hideous for her ... How often does the patient wife quietly steal from the chamber of horrors to seek shelter by the bed of her sleeping children.

Lawson's friend Thomas Walker, the one-time medium of choice for combustible Canadians, demanded divorce reform from his seat in the Legislative Assembly. He, like Lawson, believed women should be able to divorce drunks, having himself forsworn alcohol in 1892 after shooting a clergyman while pissed.[26]

---

25 Lawson wrote under the pen-name Dora Falconer until 1891, with many other *Dawn* writers also adopting pseudonyms. Pete Evans appears to have been one of them.

26 Walker moved to New Zealand, where he campaigned for temperance and elocution. Relocating to the Western Australian goldfields in 1899, he became a newspaper editor, Labor politician and one of the west's few non-Aboriginal

New South Wales was the last Australian colony to allow court-ordered divorce, and the quickest to expand it. From 1881, women, like men, were able to divorce on the grounds of adultery alone – and in 1892, Sir Alfred Stephen introduced a bill to allow divorce on the grounds of assault, desertion or habitual drunkenness or cruelty.[27] Louisa Lawson and the *Dawn* played their part in making it easier to divorce in New South Wales than any other part of the British Empire.

The workplace was another focus of the *Dawn*, which preached that women should be able to do any job their strength allowed and should receive the same pay as men for doing the same work. In country Queensland, almost a third of working women worked the land, but domestic service and clothes-making remained the two main female industries.[28] The growing profession of nursing, men agreed, was suitable for women – mainly because men had no interest in cleaning bedpans. However, women were actually going backwards in the one area of skilled employment in which they'd achieved the most success. In 1889, Victoria led the other colonies in barring married women from teaching, on the grounds that they should be at home looking after, or trying to have, their own kids, and were denying promising young men teaching work.[29]

Aboriginal rights campaigners. His early spiritualism and pyromania didn't stop him from becoming the minister for justice and education and attorney-general – the latter a post he used to suspend capital punishment and legislate against cruelty to animals. A popular speaker of the Legislative Assembly, he died in 1932, having served as the member for the goldfields electorate of Kanowna for twenty-seven years.

27   The concept of spousal cruelty was expanded over time, with English courts later finding cruelty proven in cases of 'slovenly boorishness around the house', cross-dressing, coitus-interruptus and a man demanding his wife tickle the soles of his feet. These grounds became irrelevant in Australia from 1975, when the *Family Law Act* provided for no-fault divorce.

28   In the late 1880s, the Queensland government, embarrassed by all its lady farmers and the frontier vibe they created, reclassified female agricultural workers as domestics.

29   Victoria's married women teachers were only allowed work as low-paid relief teachers until 1956, and Victorian women teachers didn't receive pay equity until 1971.

Women were, though, dominating telegraphy and the new fields of typing and telephony, with the *Worker* describing them as a 'standing menace' for being paid less than men. While the unions opposed women undercutting men's pay, they were even more opposed to wage parity. It would be better for everyone if women only worked in jobs men didn't want.

Lawson practised the values she preached, employing eleven female typesetters at the *Dawn*, attracting the enmity of Chris Watson and other Typographical Association heavies who simultaneously objected to her use of non-union labour and women joining the union. The Association leased a room opposite the *Dawn*'s office, in which male typographers shone mirrors through the *Dawn*'s windows to blind the women in an attempt to prevent them from working. It was a great wheeze. The Trades and Labour Council called on unions to boycott the *Dawn* and businesses that continued to advertise in it.

Lawson pushed back, encouraging her readers to tell advertisers they only bought their products because of the *Dawn*. The union movement, pilloried in the press and the court of public opinion, eventually ended the boycott.

The government, concerned that the *Dawn* was over-exciting the ladies, refused to recognise it as a newspaper, restricting Lawson's ability to post copies to subscribers. The government backed down when Justice Windeyer, a prominent supporter of women's suffrage, quietly pointed out that the government had never applied the reasons for refusal to other publications and threatened to call out its double standard.

The *Dawn* thrived and was influential domestically and overseas. In 1889, Lawson established the women's rights–focused Dawn Club, which met in Quong Tart's tearooms.

The suffragists got another boost in 1891, when Dora Montefiore, widow of a wealthy Jewish businessman, held the first meeting of the Womanhood Suffrage League of New South Wales in her Paddington

mansion.[30] After her husband's death in 1889, his executors informed
her that she could be her children's guardian, as her husband hadn't left
them to anyone else. Enraged that she didn't have automatic custody,
she pointed out that unmarried women had sole guardianship of their
children, meaning 'a woman is much better off as a man's mistress
than as his wife, as far as her children are concerned'. Determined to
change the law, she threw herself into the suffrage cause.

Montefiore was generally the only woman in the room at meetings
of the 1891 National Australasian Federation Convention, where she
was the plus-one of Sir George Grey, the ancient former governor of
South Australia and New Zealand. Grey advised her that Federation
provided a unique opportunity for women in each colony to 'agitate
and organise for political enfranchisement'. She got to work.

The Womanhood Suffrage League sprang out of the New South
Wales Women's Literary Society, an evening book club for society
ladies from Sydney's eastern suburbs. Lady Mary Windeyer, wife of
Justice Windeyer and a patroness of the WCTU, was the League's
president – its secretary the glamorous Woollahra singleton and
salon convenor Rose Scott, who'd embraced the suffrage cause after
politicians laughed at the suggestion that the age of consent be raised
from fourteen. Montefiore and Lizzy Ashton, the journalist wife of
artist Julian Ashton, were other League heavy-hitters, as was Louisa
Lawson, who folded the Dawn Club into the League.

The League's first resolution was:

The Commonwealth of Australia, to be 'broad based upon the
people's will', must listen to the real voice of the people, at least
half of whom are women.

---

30 *Suffragist* was the term then used to describe a person who advocated for voting
rights to be extended, especially to women. The term *suffragette* was coined as an
insult by the British press in 1906, before being embraced by the Pankhursts and
other women's voting rights activists who practised civil disobedience.

Sir Henry Parkes had failed to progress a bill extending suffrage to women in 1890, with his successor, George Dibbs, insisting, 'the bulk of women throughout the world are utterly incapable of performing the duties of men'. In 1892, J.F. Archibald pronounced:

> No amount of legislation in the world will equalize the sexes. A woman is not a man, nor is a man a woman, and things unlike cannot be compared. A man and a woman are no more equivalent quantities than half-a-mile and 4s. 8d.

Despite this, the *Bulletin* had withdrawn its opposition to the female franchise 'on the ground that the evil is evidently becoming unavoidable and must be endured in the best way possible'. New South Wales, it seemed, would be the first Australian colony to extend the vote to women beyond council elections.

The League began to fracture soon after its establishment. Dora Montefiore relocated to Europe. Lizzie Ashton was forced to resign after she called for marriage to be replaced with regularly renegotiated contracts, allowing anti-suffragists to portray the League as a cabal of frothing-at-the-mouth, free-loving feminazis. The League split over whether it should also prosecute other causes, with Mary Windeyer and Louisa Lawson both resigning from its council. Under Rose Scott's leadership, and with Lawson taking a back seat, the League lost some of its working-class appeal and progress slowed.

It would be up to South Australia to bring working-class and establishment women together to forever change the face of Australian politics.

HAIL MARY

Sixteen-year-old Edward Charles Stirling shared a ship from Adelaide to England with Catherine Helen Spence in 1864. Returning as a surgeon, he was appointed the University of Adelaide's first professor of physiology in 1882. Women topped his course in three of its first four years, but their employment options were limited.[31] As the father of four young daughters, he wanted them to live in a fairer world.

Elected to South Australia's Legislative Assembly, Stirling introduced an 1886 bill to give the vote to unmarried women with property, sensitive to the anti-suffragist argument that wives would vote as their husbands instructed, effectively giving married men two votes. The property qualification was also at odds with his belief that all women should have the vote, but he reasoned that the thin end of the wedge was better than no wedge at all.

Stirling's bill was debated in a carnival atmosphere, with MPs laughing and cracking jokes. One letter to the editor jocularly noted that if women could hang around parliament, there would be the great expense of a 'suckling room' that would draw MPs away from their important work on the off-chance they might catch a glimpse of uncorseted breast.[32]

Stirling's attempt to limit the vote to propertied women didn't appease the bill's critics and upset the United Trades and Labour Council (UTLC), which thought linking electoral and property rights might later be used to strip unpropertied men of their votes. The bill failed and Stirling was voted out of office.

---

31   Physiology was usually studied as part of a medical degree, but Australian universities still refused to let women study medicine. Forced to study in the United States, Constance Stone returned to be registered as Australia's first female doctor in 1890, with *Table Talk* running an article on her hair (dark), height (medium) and figure (trim). In 1891, Constance's sister Clara was in the first group of women to achieve Australian medical degrees, which of course didn't guarantee them work. Constance formed the Victorian Medical Women's Society, which operated out of Cole's Book Arcade, raising funds to establish the all-female Queen Victoria Hospital, which opened in 1896. Lawyers made doctors look progressive, with the University of Sydney's Ada Evans the first Australian woman to receive a law degree, in 1902, although she couldn't actually work as a lawyer in New South Wales until 1918.

32   The Australian parliament is full of tits, but women members of the House of Representatives were banned from breastfeeding in the chamber until 2016. In 2017, Greens senator Larissa Waters became the first person to breastfeed in the Australian parliament. Government did not come to a crashing halt.

On 6 June 1888, at a meeting of the Ladies Division of the Social Purity Society, Mary Lee moved that the Society 'pledges itself to advance and support the cause of woman suffrage in this colony'. Two weeks later, the Society formed the Women's Suffrage League of South Australia. Lee was appointed honorary secretary and, as for the presidency, the best woman for the job was Edward Stirling.

The League's committee had thirteen women and fifteen men. South Australian suffragists, more than their colonial counterparts, encouraged men to join the cause, calling them 'heroes in the battle' and otherwise stroking their egos. Lee wrote:

> Let husbands, brothers, fathers, be kept in mind that it is the duty of every free man to leave his daughters as free as his sons.

The month the League was formed, Robert Caldwell MP introduced a new bill to extend the vote to propertied women over the age of twenty-five, the age limitation reflecting Caldwell's view that women 'had been in the past somewhat handicapped in intellectual progress and were a few years behind their male associates in matters political'.

Alfred Catt opposed the bill on behalf of the government, contending the 'true woman, virtuous, modest and shunning publicity' had no interest in voting, with her only concern 'the welfare of her husband and children'. Although a majority of those present supported the bill, it required the backing of an absolute majority of all members because it would amend the South Australian Constitution. The bill's defeat was greeted with cheers.

Lee, pushing seventy, was the indefatigable driver and conductor of the suffragist bus, holding meetings with women and men in drawing rooms, workplaces and church halls across South Australia. Although she liked a drink, she courted Elizabeth Nicholls and the WCTU, which threw its weight behind the cause in 1889.

Women's suffrage bills failed again in 1889 and 1890, with Lee noting parliament's reluctance to debate them:

... in our own Parliament the Dog Licence Bill, the Sparrows Destruc-
tion Bill, a road or railway, a bridge or well, anything and everything
is allowed precedence of the Women's Suffrage Bill ...

In early 1890, Lee wrote a series of letters to women, published
in the *South Australian Register*. In one, she urged:

Let us be up and doing. Let every woman who can influence an
elector see that he seizes his vote as a sledgehammer and goes to
the poll resolved to dash from its pedestal of authority this hoary
injustice to womanhood ...

'Let us be up and doing' became a Lee catchphrase – more posi-
tive than 'Stop the boats' and catchier than 'Jobs and growth'. Mary
from Marketing was a canny media operator who knew how to deliver
a soundbite, and she alternately flattered and attacked her critics,
making her a difficult political target to hit.

Lee was certainly up and doing in 1890. On 14 January, the Working Women's Trade Union (WWTU) of South Australia was formed
at her urging. Lee, who emphasised the link between suffrage and
improved conditions for working-class women, was appointed WWTU
secretary, and Augusta Zadow, a German-born tailoress and anti-
sweatshop campaigner, its president. By 1891, the WWTU, UTLC
and the new United Labour Party of South Australia, which had
three seats in the Assembly, were committed to the suffrage cause.

Catherine Helen Spence attended her first Women's Suffrage
League meeting in March 1891 and was soon the League's vice-president.
Spence's involvement gave the movement greater credibility. The
Advertiser reported that her 'arguments are thoughtful and sober and
her language entirely free from the screeching hysteria that has so
often brought ridicule and contempt on the cause of "women's rights"'.

The League now swore to oppose any bill that didn't give women
the same voting rights as men. Victorian suffragists took the same
approach, with Henrietta Dugdale organising a six-week door-knocking

drive in response to Premier Munro's promise to introduce a women's suffrage bill if it could be established women actually wanted the vote. Over 30,000 women's signatures were collected by activists like 22-year-old Vida Goldstein, a private schoolgirl turned socialist slum reformer. The 'Monster Petition' was 260 metres long and took four people to carry into parliament.

Munro, good to his word, introduced a woman's suffrage bill in 1891. The reform was supported by Alfred Deakin, although he'd become more conservative on women's rights since his teenage speech on the issue. Deakin desired his daughters to 'neither be athletes nor blue stockings', believed that most women should abstain from meat, that all women should abstain from alcohol (except in medical crises), and that virginity was a girl's ticket to a successful marriage. Munro's bill failed, opposed by the conservative squatters who still dominated Victoria's Legislative Council.

Back in South Australia, Edward Stirling stepped down as president of the Women's Suffrage League in 1892, allowing him to work with animals, which were much easier to deal with than women.[33] He was succeeded by philanthropist Lady Mary Colton, who, much to everybody's surprise, appeared to be a woman. The wife of two-time premier Sir John Colton elevated the cause in the eyes of the Adelaide establishment and the colony's wowsers who, like the Coltons, abstained from alcohol, gambling, dancing and going to the theatre.

However, the League lost its trump card when the 67-year-old Spence left for a speaking tour of the United States and Canada. Spence promoted proportional representation, preached in Unitarian churches and addressed the International Conference on Charities

33 Stirling was director of the South Australian Museum and loved creeping around the bush, poking unsuspecting animals and then killing them for his collection. Stirling named and described the shy southern marsupial mole and led the reconstruction of the first full skeleton of the diprotodon – a giant, wombat-like, extremely stupid extinct marsupial. Stirling was also one of the colony's leading horticulturalists, naming one of the rhododendrons he bred 'Mrs E.C. Stirling', somewhat diminishing his feminist cred.

and Correction at the Chicago World Fair. She also exchanged intelligence with local suffragists, including ex-slave and anti-slavery campaigner Harriet Tubman. Impressed by Tubman's passion and achievements, Spence admitted 'to be a little ashamed of being so narrow in my views on the coloured question', although this didn't stop her venting about Asians and other foreign-looking types upon her return to Australia.

Things were looking up when Charles Kingston won the premiership in 1893. Kingston loved women (as often as possible). Although he'd opposed women's suffrage during the 1893 campaign, he was convinced by senior liberals and his Labor allies, as well as the WCTU, that chicks would vote for him. However, he showed uncharacteristic indecision in introducing a suffrage bill that would only pass if supported in a referendum by a majority of women ... and a majority of men.

Meanwhile, New Zealand stole South Australia's thunder by giving women the vote, after 32,000 women (almost a quarter of the colony's adult female population) petitioned parliament.[34] Henry Lawson, who was unemployed and sleeping rough in a Wellington drainage pipe, filed a report on this momentous moment for the *Dawn*.

Encouraged by the Kiwis, Mary Lee went into overdrive, touring the colony and delivering suffrage lectures to packed halls. Reading the political wind, Kingston introduced a bill that gave men and women equal voting rights, but excluded women from sitting in parliament. The Women's Suffrage League, which had never sought

---

34 New Zealanders other than Russell Crowe and Phar Lap haven't achieved much, so New Zealanders like to claim they were the first self-governing country in the world to give all women the vote in parliamentary elections. This is bollocks. New Zealand was not a self-governing country in 1893, but a British colony. New Zealand wasn't even the first British territory to enfranchise women, with the Pitcairn Islands (1838) and Isle of Man (1881) beating it to the punch. Women's suffrage was unusual, but by no means unique, in 1893. Wyoming had granted women suffrage in 1869 and Utah followed the next year, although the United States Congress revoked women's voting rights in Utah in 1887 because it considered Mormon polygamy unnatural and having several voting wives per voting husband even more unnatural.

the right for women to contest the polls, presented parliament with a petition in support of the bill. Of the petition's 11,600 signatures, 8,268 were collected by Elizabeth Nicholls and her WCTU sisters.

When the bill was debated in the Legislative Council, Ebenezer Ward realised his fellow anti-suffragists didn't have the numbers, so he attempted to spike the bill with an amendment that would allow women to run for parliament. Much to Ward's surprise, the Council supported his amendment – but the Assembly would surely vote down anything that enabled ladies to idly chatter and quilt cushions in the chamber when the bill was referred there for debate.

That debate took place in December, with Allerdale Grainger MP maintaining that 'delicate women' didn't want the vote and that their views should prevail over those of the 'screaming sisterhood'. Other opponents expressed concern that women were too emotional or uneducated to vote, would turn elections into beauty contests by voting for the most handsome candidate, would stop having children or become manly.

Spence reappeared six days before the big vote on 18 December 1894, joining Mary Lee and the other women who crowded every square centimetre of the gallery. The women cheered, danced and otherwise comported themselves in a most unfeminine manner when the Assembly passed the bill thirty-one votes to fourteen, with a distressed Grainger complaining, 'There's the hen convention.'[35]

Every South Australian woman over the age of twenty-one now had the vote, irrespective of marital status, property ownership or

---

35   Mary Lee died in poverty in 1909, as did another South Australian Mary, Mary MacKillop (though poverty, in MacKillop's case, was part of her job description). MacKillop had mounted a comeback in 1899, being elected unopposed as Mother General of the order she'd founded, and remained the boss Josephite until her death. MacKillop didn't let death stop her good works. In 1961, she cured Veronica Hopson of leukemia, and she did the same for Kathleen Evans' inoperable lung and brain cancer in 1993. MacKillop's work as Australia's leading undead oncologist was recognised by the Catholic Church in 2010, when she became the nation's first saint (the Catholic equivalent to receiving an Order of Australia).

race. And, thanks to the conservatives' spectacular own goal, every one of those women could also run for parliament, a world first.[36]

There was schadenfreude to spare in women's salons around the world when Queen Victoria, who'd written of 'this mad, wicked folly of "Woman's Rights", with all its attendant horrors', was forced to sign South Australia's suffrage reforms into law on 2 February 1895.

---

36   This didn't mean anyone would vote for them. South Australia was the last
     Australian state to vote a woman into parliament, with Joyce Steele and Jessie
     Cooper both elected in 1959.

Poets, Pests and the Perfect Loaf

You'll come a Waltzing Matilda with me.

Banjo Paterson, 'Waltzing Matilda', 1895

SLEAZE, SWAG AND SUICIDE

THE AUSTRALIA THAT ROSE FROM THE ASHES OF THE depression in 1895 was very different to the Australia of five years earlier. The economy had shrunk by 30 per cent, and Melbourne, having swapped marvellous for mediocre, was just another provincial outpost of Empire.

Andrew Barton Paterson, though, was on a high. He was moving with Sydney's fast set, was respected in sport and the law, and *The Man from Snowy River and Other Verses*, published early that year, had made him an overnight celebrity. Having cast off his cloak of anonymity, he was now known as Banjo Paterson.

Paterson deserved a holiday, so he and his fiancée, Sarah Riley, set out for Dagworth Station in central west Queensland, where Sarah's bestie, Christina Macpherson, lived with her four brothers.[1] Dagworth had been the centre of 1894's *Shearers' Strike 2*, a sequel

---

[1]   Thirty years earlier, Christina had been Australia's most famous baby, having melted the heart of Mad Dan Morgan during his hold-up of Peechelba Station. When Mad Dan allowed Christina's nursemaid to leave his hostage party to tend to her, the nurse instead raised the alarm, allowing police to shoot and behead the clinically insane bushranger and fashion a tobacco pouch from his flayed chin or scrotum (they apparently looked similar).

to the 1891 blockbuster canned by critics for its identical ending. However, there were moments of originality in the middle act, most notably the action sequence in which the striking shearers shot up the Macpherson brothers' cottage and set fire to a shed full of lambs.[2] Bob Mac (as Robert Macpherson liked to be known) and three policeman tracked the shearers, only to discover that one of them, Samuel Hoffmeister, had shot himself in the head beside a billabong. Hoffmeister had chosen death over imprisonment.[3]

One night, Christina was entertaining the household with a zither solo and Paterson offered to write some lyrics for it. Their eyes locked, the temperature in the room rose several degrees, and Sarah Riley was looking for a new bestie. Paterson's original words for 'Waltzing Matilda', sung to Christina that evening, included, 'Who'll come a Waltzing Matilda, my darling,' which have been interpreted by Australian literary scholars with too much time on their hands as an invitation for Christina to exchange her zither for a Banjo and take on the role of swagman's blanket in keeping the poet warm at night.

'Waltzing Matilda' adapted the story of Bob Mac (the squatter mounted on his thoroughbred) and the three policeman (the troopers – one, two, three) chasing down Hoffmeister (the jolly swagman), and combined it with a story Paterson heard at Dagworth about a swaggie who'd killed a sheep near a waterhole and drowned while trying to escape its angry owner. Paterson never satisfactorily explained why the swagman was jolly, when he was clearly mentally ill (he repeatedly insists that some unknown person come swagging with him,

---

2   There was also a great scene where the shearers painted their faces with mud before stealthily boarding the scab steamer *Rodney* at night, chasing fifty scabs into the Darling River, and setting the steamer alight – the only recorded act of piracy on Australia's inland waterways

3   Hoffmeister was known as *Frenchy* because he was German, just as Australians called redheads *Bluey*. Australians thought calling things something they were not was amusingly ironic, when it was just plain irritating.

irrespective of the situation) and displayed suicidal ideation. Ditto the jumbuck, which was somehow jolly *after* having been shoved into a tucker bag.

Paterson left Dagworth under a cloud. The broken-hearted Sarah called off the engagement and never married, her niece Ethel Riley claiming Paterson had also had a crack at Dagworth's sewing mistress during his visit. Christina remained unwed too, with her great-niece Diana Baillieu (mother of Victorian premier Ted Baillieu) saying Christina had never got over her affection for Paterson. The Macpherson brothers considered Paterson a cad and told him 'never to darken their doorstep again'.

Paterson returned to his bachelor life in Sydney, sharing an apartment and Japanese valet with polo player Irving Kent, riding against Harry Morant at polo and race meets, and hanging out with Morant and sheep painter Tom Roberts at Roberts' studio. He also did some legal work for Henry Lawson, negotiating two of his book contracts with publisher Angus & Robertson. Lawson's books sold poorly, while Paterson's flew off the shelf.

His literary career stuck in second gear, Lawson thought a good woman might save him. In 1896, he married Bertha Bredt, daughter of Bertha McNamara, the German-born feminist socialist bookseller dubbed 'The Mother of the Labour Movement'. Despite her friendship with Bertha senior, Louisa Lawson regarded Henry's marriage as impulsive, like her own. She disapproved and let Henry know it.

Lawson's new wife also let Henry know she disapproved of him chasing Hannah Thorburn, a young artists' model. She arranged for Archibald to send her and Henry to New Zealand, where all the artists' models were covered in wool. Henry might work as a schoolteacher and straighten himself out, Bertha thought, but the couple were soon back in Sydney, with Henry in rehab and two infants in the crib. Marriage had not improved the ailing writer's lot. Every way he turned, dark clouds gathered on the horizon.

The sun continued to shine on Banjo Paterson, although he acknowledged the creation of 'Waltzing Matilda' had left him with unhappy memories. He sold the verse to Angus & Robertson as part of a £5 'old junk' sale of his lesser works. The publisher on-sold the musical rights to Inglis & Co., which owned Billy Tea. In 1903, Marie Cowan, the wife of an Inglis accountant, set Paterson's words to music, tinkering with them to make them fit her score, and giving us the 'Waltzing Matilda' we know today. The music and lyrics were included in packs of Billy Tea, so that tea-drinking families could gather around the teapot of an evening for a sing-along about swagmen, squatters, sheep and suicide.[4]

Paterson and Cowan's song about an outback underdog who'd rather die than surrender was sung by Australian diggers at Gallipoli and the Western Front. It was sung by Australian troops on a suicide mission during the World War II Battle of Muar, and by Australian nurses as they were loaded onto a truck at Rabaul to slave for the Japanese. Most inspiringly, it was sung by Kylie Minogue at the opening ceremony of the Sydney 2000 Paralympic Games.

When Australia held a plebiscite in 1977 on whether a new national anthem should replace 'God Save the Queen', 'Advance Australia Fair' beat a fast-finishing 'Waltzing Matilda' by a nose. If that plebiscite were held today, 'Waltzing Matilda' would win by the length of the straight, which is astounding. No other people would contemplate presenting themselves on the world stage with a DIY advertising jingle about a sheep-stealing hobo who drowns himself and haunts a pond.

---

4   Australians were the largest per capita tea-drinkers in the world at the turn of the twentieth century. Most Australians had two to three large cups of tea with every meal and a quick cuppa whenever they were thirsty and near a kettle between meals. The main evening meal was commonly known as tea, and of course there was morning tea and afternoon tea. It was not 'Waltzing Matilda' that made Billy Tea popular, but the other way round.

THE DRY

As Banjo Paterson rode the rails to Sydney after his Dagworth sleazefest, he would have noticed the wide brown land flashing past his window was even browner than usual. No matter – drought was as familiar to Australians as flooding rains. However, had Paterson known the 1895 dry wouldn't break until 1903, he may not have so quickly returned his gaze to the form guide.

The Federation Drought was the drought we had to have. The worst on record, it forever killed Australian complacency about the land.[5] It also killed 49 per cent of Australia's sheep and 40 per cent of its cattle.

Overgrazing had destroyed perennial grasses, and the hard hooves of sheep and cattle, so different to the lovely soft pads of Australian marsupials, broke up the exposed topsoil. Dehydrated by drought, the soil was sucked into massive dust storms that filled dams and buried fences. The storms turned fertile farmland into barren waste, and New Zealand, where some of our best farmland was deposited, into the Land of the Long Red Cloud.

In 1902, the New South Wales government declared a public holiday for people to 'unite in humiliation and prayer' for the end of the drought – a state-sponsored rain dance. The same year, Dame Nellie Melba, returning from yet another stint at London's Covent Garden, wrote:

> I have seen with my own eyes the brown, burnt paddocks extending
> for hundreds of miles, with no vestige of grass left upon them. I have
> seen starving sheep leaning against the fences, too weak to move.

Dame Nellie donated the proceeds of her 1903 farewell perfor-mance to drought relief – like an early version of *Live Aid*, but with

---

5   The Millennium Drought of 2001–09 was almost as bad, mainly because
    Australians had to put up with millennials.

fewer starving black kids and more whinging white farmers. Actually, 'farewell performance' was pushing it, as Melba stuck to the stage like shit to a shoe. No matter how hard you tried, you just couldn't get rid of her.[6]

The only thing harder to get rid of than Dame Nellie Melba was the rabbit. Rabbits had come to Australia aboard the First Fleet, but had all been put in pies before they could get on Rabbit Tinder. In truth, the caged domesticated rabbits British immigrants brought out to eat were not particularly hardy.

Then Thomas Austin happened. Australia's biggest idiot wanted to recreate the English hunting experience at Barwon Park, his estate near Geelong. He asked his brother back in England to send him some pheasants, partridges and hares. And, oh, could he have twenty-four rabbits? Not the weak, tame ones, mind, but smart, wiry, wild rabbits that would be more of a challenge to shoot. Austin's super-rabbits were released on 25 December 1859.[7]

Austin became an enthusiastic life member of the Acclimatisation Society of Victoria, founded by *Argus* owner Edward Wilson in 1861. The aim of the Society was to 'introduce, acclimatise and domesticate useful or ornamental birds, fish, insects, vegetables and other exotic species'. Wilson helped open branches in the other Australian colonies, bar Western Australia, by the end of 1862.

While foreign people were out, foreign animals were in, with Wilson calling for monkeys to be released into the Australian bush, 'for the amusement of the wayfarer, whom their gambols would

---

6   Nellie continued to give Australian farewell performances until 1924, when she announced her final farewell performance. She then wowed Australian crowds until 1928, before returning to Europe, where she gave farewell performances until 1930. Melba was the human equivalent of a Persian rug warehouse closing sale. Her frequent and lucrative goodbyes gifting the Australian lexicon with *do a Melba*, used allusively of a person who retires but then returns to their profession, especially if done repeatedly. This once-popular phrase has now largely fallen out of use, having been made redundant by John Farnham.

7   Merry Christmas, Australia!

delight as he lay under some gum tree in the forest on a sultry day'. The governor of Victoria (also the Society's chair) didn't like monkeys, but he let Wilson import sparrows. Farmers soon started whingeing that Wilson's birds were destroying their fruit crops.[8]

Meanwhile, Austin's rabbits were getting it on, and Austin was gifting breeding pairs to friends to stock their own estates. Barwon Park became a popular hunting destination, with the *Geelong Advertiser* describing Prince Alfred's 1867 visit:

> One thousand rabbits and several parrots were killed; the Duke shot five hundred rabbits and expressed himself as highly pleased and said he had never enjoyed such a day's rabbit shooting.[9]

That was the last good press rabbits got. Rabbits were not a pest in Britain, where they had natural predators and lots of farmers to put them in pies – but in Australia, farmers were busy eliminating predators like the dingo and quoll, leaving felled trees in paddocks for rabbits to hide under, and building dams that served as drink stops for the fast-breeding little bastards.[10]

By the 1870s, rabbits had reached plague proportions and were rapidly conquering new territory, the fastest recorded spread of a

---

8   Australians also sent their own animals to Britain, with the first koala to survive the long voyage disembarking in 1881, only to die in a freak washstand accident.

9   Alfred wasn't the only European royal to enjoy wasting our rabbits. Archduke Franz Ferdinand visited in 1893, blowing away an unknown number of them, as well as at least eight koalas (they really weren't having a good time of it), kangaroos, emus, pelicans, brolgas, a pair of black swans and a platypus. He was accompanied by his overworked personal taxidermist, who'd helped Franz collect over 100,000 game trophies for his castle. Franz got a dose of his own medicine in Sarajevo on 28 June 1914, when he was shot dead by Gavrilo Princip, who should join Francis of Assisi as the patron saint of animals. After Franz's assassination, people didn't have so much time to shoot poor defenceless creatures, as they were too busy shooting each other.

10 A 1988 study found that a pair of rabbits could produce thirty-eight surviving young in a breeding season and have 15,000 descendants within three years.

mammal in world history.[11] If you were the kind of religiously and
scientifically curious person who wanted to conduct experiments on
rabbits eating their own vomit, you were spoiled for choice. By the
1880s, over a billion rabbits would call Australia home, and nine of
them could eat as much as two sheep. Rabbits entrenched themselves
on farms and stations, starving sheep and cattle. They dug out roots
and ringbarked trunks, killing the trees that offered stock shade.
Their burrowing hastened soil erosion and their chisel-like teeth
enabled them to graze close to the ground, destroying crops. When
they'd eaten everything on the surface, rabbits surprised everyone
with their facility for climbing and stripping fruit trees. Semi-arid
areas they ate out were colonised by pine scrub, just about the only
plant rabbits didn't find tasty. The scrub further reduced land carrying
capacity and had to be controlled by cutting, an expensive exercise.

Farmers laid down traps and strychnine baits, dug up warrens or
pumped them full of poison gas, loosed their hounds and shot anything
with a fluffy tail. Nothing worked. The rabbit army, with a seemingly
inexhaustible supply of new recruits, continued its inexorable spread
north and west. Aboriginal people were rabbit collaborators, carrying the wonderful fast-breeding and easy-to-catch animals into their
remote hunting grounds.

Hiring rabbiters to clear the land and then fencing it with wire
and fine netting seemed the only solution, but for many it was a pro-
hibitively expensive one. During the Federation Drought, the wind
blew sand drifts against these fences, providing ramps for the rabbit
army to reclaim lost territory. And rabbits were cunning – when the
Christian socialists of Murtho rabbit-fenced their crops, commando
rabbits got in by scaling a 37-metre cliff.

While rabbits ruined some people, they were a goldmine for others. Rabbiters received a bounty for each pair of bunny ears handed

---

11   Thomas Austin never got to appreciate how badly he'd fucked up, as he died of
     dysentery in 1871.

in. Not wanting to damage their revenue stream, they then released the now earless rabbits to keep breeding. When paid by a farmer to trap rabbits, they'd free their prisoners into an as yet rabbit-free area and offer their services to the stunned locals. Rabbiters could earn several times the wage of a skilled tradesman, and colonial governments, hoping for a rabbit-led recovery from the 1890s depression, encouraged unemployed city folk to hunt bunnies in the bush, with the *Age* helpfully publishing 'Work for the Unemployed – How Rabbit Trappers Work'.

There was also money to be made in rabbit skin, fur and meat. Skins were exported to Britain to make imitation sealskin garments, and fur was used for bedding. The soft fur closest to the skin made felt for gloves, hats and billiard tables. In 1892, local hatmaker Benjamin Dunkerley invented new machines to domestically produce felt, which he used to manufacture Akubra hats. Rabbit meat canning factories followed the rabbits west, and six million frozen bunny carcasses were shipped to Britain in 1900 alone.

The pleasure and pain rabbits provided led to confused government policy. Victoria encouraged rabbicide in most areas, but banned eradication attempts within 10 miles of railway lines and 20 miles of freezing works to support the rabbit meat industry. These rabbit safe zones provided staging grounds for rabbits to launch further assaults on farmers.

In 1887, Sir Henry Parkes offered a £25,000 prize for 'any method or process not previously known in the colony for the effectual extermination of rabbits'. A biological solution looked promising and French microbiologist Louis Pasteur sent his nephew Adrien Loir Down Under to infect Aussie rabbits with chicken cholera.[12] A laboratory was built on Rodd Island in Sydney Harbour, where Loir's experiments determined that rabbits could not transmit chicken

---

12 What could possibly go wrong in encouraging a deadly disease to jump the species barrier?

cholera, but chickens could. At the frantic urging of the local poul-
try industry, Loir's project was shut down.[13] The £25,000 remained
unclaimed.[14]

In 1888, Parkes and some of his fellow premiers established a Royal
Intercolonial Rabbit Commission to advise on rabbit control. Victoria's representative was Australia's largest barbed wire importer, so it's
not entirely surprising the Commission recommended the colonies
build massive barbed wire–topped fences to stop rabbit immigration.
The spectacularly unsuccessful rabbit-proof fence built by Western
Australian was bigger than the Berlin Wall – at 1,834 kilometres long,
it would have stretched from Berlin to Athens.

The other answer to the rabbit problem was to 'acclimatise' more
foreign animals that might eat rabbits. Cats were loaded onto trains
and dropped off along the tracks in the interior. Foxes were encouraged to go after rabbits until they, too, reached plague proportions
and had a bounty put on their heads. Both cats and foxes ravaged
small native animals such as the bilby, an unassuming marsupial that

---

13 It would take until 1950 for the Commonwealth Scientific and Industrial Research
    Organisation (CSIRO) to initiate a biological solution, with myxomatosis the
    first virus in the world to be intentionally introduced into the wild to eradicate a
    vertebrate pest. After rabbits developed immunity to it, the CSIRO continued to
    make life as miserable (and as short) as possible for Flopsy, Mopsy and Cottontail
    through the accidental 1991 release of calicivirus, which younger readers may be
    surprised has nothing to do with *Game of Thrones*.

14 However, there was a massive silver lining for Loir when he discovered that
    'Cumberland disease', which had been decimating Australian sheep and
    cattle, was anthrax. Loir proposed a vaccine trial, and Parkes hid a telegram
    from Pasteur forbidding it to proceed until he and Loir were given the rabbit
    reward money. Australia got an anthrax vaccine, and the French government
    demanded an official apology for Parkes' subterfuge. Parkes smoothed things
    over by establishing the world's second Pasteur Institute on Rodd Island, which
    produced a lot of money-making vaccines and treatments for Australian farm
    animals. Loir was glad he stayed. Visiting French superstar Sarah Bernhardt
    threatened to leave Australia in 1891, after her two pet dogs were taken away
    to be put down for breaching quarantine. Loir saved the day by offering Rodd
    Island as a quarantine facility, before embarking on a passionate affair with the
    grateful actress. It's sadly unknown if Johnny Depp would have put out if he'd
    received similar treatment from Barnaby Joyce.

has 'victim' written all over it.[15] Ferrets, weasels and stoats were also released, but didn't enjoy the Australian climate. Plans to introduce rabbit-munching iguanas and meerkats were quietly shelved.

The Federation Drought dried out waterholes, leading to a decline in rabbit numbers, although the bunnies would bounce back when the rains returned. Still, there were enough rabbits remaining to make the drought even worse. The damage they caused took the margin out of marginal properties, with no one wanting to buy the dustbowls they left behind. Pastoral leases weren't renewed, with some five million acres abandoned in the western division of New South Wales alone between 1891 and 1901. As pastoral leases were the major source of government revenue, colonial budgets were hit hard. At the turn of the twentieth century, drought, rabbits and depressed wool prices resulted in more than 50 per cent of the remaining leaseholds being repossessed by banks or large pastoral companies. Many leases were broken up, with smaller-scale mixed farming replacing grazing. The age of the squatter was at an end.

Banjo Paterson's 1902 'It's Grand' told the tale of these hard, dry years for man and bunny alike:

> *It's grand to be a squatter*
> *And sit upon a post,*
> *And watch your little ewes and lambs*
> *A-giving up the ghost.*
>   ....
> *It's grand to be a Western man,*
> *With shovel in your hand,*

---

15 Baby bilbies don't recognise foxes as predators and will happily trundle out of their burrows to play with them. Scientists are now trying to condition captive-bred bilbies to recognise foxes and cats as bad by presenting them with a model fox or cat and shooting them in the face with a water pistol. It's hoped that when they're released into the wild, they'll let their children know how bad cats and foxes (or at least water pistols) are.

To dig your little homestead out
From underneath the sand.

....

It's grand to be a rabbit
And breed till all is blue,
And then to die in heaps because
There's nothing left to chew.

...

It's grand to be a lot of things
In this fair Southern land,
But if the Lord would send us rain,
That would, indeed, be grand!

THE BARRY WHITE OF WHEAT

William Farrer was the Barry White of wheat, with an unrivalled ability to get the grain in the bedroom mood. Before Farrer came along, wheat sex in Australia was white bread – but Farrer encouraged previously shy Australian wheats to partner-swap with exotic foreign wheats. While the rest of Australia obsessed about racial purity, Farrer promoted wheat miscegenation. His most famous wheat, Federation, was the offspring of a fair-dinkum Aussie-grown wheat, Purple Straw, and the sultry Yandilla, the love child of a Canadian wheat and an Indian wheat that Farrer had helped to hook up in the early 1890s.[16]

One might expect a grain-sex addict like Farrer to have been a party boy, but his research partner and occasional *Bulletin* poet Frederick Guthrie said of him, 'Of a highly sensitive disposition, he was by nature extremely reserved and reticent towards comparative strangers.' The problem was 'the crazy faddist' could only talk about

---

16   Farrer gave some of his wheats distinctly human names – Bobs, Florence and
      Pearlie White, the last named for a neighbourhood child who told him his work
      with wheat was really interesting.

wheat, which was limiting in most social situations – but it made him
a hit at the annual Intercolonial Rust in Wheat Conferences held
between 1890 and 1896.

Black stem rust is basically wheat thrush, a fungal infection that
makes wheat less sexy, and annual rust conferences were held because
the fungus was destroying Australian crops. Things were so dire in
1889 and 1896 that Australian millers had to import grain.

Farrer had not always been interested in wheat, as evidenced by
his novelly punctuated 1873 *Grass, and sheep-farming: a paper: speculative
and suggestive*. In 1882, his new wife was gifted a farm by her father,
which Farrer named Lambrigg after his northern England childhood
home. Farrer tried to grow grapes on the property near Tharwa (now
in the Australian Capital Territory), but the soil was unsuitable.

FIG. 10: 'I LIKE TO WATCH.'

So he turned to wheat, setting himself the unambitious-sounding goal of producing a good loaf of bread, which he would achieve by becoming a 'scientific gardener'.

Farrer was one of the few people in the world who'd read the work of Gregor Mendel, now regarded as the father of modern genetics. In Farrer's day, most people who'd heard of Mendel knew him only as the abbot of St Thomas' Abbey in Brno, Moravia (now in the Czech Republic). The monk experimented with bees ('the dearest little animals'), but the other monks, tired of being stung, demanded he study something else. He chose heredity in mice, but his bishop didn't like him looking at animals having sex. Mendel therefore turned to plant sex – between 1856 and 1863, he hung out in the abbey's garden, crossbreeding pea plants with different characteristics to determine how those characteristics presented in their offspring.

Farrer, convinced that the European-descended wheat favoured by Australian bakers was unsuited to local conditions, started crossbreeding other wheat varieties, selecting the offspring that appeared most resistant to rust and drought and made the tastiest bread.[17] Guthrie, a University of Sydney chemist, devised miniature mills and bakeries that could process as little as 50 grams of grain to determine which grains baked best. It was a unique partnership between an agricultural botanist and a chemist at the time.

Farrer wasn't paid for his work until 1898, when the New South Wales government concluded the twin problems of drought and rust warranted an in-house wheat freak. Such was Farrer's obsession with finding the perfect loaf that he refused to return to England to inherit his wealthy uncle's estate, choosing bread over dough.

Farrer was disappointed that his most famous wheat strain, named in 1900 in anticipation of Federation, had 'an unattractive appearance

---

[17]   Farrer also worked on developing strains that were resistant to bunt and smut-ball (wheat diseases have truly evocative names). He used his wife's hairpins to transfer pollen between plants. Mrs Farrer's views on this practice are unknown.

in the field'. But farming wasn't a beauty contest and, after it was made available to farmers in 1903, Federation wheat – with its high yield, tasty grain, and greater resistance to rust and drought – became Australia's favourite crop. Federation and other Farrer-bred grains allowed farmers to grow wheat in a greater range of conditions, with New South Wales' yield quadrupling between 1897 and 1915.

Combined with other 1890s agricultural reforms, including the introduction of superphosphates and bare fallowing, Farrer's wheats powered the Australian economy.[18] Despite the drought, Australian wheat production grew by 20 per cent between 1891 and 1900.

In 1900, statistician Timothy Coghlan wrote, 'From primary industries Australia produces more per inhabitant than is produced by the combined industries of any other country.' Australians had better bread than anyone – and they drank more tea and ate more meat.[19] By the time the colonies federated on 1 January 1901, agriculture and pastoralism had helped make them the richest people in the world.

---

18   Bare fallowing involved ploughing crop remnants back into the earth in early spring, keeping the field clear during summer and sowing during autumn. No one knew why this worked, but it did. We now know the nitrogen produced by the ploughed-back material takes about six months to break down and provide nutrients for the next crop. The previous practice of having cows shit all over your wheat field in the off-season provided nutrients, but by sowing time, most of them had leached away.

19   In 1901, Australians ate an average 264 pounds of meat a year, much higher than the 150 pounds eaten by Americans and the 109 pounds consumed by Brits. Australian per capita meat consumption was four times that of the sausage-loving Germans and ten times that of the anaemic Italians.

II

These Are the Times that Try Men's Souls

These are the times that try men's souls.

Thomas Paine, *The Crisis*, 1776

and

Alfred Deakin, *The After-Dinner Speech*, 1898

THE PASSING OF THE BATON

SIR HENRY PARKES, LIKE HIS TOTEM ANIMAL THE RABBIT, was feeling the heat as the Federation Drought baked the continent he'd come to love.

Still smarting that his one-time ally George Reid had spiked the wheels of Federation, Parkes allied himself with former enemy George Dibbs and stood for Reid's seat in the 1895 election. He was thrashed, as he was in an 1896 by-election in which he secured less than 7 per cent of the vote. Seen as a destabilising influence by his former colleagues, the eighty-year-old was given a parliamentary payout on the condition that he never contest an election again.[1]

Cancer had claimed Nellie, aged just thirty-eight, during Parkes' campaign against Reid. The widower mourned three long months, before marrying Nellie's maid, 23-year-old Julia Lynch. Parkes told his

---

1   In today's less nepotistic times, political has-beens and embarrassments are given ambassadorships.

daughters of his new love on his wedding day. They refused to attend the service and had moved out by the time their father and the new Lady Parkes returned home, as had Parkes' housekeeper, who couldn't abide working for a woman so recently part of 'staff'. The papers had a field day with the 'giddy old octogenarian' and 'lover of riper years'.

Parkes was confined to bed with pneumonia in April 1896. On the twenty-fifth of that month, he saw his dream of universal suffrage realised when South Australian women headed to the polls for the first time, some of them daringly riding bicycles.[2] Two days later, after a tearful reconciliation with Reid, the Father of Federation breathed his last.

The depression and Parkes' earlier reluctance to take on Reid had slowed, but not stilled, the federal push. Alfred Deakin had banished himself to the backbench to prosecute the cause, firing up the Australian Natives' Association (ANA) with an 1893 speech that declared Federation was 'the one ideal worth living, working and if necessary dying for' – an argument that's easier to maintain if you believe that death is just another road stop on life's eternal highway.

Deakin saw Federation in religious terms, praying that it 'might be the means of creating and fostering throughout all Australia a Christ-like citizenship'. Nationalism, he believed, could unite people in a common moral purpose as religion had once done. It was this need for community, for belonging, that drove Deakin. In this,

---

2   In 1896, the *Dawn* editorial 'Learning to Ride the Bicycle' recommended ladies take up riding for the independence it offered. Bicycles, unlike horses, couldn't be ridden side-saddle, and some doctors were concerned that sitting on a seat and pedalling would excite women into orgasm, plaguing society with 'over-sexed females'. Others believed that cycling, like studying at university, would deform the womb and increase rates of miscarriage and maternal death. Women were also warned they might fall victim to 'bicycle face', a permanent distortion of the features caused by the strain of pedalling. The bicycle later gifted women the best of feminist slogans: 'A woman needs a man like a fish needs a bicycle.' Although often attributed to US feminist Gloria Steinem, it was coined in 1970 by Sydney's Irina Dunn, later a senator for the Nuclear Disarmament Party, who scrawled it on lavatory doors at the University of Sydney and a Woolloomooloo wine bar.

he was profoundly influenced by his old debating master, Charles Pearson, whose 1893 *National Life and Character: A Forecast* inspired international statesmen including Britain's prime minister William Gladstone and US president Theodore Roosevelt.

Pearson's book shocked Western leaders because it challenged the conventional wisdom that 'the Aryan races' and 'Christian faith' would maintain their global dominance. The inferior 'black and yellow' races were catching up, and their rapidly increasing populations (and, in China's case, its industrialisation) would help them escape the 'tutelage' of the master race. The West was 'stationary', with declining birthrates and an addiction to state socialism that neutered the bold individualism societies needed to thrive. The future of the West, Pearson contended, depended on stronger national feeling. Only patriotism, instilling a desire to protect a nation's character at any cost, would keep the black and yellow hordes at bay.[3]

Deakin pursued Federation with the zeal of a sinner granted a glimpse of Heaven, but he needed others to share his vision. He encouraged local Federation Leagues to mobilise ordinary citizens in the great cause and convinced Edmund Barton to establish a central Australasian Federation League in Sydney. The League's first meeting was infiltrated by Labor republicans holding forged tickets, with John Norton again the instigator. After the meeting endorsed Norton's motion that Federation proceed on a 'republican basis', a furious Barton shut it down and convened one free of Norton and his traitorous ilk. Loyalty to queen and mother country were central to the Australia that Barton and Deakin wished to build.

Popular involvement in Federation got a boost in July 1893, when federalists from both sides of the Murray gathered in the border town of Corowa. There, John Quick, a representative of the Bendigo

---

3   Students who plagiarise Pearson's work are guaranteed a high distinction in Australian university courses sponsored by the Ramsay Centre for Western Civilisation.

ANA, shared his brainwave: the voters of each colony should elect representatives to a convention to draft a Constitution, which would then be put to a referendum. The people, rather than politicians, would determine Australia's future.

Quick's approach was far more participatory than that of the United States, which had inspired Australia's federal push. The United States gave the people a voice by inviting the politicians of twelve states to appoint seventy-four delegates to nut out its Constitution, but nineteen delegates failed to attend and only thirty-nine signed the final document. It was not so much 'We the people' as 'We the people who could be bothered showing up and could find a pen'.

In 1894, Deakin held onto his seat of Essendon and Flemington, surviving the challenge of a popular Essendon footballer who argued the electorate needed new blood.[4] Deakin was criticised for refusing to lead a Liberal government, gifting the premiership to fellow Liberal George Turner, whom he bitchily described as:

> the ideal bourgeois who married early and who was in dress, manner and habits exactly on the same level as the shopkeepers and prosperous artisans who were his ratepayers and constituents.

Deakin divided his time between chairing the Federation League of Victoria and serving on the new Anti-Sweating League. In 1895, he called on the parliament to improve the lot of the 'thousands of helpless, honest, hopeless, half-starved women' in the garment industry. He said of the privileged, 'Let them see that the clothes they wore ... did not come to them stained with the blood from the martyrdom of the toiling masses.' The great Liberal hero sounded more Marx than Menzies.

The changes to the *Factory Act* that Deakin helped steer through parliament established boards to set wages and conditions in key

---

4   With peptides in it.

industries. The reforms didn't just protect women and kids, but men too – a world first. Deakin had the stamina to lead on both Federation and workers' rights, thanks to the efforts of the magnetic healer and clairvoyant he visited each week.

In 1895, George Reid convened his fellow premiers to progress Quick's Corowa plan. The Judas of Federation would recast himself as Australia's saviour, claiming credit for the reform that Parkes had failed to deliver. Reid and the premiers of Victoria, South Australia and Tasmania agreed to hold popular elections for an Australasian Federation Convention.

John Forrest was having none of it – Western Australia's representatives would be appointed by parliament (John Forrest) and led by the best man for the job (John Forrest). Queensland decided not to participate, as Premier Sir Hugh Nelson opposed Federation and had his hands full with redneck separatists who wanted to establish breakaway colonies in central and northern Queensland, so they could enslave Pacific Islanders and shoot Aboriginal people without any interference from the handwringers down in Brisbane.[5]

South Australia's premier, Charles Kingston, refused Catherine Helen Spence's demand that the colony's Convention representatives be elected through 'effective voting', Spence's rebranded name for proportional representation. Queensland had already experimented with the first element of Spence's system, the single transferable vote, in allowing voters to preference another candidate if their favourite was out of the race. The pineapple colony's rejection of the traditional 'first past the post' system meant it would no longer elect the most popular candidates, but the least unpopular ones.[6]

---

5   George Christensen breathed life into the separatist corpse in 2016, endorsing North Queensland's split from Queensland, although he is yet to call for its federation with the Philippines.

6   Single-candidate preferential voting is today regarded by most countries as a glass-half-full approach to choosing society's leaders ('Congratulations, you're the least hated politician in the electorate!'). Although a global rarity, the system is now used in most Australian lower house elections.

Spence's argument fell on deaf ears. Sure, the new name might be catchier, but in the days before Antony Green, nobody could understand what she was on about. After calling Kingston 'spineless', Spence decided to run for the Convention and enshrine effective voting in the Constitution. The first female candidate in Australian political history, labelled 'the best man of the lot' by one liberal organisation, polled well back in the field.

Given the plan was to give the people ownership of the Constitution, it was surprising that all but one of the Convention representatives were current or former politicians. Edmund Barton, now 'the acknowledged leader of the federal movement in all Australia', was elected to chair the Convention's constitutional and drafting committees. Billy Trenwith was the only Labor representative, with Victoria's other attendees Liberals who largely deferred to Deakin. Most attendees had liberal sympathies, although conservatives were represented. With Tasmania's Andrew Inglis Clark visiting America, republicans would have no voice in framing the Constitution. Nor would women, although the *Dawn* and suffragists from across the colonies lobbied Convention candidates to build universal suffrage into Australia's foundation document.

The Australasian Federal Convention met in Adelaide, Sydney and Melbourne between March 1897 and March 1898. Deakin enjoyed the Adelaide sittings, staying at the seaside resort of Largs Bay so he could enjoy a skinny dip each morning (he was an enthusiastic naturist), before cycling the 14 kilometres to the South Australian parliament.[7] Refreshed and invigorated, he'd then throw himself into negotiating the terms of the Constitution.

So what did Deakin, Barton and the other founding fathers come up with?

---

7   Deakin had maintained a rigorous morning exercise regime since his days at Melbourne Grammar – playing hockey with his daughters, skipping backwards, chopping wood, clearing scrub, swimming, or riding a horse or bicycle. Deakin had succumbed to the Australian cycling mania of the mid-1890s, the subject of

THE AUSTRALIAN CONSTITUTION FOR DUMMIES

The Commonwealth of Australia, the nation formed through the federation of Britain's Australian colonies, has a Frankenstein Constitution stitched together from parts of the British, US, Swiss, Canadian provincial and Australian colonial Constitutions, embalmed in nationalism and shocked into life with the electricity of racism.

The British Constitution is like a box of papers from a deceased estate garage sale, with some of its contents now lining the bottom of the budgie's cage. Nobody's really sure what documents it contains, but some of those that are known – like the one that established a whole new Church because the king wanted to root around, or the one that says all British monarchs have to be non-Catholic descendants of a dead German lady – seem pretty shitty. The British call their seemingly random collection of royal charters, parliamentary acts, court judgements and conventions a Constitution because they don't like to admit they don't have a proper one.

The Australian Constitution borrowed bits of Britain's Westminster system of government, under which members of the executive (ministers) must also be members of the legislature (parliament), thereby making the government accountable to the people (responsible government). The United States, in contrast, grants executive power to the president and the cabinet secretaries he appoints from outside the legislature – i.e. his golf buddies, political donors and people who've got a copy of the video of him wearing a nappy while being spanked by Russian prostitutes (irresponsible government).

Banjo Paterson's 1896 'Mulga Bill's Bicycle', the opening lines of which remain relevant to today's middle-aged men in lycra:
> 'Twas Mulga Bill, from Eaglehawk, that caught the cycling craze;
> He turned away the good old horse that served him many days;
> He dressed himself in cycling clothes, resplendent to be seen;
> He hurried off to town and bought a shining new machine;
> And as he wheeled it through the door, with air of lordly pride,
> The grinning shop assistant said, 'Excuse me, can you ride?'

Notwithstanding their love for Britain, the fathers of the Australian Constitution looked mainly to the United States, which had a single document helpfully labelled 'Constitution' and, like the planned Australia, was a federation.

The US and Australian Constitutions both establish a federal legislature comprising a House of Representatives and a Senate (together known as parliament in Australia and Congress in the US); an executive that applies the legislature's laws; and an independent federal court that can declare those laws unconstitutional. This is different to the British system, where parliament can make whatever laws it pleases – it can amend the Constitution on a whim, call black white, and decree that all Scotsmen living in Manchester must wear pink tutus and call themselves Tiffany.

As in the United States, Australia's House of Representatives represents the people, with a state's population determining the number of seats its people have; and the Senate represents the states, which each have an equal number of senators to prevent the larger states from stealing the smaller states' lunch money. However, the Federal Convention rejected the US model of state governments choosing their own senators, with representatives of both Australian houses to be 'directly chosen by the people'.[8] The British House of Lords, in contrast, comprises Anglican bishops, inbred aristos who inherited Daddy's estate, and the PM's chums from Eton, with a surprisingly large crossover existing between these three groups.

In the United States, the people's and states' houses are equally powerful, but in Australia, only the House of Representatives can introduce laws for taxation or government spending. While the Senate can veto these 'money bills', the smaller states were worried that funding decisions would be dominated by the larger ones. These

---

8   This didn't stop Australian prime minister Paul Keating from referring to Australian senators as 'unrepresentative swill'. The United States adopted the Australian approach of direct representation in 1913.

concerns almost derailed Federation, but Deakin insisted they were overblown, predicting that politicians would vote in accordance with their political parties or philosophies, rather than their state of origin. He took a few Tasmanian delegates out for drinks and proposed that the Senate be able to make recommendations on money bills. Deakin's compromise passed by a single vote, saving the federalists' bacon.

The Australian Constitution talks a lot about the Queen.[9] She's actually an unelected third house of parliament, which isn't a problem because she never turns up for work. She's also the Australian head of state and all executive power of the Commonwealth vests in her, but she lets her flunky, the Governor-General, do her Australian queening.

The Governor-General appoints ministers to do all the hard bits of governing for him, leaving him with the important tasks of signing any little bits of paper they give him, dressing neatly, mixing drinks for foreign dignitaries and successful Australian sportspeople, and refraining from doing anything remotely controversial or useful.[10] He and the Queen are meant to discharge their constitutional duties in accordance with the advice of ministers and the prime minister, but this is tricky because the prime minister doesn't constitutionally exist (the PM is like the Governor-General's imaginary friend).[11]

---

9   You'll notice that this book generally refers to 'the queen' and 'the governor-general', in keeping with my republican principles and publisher's style guide. However, the Constitution gives these important folk capital letters, so please don't write me outraged letters about inconsistency of style.

10 The Constitution casually presumed the Governor-General and all MPs and public servants would be men. Only one of Australia's twenty-seven governors-general, Dame Quentin Bryce, appointed in 2008, has not been a 'him'.

11 People who design constitutions don't like to acknowledge there are massive holes in them, so they Spakfilla the gaps with 'constitutional conventions' – 'No, we didn't forget the prime minister or cabinet. They are conventions, and it's also a convention for the Governor-General to do whatever the prime minister says, except when exercising reserve powers, which are far too complicated to explain.' Convention is clearly a wonderful thing and the system basically works, except when the Governor-General mixes drinks for himself, as Sir John Kerr was wont to do.

Australia's founding fathers chose not to follow the American path of incorporating citizens' rights and freedoms into the Constitution.[12] They were disciples of Jeremy Bentham, who contended individuals only have those rights and freedoms granted to them by the state, while Americans preferred John Locke's view that individual rights and freedoms are inalienable. The founders' approach, coupled with their decision to lock the Constitution up tighter than Houdini at a key party, means Australia is now the only democratic country in the world without some kind of Bill of Rights.

The founders reasoned that if the people were to approve the Constitution, they should also approve any changes to it. They therefore required changes to be approved by a referendum attracting the support of a majority of Australian voters and a majority of voters in a majority of states, unlike Britain, which required parliamentary approval, or the United States, which required the support of two-thirds of Congress. Australia's unhelpful referendum arrangements were copied from the Swiss. It would have been better if the founding fathers had instead made the Constitution out of chocolate.[13]

---

12   OK, the Australian Constitution does contain a few *very* limited rights and freedoms: the right to trial by jury for Commonwealth indictable offences (the Commonwealth has a corresponding right to make all its offences non-indictable); the right to just compensation for acquisition of property (just watch *The Castle*); the right against discrimination on the basis of out-of-state residence (nobody knows what this means); an implied freedom of political communication ('Peter Dutton is a tool'); and a limited freedom of religion. This last freedom was added to reinforce the principles that there should be no state religion (as there was in Britain where the monarch was head of both the state and the Church of England), no religious discrimination for public office and no prohibition on the exercise of a religion (although Satanists obviously couldn't wander about sacrificing babies). The late addition was considered necessary after an Adelaide lawyer successfully campaigned to have God mentioned in the draft preamble to the Constitution, upsetting plans for Australia's foundation document to be completely silent on religion.

13   Only eight of forty-four referendum proposals have been approved, with Prime Minister Sir Robert Menzies observing, 'to get an affirmative vote from the Australian people on a referendum proposal is one of the labours of Hercules.'

The Constitution left custom and excise duties to the Commonwealth and, to the amusement of generations of law students, provided that 'trade, commerce and intercourse among the States shall be absolutely free'. As intercolonial duties were a significant source of colonial revenue, particularly for the smaller colonies that had already sold or leased all their land, Tasmanian representative Edward Braddon convinced his colleagues to support 75 per cent of Commonwealth duties being returned to the states.

Defence, one of the key drivers of colonial union, would be a Commonwealth responsibility, with the Governor-General commander in chief of Australia's military and navy, which allowed him to play dress-up with lots of braids and ribbons. Amazingly, after all the hoo-ha about different-width train tracks, the colonies refused to give the Commonwealth control of railways, other than for naval or military transport, unless the future states consented. The track addicts just couldn't break their habit.

Unlike Canada, where the Constitution provides for separate federal and state powers, the Australian Constitution allows federal and state governments to act in many of the same areas, with federal laws only overriding those of a state where there is an inconsistency. This enables both state and federal governments to avoid responsibility when anything is unpopular or expensive, and to blame each other whenever anything goes wrong.[14]

The Commonwealth was given the power to be racist. Its responsibility for immigration would allow it to keep coloured people out – and its power to make special laws for the people of any race would allow dusky folk who'd somehow managed to sneak in to pay special taxes, be barred from certain jobs, imprisoned in camps or deported. Premier Charles Kingston thought special laws for those foreigners already in Australia were unfair:

---

14   'Sure, the Constitution says we have quarantine powers, but it doesn't say we have to use them, so why don't you have a go?'

If you do not like these people you should keep them out, but if you
do admit them you should treat them fairly – admit them as citizens
entitled to all the rights and privileges of Australian citizenship.

Kingston's plea that Australians should only be half racist fell on
deaf ears. For their part, Queenslanders were also concerned that
the race powers would be used to keep Kanakas out of their sugar
plantations. They didn't want other racists using the Commonwealth's
racist powers to restrict the freedom of Queensland racists to be racist. However, as the Queenslanders hadn't bothered showing up to
the Convention, their views were given short shrift.[15]

There was one race that the Commonwealth didn't want a bar
of. The Constitution prevented the federal government making any
special laws for Aboriginal people. Australia was the future and the
future was white – the states would be responsible for their own
Aboriginal people until they died out or interbred with sufficient
generations of white folk for their descendants to achieve whiteness.

To put the cream icing on the vanilla cake, the Constitution
provided, 'In reckoning the numbers of the people of the Commonwealth, or of a State or other part of the Commonwealth, aboriginal
natives should not be counted.' This was to prevent states with large
numbers of Aboriginal people from gaining additional parliamentary
seats and funding, both of which were linked to a state's population.
Aboriginal people parked in reserves didn't need to talk to their MP
or access government services, so it was only fair that states didn't
receive extra seats or money for them.[16]

---

15 The Commonwealth's power to be racist has never been referred for the
    reconsideration of the Australian people at a referendum, despite numerous
    recommendations to this effect – probably because it would be a bit embarrassing
    if Australians voted 'No'.

16 Just about every modern resource says the purpose of this provision was to exclude
    Aboriginal people from being counted in the census. It had nothing to do with the
    census. Aboriginal people have been counted in all Australian censuses, although
    some census collectors didn't try very hard to find them. Aboriginal population
    numbers were, however, placed in separate tables before 1967 so that Aboriginal

While the Constitution was heavy on race, it was light on gender. The Queen was the only woman mentioned in the Constitution, which upset Charles Kingston and his predecessor Frederick Holder, whose wife, Julia, was a committed suffragist. The South Australians wanted to protect women's voting rights, with Holder moving that the Constitution provide 'every man and woman ... shall be an elector'.

Barton, who believed a woman's place was in the home, not the House, successfully opposed the motion. Holder suggested a compromise – that the future federal parliament would determine voting rights, but that no adult who could vote at elections for the largest house of parliament in a state could be prevented from voting in Commonwealth elections.

Barton pointed out that, as it had already been agreed that the Constitution would require uniform electoral laws for choosing senators, this would effectively give all women the Commonwealth vote. Holder and Kingston threatened that South Australia would vote against joining the Commonwealth unless Holder's clause was included. Barton, realising it would be better to have women in than South Australians out, convinced his fellow anti-suffragists to back Holder.

After a year of debate, it was time for the draft Constitution to be put to the Australian people.[17]

---

people could be excluded from counts used for electoral and funding purposes. Embarrassingly, Australian governments couldn't agree on what the Constitution actually meant by 'aboriginal native'. At first, Attorney-General Alfred Deakin advised it meant 'full-bloods' but, in 1929, the government decided 'half-castes' were 'aboriginal natives' too. In 1967, 90.77 per cent of Australians voted to remove these discriminatory provisions, the largest 'Yes' vote in an Australian referendum.

17   Except for the women outside South Australia. And Aboriginal people from Queensland and Western Australia, and those in New South Wales and Victorian reserves. And the Asians who were barred from voting. And the itinerant workers who weren't able to provide an address (which left a lot of swagmen unjolly). But apart from them and a few others, all the Australian people.

THE PEOPLE DECIDE

Queensland, a non-starter at the Convention, agreed to join the other colonies in voting on the draft Constitution. John Forrest, however, held back.

Gold had made Western Australia the most prosperous colony, and John's brother Alexander led the anti-federalists who warned Australia would pillage the west's mineral wealth and redistribute it to the eastern states.[18] As Australia's least populous colony, Western Australia would have fewer parliamentary seats than the others, and western farmers were concerned that post-Federation tariff increases would drive up the price of farm machinery. There was a lot of sand between Perth and the eastern colonies, so isolationism had become a default position. There would be no Western Australian referendum.

Voters in the other colonies were simply asked, 'Are you in favour of the proposed Federal Constitution Bill?' No voter was more enthusiastic than Thomas Hinton, a Tasmanian engine driver who posed for fifteen photographic portraits, standing proudly in front of an assortment of homemade federalist and nationalist symbols, Australian flora and stuffed native animals. Hinton's admission papers to the New Norfolk Hospital for the Insane recorded his 'mania for having his photograph taken in all sorts of dress and without dress', and that he'd 'been sending indecent photos to a Miss Headlam', who'd been unimpressed by his patriotic fervour.

Australia's churches endorsed the bill, it being God's will that the colonies unite and keep the coloured sons of Ham out of the new Israel. Most women also supported it, but there were plenty of anti-billites, as opponents of the proposed Constitution were known. New South Wales suffragist Rose Scott wanted 'a Federation of men and women

---

18   Western Australia has continued this whinge for over a century. When the mining industry booms, it complains about its GST contributions subsidising the other states, and when the industry is in the doldrums, it holds out the begging bowl and demands that the other states subsidise it.

FIG. 11: MISS HEADLAM SWIPED LEFT AFTER RECEIVING
AUSTRALIA'S FIRST DICK PIC.

in all things ... a socialism of Love', but a centralised government, far from women's centre of power (the home), could only diminish women's influence. Republicans such as John Norton opposed the bill because it enshrined the primacy of the British monarchy.

Labor, while supporting Federation, opposed the bill for its failure to acknowledge the core Labor principle of 'One Person, One Vote', with voting eligibility to be determined by future federal parliaments. The bill also gave too much power to the Senate – the smaller, more conservative states would have a proportionally greater say than the progressive ones in which Labor had a foothold. Federation, Labor argued, was also a distraction from the main game of freeing workers from the chains of capital. The Fat Man was recruited to the 'No' campaign, with 'Fighting Fat Man Federation' a catchy slogan.

Victorian Labor leader Billy Trenwith supported the bill, despite his reservations. Labelled a 'political blackleg', he resigned the leadership and drifted into the orbit of the Liberal Protectionists who dominated Victorian politics. Chris Watson, a prominent 'No' campaigner, supported the idea of participatory democracy by way of referendum. If the people decided in favour of Federation, then he would respect the people's will. Diehards like Billy Hughes, in contrast, were not prepared to let the people get in the way of principle or power.

David Syme and the *Age* opposed the bill. Syme argued it would lower tariffs and harm Victorian manufacturers, although Deakin believed that Syme, who'd pulled the strings in local politics for decades, feared a loss of influence when Victoria was just another fish in the federal pond. Syme told Deakin to restrain the rabid dogs of the Australian Natives' Association, who were off the leash and barking for the bill.

Deakin went to the ANA annual conference at Bendigo. At the conference banquet, Liberals Henry Bournes Higgins and Attorney-General Isaac Isaacs urged that Federation be delayed, their reasons similar to those of Labor. Deakin stood and called on those attending to be 'filled with zeal and bearing the fiery cross of Federation', fiery crosses being something the white supremacists of the ANA could rally around. He thundered and cajoled:

> 'These are the times that try men's souls.' The classes may resist us; the masses may be inert; politicians may falter; our leaders may sound the retreat. But it is not a time for surrender. Let us nail our standard to the mast. Let us stand shoulder to shoulder in defence of the enlightened liberalism of the constitution.

The crowd went crazy. Tables were banged. Forks clattered against glasses. Some bread rolls were probably thrown. *Advance Australia*, the ANA journal, described the event as 'being like the "new baptism" when the disciples of Jesus were filled with the holy spirit', later writing of 'the Gospel of Federation'. Alfred Deakin, High Priest of the Church of Australia, had reaffirmed the faith of his flock.

Premier Turner and his ministry had been spooked by Syme, worried the puppet-master would cut their strings if they danced to their own tune. However, ANA-organised town hall meetings held across the colony, addressed by Deakin in full Joan of Arc mode, changed the political calculus. Turner declared support for the bill, and Syme, so used to leading, assumed the unfamiliar role of penitent follower. With Victoria on side, Deakin campaigned for the bill in Queensland.

The main opposition to the bill came from an unlikely source. The New South Wales premier's speech on the bill listed all of its perceived defects, before Reid limply concluded, 'I consider my duty to Australia demands me to record a vote in favour of the Bill.' While the other colonies required only majority support in the referendum, New South Wales insisted on at least 80,000 'Yes' votes. The apathy induced by Reid's 'Yes-No speech' meant that although 52 per cent of voters ticked 'Yes', the referendum failed by 8,504 votes.

The percentage of voters in support of the bill were: South Australia (67 per cent), Tasmania (81 per cent) and Victoria (82 per cent), with Queensland deferring its referendum until 1899. Reid had his fellow premiers over a barrel and, with all the cunning of a shithouse rat, promised to block further attempts at Federation unless the draft Constitution was changed in New South Wales' favour.

First, Melbourne wouldn't be the national capital – the capital would be in New South Wales, befitting its status as the foundation colony. Second, the requirement that 60 per cent of MPs support a previously blocked bill in a joint sitting of parliament would give too much power to an obstructionist Senate – it would be a simple majority, or he'd walk. Third was the Braddon clause that required 75 per cent of Commonwealth duties to be returned to the states. Reid, a free trader to his duty-free bootstraps, said Australians would have to wean themselves off tariffs and the 'Braddon Blot' would need to be erased after ten years.

The other premiers reluctantly accepted Reid's terms, although the disappointed Victorians insisted that if Melbourne wasn't to be the capital, then Sydney wouldn't be either. It was agreed the capital would need to be at least 100 miles from Sydney and 100 square miles in size. A shiny new metropolis, Melburnians reasoned, might at least dim the influence and self-importance of Sydney – and until it was established, Melbourne would host the Commonwealth parliament and serve as interim capital.

In 1899, the colonies held referenda on the new draft of the Constitution – except Western Australia, which was still sulking in its sandpit. The people of each participating colony voted to federate.

As the nineteenth century drew to a close, the political landscape was changing. Alliances shifted as politicians prepared for a new power dynamic. Should an MP be loyal to his colony, his party, his political philosophy or his conscience in these uncertain times?

In the 1899 Queensland election, Labor ran on a platform of 'A WHITE AND UNFETTERED QUEENSLAND'. Andrew

Fisher alleged his rival for the seat of Gympie employed black workers, cared little that white women might be raped by Kanakas, and was a secret supporter of leprosy.[19] The success of Labor's smear campaign enabled its leader, Andrew Dawson, to head the world's first Labor government, although the coalition of anti-Labor forces formed in response meant it was in power for only six days.

South Australia's Vaiben Solomon led a loose alliance of conservatives, unkindly dubbed the 'Forlorn Hope', dedicated to ending Charles Kingston's liberal reign. On the same day that Labor took power in the north, Solomon seized the South Australian premiership, still the only Jewish person (and the only person to nude up and paint himself black for a laugh) to lead an Australian government. His rule lasted only seven days, but at least he was able to shed the 'Black Solomon' nickname. For leading South Australia's shortest ministry, he was thereafter known as 'Sudden Solomon'.[20]

The rise and fall of governments, and the casting down of great men, were portents of the colonial end of days. So too were the hoof-beats of War, Pestilence and Death that beat an infernal staccato on the drought-cracked land as the second hand of the century clock ticked inexorably towards midnight.

BOERED TO DEATH

Banjo Paterson started his writing career by opposing the involvement of Britain and New South Wales in an African war. Fourteen years later, the thought of another such war excited him. On 11 October 1899,

---

19   Fisher was a mild-mannered, generally likeable Presbyterian Sunday school teacher who didn't drink or swear. He couldn't bear rudeness and was upset when others used intemperate language like 'Shut up!'. Yet he could accuse a rival of plotting to spread leprosy and damn Pacific Islanders as rapists. Andrew Fisher is otherwise best known as the Australian prime minister with the tallest wife, with Margaret Fisher, at six-foot-three, more than an inch taller than Margaret Whitlam.

20   Dawson and Solomon make Anthony Scaramucci look like a grizzled veteran of government.

Boers seized a British train after Britain refused to remove its troops from the borders of the Orange Free State and South African Republic (which the British called Transvaal). Britain was at war with the two Boer republics and the Australian colonies wanted in on the action.

A few days after hostilities commenced, Paterson burst into the office of Sir James Fairfax, owner of the *Sydney Morning Herald*, and told Fairfax he had a new war correspondent. On 30 October, the warrior-poet sailed with a contingent of New South Wales Lancers, the first of 16,000 colonial troops to leave Australia for the Cape Colony.[21] Two months later, the *South Australian Register* reported Harry 'The Breaker' Morant's overseas deployment with the South Australian Mounted Rifles. He'd never see Australia again.

Boer means 'farmer' in Dutch. Between 1835 and 1846, Boer *Voortrekkers* (fore-trekkers or pioneers) trekked out of the Cape Colony, seized by Britain from the Dutch during the Napoleonic Wars, to establish Boer republics where they could farm and trek without British interference. In 1868, the British discovered the Boers were farming and trekking over a massive diamond deposit. Britain took over the South African Republic in 1877 and was surprised when the Boers rebelled, won the First Boer War, and reasserted their independence.[22]

After Australian prospector George Harrison (not to be confused with the Beatle) discovered gold near present-day Johannesburg in 1886, Prime Minister Cecil Rhodes of the Cape Colony incited British residents in the South African Republic (*Uitlanders*) to rebel and steal it. After this failed, Britain, pretending it had no knowledge of the attempted coup, tried another tack. It claimed the Boers were

---

21   Six hundred and forty-nine Australian soldiers would die during the Boer War and a further 735 would be seriously wounded.

22   Those who are critical of Britain's attempt to seize Boer lands should remember the Boers seized those lands from the Zulu, Ndebele and other African peoples. The Great Trekkers also took their *inboekelinge* (black 'child apprentices') with them and forcibly recruited more juvenile not-slaves from the people they displaced. The fact that the British were dicks doesn't mean the Boers weren't.

denying taxpaying *Uitlanders* equal voting rights – and made it clear British troops might need to assist the Boers to embrace democracy.[23] Presidents Paul Kruger of the South African Republic and Martinus Steyn of the Orange Free State feared Britain's refusal to move its troops meant invasion was imminent. The best form of defence, they decided, was attack.

When Paterson arrived at Port Elizabeth, the British treated him and the Lancers with disdain. He wasn't even the best-known Australian writer in the Cape Colony. The Swiss-born Louis de Rouge-mont, real name Henri Louis Grin, was a spiritualist showman and one-time butler to the governor of Western Australia. *The Adventures of Louis de Rougemont, as Told by Himself*, the surprise literary hit of 1899, recounted Louis' three decades living with Aboriginal tribes who worshipped him as a god, his riding of giant sea-turtles and his encounters with flying wombats. Members of the British establish-ment were divided on whether de Rougemont's adventures were fact or fiction, until an old acquaintance outed him as Grin. Fleeing to the Cape, de Rougemont sold out theatres with his show *The Greatest Liar on Earth*.[24]

Paterson was embedded with Lieutenant General John French's cavalry troops. Being a war reporter was risky, with William Lambie of the *Age* gunned down in a Boer ambush, the first Australian to die

---

23   Dora Montefiore, the genteel society matron who'd founded the Womanhood Suffrage League of New South Wales, was now an English socialist engaged in an affair with a married Labour man thirteen years her junior. Her October 1899 pamphlet, *Women Uitlanders*, highlighted Britain's hypocrisy in threatening war over the voting rights of a few British men on another continent, while denying those rights to women at home. Montefiore's subsequent civil disobedience campaign for British women to refuse to pay taxes until they could vote influenced a Cape Colony lawyer who'd recruited 1,100 of his fellow Indians to support British troops against the Boers. His name was Mohandas Gandhi.

24   De Rougemont was booed off stage during a later Australian tour, his fantastical tales having made a laughing-stock of his adopted home. In 1906, he appeared at the London Hippodrome to demonstrate his sea-turtle riding skills. He resurfaced during World War I as the inventor of a useless meat substitute and died in 1921 as Louis Redman, a poor handyman.

in the war. Seven of sixty Boer War reporters died within the first
six months of hostilities, with Paterson narrowly avoiding serious
injury when hit in the ribs by a ricocheting bullet during the British
assault on Pretoria.

Paterson's early reporting and poems were jingoistic, as these
lines from 'With French to Kimberley' attest:

> *His column was five thousand strong – all mounted men – and guns:*
> *There met, beneath the world-wide flag, the world-wide Empire's*
> *sons;*
> *They came to prove to all the earth that kinship conquers space,*
> *And those who fight the British Isles must fight the British race!*

Paterson's readers back home lapped this up. Australians over-
whelmingly favoured the campaign, with churches declaring the war
just and colonial politicians and newspapers using it to fan the flames
of nationalism in the lead-up to Federation.

There were opponents of the South African venture. Most Labor
leaders saw it as a distraction from the real war between labour and
capital. While they were generally cautious in their condemnation,
J.F. Archibald was not, calling it 'a war of plunder and imperial aggran-
disement'. His interview with the *San Francisco Examiner* received
international attention:

> The Boers are fighting for their rights, the same as the thirteen
> colonies did during the American revolution. It is monstrous that
> Australia should send soldiers to South Africa to help Britain wage
> this unholy war.

The Boers proved a well-armed and difficult foe. Being farmers,
they knew how to shoot and ride. Most fought in civilian militias
known as *kommandos* (source of the English 'commando') and were able
to blend into the population. They launched ambushes and lightning
raids and, when defending, fired on the British soldiers ordered to

march against their entrenchments in tight formation. The Australian troops performed better than the English Tommies. They advanced in loose formation, sought cover and used their horses for transport, rather than vainglorious cavalry charges. Like Paterson and Morant, many of the Australians were experienced riders who could match it with the Boers.

By the end of 1899, it was clear the Boers were outnumbered, and the republics largely abandoned offence for defence. Paterson distinguished himself during the conflict, riding 40 kilometres to scoop the other correspondents with news that French had broken the siege on Kimberley, earning him an international Reuters contract. Whipping his horse as the Boer forces evacuated Bloemfontein, he was the first of the British contingent into the city, bringing out the mayor to surrender to Lord Roberts, commander-in-chief of the British forces.

During his nine months in South Africa, Paterson befriended Rudyard Kipling and Winston Churchill, the *Morning Post* correspondent who downed a bottle of beer each breakfast. Paterson described Churchill as possessing 'the most curious combination of ability and swagger', and as one of the three greatest men he'd ever met. The Australian mixed with Colonel Neville Chamberlain (aide-de-camp to Lord Roberts and the inventor of snooker) and Major-General Hector 'Fighting Mac' MacDonald, the Boer War hero who'd shoot himself in 1903 after it was announced he'd be court-martialled for buggering Ceylonese boys.[25]

Paterson's initially jingoistic reporting soon displayed more balance than that of most correspondents. He humanised the enemy, writing that the first prisoner of war he met was nothing like the 'wild and

---

25   MacDonald, who remained a national hero in Scotland, was a Highland Elvis – with reports he'd faked his own death and been sighted in China. During World War I, the German High Command sought to demoralise Scottish troops by spreading the rumour that Fighting Mac had defected and become General August von Mackensen, one of the Kaiser's most feared commanders.

hairy' Boer of war propaganda, but a doctor with an English degree who could make a fifty break at billiards. He interviewed enemy fighters and his reporting noted the futility of a war in which Britain would need to garrison the Boer territories to retain them. Paterson was no fan of Lord Kitchener, Lord Roberts' coldly calculating chief of staff:

> As far as mobility of expression goes, you could put Kitchener's face
> on the body of the Sphinx, and nobody would know the difference.
> He has the aloof air and the fixed expression of a golf champion.

Paterson accused Kitchener of tactics that wasted the lives of his men, but his heart was broken by Kitchener's scorched earth policy, initiated after the Boers were reduced to small roving guerilla bands. Boer farms were burned, their fields salted, wells poisoned and livestock slaughtered. Paterson saw 'women and children turned, homeless and crying, out onto the open veldt', before being interned in concentration camps. Over 21,350 children and 5,000 women died in the camps, mostly from disease and starvation.

The first Australian troops to see combat overseas were involved in these shameful operations, characterised by the British as a humanitarian response to care for displaced persons. Back in Sydney, J.F. Archibald laid into a group of diners at a restaurant who accused him of being a Boer sympathiser:

> By George, if you people got what you deserved you'd have your farms
> burnt and your daughters raped and your sons sent to concentration
> camps and your country given over to a load of boodling profiteers.

Paterson returned home in September 1900, with the British operations having twenty months left to run. He embarked on a national lecture tour, in which he was critical of the war and its conduct, and penned 'Now Listen to Me and I'll Tell You My Views', an anti-war poem in which he accused Joseph Chamberlain, secretary of state for the colonies, of being 'a Birmingham Judas' who'd led the colonies into a war with no exit plan. It was more 'El Mahdi to the Australian Troops' than 'With French to Kimberley':

> And next let us join in the bloodthirsty shriek, Hooray for Lord Kitchener's 'bag'!
> For the fireman's torch and the hangman's cord – they are hung on the English Flag!
> In the front of our brave old army! Whoop! the farmhouse blazes bright.
> And the women weep and their children die – how dare they presume to fight!

Still, the words of Paterson and Archibald did little to dampen the martial enthusiasm of an Australian people joined closer together, and closer to Britain, by the bonds of war. The children had shown mother they could fight and were worthy of venturing out into the world on their own.

CHINESE MORRISON IN FISTS OF FURY

Australian troops would not just see action in South Africa in 1900. They'd also invade China – a pre-emptive strike against the would-be invaders of White Australia.

George Ernest Morrison, the one-time Australian adventurer and undercover blackbirder, knew trouble was brewing in April 1900 when members of the Society of the Righteous and Harmonious Fists were sighted near the imperial capital of Beijing (known by Westerners as Peking). Morrison had left his job as a Ballarat surgeon to walk, ride and riverboat the 4,828 kilometres from Shanghai to Rangoon, wearing a Chinese peasant hat with fake pigtail attachment to make his towering, European frame less conspicuous. *An Australian in China* was another publishing success, securing him a gig as the *Times*' Eastern correspondent and the British secret service's man on the ground in French Indochina.

In 1897, 'Chinese Morrison', as he'd become known, was appointed the *Times'* first permanent Beijing correspondent and was well on his way to becoming the West's leading expert on all things China.

The Society of the Righteous and Harmonious Fists (a.k.a. the Plum Blossom Fists, a.k.a. the Fists of Harmony and Justice, a.k.a. the Militia United in Righteousness) was a not-very-secret Chinese secret society, as it's hard to conceal an organisation with so many names and tens of thousands of members who run around doing crazy Bruce Lee shit while screaming, 'Exterminate the foreigners!' The Fists' martial arts skills led to them being known as 'Boxers' in the West.

The Boxers were Chinese who hated Australians even more than Australians hated Chinese, which was saying something – although, in fairness, Australians only hated coloured foreigners, while the Boxers hated them all.

After the Second Opium War ended in 1860, China was forced to grant foreign missionaries the rights to preach and purchase land. The Boxers particularly hated these missionaries and their local followers, believing they'd corrupted Chinese morals and values. The Boxers also particularly hated the French, who'd taken control of Indochina and Zhanjiang; the Russians and British, who'd demanded additional territory and exemptions from Chinese law; the Japanese, who'd defeated China in the First Sino–Japanese War of 1895; and the Germans, who in 1898 had attacked and permanently occupied a Chinese naval base in Tsingtao.[26] The Boxers hated all other foreigners as a matter of general principle.

These Fists of Fury believed spirits possessed them while pulling martial arts moves, making them invulnerable to the white man's weapons. They also believed that, when the call came for the Boxers to purify China of all foreigners, millions of soldiers would descend

---

26 On the plus side, the Germans taught the Chinese to brew one of the world's tastiest beers.

from Heaven to join them. These beliefs made the Boxers extremely dangerous to their enemies and even more dangerous to themselves.

In January 1900, Empress Dowager Cixi issued edicts in defence of the previously outlawed Boxers. This upset the Western powers, who objected to the Boxers burning down their churches and inserting swords into their missionaries. After Boxers were seen near Beijing, the Eight Powers (Britain, Russia, the United States, France, Germany, Japan, Austria-Hungary and Italy) sent troops to guard their embassies in the capital's Legation Quarter.

On 11 June 1900, a Boxer appeared in the Legation Quarter in full foreigner-killing martial arts regalia. A Japanese diplomat was torn limb from limb and nearby churches were set ablaze. Meanwhile, German ambassador Baron Clemens von Ketteler beat a Boxer boy with his walking stick before shooting him dead. This triggered thousands of Boxers, joined by Imperial Army soldiers, to riot through Beijing, burning more churches and Chinese Christians. Then things went south.

The Imperial Court was split, with Prince Duan taking charge of the Foreign Office, which he tasked with killing foreigners. Duan became the effective leader of the Boxers. Empress Dowager Cixi and many others within the imperial government and army fell in behind the Boxers after Vice-Admiral Edward Seymour led a multinational force of 2,300 men to reinforce the embassies. Western and Japanese warships then attacked Chinese coastal forts to reinforce Seymour. Cixi ordered an attack on Seymour's troops, forcing them back to their base, and imperial troops and Boxers besieged the embassies.

Cixi demanded all foreigners leave Beijing under Chinese army escort. Ambassador von Ketteler set out for the palace to protest the expulsion. He was stopped by a captain of Prince Duan's Tiger Spirit Division, who shot him at point-blank range.

On 21 June, ten days after the first skirmishes, Cixi declared war against all foreign powers in China. Morrison was one of 882 foreigners and 3,000 Chinese Christians besieged in the Legation Quarter. During the conflict, Morrison, though not a soldier, led British,

German and American troops in rescuing more than 100 Chinese Christians. He shot six Boxers in one skirmish and, on 16 July, took a bullet himself. He was amused at the glowing obituary his own newspaper printed in response to his supposed death.

More than 40 per cent of the Legation guards were dead or injured by the time an armistice was declared. China was worried about the international blowback – which came in the form of 55,000 troops, drawn from members of the Eight Powers and Chinese defectors. New South Wales sent its Marine Light Infantry, a force of 260 soldiers and sailors; Victoria sent 200 men; and South Australia sent its entire navy (one gunboat).

In August 1901, Cixi fled Beijing by oxcart dressed as a peasant. The international occupying forces hunted and summarily executed Boxers, raped women and massacred entire villages. The imperial palaces and other Beijing institutions were looted, with Britain criticising the looters of other nations while boasting, 'Looting on the part of British troops was carried out in the most orderly manner.'[27] The British embassy held almost daily loot auctions, a recovering Morrison one of the most prominent bidders. He was on his way to assembling the largest Asiatic library the world had ever seen.

Cixi ended the occupation by signing the Boxer Protocol, which required the execution of some of the government officials who'd aided the Boxers, placed the Legation Quarter under foreign control, provided for a permanent foreign troop presence in the capital and required China to pay more than its annual revenue to members of the Eight-Nation Alliance, although it was graciously given thirty-nine years to cough up. The Chinese had again been humiliated by the West, Russia and Japan – and they would not forget it.[28]

---

27   Knowing the British, their looters probably queued.

28   Modern China uses 'the Century of Humiliation' by foreign powers, starting with the 1839 British invasion of China during the First Opium War, as a justification for its territorial claims and continued rise, and as a rebuttal to any Western claims of moral purity.

Australian troops played a relatively minor role in the occupation.
They engaged in a few light skirmishes, shot some Chinese prisoners
and performed police, guard, fireman and railway duties in Beijing
and Tientsin. As in the Sudan, they suffered no battlefield casualties,
although six servicemen succumbed to injury and disease.

PLAGUE, POMMYLAND, PERTH AND THE PATH
TO POWER

Disease was the number one concern in Sydney after dockworker
Arthur Paine was diagnosed with bubonic plague on 19 January 1900.
The plague was the Donald Bradman of diseases – with the Black
Death of 1346–1353, which claimed up to 200 million lives, the most
fatal pandemic in recorded history.

The New South Wales government employed 3,000 ratcatchers
to capture the rodents believed to have brought the Black Death to
White Australia. Dead rats were deposited at a purpose-built dead rat
depot on Darling Island, while children were given sixpence for each
dead rat delivered to a furnace near Circular Quay – like aluminium
can recycling today, although considerably more lethal.

The plague changed the face of Sydney. Slums were razed and
earth floors cemented in an attempt to rat-proof buildings, improving
housing for the workers left behind as wealthier residents escaped
the waterfront for the relative safety of the suburbs.[29] Streets were
disinfected and quarantine stations established for plague victims and
their close contacts, with those placed in quarantine compensated
for lost income. The government appointed Sydney Medical School
graduates to form a new public health department. Premier William
Lyne was applauded for these measures, even the one that brought
Sydney's children into contact with the world's most feared disease.

29   Politicians, like rats deserting a sinking ship, swarmed out of Parliament House,
     which was closed for six months.

The plague crept into the suburbs, claiming 103 victims in 1900. Sydney's people were luckier than its rats, with over 100,000 rodents falling victim to ratcatchers and enterprising kids.[30] There were twelve major plague outbreaks between 1900 and 1925, most of which hit Sydney – but Melbourne, Adelaide, Fremantle and North Queensland were also affected. Australia, unable to isolate itself from the rest of the world, would have to learn to live with disease.

Henry Lawson escaped the plague by sailing for London in April 1900. London, Bertha Lawson reasoned, was 10,000 miles away from Hannah Thorburn, and Henry, desperate enough to sell out to the London publishers he'd long derided, thought the move might kick-start his international literary career. Having drunk all his money, Henry's trip was paid for by the art-loving New South Wales governor Lord Beauchamp, described by Norman Lindsay as 'the only English Governor who had ever given a glance at what culture this country might have had' and 'a kindly man, for all the peculiar physiological and psychological quirks in his make-up'.[31]

Lawson had some literary success in London, finding a publisher for two collections of his stories. However, his greatest achievement was getting his publisher to back *My Brilliant Career*, for which he wrote the preface. Miles Franklin, whom Lawson believed to be a man, sent him the manuscript rejected by Australian publishers, with

---

30   Anyone who's read *The Pied Piper of Hamelin* knows that ratcatchers and children traditionally don't mix, but in Sydney they proved a powerful combination.

31   This was a reference to Beauchamp's homosexuality. In 1931, Beauchamp, presumed to have been the model for Lord Marchmain in Evelyn Waugh's *Brideshead Revisited*, was forced to resign as Liberal Party leader in the House of Lords. Beauchamp's brother-in-law, the Duke of Westminster, had outed him to King George V, who was rumoured to have responded, 'I thought men like that shot themselves.' Countess Beauchamp had no idea what homosexuality was, initially believing her husband had been accused of being a bugler. After the countess obtained a divorce and Beauchamp left England to tour the world with a succession of artistic younger men, his brother-in-law wrote to him, 'Dear Bugger-in-law, you got what you deserved. Yours, Westminster.'

Lawson replying, 'Dear Sir ... the first great Australian novel.'[32] The novel bought Franklin instant acclaim, although her royalty payments for the first year were about the annual wage of an unskilled worker in the clothing trade.[33]

Lawson's personal life in London was less successful. The Lawsons moved in with Edith Dean, who'd calmly handed her first husband, Australian poet Francis Adams, the revolver he'd used to shoot himself. Dean, returning from a three-week holiday, recounted how she'd found Henry 'in lodgings with *my* servant' and Bertha in Bethlem Asylum. A remorseful Henry, his marriage damaged beyond repair, later wrote, 'That wild run to London/ That wrecked and ruined me.'

Alfred Deakin also travelled to London in early 1900, part of the delegation to negotiate passage of the Australian Constitution through the British parliament. Led by Edmund Barton, the delegation included South Australia's Charles Kingston, Queensland's James Dickson and Tasmania's Sir Philip Fysh.

Deakin regarded Dickson and Fysh as 'vacillating and self-interested' – easy prey for Joseph Chamberlain, the devious secretary of state for the colonies, who wanted to amend the Constitution in Britain's favour. Deakin informed Chamberlain that any amendments would need to be put to the Australian people in a referendum, which might derail Project Australia.[34] Chamberlain, like his Nazi-appeasing son Neville, backed off.

When Deakin, Barton and Kingston received the news that Britain had consented to the establishment of a new Australian nation, they joined hands and whirled each other around their hotel room in an

---

32   Serial sleazebag Norman Lindsay didn't mistake the 22-year-old novelist for a man, describing her as 'very short but pleasingly plump ... and a superb mass of black hair in a cascade that reached her pert rump'.

33   This is a lot more than most Australian writers earn.

34   This might charitably be described as a 'white lie', as the one amendment the delegation and Chamberlain agreed to was never considered by the Australian people.

impromptu dance.[35] They would return home to a rockstar reception.

On 9 July 1900, Queen Victoria signed the *Commonwealth of Australia Constitution Act* – the British Act that would establish the Australian nation. It began:

> WHEREAS the people of New South Wales, Victoria, South Australia, Queensland, and Tasmania, humbly relying on the blessing of Almighty God, have agreed to unite in one indissoluble Federal Commonwealth under the Crown of the United Kingdom of Great Britain and Ireland ...

Western Australia had missed roll call, but would be able to attend class in 1901 if John Forrest signed its late slip.

Forrest had a miner problem – the gold rush had trebled Western Australia's population between 1893 and 1900, and the 'Outsiders', as the easterners who'd flocked to Kalgoorlie and Coolgardie were known, were now sitting on all the colony's riches. While the pre-rush Western Australians were cargo cultists who worshipped Forrest as an infrastructure god, the miners knew it was the wealth they dug up that allowed him to deliver railways, pipelines, ports and dams to his primitive followers. In early 1900, mining town representatives petitioned Queen Victoria to secede from Western Australia, with the new goldfields state of Auralia, capital Kalgoorlie, to join the new nation. Western Australians, stripped of their gold, would be left groping sand.

Forrest thought that women might weaken the electoral power of the miners, who had Labor, as well as secessionist, sympathies. Just as a ladies' book club had birthed the Womanhood Suffrage League of New South Wales, the ladies of the St George's Reading Circle formed Perth's Karrakatta Club in 1894. Australia's first 'proper' women's social club involved itself in women's and social justice issues, and many of its founding members – including its first secretary,

---

35   Come on baby, do the Federation.

Edith Cowan – suggested that women should have the vote.[36] Much
to their surprise, John Forrest, a vocal anti-suffragist, acquiesced in
August 1899. There were few women on the goldfields (if you ignored
all the prostitutes) and Forrest believed that the women of the more
established urban and farming districts would back his conservative
West Australia First agenda.

However, when a woman on the other side of the world signed off
on Federation, Forrest knew his people had to join Team Australia.
He sought last-minute concessions from his fellow premiers, most
notably the construction of an east–west railway across the continent.
He was rebuffed, but still led the 'Yes' campaign in a snap referendum.

On 31 July 1900, 69 per cent of Western Australians voted to
join the 'indissoluble Federal Commonwealth'.[37] With the last piece
of the Australian puzzle in place, a relieved Alfred Deakin said of
Federation, 'its actual accomplishment must always appear to have
been secured by a series of miracles.'

Deakin reported another miracle upon his return from Britain –
he'd underspent his parliamentary travel allowance. Deakin's refund
of £450 of the £1,000 allocated embarrassed Barton and Kingston,
who'd each blown more than £1,500 on the trip. However, Deakin
didn't disclose that he'd accepted a £500 annual retainer from the
Morning Post. For the next thirteen years, Deakin reported anonymously as 'the Australian correspondent' for the conservative English
newspaper. He went to great lengths to conceal his role, filing some

36   Cowan, who'd developed an interest in social justice after her father was hanged
     for the murder of her stepmother, became Australia's first female MP when
     elected to the Western Australian Legislative Assembly in 1921. You can check her
     out on the Australian $50 note.

37   They later voted to dissolve it. Western Australia is the only state to have ever
     asked to leave Australia, recording a 68 per cent vote in favour of Wexit in a 1933
     state referendum. However, the Australian Constitution is like a Venus flytrap –
     it allowed states to enter the Commonwealth, but provided no mechanism for
     them to leave. Western Australia asked Britain to recognise it as the new British
     dominion of Westralia, but the British House of Commons decided it had no
     power to grant this request.

of his copy in code, using the name 'Andrew Oliver' in telegraph communications and having his daughters address his mail to the paper, in order to prevent postal staff familiar with his handwriting from asking embarrassing questions. Deakin the politician was a protectionist, while Deakin the reporter was a free trader. He wrote pieces that were critical of Barton and other allies – and sometimes even of himself, such as:

> For reasons known only to himself, which are a perpetual subject of controversy in our Press, Mr Deakin pursues his enigmatic methods of action.

It was relatively easy for Alfred Deakin, whose writing hand had been possessed by the spirit of John Bunyan, to find that hand possessed by a different manifestation of Alfred Deakin. His role for the *Post* would not be revealed until he himself joined the spirit world.

Deakin had his eyes on the federal election that would be held in March 1901. Labor had started planning for a federal Labor Party in January 1900, with the first item on Labor's platform, 'Electoral Reform, providing for one adult, one vote'; and the second, 'Total exclusion of coloured and other undesirable races'. In late 1900, Deakin formed the National Liberal Organisation, which united the various Liberal factions in Victoria and which he hoped might form the nucleus of a national progressive party. Deakin, who'd decided to run for the ANA stronghold of Ballarat, started selecting Liberal candidates.

As elections wouldn't be held until after Federation, the incoming governor-general, Lord Hopetoun, needed to appoint an interim prime minister to consult with colonial premiers in forming a ministry of 'first class men from each of the colonies'. It was expected that Edmund Barton would get the nod, but Hopetoun opted for New South Wales premier Sir William Lyne.

Deakin described Lyne as 'a crude, sleek, suspicious, blundering, short-sighted, backblocks politician ... his politics are a chaos and his career contemptible'. Despite having the support of David Syme and offering the press baron two nominees in his ministry, Lyne, who'd voted against Federation, couldn't secure the backing of his federalist peers. Hopetoun, whose first official act in Australia was memorialised as 'the Hopetoun Blunder', went with Plan B – he invited Barton to form the first Australian ministry.

Barton's 'Cabinet of Kings' included Deakin as his deputy and attorney-general, and recent or serving colonial premiers Charles Kingston, John Forrest, George Turner and James Dickson. Lyne, hesitant to join 'because of the political hostility evinced' by Deakin, was nevertheless encouraged into the fold in a show of national unity. Writing anonymously for the *Morning Post* on New Year's Eve, Deakin said of Australia's first ministry, 'It may now be classed as a comedy, because of its happy ending, though it began like the prologue to a tragedy.'

Alfred Deakin went to bed a happy man. It would be his last night in colonial Australia.

12

One Nation

Australia for the White Man

The Bulletin's masthead, 7 May 1908 to 30 November 1960

CELEBRATION OF A NATION

MORE THAN A QUARTER OF A MILLION SYDNEYSIDERS, some still drunk from their New Year's Eve revels, lined the 8-kilometre route from the Domain to Centennial Park on the first day of the twentieth century. They clambered atop awnings, waved Federation flags from rooftops and windows and generally carried on like galahs.[1] They were watching the Great Inaugural Procession, the first event of the 'Commonwealth Celebrations' held to mark the federation of Britain's six southern colonies into the Commonwealth of Australia.

Two hundred mounted police led the procession, confirming the new Australia would be a nation of law and order and horses. It was followed by the first of the allegorical cars (as floats were then known), featuring a young woman in white classical robes (representing 'Australia') surrounded by trade unionists dressed as shearers, miners and other horny-handed sons of toil (representing the workers who wanted to get 'Australia' pissed at the Centennial Park after-party).

---

1   *Galah* is Australian slang for a fool, deriving from the small pink and grey cockatoo of the same name that's unfairly maligned for its stupidity. The term has largely fallen out of use, despite the best efforts of Alf from *Home and Away*.

The floats and marchers were ranked in reverse order of importance, with members of Barton's incoming cabinet the last act before
Governor-General Hopetoun's grand finale. Everyone who was anyone
featured in the 10,000-strong parade, except for the governors of the
new Australian states, who'd withdrawn in a huff as they believed
the new nation diminished their independence and authority, and
Cardinal Moran, who'd withdrawn in a huff after being told that, as
a Catholic, he'd have to walk in front of Anglican Archbishop Smith.[2]

Australia was born in war, and Hopetoun, as head of its armed
forces, was escorted by troops from the New South Wales Lancers,
soon to join their fellows in South Africa. They were part of a broader
military contingent, with troops from all over Australia, New Zealand
and the United Kingdom receiving rapturous applause. But what's
this? There were some coloured folk in the parade! Troops from Her
Majesty's Indian regiments were marching with our boys ... but it was
a party and it would be rude not to give the Hindoos a cheer.

The procession passed under ten triumphal arches, each with
its own theme. There were the Wool, Wheat and Coal Arches; the
German, French and American Arches (the last described as 'loud'
by the *Bulletin*); the Melbourne Arch; the Soldier's Arch; and the
Citizen's Arch. The final arch, at the entry to Centennial Park, was
topped with the slogan, 'ONE PEOPLE'.

More than 60,000 revellers assembled in the park to hear a ren-
dition of 'Advance Australia Fair' and watch the inauguration of
Australia take place in the Federation Pavilion, a 14-metre-tall domed
octagon described by the *Sydney Morning Herald* as 'pure whiteness

---

2   As Aboriginal people weren't anyone, they weren't invited. However, a few were
     shipped in from Queensland for a 7 January celebratory re-enactment of Cook's
     landing at Botany Bay, in which they wore feathered headdresses and other
     untraditional traditional costumes. The *Ovens and Murray Advertiser* explained
     the lack of Aboriginal people in the inauguration celebrations: 'very few of the
     aboriginals are left to witness this our crowning day, to witness the triumph of the
     white race.'

and chaste beauty'.[3] Inside the pavilion sat the Federation Stone, a sacred symbol of Australian unity that no Australian has ever heard of. The inauguration took place at 1 p.m. on 1 January 1901, which would have thrilled the numerologist in Alfred Deakin.

The inauguration was a staid affair after all the pomp and pageantry of the procession. Hopetoun read Queen Victoria's proclamation that Australia was a nation, swore a couple of oaths, then joined Deakin and other members of Barton's cabinet in signing an oath of allegiance to the Commonwealth.[4] The oaths were signed using the same pen, inkstand and table that Victoria had used to sign the *Commonwealth of Australia Constitution Act*, which was a nice touch. A 21-gun salute finished things off, and there you have it – a nation was born.[5]

Australia's only film production company, the Salvation Army, had been hired to film the procession and inauguration, getting the separation of church and state in Australia off to a rocky start.[6] This was the first time in history that the birth of a nation had been filmed. *Inauguration of the Commonwealth*, Australia's first feature-length

---

3   The symbolism of pure whiteness was self-explanatory, but the *Herald* failed to explain how a pavilion can be 'chaste' and what sort of twisted sicko would want to root a building.

4   An Australian oath is known as a 'ken oath.

5   Although not a sovereign state. Australia could not make war or peace with foreign powers, and all foreign communications had to be approved by the Colonial Office. Australians were British citizens until Australian citizenship was introduced in 1949, and they remained British subjects until 1984. Britain's Privy Council could hear appeals of some Australian High Court judgements until 1975 and all state Supreme Court judgements until 1986. Britain could also override state laws it found 'repugnant' until 1986, when the British and Australian *Australia Acts* finally made Australia a sovereign state (although it retained a foreign sovereign).

6   The Salvos embraced modern technology in winning new converts, showing short religious films at church information evenings from 1897. In 1900, they began a twenty-year tour of *Soldiers of the Cross*, a two-hour multimedia epic that included thirteen short films about Christian martyrs, most of which were shot on a suburban Melbourne tennis court, interspersed with slides and songs. The Salvos' Australian Commandant, backed by an orchestra, providing a live evangelical narration.

documentary, rated its tits off. The most widely distributed Australian film of its time, it played to audiences in New Zealand, the UK and Canada.

As the members of Barton's cabinet departed to be sworn in as ministers of the Commonwealth of Australia, many in the crowd drifted into the city to witness the 'blaze of illumination' that 'transformed night into day'. Buildings on the city's gas-lit streets were dusted with electric bulbs, amazing passers-by, and fireworks painted the Southern Cross–hung sky red, white and blue.

The festivities lasted eight days, with processions, banquets, picnics, concerts, theatrical revues, harbour and river cruises, cricket and rifle matches, athletics and swimming carnivals and cycling races held across Australia.

The party atmosphere was dampened on 22 January 1901, when 81-year-old Queen Victoria breathed her last after almost sixty-four years on the throne.[7] Victoria, dressed in a white dressing gown (a pleasant change from her usual black) and her wedding veil (just plain weird), was lowered into her coffin by her sons Edward and Arthur, and by her eldest grandson, Kaiser Wilhelm II of Germany. In accordance with her secret instructions, Victoria was buried with John Brown's mother's wedding ring on her finger, a lock of Brown's hair in her hand, a photo of Brown and one of his pocket handkerchiefs, having directed that the latter be 'laid *on* me'. She also asked to be buried with family photographs, a shawl made by her daughter Alice, a handkerchief and cloak of Prince Albert's, and a plaster cast of Albert's hand that she'd always kept near her (beyond just plain weird).

The *Bulletin* soon tired of all the letters it received about the dead queen, explaining:

7　The Australian Constitution provided that a reference to 'the Queen' included her heirs and successors, otherwise Australia's entire system of government would have collapsed after just three weeks.

We've printed all necessary valedictory verse to Queen Victoria. She was a good woman, and thank goodness, there are millions of women left just as good.

On Victoria's successor, Edward VII, the paper sniffed:

It has been found convenient to have some nominal head of state, and a life monarch saves the cost and trouble of the periodical election of a president. The hereditary principle may be ridiculous, but the official antics of a British sovereign demand so little ability that even the hereditary principle supplies good enough men and women nowadays.

Australia had grown from four colonies to six during Victoria's reign, with the last two – Victoria and Queensland – named in her honour. Free men strode purposefully where convicts had shuffled in irons. Black people had been replaced by white sheep. Women had chipped away at the imprisoning walls of the domestic sphere, and workers had placed their dusty bottoms on the benches of power. A nation had been born.[8]

And while Victoria's southern subjects shed a tear, their eyes were cast not to the past, but to the green and golden future that awaited them. The time for mourning had passed. There was work to be done.

TAKING CARE OF BUSINESS

Alfred Deakin believed that once Federation was achieved, it was the duty of those who'd argued for it to make it work. Institutions needed to be built, laws needed to be passed and coloured folk needed to be deported.

Deakin helped Barton develop the Liberal Protectionist agenda for the federal election to be held in March 1901. Barton promised

---

8   You can achieve a lot if you live long enough and leave all the details to someone else.

a national capital and High Court, a 'moderately protectionist tariff' and a uniform postage system.[9] He committed to universal suffrage and the arbitration of industrial disputes, and to build Forrest's Trans-Australian Railway, which Forrest's engineering go-to guy, Charles Yelverton O'Connor, was asked to plan.[10] But Barton's masterstroke was a proposed ban on Asian and Pacific Islander immigration. By adopting Labor's policy, he removed its principal campaign advantage and increased the likelihood of it supporting the Liberal Protection-ists in a hung parliament.

Queensland Labor's 1901 election candidates branded themselves as 'White Australia Labour'. In his run for the Senate, James Stewart urged that all black labour be swept into the sea or shot down. The election, Labor insisted, would be a referendum on White Australia.

As there were no Commonwealth voting laws, the election was run according to the laws of each state. Turnout was poor, at less than 60 per cent – and even poorer when you consider that 100 per cent of the women outside South Australia and Western Australia couldn't vote. The Liberal Protectionists won thirty-one House of Representatives

---

9   Louisa Lawson intended to be a beneficiary of postage reform. In January 1901, the Commonwealth asked the former postmistress to demonstrate the improved mailbag fastener she'd designed to refute claims that women were incapable of invention. Lawson's fastener was already in use throughout New South Wales, but the recently appointed New South Wales postmaster-general, an implacable opponent of women's suffrage, conspired with a rival manufacturer to infringe Lawson's patent and provide him with replica fasteners. Lawson sued and received compensation from the government, but the Commonwealth didn't want to deal with a pushy woman prepared to embarrass important men in court. Lawson lost the contract that would have set her up for life.

10 The overstretched O'Connor was being hounded by the Western Australian press for his management of the Coolgardie Water Supply Scheme. On 8 March 1902, O'Connor successfully pumped water through the most difficult stretch of pipe, but discovered a small leak. Two days later, he rode his horse into the sea near the new harbour he'd constructed at Fremantle and shot himself. O'Connor's fail-safe combination of Australia's most dangerous animal, drowning and a revolver was a testament to his project management skills, which were confirmed on 24 January 1903, when the scheme went live and was recognised as one of the modern engineering wonders of the world.

seats, George Reid's Free Traders twenty-eight, and Labor sixteen, after two independents joined it. In the Senate, James Stewart and Labor's seven other members held the balance of power.

Many Labor MPs, including Chris Watson, Andrew Fisher, Billy Hughes and William Spence, were tough negotiators. Their skills, honed in resolving industrial disputes, translated to the parliament, helping Labor to horse-trade to advance its agenda. Gregor McGregor, the party's Senate leader, explained Labor was 'for sale, and we will get the auctioneer when he comes, and take care that he is the right man'. Barton's placing White Australia at the centre of his campaign made him the right man, with his commitment to universal suffrage and federal arbitration a bonus. Deakin wrote of Labor in the *Morning Post*: 'They help to demoralise politics by bartering their tally of votes for concessions to their class and by their indifference to all other issues.'

This suited Deakin, who was naturally drawn to compromise. Watson, elected as Labor leader, was cut from similarly pragmatic cloth. The two men, who liked and admired each other, would pursue consensus in laying the foundations of modern Australia.

With the election out of the way, Barton got down to the important business of choosing a flag. He announced the Federal Flag Design Competition and, discovering that a Melbourne journal was running a similar one, merged his with it. The journal and the government each offered the winner £75, and the Havelock Tobacco Company threw in £50, getting the separation of big tobacco and state in Australia off to a rocky start.

The largest of the 32,823 entries was 60 square metres, the smallest the size of a postage stamp. The entries included a six-tailed kangaroo, an overweight kangaroo firing a gun at the Southern Cross, and a motley collection of native animals playing cricket with a winged cricket ball that looked exactly like the golden snitch from *Harry Potter*. Sadly, none of these won, with the prize money split among five entrants with remarkably similar designs – a Perth artist, a Melbourne architect, a New Zealand ship's officer, a fourteen-year-old Melbourne schoolboy and a Sydney teenager apprenticed to an optician.

The federal flag, modelled on the winning entries, was essentially the old 1870 Victorian blue ensign minus the crown, with a six-pointed Commonwealth Star added to represent the Australian states. A red version of the flag was authorised for merchant vessels. The *Bulletin* was unimpressed with the Union Jack in the federal flag's top-left corner:

> ... the future emblem of the Commonwealth is vulgar and ill-fitting –
> a staled réchauffé of the British flag, with no artistic virtue, no
> national significance ... Minds move slowly: and Australia is still
> Britain's little boy ... That bastard flag is a true symbol of the bastard
> state of Australian opinion ...

Edward VII finally approved the design in 1903. However, the king thought the different number of points on each Southern Cross star looked fiddly, so he insisted that all but the smallest have seven points.[11] State governments and the Australian people were forbidden from flying the blue version of the flag, as it was reserved for Commonwealth government and navy use (later expanded to the military generally). It wasn't the Australian national flag. The Union Jack still was.[12]

---

11   This change was made, along with another in 1908, when the Commonwealth
      Star was given a seventh point to recognise Papua (south-eastern New Guinea),
      Australia's first territory – it now symbolises all of Australia's territories. In
      2015, Prime Minister Tony Abbott mused that if the Northern Territory were
      to become a state, a seventh point might be added to the Commonwealth Star.
      For a guy who loved standing in front of as many Australian flags as possible, his
      ignorance was surprising.

12   Until the 1940s, states and members of the public were only permitted to fly the
      Union Jack or red ensign. Prime Minister Robert Menzies only began to encourage
      broader use of the blue version we now know as the Australian flag after concerns
      were raised that the red ensign looked too Communist. The Union Jack remained
      the national flag until the blue ensign took its place when Queen Elizabeth II
      opened the Australian parliament on 14 February 1954. South Australia insisted on
      using the Union Jack as the Australian flag until 1956, when schools were given the
      option of flying it or the current Australian flag. People who believe changing our
      national flag is an affront to tradition have short memories.

Edward's son, the future George V, swanned into Melbourne with his wife, Mary, for Australia's second royal visit (and the first not to feature one of Queen Victoria's sons being shot). On 9 May 1901, the Duke and Duchess of Cornwall and York opened the first Commonwealth parliament, held at Melbourne's Royal Exhibition Building.[13] The cream of Australian society was in attendance. Deakin's plus one was Catherine Helen Spence, 'chairman' of the South Australian Cooperative Clothing Company, a women-only business whose workers shared in its profits.[14] The Salvation Army was there with its tambourines and cameras, but its *Royal Visit to Open the First Commonwealth Parliament* was a relative box-office flop, not least because poor lighting prevented the filming of the actual opening. The money shot was captured by Tom Roberts in his 15.5-square-metre oil painting, *The Opening of the First Parliament of the Commonwealth of Australia by His Royal Highness the Duke of Cornwall and York*. Australians, consistent with their love of small words and big things, promptly renamed it 'the Big Picture'.[15]

Henry Lawson dismissively referred to the swells and dandies who descended on Melbourne to fawn over the royals as 'the Cuff and Collar

---

13 The parliament then relocated to Victoria's Parliament House, where it sat until a new Parliament House was opened in Canberra on 9 May 1927. That new Parliament House is now known as Old Parliament House, as it was replaced by a new New Parliament House that opened on 9 May 1988. I hope that's clear.

14 Deakin had, as usual, been overdoing it, pulling all-nighters to develop the government's legislative agenda. Shortly after being sworn into the new parliament, he had an out-of-body experience at a Beethoven concert, writing that he was 'sucked upwards as if out of the body ... Quivering with energy, sensibility ... unfolding as if in rapture'. It's unknown who spiked the first parliament's punchbowl with magic mushrooms.

15 Roberts himself gave it that nickname, also referring to it as his 'Frankenstein of 17 feet'. It was difficult to imbue the painting with energy because the Exhibition Building was dark and nearly everyone, still mourning Queen Victoria's passing, was in black. Roberts employed 'artistic licence' in elevating the official dais and hanging a giant portrait of Henry Parkes above it. The painting contained 269 portraits, with Roberts meticulously collecting information on each subject's place of birth, age, height, weight and hat size. It took thirty months for Roberts to complete, with all the tiny dark portraits damaging his eyesight. The Big Picture is Roberts' most famous painting that doesn't have a sheep in it.

Push' – but outside the Exhibition Building, on the hard streets of Carlton and Collingwood, the real pushes were making their presence felt.

WRONG 'UNS

The turn-of-the-century larrikin looked leaner and meaner than his predecessors. Colourful handkerchiefs and scarves were out, dark sharp jackets and stiff-collared white shirts were in. Flamboyance, once fashionable, had made way for streamlined athleticism. One man was responsible for this change: Oscar Wilde.

The Marquess of Queensberry, who objected to Wilde's relationship with his son, Lord Alfred 'Bosie' Douglas, left a calling card at Wilde's club, addressed, 'For Oscar Wilde, posing somdomite' (sic).[16] Wilde sued for libel, ignoring his friends' advice that Queensberry was not a man to pick a fight with (the Marquess having lent his name to the rules of boxing). Queensberry found some male prostitutes willing to testify they'd had sex with Wilde, Wilde dropped the prosecution, the court found Queensberry's accusation true, Queensberry insisted Wilde be criminally charged, and Wilde was sentenced to two years' imprisonment with hard labour for 'gross indecency with another male person'.

---

16   Bosie likely contributed to Australian cricket crowds calling the newly invented googly ball a *Bosie* during the English cricket team's 1903–04 Australian tour. The right-arm wrist-spinning delivery, which turned the opposite way to the bowler's stock ball, was unleashed on the bemused Australians by Englishman Bernard Bosanquet, dubbed 'Elsie' by the crowds for the elaborate, supposedly effeminate, jumpers he wore. The unknown Australian coiner of the term *Bosie* likely connected the name and 'effeminacy' of Bosanquet with Oscar Wilde's Bosie. This interpretation is supported by Australians' other name for the googly, a *wrong 'un*. While this referred to the ball moving the wrong way, it was also slang for a criminal or homosexual. English cricket writer Justin Parkinson suggests the two Australian terms for the googly, and the application of the nickname Elsie, were attempts to 'label the whole English ruling class', who dominated English cricket teams, 'effete'. A left-arm wrist spinner's stock ball was later called a *chinaman*, a term the *2018 Wisden Cricketers' Almanack* declared was no longer appropriate following Australian cricket journalist Andrew Wu, who is of Chinese descent, suggesting (correctly) the term was 'racially offensive'. Cricket is a funny old game.

Sydney's *Truth* was at its seedy best in reporting on Wilde's trial, with one article providing a double double entendre with the subheadings 'The Beauteous and the Buoyant' and 'The Arsenal of Aestheticism'. Wilde, *Truth* reported, 'had been adjudicated by the Court to be something lower than the beasts of the field; a creature for whose peculiar offending in Australia the lash would be the punishment'.

The Wilde trial changed views on 'inverts', as homosexuals were then known. Sexual offence laws had traditionally focused on acts, not inclinations. During the trial, the prosecutor asked Wilde to explain 'the love that dare not speak its name', the quote drawn from Bosie's 1892 poem 'Two Loves'. Wilde launched a passionate defence of 'such a great affection of an elder for a younger man', citing Shakespeare, Michelangelo and Plato as exemplars of such 'innocent' and 'intellectual' love. Wilde spoke not of acts, but of feelings. Those who read reports of the trial were left with the overwhelming impression that an invert might not just do a thing – he might *be* a thing.[17]

The larrikins didn't want to *be* the thing that Oscar Wilde was, but unfortunately they and the Irish playwright shared the same stylist. The answer was to de-camp, with flash dress disappearing virtually overnight.

Larrikins had also moved on from their street-trader roots. They were more traditionally working class, labouring in factories, abattoirs and brickworks. In Victoria, Australian Rules football had overtaken boxing as the discerning larrikin's sport of choice. Its professional

---

17   A more nuanced view of homosexuality was provided by Havelock Ellis, the English physician who in 1896 popularised the term *homosexual* in *Sexual Inversion*, the first English medical textbook on homosexuality. Ellis didn't characterise homosexuality as immoral, or as a disease or a crime, but in psychological terms. Ellis' 'life task' of studying sex was revealed to him in New South Wales, where he worked as a teacher in bush schools for over three years. Ellis' own sex life was unconventional – he developed 'an affection' for a 10-year-old Australian girl he taught; was a virgin when he married the lesbian women's rights campaigner Edith Lees; and suffered impotence until the age of sixty, when he discovered he could become aroused by women urinating. Sigmund Freud, another weird cat, kept a photo of Ellis on his office wall (probably next to one of his mother).

nature allowed working-class men to play competitively, something that would prove impossible north of the border until rugby league broke away from amateur rugby union in 1908.

Pushes became associated with football clubs. Larrikins' donahs or tarts sometimes attended games, with a brawl erupting at an 1896 North Melbourne–Collingwood match, in which women punched the umpire and stuck hatpins into players from the rival team.[18]

In 1899, the Crutchy Push (a.k.a. the Crutchy Gang, a.k.a. the North Melbourne Crutchies) turned up at Footscray, their hats and suits festooned with blue and white streamers, to barrack for the North Melbourne Shinboners (now the Kangaroos), a name that reflected the club's abattoir worker origins. Not wishing to pay the entrance fee, the Crutchies scaled a fence, leading to an exchange of blows with the officials and police who tried to stop them.

Crutchy Valentine Keating had earlier assaulted Senior Constable Healey. During Keating's trial, Healey testified he'd been unable to catch his assailant – 'he was off like a flying kangaroo – although he goes on a crutch!'

In this, Keating was by no means unique. Every push member was an amputee, making their escape and fence-scaling skills all the more impressive. The *Argus* called the Crutchies 'an extraordinary combination of one-legged youths', and the *Sydney Morning Herald* explained:

> The Crutchy Push, with one exception, consisted of one-legged men. The exception was a one-armed man who kept half a brick in his sewn up empty sleeve.

Keating was convicted of assaulting police on eight occasions, in keeping with the Crutchies' reputation as Melbourne's most vicious push. The unipedal standover men demanded money, food and drink from pubs, shops and passers-by, and those who didn't pay soon learned

---

18   *Tart*, then a largely non-pejorative Australian slang term for 'girlfriend', was probably a contraction of *jam tart*, rhyming slang for *sweetheart*.

that a crutch made a deadly weapon. One of Keating's in-laws, a fellow Crutchy, gave Keating's career a leg-up in 1901 when he battered push leader George Hill to death. Keating now ruled the push.

That year, Victorian premier Alexander Peacock promised to increase police numbers 'to deal with pushes such as the Crutchies and Flying Angels', the latter a South Melbourne gang that took its name from its members' favourite amusement park ride (a type of flying fox). The pushes had changed – there was less musical theatre and more fighting.[19] The shift was clear from the names they adopted: the Fitzroy Murderers, the Dirty Dozen and the Devil's Thirteen. And while the pushes assaulted police, rival football fans, union picnickers, and tambourine-playing god-botherers, most of all they assaulted each other. An incursion onto another push's turf would inevitably result in a melee, with flying fists and boots, fence palings, bicycle chains and, of course, crutches.

The larrikins gained international attention after Britain's influential *Blackwood's Magazine* published Ambrose Pratt's '"Push" Larrikinism in Australia' in 1901. Pratt, a Sydney solicitor turned London journalist, claimed to have been initiated into a Rocks push by its 'king', after agreeing to work as its lawyer. The pushes, Pratt claimed, owned large clubhouses and controlled Australian organised crime (like bikies, but without the bikes). They pulled the strings of politicians and murdered police. Their members swore oaths of sobriety and monogamy, and were whipped to death with sand-filled socks if they broke them. Pratt wrote the article to generate interest in his larrikin-themed potboiler novels, but it was taken as gospel by many readers. Australians, of course, knew it was bollocks, with the

---

19 While larrikins may have been less music hall, music halls were more larrikin. From the late 1880s, Will Whitburn and other music hall artists wore flared trousers, bootlace ties and other increasingly old-school larrikin attire while singing comic ditties like 'The Larrikin Hop' (particularly apt for the Crutchies). Whitburn was admired for performing some of his larrikin routines in blackface, another late-nineteenth-century Australian music hall staple.

Sydney Morning Herald observing, 'Not since the world was enlightened as to the flying habits of the wombat has so much information of the fancy kind been unloaded on a startled world.'

FIG. 12: THE FLYING ANGELS AND CRUTCHY PUSH FOUGHT FOR CONTROL OF THE MEAN STREETS OF MELBOURNE.

Still, it was widely agreed that larrikins were a menace, capable of any depravity. 'The Bastard from the Bush', a turn-of-the-century adaptation of Henry Lawson's 'The Captain of the Push', tells the tale of 'Foreskin Fred', the Bastard from the Bush, who joins a city push to show the larrikins he is harder and meaner than them. It was passed on verbally for obvious reasons, as this extract attests:

> *'Are you game to smash a window?' asked the Captain of the Push;*
> *'I'd knock a fucking house down,' said the Bastard from the Bush.*
> *'Would you take a maiden's baby?' asked the Captain of the Push;*
> *'I'd take a baby's maiden,' said the Bastard from the Bush.*
>
> *'Would you bash a bloody copper, if you caught the cunt alone,*
> *Would you stoush a swell or Chinky, split his garret with a stone,*

Would you make your wife a harlot, and swear off work for good?'
Again that bastard's voice rang out, 'My fucking oath, I would!'[20]

The author of this fine example of Australian verse is uncertain, although children's author Harold Lindsay maintained Lawson 'wrote the obscene version himself and circulated copies among his friends'.

The larrikins who roamed and hopped Australia's inner-city streets at the nation's birth had lost the cheeky innocence of their antisocial antecedents. The singing and dancing youth had become the irredeemable gang rapist, the dandy the damned, the grocer the gross. We should remember this when our politicians deliver empty soundbites that invoke the Australian larrikin spirit.

MAKE AUSTRALIA WHITE AGAIN

There was nothing empty about Edmund Barton's 5 June 1901 sound-bite that a bill would be introduced 'to place certain restrictions on immigration, and to provide for the removal from the Commonwealth of prohibited immigrants'.

A month earlier, two great dragons had snaked through Melbourne's streets in pursuit of a twirling cacophony of Chinese dancers and musicians, part of the city's celebrations to honour the visiting royals. A massive Chinese arch, erected between two pagodas, carried a banner reading, 'Welcome by the Chinese Citizens'. If Barton had his way, there'd be a much smaller Chinese welcome for the next royal tour.

Banjo Paterson wanted Australia to keep the Chinese out and the Chinese to let him in. Sir James Fairfax had asked him to report

---

20 The C-word was used at the turn of the century, albeit infrequently and not in polite company. Both Brits and Australians adopted rhyming slang, so they could allude to the C-word without feeling too naughty. Brits used the term *berk*, a contraction of *Berkshire Hunt*, while an Australian might call a person they disliked a *drop kick*, an Australian Rules–inspired contraction of *drop kick and punt*.

on the troubles of the Far East and secured him first-class passage
to Hong Kong. Steaming up the Australian coast, Paterson told his
readers, 'north of Rockhampton the coast towns are already hotbeds
of Oriental fecundity'. Comparing the fast-breeding coloured folk to
the rabbit, he warned:

> Only eight days' steam from our Northern Territory there lies
> the great seething cauldron of the East, boiling over with parti-
> coloured humanity – brown and yellow men by the million, and
> they are quite near enough to do us a lot of harm if their ideas
> run that way.

In Hong Kong, Paterson bemoaned the lack of horses – 'Chinese
coolies' with chairs and rickshaws having stolen their jobs. He visited
Shanghai's opium dens and Chefoo's bars, meeting Chinese Morrison
in one of the latter. Morrison, whom Paterson rated as the greatest
man he'd ever met, expressed regret that Britain had not colonised
the Yangtze Valley, which would have given it control of China's
most fertile land and main inland trade route. Paterson concluded
his piece on Morrison, 'We should have walked in and taken the boss
mandarin's seat at the top of the table.'[21]

While Paterson filed reports from China, the Australian parliament started debating the Immigration Restriction Bill. Colonial
Secretary Chamberlain had asked Australia to make its racist law
look less racist, as Britain headed an empire 'whose traditions make
no distinctions in favour or against race or colour'. Laws based on
those criteria, Chamberlain advised, would offend Britain's Indian
citizens, and the citizens of its new ally, Japan.

Mississippi had shown the world how to be sneakily racist in 1890.

---

21   Morrison did just that. He backed the revolutionaries during the 1911 Chinese
Revolution, was appointed a political advisor to the president of the new Chinese
Republic, was instrumental to the Chinese joining the Allied powers in World
War I, and represented China at the 1919 Paris Peace Conference.

Precluded by the US Constitution from denying black people the vote on racial grounds, it set about denying them the vote on education grounds. Mississippi would only register a voter 'able to read any section of the Constitution, or be able to understand the same when read to him, or to give a reasonable interpretation thereof'. This test was selectively applied, so that an illiterate black person might be asked to read a complex constitutional provision, while an illiterate white person could pass by saying, 'That there says I can carry me a gun. I call this li'l baby Mary-Jo. She be real purdy.'

Britain's South African colony of Natal adapted Mississippi's approach, asking coloured would-be immigrants to complete an application form in a European language of the immigration official's choosing. In the late 1890s, New South Wales, Western Australia and Tasmania, at Chamberlain's suggestion, adopted Natal's model in asking certain coloured immigrants to pass a comprehension test (although Western Australia's test was always in English).

Barton's original bill proposed an English dictation test of fifty words, but this worried most MPs. What if proper white French, German or Welsh people were given the test, and Australians wishing to travel overseas were then asked to sit tests in French, German or, God forbid, Welsh? Others, such as Labor's King O'Malley, pointed out that cunning Asians would simply become proficient in English:

> ... the education test proposed will not shut out the Japanese if they desire to come to Australia. It will not shut out the Indian 'toff' who becomes a human parasite preying upon the people of the country. It will not shut out the intellectual Afghan. We have more to fear from the educated coloured people than from the ignorant coloured people, because the latter will not attempt to mingle or associate with the white race.[22]

---

22 This was rich coming from O'Malley as, like Chris Watson, he'd lied about his own foreign origins. O'Malley pretended to be from Canada, part of the British Empire, while he was almost certainly born in Kansas. Both O'Malley and Watson

Parliament ultimately settled on a dictation test in any European language, changed to any language in 1905, so that a Chinese person could be refused entry if he or she couldn't take down an extract from *Pride and Prejudice* in Swahili.

Labor originally opposed the dictation test. Why should Australians ~~kowtow~~ bow to Britain and hide their racism? Why couldn't they call a spade a spade, and a wog a wog? Why not be honest and admit – no, embrace – racist motivation and explicitly exclude Asians, Africans and Pacific Islanders? But rather than hold up the bill, Labor ultimately supported the test.[23]

Some historians (Keith Windschuttle, you know who you are) contend that the White Australia policy, of which the *Immigration Restriction Act* was the centrepiece, had a 'legal and economic basis' and was not grounded in racial prejudice. Labor leader Chris Watson would have bristled at this contention:

> The objection I have to these mixing of the coloured people with the white people of Australia ... lies in the main in the possibility and probability of racial contamination ... The question is whether we should desire that our sisters or our brothers should be married into any of these races to which we object.

Debate on the bill was filled with calls to protect Australia from 'alien invasion', the 'race taint' and Chinese vegetables; to stop Assyrian hawkers from pestering Australian women and children;[24] to prevent

---

were constitutionally ineligible to sit in parliament, as they'd never taken out British citizenship.

23   The *Immigration Restriction Act* wasn't entirely racist, as it also barred the entry of disabled people, idiots and the insane, prostitutes and pimps, people suffering from venereal disease or other dangerous infectious diseases, and certain criminals and contracted manual labourers.

24   Australia's Assyrians were mostly from modern Lebanon. The 1869 opening of the Suez Canal disrupted international trade routes through Lebanon, resulting in significant Lebanese migration, augmented by Maronite Christians fleeing Islamic Ottoman rule. Many Lebanese became tailors or hawkers in Queensland

the creation of ghettoes; to avoid the United States' 'Negro problem'; and to not inhibit 'the very process of natural selection on which the evolution of the higher type depends' – this point reflecting many MPs' concerns about interbreeding. Opposition leader George Reid welcomed the unanimity of view that 'the current of Australian blood shall not assume the darker hue'. Charles McDonald was worried about Australia turning into *Mongrelia* and fellow Labor MP James Ronald warned:

> Let those people come in here and our race will become piebald in spite of our efforts to prevent it. Let us keep before us the noble idea of a white Australia, a snow white Australia ...[25]

Barton had this to say:

> I do not think either that the doctrine of the equality of man was really ever intended to include racial equality. There is no racial equality. There is basic inequality. These races are, in comparison with white races – I think no one wants convincing of this fact – unequal and inferior.

Deakin, responsible for progressing the Act through parliament, was more nuanced in his xenophobia. He didn't believe the Asian races were unequal or inferior, warning:

> It is not the bad qualities, but the good qualities of these alien races that make them dangerous to us. It is their inexhaustible energy, their power of applying themselves to new tasks, their endurance, and low standard of living that make them such competitors.

---

or New South Wales rural communities. Australians were particularly concerned by Asians like the Lebanese, who were sneakily able to conceal their Asianness by not looking Asian.

25   So we keep the Asians out, but let the dwarves in?

Racism, Deakin believed, was a virtue. It would elevate and unite Australians:

> The unity of Australia is nothing, if that does not imply a united race. A united race means not only that its members can intermix, intermarry and associate without degradation on either side, but implies one inspired by the same ideas, and an aspiration towards the same ideals, of a people possessing the same general cast of character, tone of thought ... Unity of race is an absolute essential to the unity of Australia.[26]

Bruce Smith, the one-time union-busting shipping magnate, now a Free Trade MP, was one of two politicians who spoke out against the White Australia policy, calling the danger of 'hordes of Asiatics' to 'the purity and whiteness of the Australian Commonwealth' 'a fairy story'. Fellow Free Trader Donald Cameron argued:

> ... no race on the face of this earth has been treated in a more shameful manner than have the Chinese ... they were forced at the point of the bayonet to admit Englishmen and other Europeans into China. Now if we compel them to admit our people into their land, why in the name of justice should we refuse to receive them here?

Cameron's attempt to appeal to the Australian sense of fair play failed.

Edward Cole was one of the few Australians who challenged White Australia. In *A White Australia Impossible*, he wrote:

> 'God hath made of one blood all nations of men for to dwell on the face of the earth.' 'Do unto others as ye would they should do

---

26 Deakin was as committed to keeping Australia free of inappropriate foreign books as he was inappropriate foreign people. On 8 July 1901, he approved the seizure of a shipment of dirty French novels by de Kock and Balzac. Even the authors' names were dirty, but that's the French for you.

unto you.' These just and humanitarian doctrines were taught by two Asiatic, coloured men, Jesus and Paul.

Cole pointed out that the Second Coming wouldn't occur in Australia, as Jesus would be turned back at the border.[27]

The media was all aboard the white train, and a 'Buy White' campaign allowed companies to market their racist credentials. Parsons' Starch declared itself 'A White Australian', and customers of Brisbane's M. Finucan Bros. could rest assured they wouldn't catch leprosy from the company's White Australian Sliced Pineapples in Syrup, as the only yellow thing on its production line was the fruit. The White Australia Game ('Place the Four Coloured Men on the Circles in Australia, the Four White Men Outside') provided fun for the whole family as they moved the White Men in and the Coloured Men out.

Coloured men were fair game. In 1902, Mei Quong Tart was the victim of a serious assault in Sydney's Queen Victoria Building, where he had his office and largest tearoom. His wife believed the attack was racially motivated. Australia's 'most popular Chinaman' never fully recovered and died the next year.

The first person to fail the dictation test was an Indian British citizen and former British soldier. He was roped, dragged back onto the boat that brought him here and sent back to where he came from.[28] Some non-white people, like Javanese and Timorese pearl divers, were allowed into isolated regions to perform work white people refused

27 Cole's opposition to White Australia earned him a rockstar reception during a 1903 visit to Japan. During his twilight years, Cole turned his attention to publishing gardening books and compiled *The Cream of Human Thought Library*, a series of books containing select passages drawn from his lifetime of reading. He died in 1918, his literary empire broken up and sold off.

28 Forty-six non-white immigrants passed the dictation test between 1902 and 1903, six between 1904 and 1909, and none between 1910 and its repeal in 1958. After World War I, the test was used to exclude Germans, Austrians, Hungarians and Bulgarians until 1926, and Turks until 1930. In 1930, it was applied to two boatloads of Italians who looked a bit swarthy.

to undertake. As the years passed, Kalgoorlie's Japanese prostitutes started to look a bit long in the tooth, but every once in a while some new girls appeared and not too many questions were asked.

The Act's companion legislation, the 1901 *Pacific Islands Labourers Act*, codified the government's 'Bye Bye Blackbird' policy, which was phased in to give Queensland's sugar planters time to find some new people to exploit. The importation of Islander labour was banned from 1904, and over 7,200 Pacific Islanders, some whose families had lived in Australia for generations, were forcibly deported from 1906.

Further laws were introduced to whiten Australia. The government could only issue mail contracts to ships employing all-white crews. New camel charges were levied, with the humped scabs that stole Aussie horses' jobs forbidden from being driven within 20 yards of the centre of a road or track. Afghan freight companies suddenly discovered they owned a fleet of highly taxed off-road vehicles. Unable to compete with white guys with horses, they shut down.

There were 80,000 'coloured aliens' among Australia's 4 million non-Indigenous people when the White Australia policy took effect. They were barred access to health and welfare services and, in some areas, from working in certain occupations or owning land. From 1903, natives of Asia, Africa or the Pacific Islands (except New Zealand) could no longer apply for British citizenship in Australia.

New Zealanders aside, Australians' neighbours were Asians and Pacific Islanders. Australians told them all they were inferior, before shutting them out. Australia turned its back on the world, gazing inwards at its spectacular whiteness. It lost trade, industrious and innovative workers, and much of its international reputation. Australia had the highest GDP per capita and standard of living in the world when the White Australia policy was introduced in 1901. By the time the Whitlam government introduced a colour-blind immigration policy in 1973, it was a minnow in the global pond.

THE VOTERS AND THE VETOED

The 1902 *Commonwealth Electoral Act* contained forty pages of rules for running federal and state elections. Sir William Lyne, minister for home affairs, attempted to make the Act 'the freest, most liberal and democratic measure' ever considered by a parliament.

William Boothby, who'd given the world the modern secret ballot and South Australian prisoners a new lubricant, had his olive oil–stained fingerprints all over the Act.[29] In 1896, he'd given South Australia the world's first non-partisan, government-resourced, full-time central body to manage elections and electoral boundaries. Lyne accepted Boothby's advice to adopt his model for all Australian federal and state elections, in stark contrast to the United States, where political parties controlled state and local electoral processes and rorted the system to their hearts' content (and still do). Boothby's innovations of postal voting and continuous electoral enrolment were also picked up. People could vote anywhere in their district, abandoning the British requirement that they vote at the booth nearest their home. The Act also required assistance be given to illiterate and blind voters, another world first.

Preferential voting, modelled along Queensland lines, was to be used for House of Representatives elections – and, amazingly, proportional representation by way of a single transferable vote was to be used in electing senators! Catherine Helen Spence clicked her comfortable heels with joy – until the Cambridge mathematician responsible for the model's detail briefed the Senate with eight pages of incomprehensible calculations. Labor declared 'the fancy method of voting' too confusing and withdrew support for Spence's scheme.[30]

---

29 See Chapter 2, footnote 14, for a summary of Boothby's contributions to the olive industry and prisoner welfare.

30 Spence had some joy, in that Andrew Inglis Clark trialled proportional representation for Tasmanian elections in 1896, with the Hare-Clark system, as it's now known, used in Tasmania from 1909 (and in the Australian Capital Territory

While the *Electoral Act* addressed how people would be heard in elections, its companion, the *Commonwealth Franchise Act*, addressed *who* would be heard. At only one page long, it was one of the shortest acts in Australian history, but its legacy would be long lasting.

The Franchise Bill proposed the federal vote for all adult Australian residents, except those of unsound mind, guilty of treason, or facing or serving a prison sentence of at least a year. Some MPs were concerned that women who weren't mad or bad would be able to vote.

In 1900, Victorian MP Frank Madden warned that giving women the vote 'would abolish soldiers and war, also racing, hunting, football, cricket and all such manly games' (apparently a bad thing). Senator Simon Fraser, a fellow Victorian, mused during debate on the bill, 'If I were a woman I should infinitely prefer the position of looking up to man as my director, my guide and adviser.' Still, Fraser joined all his fellow senators and most lower house MPs in voting for women's suffrage.[31]

Australian women had achieved the vote without chaining themselves to fences, throwing cobblestones at police, setting fire to buildings, going on hunger strikes or being trampled to death by racehorses, campaign strategies adopted by British suffragettes.

---

from 1995). Similar systems (although weighted more towards parties than candidates) are now used for Senate and most state upper house elections. Hare-Clark was also known as Hare-Spence in the early 1900s, but people ultimately felt more comfortable using a voting system named after two men.

31   The year 1902 was a good one for Australian women. The *Commonwealth Public Service Act* provided female telegraphists and postmistresses with the same pay as their male counterparts (although some of the gloss wore off when married women were barred from the public service two years later). Vida Goldstein, who'd helped compile Victoria's monster suffrage petition, was elected to the first conference of the International Woman Suffrage Alliance, held in Washington. The youngest attendee, she was appointed conference secretary and was the first Australian to meet an American president at the White House. President Theodore Roosevelt, a suffragist, was impressed. So too was *Table Talk*, which reported on how Goldstein was 'always very prettily and stylishly gowned' and was 'really a smart, pretty girl, the very opposite to what one unconsciously expects in a woman's suffrage advocate'.

Deakin boasted Australia had 'the broadest franchise in the world' after Australian broads achieved the vote, although it would take until 1908 for Victoria, Australia's last man shed, to allow women to participate in state elections.[32] Still, Victoria was well ahead of the global pack. American women wouldn't enjoy equal suffrage until 1920, and Britain's women had to wait until 1928.

However, the Act's enfranchisement of women came with an *. What the good parliament giveth, it also taketh away. The Constitution provided:

> ... if by the law of any State all persons of any race are disqualified from voting at elections ... then, in reckoning the number of the people of the State or of the Commonwealth, persons of that race resident in that State shall not be counted.[33]

If the Constitution contemplated racial discrimination in state elections, then why would those who'd championed White Australia give Australians 'a piebald ballot box'? The Senate, responding to an amendment proposed by Western Australian senator Alexander Matheson, enthusiastically excluded natives of Asia, Africa and the Pacific Islands (except New Zealand) from the federal vote. However, Matheson's following comment excited more debate:

> Surely it is absolutely repugnant to the greater number of people of the Commonwealth that an aboriginal man, or aboriginal lubra or gin – a horrible, degraded, dirty creature – should have the same rights, simply by virtue of being 21 years of age, that we have, after some debate today, decided to give our wives and daughters.

---

32 Henrietta Dugdale, the mother of the Australian women's suffrage movement, eighty-one and still going strong, went to the Victorian polls for the first time that year.

33 The US Constitution prohibits race-based voter discrimination, but the Australian Constitution enshrines it. This provision, like the Commonwealth's race power, has never been put forward for repeal at a referendum – again, probably because it would be a bit embarrassing if Australians voted 'No'.

The good senator pointed out that the Constitution provided that 'aboriginal natives' weren't to be counted in reckoning the number of the people of the Commonwealth, to ensure they weren't considered in determining electorates. If they weren't to be considered in determining electorates, it followed they shouldn't be considered in determining elections.

Matheson had precedent on his side. Western Australia and Queensland had already barred Aboriginal people from voting. New South Wales and Victoria excluded those receiving government aid, which meant Aboriginal people in reserves or government-funded missions had no vote. Tasmania hadn't considered Aboriginal voting because it believed it had got rid of all its Aboriginals. South Australia was the only state to passionately defend Aboriginal equality at the ballot box.

Matheson also had prejudice on his side. When a sympathetic comment was made about Aboriginal people, he retorted, 'Cannibals', and Liberal senator James Walker's protest that '100,000 aborigines in Australia' would be disenfranchised was met with, 'We are aware of that fact, and it is very regrettable, and the only consolation we have is that they are gradually dying out.'

Senator Richard O'Connor, government leader in the Senate, vehemently opposed Matheson's amendment to exclude Aboriginal people from the federal vote:

> It would be a monstrous thing, an unheard of piece of savagery on
> our part, to treat the aboriginals, whose land we are occupying, in
> such a manner as to deprive them absolutely of any right to vote in
> their own country ...

The Senate narrowly rejected Matheson's amendment, but the tide against Aboriginal voting became a tsunami when the bill was referred to the lower house. Hugh Mahon, Labor member for Coolgardie, mused it would be 'distinctly dangerous' to allow squatters 'to muster up their niggers and drive them to the polling both to vote'. Chris Watson agreed that Western Australian and Queensland Aboriginal people 'were practically the slaves of those squatters', who could use them 'to turn the tide of an election'. 'Savages and slaves' would 'be running electorates', Watson warned, abandoning Labor's core principle of 'One Person, One Vote' with remarkable ease.

Radical liberal lawyer Henry Bournes Higgins proposed an amendment to exclude Aboriginal voting, stating, 'It is utterly inappropriate to grant the franchise to the aborigines, or ask them to exercise an intelligent vote.' Tasmania's Edward Braddon ruminated:

> As an argument for including Australian aborigines ... we are told we have taken their country from them. But it seems a poor sort of justice to recompense those people for the loss of their country by giving them votes.

It would be a better sort of justice to give them nothing at all.

Every Liberal Protectionist backed Higgins. Hugh Mahon, whose democratic principles were stronger than his fear of an Aboriginal–squatter electoral alliance, was one of only five lower house MPs to support Aboriginal voting rights. He was joined by James Ronald (the champion of 'a snow white Australia'), Billy Hughes, Free Trader Henry Willis and Aboriginal impersonator Vaiben Solomon.

Whether Barton and Deakin would have opposed Higgins' amendment is unknown, as neither was in the chamber. Deakin had earlier expressed hope that:

> ... in their last hours [Aboriginal people] will be able to recognise not simply the justice but the generosity of the treatment which the white race, who are dispossessing them and entering into their heritage, are according them.

Perhaps he would have voted for generosity and justice, but he may well have made a pragmatic decision to not waste political capital on a people he believed faced inevitable extinction.

When the bill containing the Aboriginal voting exclusion was returned to the Senate, a disconsolate O'Connor said, 'It is not worthwhile, for the sake of this particular provision, to stand out for our own way and so run the risk of losing the Bill.' For the sake of political expediency, he did 'a monstrous thing' – and while the Australian-born children of other barred races could vote, Aboriginal exclusion was inter-generational.

The constitutional provision designed to protect women from being stripped of pre-existing voting rights meant the *Franchise Act* couldn't bar those Aboriginal people already on state electoral rolls. Still, electoral forms didn't alert them to their rights. Aboriginal Australians were not all entitled to the federal, Western Australian and Northern Territory vote until 1962, or the Queensland vote until 1965.

The First Australians were the last to have a say in the future of Australia.

THE FINAL STANZA

Harry Harbord Morant would have no say in the future of Australia, or of anywhere else.

After arriving in South Africa in 1900, Morant worked as a dispatch rider, riding with dispatch from his Cape Town hotel when asked to settle the bill. The account was sent to a confused Admiral Morant, who the scamming warrior poet continued to claim was his father. Morant took leave and may or may not have travelled to England with his friend Captain Percy Hunt. It was always difficult to separate fact from fiction with The Breaker.

By April 1901, Morant was back in South Africa as a lieutenant with the Bushveldt Carbineers, a British irregular mounted infantry regiment. Captain Hunt, now Morant's commanding officer, was shot during a raid on a Boer farm, his body allegedly stripped and mutilated. According to fellow Carbineer, Australian lieutenant George Witton,

Morant was 'a man demented' after Hunt's death and declared he'd take no prisoners in pursuing the *kommandos* who'd shot his friend. Morant ordered a firing squad to execute a wounded Boer prisoner, and the Carbineers later executed eight captured Boers, including four Dutch schoolteachers. Morant arranged the assassination of a Lutheran missionary who knew of the murders, and ordered the execution of another three Boers – a farmer and his sons, aged sixteen and twelve, who'd surrendered to seek medical treatment.

On 4 October 1901, Trooper Robert Cochrane, a Western Australian Carbineer, wrote a letter to the British command accusing Morant and others of shooting Boer prisoners. It was signed by fourteen other Carbineers, mostly Australians. The letter charged a fellow Australian, Lieutenant Peter Handcock, with murdering the missionary on Morant's orders and killing a fellow Carbineer who'd told the wives and children of Boer prisoners that their husbands and fathers had been executed.

Morant and several other officers faced courts martial for murder, but only Morant, Handcock and Witton were punished.[34] More senior British officers, who were undoubtedly culpable in ordering or concealing the murder of Boer prisoners, quietly slunk into civilian life. Morant didn't have a life to slink into, as he and Handcock faced the firing squad on 27 February 1902. His last words, as reported by the *Argus*, were 'Take this thing [the blindfold] off. Be sure and make a good job of it!'[35]

The *Bulletin* was used to its poets shooting themselves, but objected to the British Army doing the job for them. It took the line, adopted

---

34   Morant and Handcock were found not guilty of murdering the missionary, although several Carbineers attested to their guilt. There is debate as to whether Morant and his co-accused had orders to 'take no prisoners'. There is, however, a distinction between 'take no prisoners' and 'take prisoners, then shoot them', which is what Morant, Handcock and Witton did.

35   The line from the 1980 film *Breaker Morant*, 'Shoot straight, you bastards! Don't make a mess of it', was better.

by many Australians, that our boys had been scapegoated to conceal
the wrongdoings of British higher-ups, glossing over the fact that our
boys had been convicted on evidence provided by our boys.[36] Banjo
Paterson, who'd enjoyed Morant's company (at least where horses were
involved), took a less charitable view. He believed that Morant, after
the first murder, was 'drunk with his one day of power', and wrote:

> For years he had shifted and battled and contrived; had been always
> the under-dog, and now he was up in his stirrups. It went to his
> head like wine.

Paterson had sailed for England after his China sojourn. His offer
to be the *Times'* Australian correspondent was knocked back, but he
got to hang out with Rudyard Kipling and go for a spin in his new
chauffeured motorcar. He returned to Sydney after diving for pearls
off Thursday Island.

In 1902, Paterson published *Rio Grande's Last Race and Other Verses*,
another collection of poems about horses, racing and chiselled and
grizzled bushmen – but the formula seemed a little stale, and new
Australian writers were coming onto the scene. The *Bulletin's* literary editor, Alfred George Stephens, had spent the previous five years
editing *Such Is Life*, the debut novel of sixty-year-old mechanic and
former bullock driver Joseph Furphy. The darkly humorous account
of Tom Collins' interactions with a cast of rural oddballs was a mas-
terwork of intellectual anti-intellectualism, a style later embraced by
generations of Australian satirists.[37]

---

36 Lieutenant Witton served two years of his life sentence before King Edward
    VII, who'd been petitioned by 80,000 Australians, ordered his release. Peter
    Handcock, the only Australian ever executed for war crimes (Morant being a
    Brit), had his name added to Bathurst's war memorial in 1964. Australians have
    historically been keen on holding Germans and Japanese accountable for their
    war crimes, but some are less enthusiastic in questioning the honour of Australian
    soldiers, even when other Australian soldiers who served with them question it.

37 *Tom Collins* was the name of an imaginary person, with Americans hoaxing their
    friends from 1874 by asking, 'Have you seen Tom Collins?' When the friend said

Stephens also rated Miles Franklin's *My Brilliant Career* as 'the very first Australian novel', even though he believed women writers never lived up to their promise due to a lack of red blood corpuscles.

Paterson rated Franklin too. He attempted to seduce her in 1902, offering to find her an Australian publisher and do her legal work for free. Franklin, still living on her parents' struggling country property, wrote to him, saying she wished she had a recording of his voice. Paterson replied he wished she was back at his flat, reading his poetry (not her work) and singing to him while playing the piano. When Paterson said he wanted her to come with him 'to paradise in the South Pacific', she told him she'd fantasised about dressing up as his valet (presumably not the Japanese one, as she was a card-carrying racist). Paterson then refused to take her on a trip to Fiji, but sent her £5 to visit him in Sydney. When Franklin turned up, he was covering a shearing strike in the country. Franklin returned the £5 with interest and made it clear she'd lost hers. However, she remembered Paterson as 'the most sophisticated man who ever attempted to woo me sexually'.

Paterson, approaching forty, was tiring of bachelor life. He turned his attentions to Alice Walker, the daughter of a Tenterfield grazier, marrying in 1903. He'd given up the law months earlier and become editor of the *Evening News*. In the first days of his watch, the paper broke stories with headlines like 'Beat His Wife with a Shovel' and

---

he didn't know Tom Collins, the hoaxer would outline the outrageous things Tom Collins had said about him, causing the friend to ask others, 'Have you seen Tom Collins?' in order to find and punish him. As a result of 'The Great Tom Collins Hoax of 1874', an enterprising barman named a tall gin cocktail a Tom Collins and gave it to every customer who asked, 'Have you seen Tom Collins?', then charged them for the drink. In Australia, *Tom Collins* came to mean a tall story, *Such Is Life* being full of such tales. Australians later replaced the term with *furphy*, which, furphy that it may seem, had nothing to do with Joseph. The term derives from the water carts manufactured by Joseph's brother John that bore the inscription 'J. Furphy & Sons'. During World War I, Australian troops exchanged rumours and gossip while waiting for their water ration from a 'furphy'. The bullshit spun near a furphy meant the name was adopted for a tall story.

'Shot Himself at 77. Eccentric Suicide. Died to Escape Fleas'. Banjo Paterson was as happy as a dog with two tails.

Henry Lawson was not. Bertha and the kids had sailed home from London with his former love interest, Mary Gilmore, who'd tired of being cold and poor in Patagonia. Henry joined them in Colombo, but his drinking hindered reconciliation. Back in Australia, he'd hoped to reconnect with Hannah Thorburn, only to discover she'd died six weeks earlier, most likely from a botched abortion. His poem 'To Hannah' would have also done his marriage no favours:

> *Spirit girl to whom 'twas given*
> *To revisit scenes of pain,*
> *From the hell I thought was Heaven*
> *You have lifted me again;*
> *Through the world that I inherit,*
> *Where I loved her ere she died,*
> *I am walking with the spirit*
> *Of a dead girl by my side.*

And if you think that's miserable, Lawson was just warming up. Police informed him that Bertha, again pregnant, had left him, alleging domestic violence and desertion, both grounds for divorce, thanks to the work of his mother. Two days later, Lawson threw himself off a 30-metre cliff at Manly. He survived after landing on a bed of sand between the rocks, sheepishly reporting, 'Broke ankle and lost one eyebrow. (Pipe, tobacco and matches safe),' and writing to his publisher, 'I wasn't a success as a flying machine, was I?' His subsequent poem, 'Lawson's Fall', captured this blackness, but not its humour:

> *Twas the white clouds flying over, or the crawling sea below, –*
> *Or the torture of the present or the dreams of long ago,*
> *Or the horror of the future born of black-days, fate – or all –*
> *Never mind! The gods who saw it know the cause of Lawson's fall.*

In the week of Paterson's honeymoon, Bertha filed for divorce, detailing Lawson's habitual drunkenness and physical and mental assaults. Their child was stillborn and Henry was remanded in the Royal Prince Alfred Hospital for treatment for alcoholism. After his release, he could be found among Sydney's rough sleepers, shouting incoherently outside the *Bulletin*'s office or begging for booze money at Circular Quay. Although there were flashes of sobriety and genius, they became rarer and further apart. Drink, self-loathing and despair had conquered Australia's greatest writer. He was only thirty-five.

HE IS RISEN

Alfred Deakin was a man of principle. One of the government's first proposals in 1902 was to raise MP allowances from £400 to £600 a year, more than six times what most breadwinners earned. Deakin resigned in protest. Barton refused his resignation and dropped the pay rise.

Barton was also having a pay dispute with his governor-general. Lord Hopetoun enjoyed a salary of £10,000 a year and wanted an £8,000 increase to cover 'various unavoidable expenses'. In fairness, he did have to mix a lot of drinks and maintain homes in both Sydney and Melbourne, as Victoria and New South Wales couldn't agree which state should host the governor-general before the national capital was built. Barton put the increase to parliament, where every single speaker opposed it.

Lord Hopetoun took his drinks trolley back to London and was replaced by Lord Hallam Tennyson. A part of Deakin was thrilled: Hallam was the eldest son of Alfred, Lord Tennyson, the great poet after whom Deakin was named. Tennyson junior was also a writer (having penned a two-volume biography of his father and a new interpretation of *Jack and the Beanstalk*), as well as an artist, having co-designed the South Australian flag and seal. Like Deakin, he was also a prominent campaigner for Imperial Federation.

Tennyson, however, had proven himself an enemy of Deakin's vision of Australian Federation. As governor of South Australia, he'd championed strong states and a weak Commonwealth, and supported South Australian chief justice Sir Samuel Way's campaign to neuter Australia's High Court, which Way thought 'was no more needed than the fifth wheel to a coach'.

South Australia was displaying an alarming degree of independence. In 1901, the Dutch consul asked it to honour the Anglo-Dutch convention by apprehending sailors who'd deserted a Dutch vessel, the *Vondel*, for the dubious pleasures of Adelaide. South Australia refused and the Netherlands complained to Britain, which asked Deakin, who was acting prime minister at the time, what the hell was going on. Deakin sought an explanation from South Australia, which responded that it would only explain itself to Britain if Britain asked it directly. South Australia regarded itself as a state of the British Empire. Things might be different if Australia was an independent sovereign nation, but it was not – it was, like South Australia, an imperial dominion and shouldn't get too big for its boots. It took until 1903 for Chamberlain to end the constitutional crisis, ruling:

> ... the people of Australia form one political community, for which the Government of the Commonwealth alone can speak, and for everything affecting external states or communities which takes place within its boundaries that Government is responsible.

The states also felt that the watered-down 1902 *Customs and Tariff Act* would strip them of resources. Labor, in a precursor to the Goods and Services Tax (GST) debates of 1999, argued for 'a free breakfast table', with no tariffs payable on common foods. The House of Representatives agreed household staples, including kerosene and tea, should be duty free. The Senate wanted ninety-three changes to the duties approved by the House, with raisin, peel and ginger taxes to be reduced by a third.[38] The duty on dogcarts would need to be reduced by a fifth.[39] Deakin, presented with a tariff that was less protectionist than he'd hoped, encouraged government members to accept most of the Senate's changes. He wanted to put the defining political conflict of the nineteenth century to bed and enable the Commonwealth to start raising revenue.

Deakin was not keen on talking about his spiritualist beliefs, which his political rivals had used against him. He'd stopped his *Lucifer* subscription after stepping back from Theosophy and had joined Charles Strong's Australian Church, a free-thinking congregation that focused on earthly good works rather than eternal salvation. Deakin was upset by the 1903 publication of *Human Personality and Its Survival of Bodily Death*, a popular international work on psychic research that detailed Pattie Deakin's extraordinary communications with Shakespeare and other prominent members of the unliving community. The raising of the ghosts of his spiritualist past might derail his ambitions to lead Australia's living.

Deakin's passage of the Judiciary Bill through parliament in July 1903 gave that ambition new life. The establishment of the High Court would remove the one obstacle to his prime ministership: Edmund Barton.

Barton was not the most effective politician, having left much of the detail of governing to Deakin. Deakin praised Barton for 'his Apollo-like brow and brilliant capacities', but saw him as 'chained to the earth by his love of good living'. Barton had a small bachelor flat in Parliament House where he cooked chops and boiled billy tea in his fireplace, but his choice of residence also gave him unrivalled access

---

38 Liberal leader John Hewson lost the unlosable 1993 Australian federal election because he didn't know how his proposed GST would affect such cake ingredients. Deakin, whose healthy diet meant he wasn't keen on cakes, nevertheless understood it was important to sweat the detail.

39 Billy Hughes and other little people would have been fans of lowering the dogcart tariff.

to the parliamentary cellar. The head of Toby Tosspot's department, Atlee Hunt, while acknowledging his boss' 'brilliancy of perception', complained of 'his habit of taking so much to drink that he becomes slow of comprehension and expression', his 'want of personal energy' and 'his disregard of time, both his own and other people's'. It was time for Barton to move on, and the thought of slipping into a red dress and a wig excited him. He would resign for a position on the High Court bench, and Deakin, with Labor's support, would succeed him on 24 September 1903.

And lo, it came to pass, as prophesied by the restless shades of the long departed, that a child born unto a humble costermonger would rise to greatness. Two score and seven would his years number when first he led the six tribes of Australia that had become one. Thrice would he wield the sceptre of power, seven years would he rule: three and seven being the numbers most pleasing to the Lord. His shield, bearing the kangaroo and emu sigil of his house, would defend white Australia from the green vegetables of the yellow men. He would tend his flocks to clothe the weak, and grow wheat to feed the hungry. He would remake Australia in his own image. So it was foretold, and so it was.

And it was good.

Acknowledgements

Australia is the girtest it has been in generations, its island status both a boon and a brake as it wrestles with Covid-19. The drawbridge of Fortress Australia has once again been raised. It's a good time to look inwards, without losing the perspective necessary to engage with the world, and learn the lessons of the past.

In writing *Girt Nation,* I was struck by the similarities between the public and health responses to the current pandemic and Sydney's 1900 bubonic plague outbreak. There are also parallels between *China virus* and *kung flu,* and some earlier Australians' belief that the Chinese deliberately spread leprosy and other diseases. There were real tensions among the Australian colonies in the lead-up to Federation and, while they may have been buried, Covid has proven that unlike Alfred Deakin's closest advisors, they were never dead. History repeats, even if it plays at a different tempo.

Cicero, who knew a thing or two about history, wrote, 'History is the witness that testifies to the passing of time; it illuminates reality, vitalises memory and provides guidance in daily life.' History is useful. It's not just about the past, but about the present and, perhaps even more importantly, the future. History is not all about what happened, or even how it happened. Good history is about *why* it happened – it is the *why* that provides guidance.

It's important to understand First Nations dispossession and White Australia because their echoes can still be heard today (the view that the White Australia policy was motivated purely by labour and economic concerns is, I hope you'll agree after reading this book, complete bollocks). We must reconcile with our past to understand present consequences and inoculate ourselves against future missteps.

In 1996, then prime minister John Howard told us we should feel 'comfortable and relaxed about our past, as the balance sheet of our history is one of heroic achievement'. Australians have had more than their fair share of heroic achievement, and *Girt Nation* reflects that. However, Howard's 'Bex, a cuppa and a good lie-down' approach to Australian history was designed to gloss over the catastrophic impact white settlement had on First Nations Australians.

The Howard approach is an unabashedly nationalist one, which is unsurprising given Australia's early historians adopted a nationalist narrative of hardy pioneers conquering the convict stain, the bush, First Nations people (although best not to dwell on them too much), the tyranny of distance, tough mallee roots and all sorts of other seemingly insurmountable obstacles, to build a nation that was the envy of the world. This was the Australian history that John Howard and I were taught at school.

The rise of history as a discipline accompanied the rise of the nation-state and, in Australia, the Federation movement. History was used as a tool to justify nations, and what they did.

The great British military historian Sir Michael Howard argued that historians should challenge, and even explode, national myths. The *Girt* books are a reaction against the nationalist history I was weaned on. They are anti-nationalist histories, if you will – but they are not anti-Australia. They are pro-Australia – an Australia that is reflective, inquiring and forward-looking. They are also intended to speak truth to power and make you laugh.

There is an increasing tendency among some Australian politicians and the Murdochracy to promote a particular version of history as gospel. It is this history – one drunk on nationalism and high on Enlightenment thinking – that they insist be taught to our children. This is the 'authorised history' of Australia.

The *Girt* books are *The Unauthorised History of Australia* because history should not be authorised. They are an attack on the idea that there is one history or one truth. If you believe there is one truth, or wish to promote a single view, then tolerance of difference and dissent diminishes. This empowers those with authoritarian urges to not just reinvent the past, but also the present (please read George Orwell's *1984*).

I find the growing intolerance of dissenting views in Australia distressing. I believe in freedom of speech and expression, even where that speech or expression is hurtful to some (but like everyone, I have my own lines in the sand). I dislike mob pile-ons and cancel culture, whether practised by 'the right' or 'the left'. Suppression of debate, of alternative views, leads to book burnings (please read Ray Bradbury's *Fahrenheit 451*). If anyone doesn't like my snarks on this, they can cancel me and burn mine.

One of the joys in researching this book has been questioning my political assumptions. I didn't expect to like Alfred Deakin much, let alone build a book around his life. However, here I am at the end, and I find him the most impressive and influential (if odd) Australian political figure I've studied. He had personal integrity, compassion and a radical progressive vision, fuelled by reformist zeal. We should have more of it.

Another joy was reading Henry Lawson, whom, I must confess, I'd never appreciated. I do now. He really let it all hang out and had a wonderful rhythm to his words. I didn't think I'd be quoting so much poetry in this book, but I'm glad I did, because it's great at revealing both the personal and political. And often it just sounds good.

Thanks to Judith Brett for writing *The Enigmatic Mr Deakin*. Her *From Secret Ballot to Democracy Sausage* also got a thorough working over in writing this book. Grantlee Kieza's *Banjo* was never far from my keyboard, and Melissa Bellanta's *Larrikins: A History* is history at its music hall, street-fighting best. Sylvia Lawson's *The Archibald Paradox* and Susan Magarey's *Unbridling the Tongues of Women*, a romp through the life of Catherine Helen Spence, were informative and surprisingly fun. Clare Wright's *You Daughters of Freedom* and Audrey Oldfield's *Woman Suffrage in Australia* were inspirational. Nick Dyrenfurth's *Heroes and Villains: The Rise and Fall of the Early Australian Labor Party* and *Mateship: A Very Australian History* make me glad that 'I am not now and never have been a member of the Labor Party'. Meredith Lake's *The Bible in Australia* and Tom Frame's *Losing My Religion: Unbelief in Australia* brought me closer to God, Frank Bongiorno's *The Sex Lives of Australians* brought me closer to sex, and Richard Broome's *Aboriginal Australians: A History Since 1788* brought me closer to tears. Catherine Jinks' *Charlatan* and Catie Gilchrist's *Murder, Misadventure and Miserable Ends* taught me there are a lot of dangerous nutters out there. Kel Richards' *The Story of Australian English* is honoured in every chapter, and I wish I'd written Titus O'Reily's *A Thoroughly Unhelpful History of Australian Sport* because it's just so damned good. Robert Macklin's *Dragon and Kangaroo* deserves a special mention, as does *The Life and Adventures of Morrison of China*, which he co-wrote with Peter Thompson. The National Library of Australia's Trove database of newspapers and journals and Project Gutenberg are excellent online repositories of primary sources.

Thanks again to Ad Long for his illustrations and his patience, and to Hilary Davidson for her occasional fashion advice (for the book, not me personally, as I'm beyond redemption). Chris Feik and Jo Rosenberg showed admirable sangfroid as editors, particularly given my approach to deadlines, split infinitives (I like them), prepositions (I don't like them as much as they do), and the Oxford comma. The other happy and talented folk of Black Inc. are also always a pleasure to deal with. A big shout-out to Charles Firth for being an early reader and assisting with publicity, and to Frank Bongiorno for reading the manuscript and offering sage historical advice. Thanks also to

Susan Carland, Mark Humphries, Osher Günsberg, Wendy Harmer, Mikey Robins and David Astle for agreeing to read the first proofs.

Thanks to Elissa McKeand and Foxtel for trusting me with a TV writing and presenting gig on *Aussie Inventions that Changed the World* between *True Girt* and *Girt Nation*, and to the good folk of TEDxSydney for giving me a stage to strut. And a huge thank you to my readers for telling me to write a third *Girt* book, because I really needed a kick up the arse.

I started writing the first chapter of *Girt Nation* in May 2020 and finished the last in July 2021. I went from being as fit as I've ever been at the beginning of the project to being decidedly slow and stodgy at the end (I've grown a little lap-lap and think I might keep it). Working on the book helped me take my mind off a hard year. In the first few months of 2021, I lost my mother, my much-loved 21-year-old cat and my rowing partner, Frazer Allan.

Covid makes you do stupid things. Coming out of Sydney's first lockdown, I learned to row – and then decided to row competitively. I am not very good at it, although I was once in a boat that narrowly beat The Fossils, a crew of men in their seventies and eighties. The way I look in my lycra race suit has earned me the name 'Beast' at Leichhardt Rowing Club. Frazer, superbly fit, was Beauty to my Beast. He, and the other learn-to-row chaps from the Dictators, Chris Morsley and Aaron Kingston, have been an enormous amount of fun, both on and off the water, as have our coaches Marg, Kerry, et al. Frazer had a great sense of humour for a New Zealander and was kind enough to row in a double with me, a brave and foolish call. Frazer left us far too soon and this book is dedicated to him.

Heartfelt thanks to Alison for having a wonderful sense of humour and an ability to see the world in shades of grey and in vibrant colour, for her constructive advice on tone and grammar, and for being my wife. She'll soon have finished her own book and I can't wait to read it. To Arabella and Dalton, who have never shown the slightest interest in reading my books – you are everything to me and I promise to embarrass you for as long as I live. I can hear you doing your lockdown lessons as I type this, so it's time to finish up here, take off all my clothes and streak across your Zoom feeds.

David Hunt, in study without cat, July 2021

Index

Before GIRT NATION,
there was GIRT and TRUE GIRT

Read Volumes 1 and 2
of the Unauthorised History of Australia

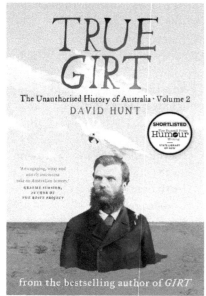

'David Hunt knows how to make the most
of history's juicy bits' *THE AGE*

BLACKINCBOOKS.COM

Lightning Source UK Ltd.
Milton Keynes UK
UKHW021821091122
411907UK00008B/1134